SOMETHING ABOUT THE AUTHOR®

Something about
the Author *was named
an "Outstanding
Reference Source,"
the highest honor given
by the American
Library Association
Reference and Adult
Services Division.*

ISSN 0276-816X

SOMETHING ABOUT THE AUTHOR®

**Facts and Pictures about Authors
and Illustrators of Books for Young People**

VOLUME 117

GALE GROUP

*Detroit
New York
San Francisco
London
Boston
Woodbridge, CT*

STAFF

Scot Peacock, *Managing Editor, Literature Product*
Mark Scott, *Publisher, Literature Product*

Sara L. Constantakis, Melissa Hill, Motoko Fujishiro Huthwaite, Simone Sobel, *Associate Editors*; Kristen A. Dorsch, Erin E. Hockenberry, Justin Vidovic, *Assistant Editors*

Alan Hedblad, *Managing Editor*
Susan M. Trosky, *Literature Content Coordinator*

Victoria B. Cariappa, *Research Manager;* Tracie A. Richardson, *Project Coordinator;* Maureen Emeric, Barbara McNeil, Gary J. Oudersluys, Cheryl L. Warnock, *Research Specialists;* Tamara C. Nott, *Research Associate;* Nicodemus Ford, Tim Lehnerer, Ron Morelli, *Research Assistants*

Maria L. Franklin, *Permissions Manager;* Edna Hedblad, Sarah Tomasek, *Permissions Associates*

Mary Beth Trimper, *Composition Manager;* Dorothy Maki, *Manufacturing Manager;* Stacy Melson, *Buyer*

Michael Logusz, *Graphic Artist;* Randy Bassett, *Image Database Supervisor;* Robert Duncan, *Imaging Specialist;* Pamela A. Reed, *Imaging Coordinator;* Dean Dauphinais, Robyn V. Young, *Senior Image Editors;* Kelly A. Quin, *Image Editor*

Library of Congress Catalog Card Number 72-27107

ISBN 0-7876-4035-2
ISSN 0276-816X

Printed in the United States of America

10 9 8 7 6 5 4 3 2 1

Contents

Authors in Forthcoming Volumes viii
Introduction ix
Acknowledgments xi

W

Authors in Forthcoming Volumes

Below are some of the authors and illustrators that will be featured in upcoming volumes of *SATA*. These include new entries on the swiftly rising stars of the field, as well as completely revised and updated entries (indicated with *) on some of the most notable and best-loved creators of books for children.

*Jim Arnosky: An inveterate observer of nature and a skilled artist, Arnosky is the creator of the popular *Crinkleroot* nature book series. His books present a variety of nature facts, from how to fish to how to draw natural landscapes. Several of Arnosky's books, including *Drawing from Nature* and *Sketching Outdoors in All Seasons*, have inspired a four-part television series produced by Public Broadcasting System (PBS).

*Eileen Charbonneau: Charbonneau is an historical fiction writer whose books, including *Honor to the Hills* and *The Connor Emerald*, have attracted a wide range of readers. A multiracial author of Irish, Slovene, French, Canadian, and Native American ancestry, Charbonneau is the product of a diverse ethnic heritage that has helped to shape one of the prevalent themes in her books: society's critical need for racial tolerance and understanding.

Dennis Foon: A long-time children's advocate and a major talent in children's theater, Michigan-born Canadian playwright Foon is noted for creating plays that help children to cope with a complex and often frightening world. His play *Invisible Kids* won the 1986 British Theatre Award for best production for young adults.

Gail Gauthier: Gauthier is a children's writer noted for her off-beat and humorous stories. Her book *My Life Among the Aliens* was cited by Bank Street College as a "children's book of the year" and is a prime example of the author's ability to present fantastic situations as if they are common occurrences.

*Florence Parry Heide: For over thirty years, Heide has enjoyed a successful career as a children's writer. She has published scores of books, most of which demonstrate her capacity to find humor in the often difficult and confusing situations of a child's life. Heide's most recent works include *Tio Armando* and *The House of Wisdom*.

George R. R. Martin: One of the most important contemporary science fiction writers, Martin has earned multiple Nebula and Hugo awards for his novels. Many of his books have been translated into fourteen languages, and one of his earliest works, *The Armageddon Rag*, has achieved cult status.

P. J. Petersen: A prolific and popular author of fiction for children and young adults, Petersen is recognized for writing fast-paced, appealing books with serious themes that he lightens with optimism and humor. Petersen's books also address more subtle youth issues, such as adolescent self-esteem and deciding how to treat a classmate with cancer.

Randy Powell: Powell is a young adult author known for creating adolescent characters who struggle with their identity and purpose. Powell's books, including *Dean Duffy* and *The Whistling Toilet*, are famed for using sports as a metaphor through which the protagonists combat and, ultimately, overcome their problems.

Spider Robinson: Known for his ability to predict popular technological trends, Robinson is a prolific science fiction writer famous for books like *Time Pressure* and *True Minds*, which show Robinson's faith in the human mind and its power to create a better world.

*Charles Schulz: Creator of the beloved "Peanuts" comic strip, Schulz delighted generations of children and adults with popular cartoon characters like Snoopy, Charlie Brown, Lucy, and Peppermint Patty. The most successful comic strip in history, "Peanuts" spawned numerous books and television specials and recently celebrated its fiftieth anniversary. Schulz's last original "Peanuts" cartoon was published just one day before his death in February 2000.

Judy Walgren: Writer and photojournalist Walgren was awarded a 1994 Pulitzer Prize for documenting through photographs the violent human rights abuses against women throughout the world. She is also the author of *The Lost Boys of Natinga: A School for Sudan's Young Refugees,* for which she contributed photography.

Introduction

Something about the Author (*SATA*) is an ongoing reference series that examines the lives and works of authors and illustrators of books for children. *SATA* includes not only well-known writers and artists but also less prominent individuals whose works are just coming to be recognized. This series is often the only readily available information source on emerging authors and illustrators. You'll find *SATA* informative and entertaining, whether you are a student, a librarian, an English teacher, a parent, or simply an adult who enjoys children's literature.

What's Inside SATA

SATA provides detailed information about authors and illustrators who span the full time range of children's literature, from early figures like John Newbery and L. Frank Baum to contemporary figures like Judy Blume and Richard Peck. Authors in the series represent primarily English-speaking countries, particularly the United States, Canada, and the United Kingdom. Also included, however, are authors from around the world whose works are available in English translation. The writings represented in *SATA* include those created intentionally for children and young adults as well as those written for a general audience and known to interest younger readers. These writings cover the entire spectrum of children's literature, including picture books, humor, folk and fairy tales, animal stories, mystery and adventure, science fiction and fantasy, historical fiction, poetry and nonsense verse, drama, biography, and nonfiction.

Obituaries are also included in *SATA* and are intended not only as death notices but also as concise overviews of people's lives and work. Additionally, each edition features newly revised and updated entries for a selection of *SATA* listees who remain of interest to today's readers and who have been active enough to require extensive revisions of their earlier biographies.

New Autobiography Feature

Beginning with Volume 103, *SATA* features three or more specially commissioned autobiographical essays in each volume. These unique essays, averaging about ten thousand words in length and illustrated with an abundance of personal photos, present an entertaining and informative first-person perspective on the lives and careers of prominent authors and illustrators profiled in *SATA*.

Two Convenient Indexes

In response to suggestions from librarians, *SATA* indexes no longer appear in every volume but are included in alternate (odd-numbered) volumes of the series, beginning with Volume 57.

SATA continues to include two indexes that cumulate with each alternate volume: the Illustrations Index, arranged by the name of the illustrator, gives the number of the volume and page where the illustrator's work appears in the current volume as well as all preceding volumes in the series; the Author Index gives the number of the volume in which a person's biographical sketch, autobiographical essay, or obituary appears in the current volume as well as all preceding volumes in the series.

These indexes also include references to authors and illustrators who appear in Gale's *Yesterday's Authors of Books for Children, Children's Literature Review,* and *Something about the Author Autobiography Series.*

Easy-to-Use Entry Format

Whether you're already familiar with the *SATA* series or just getting acquainted, you will want to be aware of the kind of information that an entry provides. In every *SATA* entry the editors attempt to give as complete a picture of the person's life and work as possible. A typical entry in *SATA* includes the following clearly labeled information sections:

- *PERSONAL:* date and place of birth and death, parents' names and occupations, name of spouse, date of marriage, names of children, educational institutions attended, degrees received, religious and political affiliations, hobbies and other interests.

- *ADDRESSES:* complete home, office, electronic mail, and agent addresses, whenever available.

- *CAREER:* name of employer, position, and dates for each career post; art exhibitions; military service; memberships and offices held in professional and civic organizations.

- *AWARDS, HONORS:* literary and professional awards received.

- *WRITINGS:* title-by-title chronological bibliography of books written and/or illustrated, listed by genre when known; lists of other notable publications, such as plays, screenplays, and periodical contributions.

- *ADAPTATIONS:* a list of films, television programs, plays, CD-ROMs, recordings, and other media presentations that have been adapted from the author's work.

- *WORK IN PROGRESS:* description of projects in progress.

- *SIDELIGHTS:* a biographical portrait of the author or illustrator's development, either directly from the biographee—and often written specifically for the *SATA* entry—or gathered from diaries, letters, interviews, or other published sources.

- *FOR MORE INFORMATION SEE:* references for further reading.

- *EXTENSIVE ILLUSTRATIONS:* photographs, movie stills, book illustrations, and other interesting visual materials supplement the text.

How a SATA Entry Is Compiled

A *SATA* entry progresses through a series of steps. If the biographee is living, the *SATA* editors try to secure information directly from him or her through a questionnaire. From the information that the biographee supplies, the editors prepare an entry, filling in any essential missing details with research and/or telephone interviews. If possible, the author or illustrator is sent a copy of the entry to check for accuracy and completeness.

If the biographee is deceased or cannot be reached by questionnaire, the *SATA* editors examine a wide variety of published sources to gather information for an entry. Biographical and bibliographic sources are consulted, as are book reviews, feature articles, published interviews, and material sometimes obtained from the biographee's family, publishers, agent, or other associates.

Entries that have not been verified by the biographees or their representatives are marked with an asterisk (*).

Contact the Editor

We encourage our readers to examine the entire *SATA* series. Please write and tell us if we can make *SATA* even more helpful to you. Give your comments and suggestions to the editor:

BY MAIL: Editor, *Something about the Author,* The Gale Group, 27500 Drake Rd., Farmington Hills, MI 48331-3535.

BY TELEPHONE: (800) 877-GALE

BY FAX: (248) 699-8054

Acknowledgments

Grateful acknowledgment is made to the following publishers, authors, and artists whose works appear in this volume.

ANDERSON, KEVIN J. Alvin, John, illustrator. From a cover of *Star Wars: Jedi Search,* by Kevin J. Anderson. Bantam Books, 1994. Cover art copyright © 1994 by John Alvin and Lucasfilm Ltd & TM. All rights reserved. Used under authorization. Unauthorized duplication is a violation of applicable law. / Struzan, Drew, illustrator. From a cover of *Star Wars: Darksaber,* by Kevin J. Anderson. Spectra, 1996. ®, TM, and © 1996 Lucasfilm Ltd & TM. All rights reserved. Used under authorization. Unauthorized duplication is a violation of applicable law. / Anderson, Kevin J., photograph. Reproduced by permission.

BAUER, JOAN. From a cover of *Squashed,* by Joan Bauer. Laurel-Leaf Books, 1992. Copyright © 1992 by Joan Bauer. Reproduced by permission of Dell Publishing, a division of Random House, Inc. / Ramhorst, John, illustrator. From a cover of *Sticks,* by Joan Bauer. Yearling, 1996. Copyright © 1996 by Joan Bauer. Reproduced by permission of Dell Publishing, a division of Random House, Inc. / Minor, Wendell, illustrator. From a cover of *Rules of the Road,* by Joan Bauer. G. P. Putnam's Sons, 1998. Jacket art and design © 1998 by Wendell Minor. Reproduced by permission of the illustrator. / Minor, Wendell, illustrator. From a cover of *Backwater,* by Joan Bauer. G. P. Putnam's Sons, 1999. Jacket art © 1999 by Wendell Minor. Reproduced by permission of the illustrator.

BEAGLEHOLE, HELEN. Beaglehole, Helen, photograph. Reproduced by permission.

BLUE, ROSE. All photographs reproduced by permission of the author.

BONE, IAN. Bone, Ian, photograph. Reproduced by permission.

BOUCHARD, DAVID. From a cover of *If You're Not from the Prairie. . . ,* by David Bouchard. Raincoast Books, 1994. Reproduced by permission. / Huang, Zhong-Yang, illustrator. From a cover of *The Dragon New Year: A Chinese Legend,* by David Bouchard. Peachtree, 1999. Cover illustration © 1999 by Zhong-Yang Huang. Reproduced by permission. / Huang, Zhong-Yang, illustrator. From an illustration in *The Mermaid's Muse: The Legend of the Dragon Boats,* by David Bouchard. Raincoast Books, 2000. Text © 2000 by David Bouchard. Illustrations © 2000 by Zhong-Yang Huang. Reproduced by permission. / Bouchard, David, photograph. Reproduced by permission.

BRUCHAC, JOSEPH. Watling, James, illustrator. From an illustration in *The Arrow Over the Door,* by Joseph Bruchac. Dial Books for Young Readers, 1998. Text © 1998 by Joseph Bruchac. Illustrations © 1998 by James Watling. Reproduced by permission of Dial Books for Young Readers, a division of Penguin Putnam Inc.

BUCKLESS, ANDREA. Goodnow, Patti, illustrator. From an illustration in *Class Picture Day,* by Andrea Buckless. A Hello Reader! Book published by Cartwheel Books, a division of Scholastic Inc., 1998. Text © 1998 by Andrea Buckless. Illustrations © 1998 by Patti Goodnow. Reproduced by permission.

BUNTING, EVE. Wiesner, David, illustrator. From an illustration in *Night of the Gargoyles,* by Eve Bunting. Clarion Books, 1994. Illustrations © 1994 by David Wiesner. Reproduced by permission.

BURDETT, LOIS. Burdett, Lois, photograph. Reproduced by permission.

CLARK, EMMA CHICHESTER. Clark, Emma Chichester, illustrator. From an illustration in *Little Miss Muffet's Count-Along Surprise,* by Emma Chichester Clark. Andersen Press Ltd., 1997. © 1997 by Emma Chichester Clark. Reproduced by permission of Andersen Press, Ltd. In the U.S. by Random House Children's Books, a division of Random House, Inc. / Clark, Emma Chichester, illustrator. From an illustration in *I Love You Blue Kangaroo,* by Emma Chichester Clark. Andersen Press Ltd., 1998. © 1998 by Emma Chichester Clark. Reproduced by permission of Andersen Press, Ltd. In the U.S. by Random House Children's Books, a division of Random House, Inc. / Clark, Emma Chichester, illustrator. From an illustration in *More,* by Emma Chichester Clark. Andersen Press Ltd., 1998. © 1998 by Emma Chichester Clark. Reproduced by permission of Andersen Press, Ltd. In the U.S. by Random House Children's Books, a division of Random House, Inc.

COX, JUDY. DiSalvo-Ryan, DyAnne, illustrator. From an illustration in *Now We Can Have a Wedding!,* by Judy Cox. Holiday House, 1998. Text © 1998 by Judy Cox. Illustrations © 1998 by DiSalvo-Ryan, DyAnne. Reproduced by permission of Holiday House, Inc. / Fisher, Cynthia, illustrator. From an illustration in *Third Grade Pet,* by Judy Cox. Holiday House, 1998. Text © 1998 by Judy Cox. Illustrations © 1998 by Cynthia Fisher. Reproduced by permission of Holiday House, Inc. / McCully, Emily Arnold, illustrator. From an illustration in *Rabbit Pirates: A Tale of the Spinach Main,* by Judy Cox. Harcourt, Inc., 1999. Text © 1999 by Judy Cox. Illustrations © 1999 by Emily Arnold McCully. Reproduced by permission. / Cox, Judy, photograph by Walt Houde. Reproduced by permission of Judy Cox.

DILLON, JANA. Dillon, Jana, photograph. Reproduced by permission.

DUDER, TESSA. Catalanotto, Peter, illustrator. From a jacket of *Alex in Rome,* by Tessa Duder. Houghton Mifflin Company, 1992. Jacket art © 1992 by Peter Catalanotto. Reproduced by permission. / Duder, Tessa, photograph. Reproduced by permission.

FARMER, NANCY. Henry, Matthew, illustrator. From a jacket of *The Warm Place,* by Nancy Farmer. Orchard Books, 1995. Jacket illustration © 1995 by Matthew Henry. Reproduced by permission of the publisher, Orchard Books, New York./ Farmer, Nancy, photograph. Reproduced by permission.

FORRESTAL, ELAINE. Forrestal, Elaine, photograph. Reproduced by permission.

GIBBONS, KAYE. Hyman, David, illustrator. From a cover of *Ellen Foster,* by Kaye Gibbons. Vintage Books, 1987. Copyright © 1987 by Kaye Gibbons. Reproduced by permission of Random House, Inc. / From a jacket of A *Cure for Dreams: A Novel,* by Kaye Gibbons. Algonquin Books of Chapel Hill, 1991. Reproduced by permission. / Gibbons, Kaye, photograph by Jerry Bauer. © Jerry Bauer. Reproduced by permission.

GOODWIN, WILLIAM. From a cover of *Teen Violence,* by William Goodwin. Lucent Books, Inc., 1998. © 1998 by Lucent Books, Inc. Reproduced by permission.

GUIBERSON, BRENDA Z. Lloyd, Megan, illustrator. From an illustration in *Cactus Hotel,* by Brenda Z. Guiberson. Henry Holt and Company, LLC, 1991. Illustrations copyright © 1991 by Megan Lloyd. Reproduced by permission of Henry Holt and Company, LLC.

HAUGAARD, KAY. Haugaard, Kay, November 28, 1999, photograph. Reproduced by permission.

HENRY, MARILYN. Henry, Marilyn, photograph by Goodman/Van Riper Photography. Reproduced by permission of Goodman/Van Riper Photography.

HINES, ANNA GROSSNICKLE. Watson, Mary, illustrator. From an illustration in *My Own Big Bed,* by Anna Grossnickle Hines. Greenwillow Books, 1998. Illustrations © 1998 by Mary Watson. Reproduced by permission of HarperCollins Publishers.

HODGES, MARGARET MOORE. Miles, Elizabeth, illustrator. From a jacket of *Molly Limbo,* by Margaret Hodges. Atheneum Books for Young Readers, 1996. Jacket illustration © 1996 by Elizabeth Miles. Reproduced by permission of the illustrator. / Ladwig, Tim, illustrator. From a jacket of *Silent Night: The Song and Its Story,* by Margaret Hodges. Eerdmans Books for Young Readers, 1997. Jacket illustration © 1997 by Tim Ladwig. Reproduced by permission of William B. Eerdmans Publishing Co. / Rayevsky, Robert, illustrator. From a cover of *Joan of Arc: The Lily Maid,* by Margaret Hodges. Holiday House, 1999. Reproduced by permission of Holiday House, Inc. / Hodges, Margaret Moore, photograph. Reproduced by permission.

JOSLIN, MARY. Mayer, Danuta, illustrator. From an illustration in *Do the Angels Watch Close By?,* by Mary Joslin. Lion Publishing, 1997. Illustrations © 1997 by Danuta Mayer. © 1997 Lion Publishing. Reproduced by permission.

KARWOSKI, GAIL LANGER. Watling, James, illustrator. From an illustration in *Seaman: The Dog Who Explored the West with Lewis & Clark,* by Gail Langer Karwoski. Peachtree, 1999. Text © 1999 by Gail Langer Karwoski. Illustrations © 1999 by James Watling. Reproduced by permission.

KASTNER, JILL. Kastner, Jill, illustrator. From an illustration in *Barnyard Bigtop,* by Jill Kastner. Simon & Schuster Books for Young Readers. Copyright © 1997 by Jill Kastner. Reproduced by permission of Simon & Schuster Books for Young Readers, an imprint of Simon & Schuster Children's Publishing Division.

KEAMS, GERI. Keams, Geri, photograph. Reproduced by permission.

KIMMEL, ERIC A. Lloyd, Megan, illustrator. From an illustration in *Seven at One Blow: A Tale from the Brothers Grimm,* retold by Eric A. Kimmel. Holiday House, 1998. Illustrations © 1998 by Megan Lloyd-Thompson. Reproduced by permission of Holiday House, Inc.

KIRK, DAVID. Kirk, David, illustrator. From an illustration in *Miss Spider's ABC,* by David Kirk. Scholastic Press/Callaway, 1998. © by Callaway & Kirk Company LLC. Reproduced by permission. / Kirk, David, illustrator. From an illustration in *Nova's Ark,* by David Kirk. Scholastic Press/Callaway, 1999. © 1999 by Callaway & Kirk Company, LLC. Reproduced by permission.

LASER, MICHAEL. Greene, Jeffrey, illustrator. From a jacket of *The Rain,* by Michael Laser. Simon & Schuster Books for Young Readers, 1997. Jacket illustration © 1997 by Jeffrey Greene. Reproduced by permission of Simon & Schuster Books for Young Readers, an imprint of Simon & Schuster Children's Publishing Division.

LONGYEAR, BARRY B. Manley, Matt, illustrator. From a cover of *The Enemy Papers,* by Barry B. Longyear. White Wolf Publishing, 1998. Reproduced by permission. / longyear, Barry Brookes, photograph. Reproduced by permission.

MAYER, DANUTA. Mayer, Danuta, photograph by B. Baran. Reproduced by permission.

MCALLISTER, MARGARET. McAllister, Margaret, photograph. Reproduced by permission.

MCCOURT, LISA. Krenina, Katya, illustrator. From a cover of *Chicken Soup for Little Souls: A Dog of My Own,* by Lisa McCourt. Jacket design by Cheryl Nathan. Health Communications, Inc., 1998. Reproduced by permission. / Moore, Cyd, illustrator. From an illustration in *I Love You Stinky Face,* by Lisa McCourt. BridgeWater Paperbacks, 1998. Text © 1997 by Lisa McCourt. Illustrations © 1997 by Cyd Moore. Reproduced by permission of Troll Communications, LLC. / Moore, Cyd, illustrator. From an illustration in *I Miss You Stinky Face,* by Lisa McCourt. BridgeWater Books, 1999. Text © 1999 by Lisa McCourt. Illustrations © 1999 by Cyd Moore. Reproduced by permission of Troll Communications, LLC. / McCourt, Lisa, photograph. Reproduced by permission.

MCFARLANE, TODD. From an illustration in *Spawn: Book 5,* by Todd McFarlane. Image Comics, 1994, 1997. © 1997 Todd McFarlane Productions, Inc. All rights reserved. Reproduced by permission./ McFarlane, Todd, photograph,. AP/Wide World Photos. Reproduced by permission.

MCKISSACK, FREDRICK. Ransome, James E., illustrator. From a jacket of *Let My People Go: Bible Stories Told by a Freeman of Color to His Daughter, Charlotte, in Charlestown, South Carolina, 1806-16,* by Patricia McKissack and Fredrick McKissack. Atheneum Books for Young Readers, 1998. Jacket illustration © 1998 by James Ransome. Reproduced by permission of the illustrator. / Abdul-Jabbar, Kareem, photograph. From *Black Hoops: The History of African Americans in Basketball,* by Fredrick McKissack, Jr. Scholastic Press, 1999. Reproduced by permission of AP/Wide World Photos. / Regan, Dana, illustrator. From a cover of *Messy Bessey's Holidays,* by Patricia McKissack and Fredrick McKissack. Children's Press, 1999. Cover illustration © 1999 by Dana Regan. Reproduced by permission. / McKissack, Fredrick, and Patricia McKissack, photograph. Reproduced by permission.

MCKISSACK, PATRICIA. Truth, Sojourner, photograph. From a cover of *Sojourner Truth: Ain't I a Woman?,* by Patricia C. McKissack and Fredrick McKissack. Scholastic Inc., 1992. Reproduced by permission of Sophia Smith Collection, Smith College. / Pinkney, Brian, illustrator. From a cover of *The Dark-Thirty: Southern Tales of the Supernatural,* by Patricia C. McKissack. Knopf, 1998. Cover art © 1992 by Brian Pinkney. Reproduced by permission of Alfred A. Knopf, Inc. / Potter, Giselle, illustrator. From a cover of *The Honest-to-Goodness Truth,* by Patricia C. McKissack. Atheneum Books for Young Readers, 2000. Jacket illustration copyright © 2000 Giselle Potter. Reproduced by permission of Atheneum Books for Young Readers, an imprint of Simon & Schuster Children's Publishing Division. / McKissack, Patricia, photograph. Reproduced by permission.

MILLER, JUDI. Levy, Lina, illustrator. From a cover of *Purple Is My Game, Morgan Is My Name,* by Judi Miller. Minstrel Books, 1998. Copyright © 1998 by Judi Miller. Reproduced by permission of Pocket Books, a division of Simon & Schuster. / Miller, Judi, photograph. Reproduced by permission.

NELSON, JULIE. From a cover of *The History of the Los Angeles Sparks,* by Julie Nelson. Creative Education, 2000. © 2000 Creative Education. Reproduced by permission.

NILSON, ELEANOR. Nilson, Eleanor, photograph. Reproduced by permission.

OCHILTREE, DIANNE. Dun-Ramsey, Marcy, illustrator. From an illustration in *Cats Add Up!,* by Dianne Ochiltree. A Hello Reader! Math Book published by Cartwhell Book, a division of Scholastic Inc., 1998. Hello Reader! Books is a registered trademark of Scholastic Inc. © 1998 by Scholastic Inc. All rights reserved. Reproduced by permission. / Ochiltree, Dianne, photograph. Robyn Schwartz Photography. Reproduced by permission.

PALLOTTA-CHIAROLLI, MARIA. Pallotta-Chiarolli, Maria, photograph by Robert Chiarolli. Reproduced by permission.

PEARSON, KIT. All photographs reproduced by permission of the author.

POMASKA, ANNA. From a cover of *Six Full-Color Hidden Picture Puzzles,* by Anna Pomaska. Dover, 1994. © 1994 by Dover Publications, Inc. Reproduced by permission. / Pomaska, Anna, illustrator. From an illustration in *Hidden Alphabet Adventure,* by Anna Pomaska. Work in progress. Reproduced by permission of the author. / Pomaska, Anna, photograph. Reproduced by permission.

RASCHKA, CHRIS. Raschka, Chris, illustrator. From an illustration in *The Blushful Hippopotamus,* by Chris Raschka. Orchard Books, 1996. © 1996 by Christopher Raschka. Reproduced by permission of the publisher, Orchard Books, New York. / Raschka, Christopher, illustrator. From an illustration in *The Genie in the Jar,* by Chris Raschka. Henry Holt, 1996. Reproduced by permission of the illustrator. / Raschka, Chris, illustrator. From an illustration in *Arlene Sardine,* by Chris Raschka. Orchard Books, 1998. Copyright © 1998 by Chris Raschka. Reproduced by permission of the publisher, Orchard Books, New York. / Raschka, Chris, illustrator. From an illustration in *Can't Sleep,* by Chris Raschka. Orchard Books, 1999. © 1995 by Christopher Raschka. Reproduced by permission of the publisher, Orchard Books, New York.

REEVE, KIRK. Reeve, Kirk, photograph. Reproduced by permission.

RINALDI, ANN. From a cover of *Wolf by the Ears,* by Ann Rinaldi. Scholastic Inc., 1991. Cover illustration © by Scholastic Inc. Reproduced by permission. / Hussar, Michael, illustrator. From a jacket of *An Acquaintance with Darkness,* by Ann Rinaldi. Gulliver Books, 1997. Jacket illustration © 1997 by Michael Hussar. Reproduced by permission of Harcourt, Inc. / Tauss, Marc, photographer. From a cover of *Amelia's War,* by Ann Rinaldi. Scholastic Press, 1999. Jacket photograph

SOMETHING ABOUT THE AUTHOR

ADAM, Mark
    See ALEXANDER, Marc

*   *   *

ALEXANDER, Marc 1929-
    (Mark Adam, Marcus Aylward,
    Mark Ronson)

Personal

Born January 27, 1929; son of Ronald and Marie (Poole) Alexander; married Maisie Adolphus; children: Simon, Paul. *Education:* Graduated from Wellington Teachers' College, Wellington, New Zealand.

Addresses

Home—Hacienda Guadalupe, 29692 Manilva, Malaga, Spain; and Crooks Cottage, Gilsland, Cumbria CA6 7EA, England. *Agent*—Rupert Crew Ltd., Kings Mews, London WC1N 2TA, England.

Career

Writer. *Gisborne Herald,* New Zealand, subeditor; went to Europe in 1954 and worked as a reporter and feature writer for the *Reveille; Television Mail,* cofounder, 1959, became editorial director. Inaugurated *Vision* Awards, a festival for British documentary films, and *Icarus,* a poetry magazine; organizer of British Television Advertising Awards and World Newsfilm Awards.

Writings

In Ostia (poetry), Linden, 1959.
Behind the Scenes with a Fishing Fleet (for children), Phoenix, 1964.
Golden Dollar, Ward, Lock, 1965.
The Water War, Ward, Lock, 1966.
The Past, Parrish, 1965, A. Lynn, 1967.
The Rhineland, illustrated by Barbara Crocker, Rand McNally, 1967.
Hand of Vengeance, Ward, Lock, 1967.
A Fast Gun for Judas, Ward, Lock, 1968.
The Sundown Trail, Ward, Lock, 1968.
(With David Leader) *The Sportsman's Book of Records,* Clipper, 1971.
True Adventure Stories: 45 Authentic Stories, Clipper, 1972.
Haunted Inns, F. Muller, 1973.
Haunted Castles, F. Muller, 1974.
Phantom Britain: This Spectre'd Isle, F. Muller, 1975, Transatlantic, 1976.
(And photographer) *Legendary Castles of the South,* Pacific, 1977.
The Outrageous Queens, F. Muller, 1977.
The Mist Lizard, F. Muller, 1977, revised edition, Piccolo, 1980.
(And photographer) *Ghostly Cornwall,* Pacific, 1977.
(And photographer) *Legendary Castles of the Border,* Pacific, 1977.
Royal Murder, F. Muller, 1978.
Haunted Churches and Abbeys of Britain, Arthur Barker, 1978.
To Anger the Devil: An Account of the Work of Exorcist Extraordinary the Reverend Dr. Donald Omand, N.

Spearman, 1978, published as *The Man Who Exorcised the Bermuda Triangle: The Reverend Dr. Donald Omand, Exorcist Extraordinaire,* A. S. Barnes, 1980, revised British edition published as *The Devil Hunter: An Account of the Work of Exorcist Extraordinary the Reverend Dr. Donald Omand,* Sphere, 1981.

(And photographer) *Legendary Castles of Scotland,* Pacific, 1978.

Gilsland, Griffin, 1978.

The Dance Goes On: The Life and Art of Elizabeth Twistington Higgins MBE, foreword by His Royal Highness Prince Philip, Duke of Edinburgh, Leader, c. 1980.

(And photographer) *Enchanted Britain: Mystical Sites in Rural England, Scotland and Wales,* Weidenfeld & Nicolson, 1981.

British Folklore, Myths and Legends, Weidenfeld & Nicolson, Crescent, 1982.

Haunted Pubs in Britain and Ireland, Sphere, 1984.

Not after Nightfall (short stories), Viking Kestrel, 1985.

A Talent for Living, Leader, 1986.

(Contributor) Reginald Massey, editor, *All India,* Quintet and Chartwell, 1986.

Canvases of Courage, Leader, 1990.

(With Geraldine Walker) *Gilsland & Greenhead, Past and Present: A Short History and Guide of the Two Villages and Surrounding Area,* Middle March, 1995.

Painters First, Leader, 1995.

The Life of Erich Stegmann, Leader, 2000.

The Millennium People, Orion (Oslo, Norway), 2000.

"WELLS OF YTHAN" SERIES

Ancient Dreams, Headline, 1988.

Magic Casements, Headline, 1989.

Shadow Realm, Headline, 1990.

Enchantment's End, Headline, 1992.

UNDER PSEUDONYM MARCUS AYLWARD

Harper's Folly, Arthur Barker, 1984.

Harper's Luck, Arthur Barker, 1985.

UNDER PSEUDONYM MARK RONSON

Bloodthirst, Hamlyn, 1979.

Ghoul, Hamlyn, 1980.

Ogre, Hamlyn, 1980.

Plague Pit, Hamlyn, 1981.

Haunted Castles, Beaver, 1982.

Super Ghosts, Beaver, 1982.

(With Stella Whitelaw and Judy Gardiner) *Grimalkin's Tales,* Hamlyn, St. Martin's, 1983.

The Dark Domain, Century, 1984, published as *Ombres et Miroirs,* Fanval (Paris, France).

Here Be Dragons, Beaver, 1985.

Turtle Island, Target, 1986.

Whispering Corner, Arrow, 1989.

UNDER PSEUDONYM MARK ADAM

Kamikaze 214, Mortensen (Oslo, Norway), 1991.

OTHER

Also author of *Boats on Wheels,* Macdonald & Janes, and *Haunted Houses You May Visit,* Sphere; author of television documentary films *The Dance Goes On,* based on his book of the same title, 1981, *Secret Paradise,* 1983, and *Return to Eden,* 1984; author of television plays *The Barrington Case* and *The Black Tomb;* author of *Don't Turn Out the Light,* short stories published as an audio book by Telstar; author of commentary for cinema documentary *Bangladesh, I Love You,* 1980. Former editor, *International Broadcast Engineer, International Sound Engineer, International TV Technical Review, Vision,* and *Exploration;* former consultant editor, *Heritage;* editor of *Travelscope* and *Adventure Travel News.*

Alexander's fiction has been translated into nine languages.

Work in Progress

The Encyclopedia of Folklore of the British Isles, for Sutton; *Tropicana Tales* (short stories), for Griffin Press.

Sidelights

Born in New Zealand, Marc Alexander is a journalist turned author. He has written on a variety of subjects, including haunted places, adventure, and traveling. In addition, Alexander has also created the "Wells of Ythan," a fantasy series "whose plot—though it becomes more complex with each book—can be stated simply: the quest to wake Sleeping Beauty," according to Ian Covell in *St. James Guide to Fantasy Writers.* Throughout each book, Alexander toys with characters struggling to awaken Princess Livia of Ythan and free the land from the power of ruthless Regents. In the legend, the princess is not dead but lies asleep under an Enchantment. Only when the sleeping princess is bathed in water from the Wells of Ythan will peace and prosperity return to the kingdom. Claiming the characters have "astonishingly complex and troubled emotions," throughout the series, Covell suggests the "greatest strength of all is the final inversion of the series when the Enchantment's true genesis and purpose are revealed to the astonishment (one presumes) of every reader and the author himself."

Alexander once commented: "My ambition to become a storyteller began at the age of ten while I was in traction as the result of Potts' Disease. My thoughtful father kept me supplied with widely ranging books—for which I am ever grateful—and I was inspired to write a novel *Black Days in Dark Ages* (!) largely influenced by Sir Walter Scott and Dennis Wheatley. As I wrote 'The End' on page one hundred, I had not the slightest doubt that I was going to be a professional author though I had no notion of the difficulties that can beset authorship; indeed I thought it was merely a matter of mailing a manuscript to an appreciative publisher and living in style on the subsequent royalties. Yet, although I have since known the vicissitudes and pleasures of authorship, my enthusiasm for the written word remains. This is of the greatest importance as my credo is that I cannot expect my readers, whether of a biography or fantasy novel, to be absorbed by my work unless it was written with enthusiasm. I think I was most successful in this respect with my novel *The Dark Domain;* certainly of my books I enjoyed writing it the most.

"I was very fortunate that Fleet Street came before authorship. As a sub-editor I learned that my sacred prose could only improve with ruthless pruning; as a reporter I realized the value of detailed observation.

"Today I am still happy to be a journeyman story-teller, for the other part of my credo is respect for the power of narrative which is demonstrated by all the great literary works no matter how philosophical their content may be, from the Bible onwards. If I had a previous incarnation I like to think I should have been found in a square—or royal courtyard—in Old Baghdad declaiming, 'Listen, oh ye Faithful, there was once a poor sailor named Sinbad ...'"

Works Cited

Covell, Ian, "Marc Alexander," *St. James Guide to Fantasy Writers,* St. James, 1996, pp. 14-16.

*   *   *

ANDERSON, Kevin J. 1962-

Personal

Born March 27, 1962, in Racine, WI, son of Andrew James (a banker) and Dorothy Arloah (a homemaker; maiden name, Cooper) Anderson; married Mary Franco Nijhuis, November 17, 1983 (divorced June, 1987); married Rebecca Moesta (a technical editor), September 14, 1991; children: Jonathan Macgregor Cowan (stepson). *Education:* University of Wisconsin—Madison, B.S. (with honors), 1982. *Hobbies and other interests:* Hiking, camping, reading, astronomy.

Addresses

Home—Colorado. *Agent*—Matt Biales, William Morris Agency, 1325 Avenue of the Americas, New York, NY 10019.

Career

Writer. Lawrence Livermore National Laboratory, Livermore, CA, technical writer/editor, 1983–96; Materials Research Society, Pittsburgh, PA, columnist, 1988–94; International Society for Respiratory Protection, Livermore, CA, copy editor, 1989—. *Member:* Science Fiction Writers of America, Horror Writers of America.

Awards, Honors

Nominated for best small press writer, Small Press Writers and Artists Organization, 1984; Dale Donaldson Memorial Award for lifetime service to the small press field, 1987; Bram Stoker Award nomination for best first novel, Horror Writers of America, 1988, for *Resurrection, Inc.;* "Writers of the Future" honorable mention citations, Bridge Publications, 1985, 1988, and 1989; nominee for Nebula award for Best Science Fiction Novel for *Assemblers of Infinity,* 1993; Locus magazine award for best science fiction paperback novel of 1995 for *Climbing Olympus.*

Writings

NOVELS WITH DOUG BEASON

Lifeline, Bantam, 1991.
The Trinity Paradox, Bantam, 1991.
Assemblers of Infinity, Bantam, 1993.
Ill Wind, Forge, 1995.
Virtual Destruction, Ace Books, 1996.
Ignition, Forge, 1997.
Fallout, Ace Books, 1997.
Lethal Exposure, Ace Books, 1998.

NOVELS WITH KRISTINE KATHRYN RUSCH

Afterimage, Roc Books, 1992.
Afterimage/Aftershock, Meisha Merlin, 1998.

"THE X-FILES" SERIES

Ground Zero, HarperPrism, 1995.
Ruins, HarperPrism, 1996.
Antibodies, HarperPrism, 1997.

SCIENCE FICTION

Resurrection, Inc., Signet, 1988, reprinted in a tenth anniversary limited edition, Overlook Connection Press, 2000.
Climbing Olympus, Warner, 1994.
Blindfold, Warner, 1995.

Kevin J. Anderson

(Editor) *War of the Worlds: Global Dispatches* (anthology), Bantam, 1996.

"GAMEARTH" SERIES

Gamearth, Signet, 1989.
Gameplay, Signet, 1989.
Game's End, Roc Books, 1990.

FOR YOUNG ADULTS

(With John Gregory Betancourt) *Born of Elven Blood,* Atheneum, 1995.
Bounty Hunters, Bantam, 1996.

"STAR WARS" SERIES

Darksaber, Bantam, 1995.

STAR WARS: "JEDI ACADEMY TRILOGY"

Jedi Search, Bantam, 1994.
Dark Apprentice, Bantam, 1994.
Champions of the Force, Bantam, 1994.
Jedi Academy Trilogy (includes *Jedi Search, Dark Apprentice,* and *Champions of the Force,* published as one volume), Doubleday, 1994.

STAR WARS: "YOUNG JEDI KNIGHTS" SERIES

(With Rebecca Moesta) *Heirs of the Force,* Boulevard, 1995.
(With Moesta) *Shadow Academy,* Boulevard, 1995.
(With Moesta) *The Lost Ones,* Boulevard, 1995.
(With Moesta) *Lightsabers,* Boulevard, 1996.
(With Moesta) *Darkest Knight,* Boulevard, 1996.
(With Moesta) *Jedi under Siege,* Boulevard, 1996.
(With Moesta) *Shards of Alderaan,* Boulevard, 1997.
(With Moesta) *Delusions of Grandeur,* Boulevard, 1997.
(With Moesta) *Diversity Alliance,* Boulevard, 1997.
(With Moesta) *Jedi Bounty,* Boulevard, 1997.
(With Moesta) *Crisis at Crystal Reef,* Boulevard, 1998.
(With Moesta) *Trouble on Cloud City,* Boulevard, 1998.
(With Moesta) *Return to Ord Mantell,* Boulevard, 1998.
(With Moesta) *The Emperor's Plague,* Boulevard, 1998.

"STAR WARS" ANTHOLOGY SERIES

(Editor) *Star Wars: Tales from the Mos Eisley Cantina,* Bantam, 1995.
(Editor) *Star Wars: Tales from Jabba's Palace,* Bantam, 1995.
(Editor) *Star Wars: Tales of the Bounty Hunters,* Bantam, 1996.

STAR WARS: "TALES OF THE JEDI" SERIES

Dark Lords of the Sith, Dark Horse Comics, 1996.
The Sith War, Dark Horse Comics, 1996.
Golden Age of Sith, Dark Horse Comics, 1997.
Fall of the Sith Empire, Dark Horse Comics, 1998.
Redemption, Dark Horse Comics, 1999.

"DUNE" SERIES

(With Brian Herbert) *Dune: House Atreides,* Bantam, 1999.

NONFICTION

The Illustrated Star Wars Universe, illustrated by Ralph McQuarrie, with additional art by Michael Butkus and others, Bantam (New York, NY), 1995.

(With Rebecca Moesta) *Star Wars: The Mos Eisley Cantina Pop-Up Book,* illustrated by Ralph McQuarrie, Little, Brown (Boston, MA), 1995.
(With Moesta) *Jabba's Palace Pop-Up Book,* illustrated by McQuarrie, Little, Brown (Boston, MA), 1996.

OTHER

(With L. Ron Hubbard) *Ai! Pedrito!,* Bridge Publications, 1998.

Work represented in anthologies, including *Full Spectrum,* volumes I, III, and IV, *The Ultimate Dracula,* and *The Ultimate Werewolf.* Contributor of short stories, articles, and reviews to periodicals, including *Analog, Amazing,* and *Fantasy and Science Fiction.* Also author of several comic-book series. Over two dozen of Anderson's books have been translated for foreign publication.

Adaptations

Audiotape, *The X-Files: Ground Zero,* read by Gillian Anderson, Harper Audio, 1995.

Sidelights

Kevin J. Anderson is the author of a daunting array of science fiction books for young adults, and has emerged as one of the most successful writers in the genre's history. Over ten million books of Anderson's were in print by the late 1990s, and in 1998 he set the world record for largest single-author book signing while promoting his spoof-filled spy thriller, *Ai! Pedrito!,* in Los Angeles. In addition to creating original novels with themes of space exploration and new frontiers, Anderson has written many books in the "Star Wars" series for teen readers under the auspices of Lucasfilm. For a 1999 prequel to the classic sci-fi tome *Dune,* Anderson set another record when he was signed to the most lucrative book publishing contract ever drawn up for a science fiction author.

Anderson was born in 1962 and grew up in a small town in Wisconsin. He recalled in a biography published on his Web site, http://www.wordfire.com, that a television film broadcast of the H. G. Wells classic *War of the Worlds* made a tremendous impression upon his five-year-old mind. Originally a radio play, *War of the Worlds* caused a stir when first broadcast in the late 1930s, sending many Americans into a panic, believing that the Earth really was being attacked by Martians. The television movie, based on the radio play, made such an impression upon Anderson that, still too young to read or write well, he drew pictures of the movie scenes the next day.

Anderson wrote his first short story at the age of eight, and two years later he bought a typewriter with savings from his allowance. The year he entered high school, he began submitting short stories to science fiction magazines, but received nothing but peremptory rejection letters. By the time he entered the University of Wisconsin at Madison, he had begun to enjoy minor success with his fiction. After he graduated from college with an honors degree in 1982, he began working for the Lawrence Livermore National Laboratories in Livermore, California. As a technical writer at this important defense-industry complex, Anderson was exposed to ideas and technologies that fired his imagination. He also met his future wife and co-author, Rebecca Moesta, and another future collaborator, a physicist named Doug Beason.

Anderson's first published book was *Resurrection, Inc.* which appeared in 1988. Its protagonist is Francois Nathans, founder of a company that recycles human corpses. Nathans owns the technology that can animate the cadavers with a microchip, and, since their human memory has been erased, these "Servants" are used to free the living from difficult, drudge-like, or dangerous labor. When some of the Servants begin to recover their memories, they rebel. One of them possesses inside knowledge about the company because his father, once the greedy Nathans's partner, had been ousted from the partnership. "Although familiar in outline, this first effort is well plotted and lively in the telling," wrote Barbara Bannon in *Publishers Weekly.* As testament to its appeal, *Resurrection, Inc.,* was published in a tenth-anniversary edition.

Anderson's next project was a series of novels based upon the fantasy role-playing games popular with teenagers and young adults in the late 1980s. His 1989 work *Gamearth* introduced Melanie, David, Tyrone, and Scott, a quartet of students deeply involved in a Dungeons-and-Dragons style fantasy game. David begins to think that others are taking the plotted movements and created characters too seriously and wants to quit. To extricate himself, he creates a monstrous character that will destroy the other players' characters. His strategy backfires, however, and the book's ending is a cliffhanger.

In the sequel, *Gameplay,* also published in 1989, the four teens and their two-year-long role-playing game continues. Baffled by some occurrences, they come to realize through their dreams that some of the created characters have begun to make their own moves. The forces of good and evil battle, helped along by a new character who speaks only in advertising and pop-culture platitudes. "Anderson adds a delightfully fresh sense of humor in his character of Journeyman, the clay golem Melanie sends to save the day," noted a reviewer in *Kliatt.*

Beginning in the early 1990s, Anderson found success with several titles co-authored with his Livermore colleague Doug Beason. The first of these books, *Lifeline,* was published in 1991. It posits a futuristic scenario of an American base on the Moon, a corporate satellite called Orbitech, and a Soviet counterpart viewed with some suspicion. At the beginning of the story, the American government has agreed to a deal with the Philippines: to retain the leases for their military bases on the Pacific archipelago, the Philippines have been given a space station called Aguinaldo. There,

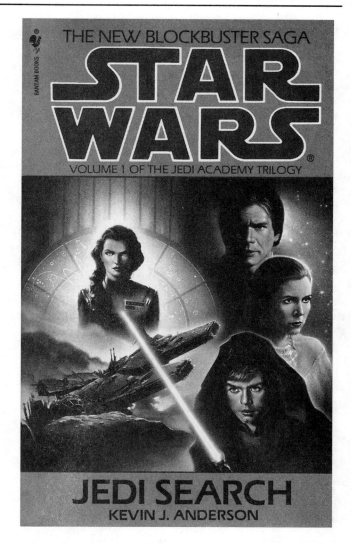

First in Anderson's "Jedi Academy Trilogy" series, Star Wars: Jedi Search *features Han Solo and Princess Leia, now married and parents of three children, with appearances by Luke Skywalker, Chewbacca, and a new teenage character. (Cover illustration by John Alvin.)*

scientist Luis Sandovaal and his team of 1,500 researchers are creating groundbreaking new scientific products. One of these is wall-kelp, a quick-growing edible that provides all necessary nutrients for humans. Aguinaldo is also home to experimental prototypes of fantastic flying creatures that can be transformed into sails for the satellites.

Lifeline's action starts with the space settlers observing nuclear mushroom clouds on Earth. The United States and the Soviet Union have attacked one another, and all space stations are stranded. The Russians on Kibalchick put themselves into suspended animation, while the Americans attempt to find a more immediate solution. When the director of Orbitech, Brahms, turns tyrannical and ejects 150 "under-performing" personnel, Duncan McLaris flees and escapes to the moon base, Clavius. Sandovaal manages to successfully send wall-kelp to the base, and to Orbitech, but then the Soviets unexpectedly awaken, and tensions mount. "The posing and solving of apparently insuperable problems keeps the reader involved in that classic way," stated Tom Easton in *Analog Science Fiction and Fact,* who found fault only with the pacing of the book, and its rapid introduction of technological innovations that come to the rescue. "At the same time, the characters are real enough to engage the reader's sympathy . . . and at the end there is a very real sense of resolution and satisfaction."

Anderson and Beason's second collaboration, *The Trinity Paradox,* appeared in 1991. The novel "demonstrates their collaborative storytelling powers much more effectively," wrote Dan Chow in *Locus.* Its protagonist is Elizabeth Devane, a radical anti-nuclear activist. She and her boyfriend plan to disable a nuclear weapon sitting unguarded in the desert of the American Southwest, but a mishap occurs. He dies, and she is catapulted back into time to Los Alamos, New Mexico, during World War II, when Los Alamos was the primary research site for

Luke Skywalker is in love with a Jedi in Anderson's **Star Wars: Dark Saber.** *(Cover illustration by Drew Struzan.)*

American nuclear weapons technology. Finding herself in the midst of the feverish race to master nuclear technology at the top-secret national laboratory, Devane realizes that she might be able to sabotage the invention of the atomic bomb.

The Trinity Paradox includes several real scientists in its plot, such as Robert Oppenheimer and Edward Teller, and the "Trinity" of the title takes its name from the site of the first successful test explosion. Devane meets English physicist Geoffrey Fox and tells him something that he in turn reveals to an old college friend now working for Nazi Germany; she also makes math errors on purpose, and attempts to assassinate Oppenheimer. Instead of stopping the Cold War, however, Devane's actions set in motion a new version of Cold War history: the outcome of World War II is affected, and nuclear technology heads in an entirely new direction. Realizing that she possesses the power to change the world, she becomes as dangerous as the scientists she considers traitors to humankind. "Hers is the most chilling of revolutionary beliefs, that with a constituency of one," noted Chow in *Locus.*

Anderson and Beason continued their successful collaboration with the 1993 novel *Assemblers of Infinity.* Set in the early decades of the twenty-first century, the plot centers around a group of scientists who believe an alien invasion may be imminent. A team of investigators is sent to a suspicious site—the Earth's base on the moon—but the mission goes awry when they die under questionable circumstances shortly after landing. Back on Earth, other researchers are positing that the relatively new field of nano-technology (machines run by microprocessors) may have something to do with that incident and a threat of invasion. Erika Trace, one of the Earth's leading names in nano-technology, is enlisted to help. There are many dynamic characters in this complex plot, and the book won praise from reviewers. *Kliatt* reviewer Bette D. Ammon noted "the premise is riveting and the technology is fascinating," and said that Anderson and Beason created a situation "utterly plausible and frightening—the stuff of which good SF is made." Rosie Peasley reviewed *Assemblers of Infinity* for *Voice of Youth Advocates* and praised its "sophisticated science fiction concepts," declaring that "the plot hums along at high speed." In a *Booklist* critique, Roland Green compared it to "the techno-thriller, sort of a Tom-Clancy-meets-space-advocacy effort."

Ill Wind was Anderson's fourth collaboration with Beason, a 1995 sci-fi eco-thriller involving a massive oil spill in the San Francisco Bay. The large corporation responsible for this disaster—eager to clean up both the spill and their corporate image as quickly as possible— unleashes an untried new microbe to do the job. Soon the uncontrollable organism begins eating everything made from petroleum products, such as gasoline and plastic. When martial law is declared and the electricity fails, a scientist and two pilots become the heroes who try to save the world.

With their 1996 book, *Virtual Destruction,* Anderson and Beason moved the action closer to home: the story is set at the Livermore Labs, from which Anderson had retired the previous year, and was a timely glimpse into how such national defense labs were forced to refocus their missions after the end of Cold War tensions. After decades of relying heavily upon federal funding to develop new weapons technology, Livermore and other facilities were challenged to find consumer and private-sector applications for their patents. The conflicts presented by this new era—specifically between profit-minded management and the more altruistic scientists—is the focus of *Virtual Destruction.*

The plots revolves around a virtual reality chamber that produces devastatingly real effects; Livermore executive Hal Michaelson is discussing with the government possible uses for this chamber in the dangerous realm of nuclear-weapons surveillance. One of Michaelson's researchers, Gary Lesserec, who has been involved with the Virtual Reality Lab from its conception, knows that this is not feasible, that even sound recordings can trick entrants. Lesserec is about to be fired when Michaelson, his boss, is found dead inside the chamber in the presence of a lethal acid. A Federal Bureau of Investigation agent, Craig Kreident, investigates and uncovers nefarious industrial espionage links to the computer gaming industry. Introducing Kreident changes the feel of the book from sci-fi thriller to detective fiction, but as Tom Easton noted in *Analog,* "[T]here's not much detecting going on here. The tale exists to give us a tour of Livermore, explicate some interesting technology, and discuss the problems the end of the Cold War has given the national labs."

For help with the details in his next book with Beason, Anderson was able to obtain an insider's visit to Kennedy Space Center in Florida. Published in 1997, *Ignition* chronicles the planning and sabotage of a joint U.S.-Soviet mission on the space shuttle *Atlantis.* The first commodore, Colonel Adam "Iceberg" Friese, suffers an accident that cancels his participation. He becomes vitally involved, nevertheless, when a band of terrorists, organized by a famous Wall Street criminal, takes the crew hostage. The pilot's former paramour, Nicole Hunter, an astronaut-turned-launch-controller, is also held hostage, but manages to help Friese battle the gang, some of whom have unusual personal quirks. The realistic details pertaining to the launch pad and pre-launch tensions—somewhat altered for security reasons—make *Ignition* "a nail biter" of a book, according to *Library Journal* reviewer Grant A. Frederickson.

Intrepid FBI agent Craig Kreident reappears in Anderson and Beason's 1998 sci-fi thriller, *Lethal Exposure.* This work is set at another government-funded research facility, the Fermi National Accelerator Laboratory in Illinois. Kreident arrives to investigate the mysterious radiation death of a renowned physicist, Georg Dumenco. A reviewer for *Publishers Weekly* observed that the authors' familiarity with the subject matter and lab environment "gives their latest [book] plenty of scientific authenticity."

Anderson is also the author of several books in the "Star Wars" series. The plots, aimed at young-adult readers, but popular with Star Wars fans of all ages, help provide panoramic details of the factions, clans, and worlds in this classic saga of good and evil. The first series is set at the Jedi Academy and begins with the 1994 novel *Jedi Search.* Heroic Han Solo is married to Princess Leia, and they have three small children. Other characters from the original 1977 film also appear, such as Luke Skywalker and Chewbacca, and a new one is introduced, the teenager Kyp Durron. Spice mines and a space battle lead to a "rollicking SF adventure," according to Ingrid von Hausen in a review for *Kliatt.* This book and two sequels written by Anderson, *Dark Apprentice* and *Champions of the Force,* were published in 1994 under the collective title *Jedi Academy Trilogy.*

Anderson has written several other "Star Wars" books that are not part of a definitive series. One such work is the 1995 hardcover *Darksaber,* in which the Empire is again attempting to resurrect its former glory. *Darksaber* introduces a new leader of the Hutt group, named Durga, and finds Luke Skywalker in love with a Jedi, Callista, whose special powers have vanished. Many other successful science fiction writers have authored titles for various "Star Wars" series, but "Anderson leads the pack in both overall popularity and sheer storytelling power," wrote Carl Hays in *Booklist.* Hays further remarked that Anderson's well-developed characters added greatly to their appeal, giving readers a far more in-depth treatment than is possible in the film plots.

Anderson has authored most of the books for the "Young Jedi Knights" series with his wife, Rebecca Moesta. In this series, the heroes are the offspring of Han Solo and Princess Leia, the teen twins Jacen and Jaina. The first book in the series appeared in 1995, *Heirs of the Force,* and places the two at the fabled Jedi Academy, founded by their uncle, Luke Skywalker. When the teens are captured by a fighter pilot from the evil Empire, they are threatened with being stranded on a jungle moon. In *The Lost Ones,* another in the series, also published in 1995, Anderson and Moesta again place Jacen and Jaina in danger. As expected, the fourteen year olds ably extricate both themselves and a friend who has been lured astray by the malevolent Dark Jedi Master, Brakiss. The Dark Jedi Force is attempting to revive the empire, creating a Second Imperium that will rule the galaxy. Hugh M. Flick, reviewing *The Lost Ones* in *Kliatt,* declared it, along with its two series predecessors, "well written and will be interesting for Star Wars fans of all ages."

The 1996 book *Lightsabers,* another in the series, features the maimed Tenel Ka, a friend of Jacen and Jaina. Tenel Ka's arm was destroyed when her lightsaber misfired, and out of shame she has exiled herself to the planet Hapes, where she is the crown princess. Jacen and Jaina attempt to help her maintain political stability on her home planet, and convince her to return to the Jedi Academy despite her accident. The fifth book in the Young Jedi Knights series, *Darkest Knight,* came in 1996. In it, Jacen and Jaina travel to Kashyyk, home of

Lowbacca and the Wookies. When the Dark Jedis of the Shadow Academy attack Kashyyk, they steal vital computer technology to help build the Second Imperium, but Jacen and Jaina preserve the galaxy once again.

Anderson has also authored several solo titles outside of the young-adult market that have garnered him definitive praise. His 1994 novel, *Climbing Olympus,* is set on the planet Mars, inhabited by three types of humans. Rachel Dycek, the United Nations commissioner there, is in charge of Lowell Base, but is about to be relieved of her duties. She was once the infamous surgeon who created "adins" (*adin* is Russian for "first"), surgically modified prisoners from Soviet labor camps. Their physiology has been altered so that they can survive on Mars, where they were sent originally to construct a colony.

After the adins rebelled and fled to another part of the planet, Dycek created the "dva" (Russian for "two"), another type of creature, but much less monstrously engineered and in possession of a higher degree of intelligence. The dvas were sent to Mars to create an infrastructure allowing average, non-modified humans to survive there. As the work nears completion, both the dvas and Dycek are being phased out. When a landslide kills a large number of the dvas, Dycek visits the site and soon learns that, although adins and dvas were sterilized, the partner of an escaped adin, Boris, is now expecting a child. On the mountain Pavonis Mons, Dycek finds the unbalanced Boris ruling over the remaining adins, and she attempts to right her past wrongs and set the planet toward a harmonious future. Reviewers praised Anderson's vividly drawn portrayals, and Russell Letson in *Locus* called Dycek and Boris "characters as compelling as the technological widgetry of survival augmentation or the extremities of the Martian landscape and climate."

Anderson's rank as a leading American science fiction writer was reinforced when he was selected to create a companion work to the classic sci-fi novel *Dune* by Frank Herbert. This honor came after he sent a letter to the literary executors of the late author "telling them of my love for *Dune* and wondering if there was ever a possibility of new books," Anderson explained in an interview published on the website http://www.anotheruniverse.com. He was teamed with Herbert's son, Brian Herbert, to write the 1999 novel *Dune: House Atreides,* and received for it the most lucrative contract ever signed by science fiction authors in publishing history.

Their task was to explain some of the relationships and feuds behind the extremely intricate plot of the original book. As *House Atreides* opens, Duke Atreides and his son Leto are attacked by arch-foe House Harkonnen. In the battle, a young boy named Duncan Idaho escapes to the Atreides side. An action of the machine planet Ix infuriates Emperor Elrood and sets in motion a long standing grudge, but Elrood's power is usurped by his own son. Meanwhile, the Bene Gesserits are about to see the fruition of their millennium-long plan to create a perfect being, Kwisatz Haderach. Central to all charac-

ters and subplots is the vast wasteland of Dune, where nothing except "Spice" lives. Authors Anderson and Herbert won praise from *Publishers Weekly* for their creation of a complex groundwork for lovers of the original *Dune.* "The attendant excitement and myriad revelations not only make this novel a terrific read in its own right but will inspire readers to turn, or return, to its great predecessor," its critic declared.

Such triumphs were not easily achieved, however. Anderson once won a tongue-in-cheek "Writer with No Future" award at a conference when he produced the most rejection slips among fellow participants. "I have now topped 750 rejections," the author said in the interview with http://www.anotheruniverse.com, "and some people look at me as an 'overnight success.' Hah! My work is very popular now, but it took me a lot of work to get here."

Works Cited

Ammon, Bette D., review of *Assemblers of Infinity, Kliatt,* May, 1993, p. 12.

Anderson, Kevin J., comments published on his Web site, located at http://www.wordfire.com.

Anderson, Kevin J., on-line interview, located at http://www.anotheruniverse.com.

Bannon, Barbara, review of *Resurrection, Inc., Publishers Weekly,* June 3, 1988, p. 83.

Chow, Dan, review of *The Trinity Paradox, Locus,* December, 1991, p. 31.

Review of *Dune: House Atreides, Publishers Weekly,* August 30, 1999, p. 57.

Easton, Tom, review of *Lifeline, Analog Science Fiction and Fact,* May, 1991, pp. 178-180.

Easton, Tom, review of *Virtual Destruction, Analog Science Fiction and Fact,* August, 1996, p. 146.

Flick, Hugh M., review of *The Lost Ones, Kliatt,* May, 1996, p. 12.

Frederickson, Grant A., review of *Ignition, Library Journal,* January, 1997, p. 141.

Review of *Gameplay, Kliatt,* January, 1990, p. 16.

Green, Roland, review of *Assemblers of Infinity, Booklist,* February 15, 1993, p. 1041.

Hays, Carl, review of *Darksaber, Booklist,* September 15, 1995, p. 144.

Review of *Lethal Exposure, Publishers Weekly,* June 15, 1998, p. 57.

Letson, Russell, review of *Climbing Olympus, Locus,* August, 1994, p. 27.

Peasley, Rosie, review of *Assemblers of Infinity, Voice of Youth Advocates,* August, 1993, p. 159

Von Hausen, Ingrid, review of *Jedi Search, Kliatt,* May, 1994, p. 13.

For More Information See

PERIODICALS

Analog Science Fiction and Fact, November, 1992, p. 161; January, 1995, p. 301; December, 1995, p. 162; October, 1996, p. 145.

Booklist, August, 1992, p. 2028; June 1, 1995, p. 1736; March 15, 1996, p. 1244; May 15, 1996, p. 1573; December 15, 1996.

Booktalker, November, 1990, p. 7.

Book Watch, December, 1995, p. 11; January, 1996, p. 10.

Kirkus Reviews, May 1, 1995, p. 570.

Kliatt, July, 1994, p. 54; January, 1996, p. 12; March, 1996, p. 13; p. 51; Spring, 1996, p. 55; July, 1996, p. 16; November, 1996, p. 11.

Library Journal, December, 1990, p. 167; May 1, 1992, p. 133; June, 1995, p. 128; October 15, 1995, p. 91; May 15, 1996, p. 86.

Locus, February, 1989, p. 21; November, 1989, p. 53; October, 1990, p. 50; November, 1990, p. 21; December, 1990, p. 19; January, 1991, p. 54; February, 1991, p. 36; December, 1991, pp. 31, 50; January, 1993, p. 27; July, 1993, p. 39; April, 1994, p. 47.

Magazine of Fantasy and Science Fiction, November, 1988, p. 28; March, 1991, p. 18.

Monthly Review, October, 1996, p. 43.

Necro, fall, 1995, p. 25; spring, 1996, p. 26.

Publishers Weekly, February 7, 1994, p. 85; March 14, 1994, p. 69; May 15, 1995, p. 60; September 4, 1995, p. 54; February 12, 1996, p. 75; April 22, 1996; p. 63; May 13, 1996, p. 30; February 3, 1997, p. 25; February 10, 1997, p. 67; January 11, 1999, p. 20.

Quill and Quire, March, 1994, p. 7.

School Library Journal, December, 1994, p. 38.

Science Fiction Chronicle, September, 1988, p. 64; March, 1989, p. 38; September, 1990, p. 38; March, 1991, pp. 28, 30; May, 1991, p. 32; April, 1993, p. 30; February, 1994, p. 5; October, 1995, p. 45; December, 1995, p. 59; February, 1996, p. 46.

Voice of Youth Advocates, February, 1990, p. 369; December, 1995, p. 283; October, 1996, p. 214.

Wilson Library Bulletin, November, 1990, p. 7.

*   *   *

ANGO, Fan D.
See LONGYEAR, Barry B(rookes)

*   *   *

AYLWARD, Marcus
See ALEXANDER, Marc

B

BAUER, Joan

Personal

Born in River Forest, IL; married; children: Jean.

Addresses

Home—Darien, CT. *Agent*—c/o Putnam Publishing Group, 200 Madison Ave., New York, NY 10016.

Career

Author. Has also worked as an advertising and marketing salesperson, a writer for magazines and newspapers, and a screenwriter.

Writings

Squashed, Delacorte, 1992.
Thwonk, Delacorte, 1995.
Sticks, Delacorte, 1996.
Rules of the Road, Putnam, 1998.
Backwater, Putnam, 1999.

Awards, Honors

Delacorte Prize for First Young Adult Novel, 1992, for *Squashed;* Top Ten Best Books for Young Adults selection, American Library Association, 1999, for *Rules of the Road.*

Sidelights

"There are two things you can count on in a book by Joan Bauer. One, it will make you laugh. And two, the girl who is telling the story will be really good at something, but not something you'd expect," Amazon.com reviewer Patty Campbell commented in a review of Bauer's 1999 novel *Backwater.* Bauer, an advertising-salesperson-turned-writer, has written five books, which have earned her a reputation as a deft spinner of engaging, off-beat tales about young adult themes.

In a 1996 *Alan Review* article entitled "Humor, Seriously," Bauer explained that she uses levity to "teach young people to use laughter against the storms of life." After quoting Mark Twain, who once said that "Humor must speak the truth," Bauer explained, "Finding that truth in characters for me evolves through a process of layering—determining where the characters have been, what they've experienced, what they've overcome and failed abysmally at—that's when the truth of who they are emerges and the voice becomes concrete." For Bauer, humor also reveals that "the person or character has moved from seeing life as a series of problems or things done to them, and has moved into greater clarity and control of the situation." Being someone who knows from first-hand experience about the trials and tribulations of a difficult youth, Bauer works to help teens through their problems and boost their self-esteem through her fiction—both as entertainment and as mild therapy for those who are coping with the problems and pressure of growing up nowadays.

Joan Bauer was born in River Forest, Illinois, the eldest of four sisters. The girls were raised by their mother, a teacher with a lively sense of humor; Bauer's father played little role in her upbringing. Responding to a question in a 1999 interview that is posted on the website of her publisher, Penguin-Putnam, the writer described her father, as "a very messed up man—an alcoholic [who was] married four times, a chronic gambler." Bauer was close to her grandmother, who lived with the family; the woman, a gifted storyteller, engaged the imaginations of her granddaughters with wonderful tales, which she told in a colorful, animated style, using a range of voices. Bauer recalled in the Penguin-Putnam interview, "[My grandmother] taught me the significance of humor and how it intersects our daily lives."

Bauer's teen years were difficult. Her grandmother suffered from Alzheimer's disease, and when Bauer was

Ellie raises a champion pumpkin in Joan Bauer's humorous, award-winning first novel.

write about kids who tend to be loners." Bauer's protagonists are consistent in that they are role models for teens as they move past their problems by working through them. Bauer told her interviewer, "My first drafts are usually quite serious because I'm getting the real serious underpinnings of the stories and characters in place." As she edits her first draft, she adds the humor, which she feels is vital to telling her stories: "I see laughter as being a bridge between pain and redemption," she says. "When we can laugh about something difficult, what we're really saying is that we've moved from the pain of it to the hope." Before she types out the story, Bauer spends a great deal of time researching occupations of her characters, activities the characters engage in, and the scenes where the action takes place. She then writes detailed biographies about her characters before she begins fleshing out the story, treating her own acquaintance with her characters as real and integral to bringing them to life in the imaginations of her readers.

Bauer's teenage daughter, Jean, and her friends help Bauer to stay current on American youth culture. Being a fan of her mother's work, Jean Bauer offers sugges-

twenty, her father committed suicide. She revealed in the Penguin-Putnam interview that day was "the saddest day of my life." Shortly before her father's death, Bauer had gone to Iowa, where he was living, to seek him out. "I confronted him on several things," Bauer told the interviewer. "I learned from that experience that there are times in life when we have choices—we can continue to be victims or we can move forward to be healthy people." Applying the same direct, proactive approach in her fiction, Bauer's characters confront problems in their relationships head-on as they attempt to deal with them.

In the Penguin-Putnam interview, Bauer explained the connection of her real-life teen experiences to her story lines this way: "Because so much was not positive for me, I want to write positive stories. Because so much was painful for me, I want to show ways to overcome pain with emotional health, relationships, and humor. Because I desperately needed ties to my father, I write a great deal about complex fathers.... Because I never had a huge group of friends when I was growing up, I

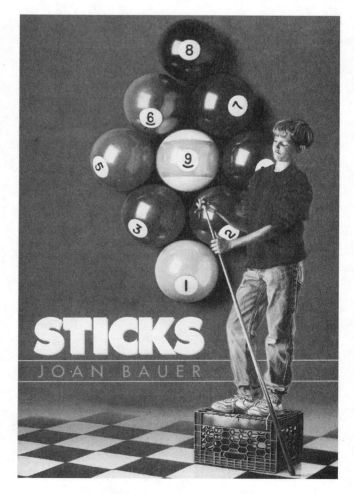

Ten-year-old Mickey is matched against the town bully in a nine-ball pool tournament in Bauer's third novel. (*Cover illustration by John Ramhorst.*)

tions and comments regarding her mother's characters, helping the author to focus on what interests teens; in her Penguin-Putnam interview, Bauer described her daughter as "one of the world's great teenagers." Placing great value on the input and response of her readers, Bauer doesn't take for granted the letters she receives from her readership.

Bauer started working at various jobs when she was still a preteen; she was an assistant typing teacher, a waitress, and a freelance writer. Bauer began a decade-long career in advertising sales in her early twenties. Although she was successful, she eventually grew frustrated with the lack of creativity in her job and, as she recalled in her Penguin-Putnam interview, she "ended up with a few ulcers and was singularly miserable. It was then that I finally began to listen to my heart, quit my job, and started writing." Bauer began in journalism, then tried her hand at screenwriting, before achieving success in young adult fiction. Like many writers, Bauer confesses to a love/hate relationship with writing. "I write because I have to," she told the Penguin-Putnam interviewer. "I

A talented shoe saleswoman, sixteen-year-old Jenna chauffeurs her boss from Chicago to Texas, confronting greed and betrayal while helping save her boss' shoe business. (Cover illustration by Wendell Minor.)

love writing, and yet there are times when it is painfully difficult. I see the world through metaphor, and stories have always been a way for me to explain the world." Bauer recognizes that writing is her forte and therefore a path she pursues naturally. During difficult periods, she said in her Penguin-Putnam interview, "My faith in God, my family, and my close friends keeps me going as a writer."

Bauer's writing debut was an auspicious one. A reviewer for the *Bulletin for the Center for Children's Books* praised *Squashed* for its "humor and tenderness," and the book won the 1992 Delacorte Press Prize for a first novel. Like all of her subsequent tales, Squashed is narrated by the chief protagonist in the first-person. Ellie Morgan is a slightly overweight teenager who is determined to raise a champion pumpkin she calls Max. Ellie is resolute in mustering up the inner strength and agricultural savvy required to successfully care for Max, who requires an exceeding amount of tender loving care. She has loved pumpkins since the first time she saw Cinderella at the age of five. Her hometown of Rock River, Iowa, boasts of its prize-winning pumpkin-growing in its motto: "Our pumpkins we prize; Our rights we will maintain." As Max already weighs three hundred pounds in August, Ellie has a good chance of winning this year's Rock River Pumpkin Weigh-In, where she could earn a dollar per pound, as well as respect in the town. Ellie's motivational specialist father, who wants more than farming for his daughter, is concerned that she is neglecting herself by devoting so much time to her pumpkin. Ellie's grandmother, in contrast, views her granddaughter's attention to Max as instrumental in helping her to build her self-esteem.

The story takes the reader through Ellie's vigorous fight to win the title. Ellie stands on watch against vandals and pumpkin bandits; she sprays and composts; she cleans Max with Windex; she warms him against the fall chill; she plays music for him and talks to him; she injects a concoction of buttermilk and Orange Crush into his stem. In the end, the ordinary girl from Iowa achieves an extraordinary accomplishment through her care of her beloved Max; she emerges as a heroine.

Bauer's second novel, *Thwonk*, teaches readers something about the ingredients for true romance—in other words, what we initially think we want in a mate may not be what can truly bring lasting happiness. A. J. (Allison Jean) McCreary is a Connecticut high-school senior with a passion for photography. When she stumbles upon a stuffed Cupid doll that magically comes to life, A. J. is offered the doll's help in one of the following areas: academics, career, or romance. She chooses the latter, specifically a love-tipped arrow for the heart of Peter Terris, a boy who is handsome, popular, and totally unaware of A. J.'s existence. She is set on Peter taking her to the school's King of Hearts Dance—hence the title "thwonk," which is the sound of an arrow shot from Cupid's bow. With the doll's help, Peter becomes pathetically infatuated with A. J., but it's not long before she finds his attentions annoying. What's more, A. J. discovers that Peter is wanting in wit and smarts, areas in which she excels. A. J.'s drollery in relating her story to readers sharply contrasts with Peter's dullness and goofiness. As the plot progresses and A. J.'s skill in photography develops, she learns more about herself and what's really important to her. Her talents are even acknowledged and rewarded by her previously distant filmmaker father.

Several reviewers praised *Thwonk* and lauded Bauer for her writing. Alice Casey Smith of *School Library Journal* praised the book as a "silly, offbeat novel ... [that] revels in the vagaries, insecurities, and uncomfortable realities of teen love." Suzanne Curley of the *Los Angeles Times Book Review* described it as "a first-class comic romance," while Deborah Stevenson of *The Bulletin of the Center for Children's Books* noted that "Bauer's forcefully funny writing remains stylish from start to finish."

By now, it was apparent that Bauer was beginning to hit her stride as a writer. *Sticks,* her third novel, was nominated for the 1998-1999 Mark Twain Award; it is another light-hearted teen novel with a message. The protagonist is ten-year-old Mickey Vernon, who dreams of winning the nine-ball tournament hosted by his family's pool hall. His rival is town bully Buck Pender. At age thirteen, Buck is bigger than Mickey and stronger than him. However, Mickey learns during the story that physical size and strength aren't everything. Superior technique and using his brain will help him beat Buck in the big tournament. As Mickey prepares for the match, his brilliant friend Arlen shows him the mathematics of pool and assists him in becoming skillful in the geometric strategy of the game. Meanwhile, Joseph Alvarez, an old friend of Mickey's late father comes to town. An old pool shark himself, he takes Mickey under his wing, in the process becoming a sort of father figure to the boy. Mickey's mother objects to her son's relationship with Joseph, forbidding it. Since Mickey narrates the story, the reader is drawn into his struggle to win the tournament from Buck while soothing the tensions between his mother and Joseph.

Reviewer Todd Morning of *School Library Journal* liked *Sticks,* writing that "the winning characterizations may make this a book to be enjoyed by kids who like pool and even some who don't." Janice Del Negro of *Booklist* echoed that assessment. "Bauer's characterizations are well drawn, their personalities three-dimensional even when they only appear briefly, and Mickey is not only a credible ten-year-old but also a likable narrator," Del Negro noted. "Good characters, humor, and an engaging plot make this a solid piece of middle-grade fiction."

Rules of the Road, Bauer's next book, is the story of sixteen-year-old Chicago-resident Jenna Boller, a young woman with a talent for selling shoes. Not only does Jenna have the knack for servicing the needs and footwear tastes of customers, she is dedicated to the business. Shortly after obtaining her driver's license, Elden Gladstone, president of Gladstone shoes, offers Jenna the job of chauffeuring her to Texas for a

Sixteen-year-old Ivy would rather study history than pursue a legal career as her family expects. (Cover illustration by Wendell Minor.)

stockholders' meeting. The novel chronicles the twosome's adventure south, during which Jenna learns about her own strengths and capabilities, while picking up important values in loyalty and service to others. Jenna is also confronted with betrayal and greed through the dirty deeds of Mrs. Gladstone's slimy son Elden, who is trying to swindle his mother out of her shoe empire through corporate takeover maneuvering. Together, Jenna and Mrs. Gladstone embark on a mission to save the business.

Along the way, Jenna befriends a salesman, a longtime member of Alcoholics Anonymous. She wishes her own father, a current alcoholic, were more like him. After the salesman is killed by a drunk driver, Jenna alerts police to her own father's drunk driving.

Reviewer Cindy Darling Codell of *School Library Journal* hailed *Rules of the Road* as "Bauer's best [novel] yet;" Candace Deisley of the *Voice of Youth Advocates* praised it as "a remarkable book, presenting lessons of respect for others, courtesy, and honesty gently, but persistently."

Backwater, published in 1999, is a tale of a sixteen-year-old girl's journey to find her roots and to discover her emotional, intellectual, and physical limits. Ivy Breedlove comes from a family of lawyers, and being an intelligent girl, she is naturally expected to pursue a legal career. However, her real passion in life is studying history. While tracing her family tree, a project started as a birthday gift for her Great Aunt Tib, Ivy discovers female relatives who were mavericks in that they followed their own interests, and left behind family expectations for them. Ivy becomes obsessed with wanting to learn more about her father's sister Josephine, "Aunt Jo"; aided by a colorful guide known as Mountain Mama, Ivy sets out to meet her. Aunt Jo is a hermit sculptor who lives in the wilderness of the Adirondack Mountains. During Ivy's quest for knowledge and historical revelation, she learns important lessons about herself and the essence of family. Reviewer Jean Franklin of *Booklist* praised the novel, saying "This warm, funny patchwork quilt of a book ... will keep readers turning the pages to the last." Franklin added that, along with *Rules of the Road,* Backwater provides "a dynamite mother-daughter book discussion."

On the strength of such comments, Bauer's five novels have won her many fans among teen readers, parents, librarians, and teachers. The author revealed in her Penguin-Putnam interview that a new book she is writing centers on a theme of honor and politics. "And yes, it's fiction," she added jokingly.

Works Cited

Bauer, Joan, "Humor, Seriously," *ALAN Review,* winter, 1996.

Bauer, Joan, interview on Penguin-Putnam Web site, located at http://www2.penguinputnam.com.

Campbell, Patty, review of *Backwater,* Amazon.com website, located at http://www.amazon.com.

Coddell, Cindy Darling, review of *Rules of the Road, School Library Journal,* March, 1998, p. 208.

Curley, Suzanne, "A Few Well-Placed Arrows," *Los Angeles Times Book Review,* February 26, 1995, p. 9.

Deisley, Candace, review of *Rules of the Road, Voice of Youth Advocates,* June, 1998, p. 120.

Del Negro, Janice, review of *Sticks, Booklist,* May 1, 1996, p. 1505.

Franklin, Jean, review of *Backwater, Booklist,* May 15, 1999, p. 1687.

Morning, Todd, review of *Sticks, School Library Journal,* June, 1996, p. 120.

Smith, Alice Casey, review of *Thwonk, School Library Journal,* January, 1995, p. 134.

Review of *Squashed, Bulletin of the Center for Children's Books,* October, 1992, p. 36.

Stevenson, Deborah, review of *Thwonk, Bulletin of the Center for Children's Books,* January, 1995, p. 158.

For More Information See

PERIODICALS

Booklist, January 1, 1995, p. 814; July, 1997, p. 1830; February 1, 1998, p. 77.

Horn Book, May-June, 1998, p. 339.

New York Times Book Review, June 20, 1999, p. 21.

Publishers Weekly, February 27, 1995, p. 104; February 23, 1998, p. 77.

School Library Journal, June, 1999, p. 126.*

—*Sketch by Melissa Walsh Doig*

*   *   *

BEAGLEHOLE, Helen 1946-

Personal

Born November 27, 1946, in New Zealand; father, a managing director; mother's name Elizabeth (Barrowclough) Bisley; married Tim Beaglehole (a university teacher and administrator); children: John, Toby, Charlotte. *Education:* Victoria University of Wellington, B.A., 1968, diploma in educational studies, 1974; Wellington Teachers College, diploma in teaching, 1978; Whitireia Polytechnic, certificate in publishing, 1995. *Politics:* "Left." *Hobbies and other interests:* Sailing, tramping, mountain biking.

Helen Beaglehole

Addresses

Home—6 Messines Rd., Wellington, New Zealand. *E-mail*—tim.beaglehole@vuw.ac.nz.

Career

Teacher, 1977-80; held advisory and assistant advisory positions with New Zealand Ministry of Commerce and Departments of Trade and Industry, Labour, and Social Welfare, between 1980 and 1989; worked as senior policy analyst for New Zealand Ministries of Commerce and Women's Affairs, 1989-94; freelance editor, 1996—; Victoria University of Wellington, Wellington, New Zealand, teacher of policy writing, 1999. New Zealand Book Council, member, 1996—, member of board of directors, 1997—. Women's Electoral Lobby, member of executive group, 1989-93. Wellington Girls' College, member of board of trustees, 1990-93. *Member:* New Zealand Society of Authors (chairperson of Wellington branch and member of national executive, 1995-97); Wellington Children's Book Group, committee member, 1995-97; Society for Research on Women, Amnesty International (New Zealand section).

Awards, Honors

Grants from QEII Writers Project, 1992, and QEII New Zealand Authors Scheme, 1994; short-listed for Aim Children's Book Award and nomination for Russell Clark Award, both 1994, for *Two Tigers;* short-listed for May Smith Award, New Zealand Society of Authors, 1994; writing fellowship, Reader's Digest-New Zealand Society of Authors-Stout Research Centre, 1995.

Writings

FOR CHILDREN

Two Tigers, illustrated by Lesley Moyes, Shearwater Books (New Zealand), 1993.
Strange Company (novel), Cape Catley (New Zealand), 1996.
Plumstones, illustrated by Craig Smith, Roland Harvey (Port Melbourne, Australia), 1999.
John's Remarkable Day, illustrated by Smith, Roland Harvey, 1999.

YOUNG ADULT NOVELS

The Family Album, Cape Catley, 1997.
because he's my brother, Mallinson Rendel (New Zealand), 1998.
hanging on letting go, Mallinson Rendel, 1999.

Contributor to periodicals, including *Education, Listener,* and *Input.* Author of "Ruth France" entry in *Dictionary of New Zealand Biography,* Vol. 5, forthcoming.

Work in Progress

A young adult novel, *C'mon In, Baby.*

Sidelights

Helen Beaglehole told *SATA:* "I wrote a lot as a child, but it was only as a parent, reading to my own children, that I thought I could do as well. I started, very much part-time, and fitted writing into a busy job and family life. Later I worked a four-day week, and my writing became a refuge from a busy office and an opportunity for access into the world that writers carry in their heads. Now I divide my time between my own writing and the writing and editing I do on contract for the government—and sailing, tramping, and mountain biking.

"My early books—the illustrated books—I conceived as a way of bridging a gap that I'd discovered with my own children. We all needed something between the two-to-three-lines-a-page books and *Winnie the Pooh.* But those books, and my later ones for older readers, all spring from passionately held beliefs: that you don't write down to children; that the tradition of stories being used to explore human conflicts or questions around the human condition should constantly be revitalized by children's authors who are writing about issues that engage and interest them; that endings should provide hope and a way to the future; and that books should offer readers a world beyond their own. Start with the familiar, if you must, but don't shackle yourself or your reader with it."

For More Information See

PERIODICALS

Magpies, March, 1999, p. 8.

ON-LINE

Victoria University of Wellington website with information on New Zealand authors located at http://www.vuw.ac.nz/nzbookcouncil.

Autobiography Feature

Rose Blue

I guess I like it here. Born and bred in New York City, Brooklyn, to be exact, I still, and in all probability always will, call this town home. My parents, the children of immigrants, were also born in New York. Mom and Dad met in a Manhattan pharmacy.

She, the pretty, fun-loving cosmetician, he the tall, handsome pharmacist, worked together, then dated, then married. Two years later, on a cold December night in Brooklyn Women's Hospital, I came upon the scene.

I was to be the only child. As I was to discover later, this is a mixed blessing. No siblings to share the attention later leads to no siblings to share the responsibility. After my entrance to this earth, my mother lost two babies. I knew early on that I was destined to be the one and only.

The Brooklyn apartment, however, did not lack for company. Upon the death of my grandparents, two uncles and one aunt moved in. The men didn't stay too long, but Aunt Lila remained throughout most of my childhood.

The extended family is a vanishing breed these days. People move and scatter throughout the country, if not the world, and communicate through long-distance phone company plans, catalogue birthday gifts, and holiday greeting cards. There is much to be said, however, for the richness of the extended family. Aunt Lila, who came to be known as Nonny when at the age of nine or ten months I pronounced the L sound as N, became in effect my second mother. She read to me, sang to me, and showered me with constant attention. Nonny served as a one-woman prekindergarten and learning center. When she overslept past 6:00 A.M. or so, I would rush over to her bed bearing her eyeglasses—a toddler alarm clock informing her that the time had come to rise and shine and pay attention to Rose. The place for aunts in the family is an exalted one, and sadly it is losing its luster in present-day society.

Lila provided reading readiness. Our twelve-year-old neighbor Anabelle did the rest. Anabelle thought I was cute. When she had nothing else to do and her apartment grew too noisy, she came downstairs and visited. Although she had many friends her own age, none lived in the building and her mother wouldn't permit her to go out to see her buddies in bad weather. So, the storm often blew Anabelle to our place.

One cold winter's day, just after my third birthday, Anabelle arrived with the first blizzard of December. She came bearing coloring books, storybooks, and other goodies. Bored with coloring and reading to me, Anabelle decided to teach me to read. It didn't take long. By the time the last flake fell and Anabelle went up for dinner, I had become a just-turned-three avid reader. I read everything I could get my hands on, including the newspapers my father brought home each day—one with his morning coffee and one on his way home from work at the pharmacy.

My education continued unabated as the autumn before my fifth birthday drew near. That would be time for kindergarten. My mother noticed that many neighbor children cried, clung to their mothers, and generally experienced severe trauma on this fateful day. She was determined not to allow this to happen to our family.

In an effort to avert such shame falling upon us, she began to campaign a year before the scheduled event. She walked past the school with me on a regular basis. This was no big trick since P.S. 103 was conveniently located across the street. She told me that when I got bigger I would be coming here.

If I was a good girl, I would play games indoors and out, and the nice teacher would give me milk and cookies. She pointed out the children at recess time, enjoying the swings, sliding boards, and seesaws in the school yard and told me that all that fun would be mine. All I had to do to be a part of that magic kingdom was wait till the proper time and be a good girl. It worked. I looked forward eagerly to the start of school, and at the appointed day, I waved my mother away eagerly and did not disgrace the family.

It was all true. This place called school was great fun. Miss Penny was very sweet indeed. She played the piano. We sang songs. She read picture books. We listened. She provided puzzles, games, toys, and tea sets. She took us to the school yard to play circle games and enjoy the equipment. And, as my mother had promised, Miss Penny served milk and cookies. The cookies were chocolate-covered graham crackers, and they were simply wonderful. I can still taste the sweetness on my tongue. I kept my part of the bargain. I was a good girl. All was right with the fun world of P.S. 103. There was one thing, however, that my mother never told me in her eagerness for me to like school. She forgot to mention that school was a place to learn. The thought never occurred to me. The rude awakening did, however, occur in Miss Higgens's first-grade class.

Miss Higgens was a tall, slender, serious of purpose, yet pleasant teacher. I liked Miss Higgens and looked forward to a year of good behavior in exchange for games and grahams. Miss Higgens launched the school year by giving out readers. She said that we were going to read the story contained therein. Then Miss Higgens proceeded to write letters on the chalkboard, sound out syllables, and speak in an extremely slow and boring fashion. I had no idea what Miss Higgens was doing or why. I looked out the window, but there was no tree in direct view. I always loved a tree outside my window. I watched the clouds pass slowly and turned them into shapes in my mind's eye. I watched the birds fly by. Miss Higgens still held forth. Miss Higgens had said we were going to read the story. I read it. Miss Higgens still spoke. I watched the clouds and birds some more. Miss Higgens still wrote on the chalkboard. I picked up my pencil, opened my notebook, and wrote a story.

Miss Higgens stood at my desk. "Rose," she said firmly but pleasantly, "you haven't been paying attention to me. How will you learn to read?"

"Learn to read?" I repeated in surprise and puzzlement. "Is that what the children are doing?"

"Yes," Miss Higgens repeated pleasantly. "I'm teaching the class to read. You're in first grade now. We come to school to learn."

I waited for that pronouncement to sink in. I was supposed to learn here, not just play and savor snacks. But didn't learning mean doing something you didn't do before?

"Miss Higgens," I said politely, "I know how to read. Anabelle upstairs taught me when I was three. I read this story just now."

Miss Higgens sighed. "We'll learn to read this story in a few weeks."

"Miss Higgens," I repeated. "You said we could read the story, so I read it." I opened the book and read the story quietly and clearly to Miss Higgens. The sweet lady was truly stunned. She didn't know what to make of this.

Then she spotted my open notebook. "What have you been doing, Rose?" she asked.

"Well, I read the story you gave us. Then I read it again. I couldn't keep reading the same story, and there was no other story to read so I wrote my own."

"You wrote your own story?" Miss Higgens picked up my notebook. "May I read it?"

"Yes, Miss Higgens," I replied.

Miss Higgens read my masterpiece and smiled cheerfully. "This is really very good. My lesson is finished. Would you like to read your story to the class?"

Visions of chocolate grahams danced in my head. I didn't want to upset the keeper of the cookies. "Yes, Miss Higgens." I rose and embarked on my first public appearance.

I was a smash. The kids loved it. They cried for more. But there was no more.

"Rose," Miss Higgens suggested, "why don't you get a special notebook just to write your stories. Write them at home, bring them to school, and read them to the class. Would you like that?"

"Yes, Miss Higgens."

The notebook was black-and-white speckled. I wrote my stories looking out my window at my tree. When Miss Higgens had lesson plans to compose or rests to take, she would ask me to read my story of the week to the class. The children sat rapt and listened. I was six years old, and I knew nothing could ever shake that certainty. It has been

Rose Blue

said that an angel appears at birth and blesses or curses some with a talent. I didn't know whether it was a blessing or a curse. I still don't know. But I know what I knew for an absolute fact at six. I was a writer. And that was that.

The word was passed in the teachers' room at P.S. 103. I provided respite for Miss Manganaro, Mr. Reich, and Mrs. Stern. I filled up my story notebooks and served as P.S. 103 writer-in-residence. My career was launched.

The remainder of my tenure at P.S. 103, as well as the rest of my childhood years, was relatively uneventful. I had many friends, played ball, jump rope, circle games, and all that traditional stuff. Mom and Nonny spoiled me. Nonny found a job as executive secretary and encouraged me in my writing. I awaited Dad's arrival from his job each twilight. He lifted me high in the air, and I reached upward in an effort to touch the leaves. I spent time at the library on the main avenue of my neighborhood, borrowing Nancy Drew, Louisa May Alcott, and whatever the children's librarian advised.

Then it was time to move up the educational ladder. The days of P.S. 103 came to a close. As seventh grade approached the days at Montauk Junior High began. It was a long walk, but we made the trek in quest of higher learning.

I recall those days as lackluster. I don't really know the reason for junior high, or middle school as it is now frequently called. Middle school seems an apt name for it—sandwiched in the middle between the childhood cocoon of elementary school and the teen years of high school.

The teachers seemed rather bored as well. I decided to join the school paper. It felt like the natural move for a writer to make. The Montauk Junior High paper was entitled, appropriately enough, *The Wigwam*. I didn't let that stop me. I became a reporter and columnist. Mr. Greenleaf, the faculty advisor, did not shine. I did my best to make my *Wigwam* days memorable. However, I did look forward to step three on the educational ladder. After graduation day at Montauk Junior High, replete with a gardenia corsage from my parents, the next step arrived. I stepped up the elevated subway stairs and took the train to New Utrecht High School.

At that time, some significant family events occurred. Nonny got married. That happy day got me my very own room. In addition, my father opened a pharmacy two blocks away from home. Mom worked with him as a salesperson. She always loved that work and always had a buoyant, outgoing personality.

Because my parents spent so much time at the store, I practically had my own apartment. I had the freedom to study and entertain friends. But family was nearby. The pharmacy was conveniently located between the subway stop to and from school, and Nonny lived in the apartment next door. One year later Nonny had a son, and cousin Bill and I remain close.

Things took a definite turn for the better at New Utrecht. The English honors program included two teachers who were truly terrific and memorable. Mrs. Rosenkans and Mr. Shlackman also served as faculty advisors on the school newspaper *NUHS* (New Utrecht High School) and *Spiral,* the literary magazine. I served on both those distinguished publications as well as *Comet,* the senior magazine. The staff was outstanding, and I number some lifelong friends from those days.

Mr. Shlackman was a charismatic teacher, a real hunk. I can picture him sitting at the edge of his desk reading Carl Sandburg's *Chicago* in a dramatic booming voice. Mr. Shlackman's class was exciting every which way. Mrs. Rosenkans had a different, but very effective, style. She was very motherly. That worked too. She got the best out of her kids, and the New Utrecht publications were superior for high-school journalism and art. She encouraged me in my writing career and told me that I had a bright future as a writer. She and Nonny were my biggest boosters. I often think of her, and that in itself is a great legacy for a dedicated teacher. The day came, however, to bid farewell to high school at a ceremony overlooking Brooklyn's Prospect Park Lake. It was time to cast my bread upon the waters.

Barnard College accepted me for admission. I decided to accept, then go on to Columbia's Graduate School of journalism for a master's degree. That would provide immediate entry into a career in journalism, or so I thought. The tuition at Barnard was high, so I thought, and so

(From left) Rose, Cousin Ruth, (standing) Aunt Lil and Cousin Claire, Cousin Bernie, and Cousin Harvey at Aunt Lil's birthday party.

thought my father. "Barnard," he said, "who has the money? And it's far. Go to Brooklyn College. It's free. And you can take the bus."

I took the bus and stepped off to a great new world. I didn't expect to—it wasn't Barnard but I loved Brooklyn College. I loved the lily pond, the rock garden, the steps of Boylen Hall, which served as the communal congregation center.

Nothing without great labor. But my primary labor was on the school newspaper, the *Kingsman.* It was a highly professional outfit for a school paper. The staff was sensational. We spent serious overtime, working far into the night at press time. It was generally accepted that killing your mother was a bad thing, but missing a deadline was a really bad thing. That work ethic remains with me to this day. I believe that I thought my primary function in college was the school newspaper, not my general education. Except for English, I could have paid more attention to my courses, but the *Kingsman* office was my home away from home. I made lifelong friends at Brooklyn College and spent a great four years there.

I learned to keep the teachers off my back early on. Mr. Bernardine, a formidable teacher in the English honors program, caused much quaking in the ranks. Mr. Bernardine could make or break your future with a lilt of his booming voice. So you want to be a professor? A scholar? A teacher? A writer? Mr. Bernardine would let you know if that was possible. You didn't even have to ask him. Few did. He volunteered the information and could cut you down in an instant. It was incredible. Years later, I met an ex-colleague who congratulated me on my work and said she wished she could be a writer. I asked her what stopped her. She was fine on the college newspaper. "Mr. Bernardine said I would never be a writer," she explained.

I heaved a sigh of sadness for Louise and a sigh of relief for myself. I took care of Mr. Bernardine quickly. His first term-paper assignment was an in-depth study of the works of a playwright of your choosing. Most everyone went scurrying to the classics. I did William Saroyan, then avant-garde and offbeat. It was an in-depth, scholarly treatise in perfect form. Why didn't Mr. Bernardine rip it apart? Why did I get an A? Because Mr. Bernardine couldn't critique it. "It's a fine paper," he said. "I'm terribly sorry that I can't discuss it with you properly because I'm not as familiar as I should be with Saroyan's work. I plan to study it now."

I smiled sweetly and spoke softly. "When you do, Mr. Bernardine," I said, "please let me know. I'd like to discuss it with you."

Since Mr. Bernardine apparently never found the time for Saroyan, he never came near me again. I got As, and I got Mr. Bernardine off my back for the semester. I was spared his prediction of my future writing career. I'll never know what his pronouncements would have been.

The famed jazz musician Fats Waller was once asked to explain his music and to offer advice to aspiring talent. He replied, "If you gotta ask, you don't got it." I wholeheartedly agree with Fats. I firmly believe that the talent must be there to begin with. Then the hard work, honed skill, passion, and determination must follow. If you got it, you gotta work at it, and no Mr. Bernardine can be permitted to derail you.

Brooklyn College yearbook photo.

College went smoothly. I worked at the *Kingsman,* hung out with friends, had a romance or two, and worked part-time at the public library next to my Dad's store. Then it happened. A ceremony was held one spring day on the Brooklyn College campus. We threw our caps high in the air. Graduation day had arrived, and it was time for us to depart. The cocoon of college was no more. The future was upon us.

After graduation, my parents treated me to a week's vacation in a Florida hotel. I remember lounging at poolside in my bathing suit when a photographer approached me. "We're doing a feature on the local newspaper. Each week we run a photo of a visitor."

"Why me?" I asked.

"We run young women for publicity. It makes a good shot. We'll give you a free photograph."

"No, thanks," I replied. "One day my name will be in a newspaper. But not because I look good in a bathing suit. When it happens, I want it to be because of something I'm proud of."

The photographer didn't get it, and neither did the other guests or my family. But I stood my ground. The photographer took my picture and gave it to me as a gift because he felt I was a person of conviction, whatever those convictions were, and I still keep that photo as a reminder of those days. Later, I was to get my name in the paper, as promised, for my work. But it was to be a long, hard row to hoe.

The first thing I did after graduation and vacation was redecorate my room. I papered the wall with rejection slips. I wrote. I submitted. I waited for the postman. He brought letter after letter stating "we regret that your submission does not meet our needs at this time."

My father began leaving the "Help Wanted" sections of the newspapers in conspicuous places around the house. When the gentle hints failed to provoke a response from his oblivious daughter, he asked point blank, "Now that college is over, what are you planning to do for a living?"

Silly question. "I'm going to be a writer," I replied.

My father smiled patiently. That was very nice indeed. However, he wished to know what I intended to do for a living. He suggested that I find a teaching job, write "on the side," and he provided me with explicit directions to the New York City Board of Education.

I was assigned to a Brooklyn junior high school as an English teacher. When I arrived, I was greeted by a most amiable young man, Mr. Russel, the assistant principal.

"Welcome to Adams Junior High," he said. "We really need a library teacher."

"There must be some mistake," I replied. "I majored in English. I'm supposed to be an English teacher." I handed him the official seal of the Board of Education edict.

He barely glanced at it. "That's nice. But we don't need an English teacher. We need a library teacher. You can do it. You're an English teacher. English. Books. Library. You'll do fine. Here are the keys. If you have trouble, call me. Good luck."

The first two periods of my teacher/librarian career went quite well. Teachers brought their classes to me, dumped the kids at the library door, and raced off for coffee. I seated my charges, gave an impromptu talk on how to use the library and the rewards of reading, and called the crew table by table to select a book. Third period arrived and so did my lesson on life in the school system.

Things went well until book selection time. It was warm for early September, and the windows were open without benefit of screens. A boy selected a book, strolled slowly and coolly back to his table, but on the way he paused to throw the book out the fourth-floor window. Horrified, I chastised him severely and used the telephone intercom to call the nice, amiable assistant principal. After all, he did instruct me to call him if I had any trouble.

"What's wrong?" he asked when he arrived. "You're doing fine. I passed the library a few times, and there was no problem."

"Well, Johnny here threw a book out the window," I replied with righteous indignation.

Mr. Russel severely chastised Johnny once again. Then he called me aside. "I don't understand," he said. "Why did you call me? You're doing very well."

"You told me to call you if I had trouble," I reminded him.

"Let me explain," he said patiently. "I'm a very busy person. Call me only when absolutely necessary. You do not have trouble. A kid throwing a book out the window is not trouble. When a kid throws another kid out the window, then you have trouble. Then you may call me."

Major lesson in education. Don't bother the bosses. They did not become bosses to be bothered. Sink or swim.

And if you want to keep your job, learn to swim. I gave myself a crash course in survival techniques at Adams Junior High, and my teaching career was launched.

While I held forth in the halls of knowledge, my Brooklyn College Kingsman crowd was pursuing other areas. Some went in search of editing jobs. I never really pursued editing with much enthusiasm. I felt that I was on the writer's side of the publishing team, not the editor's. I also never felt comfortable judging the work of other writers. I did not really care to be cast in the role of Professor Bernardine, decreeing who shall succeed and who shall fail. But editors are an invaluable part of the publishing business, and it is a noble profession.

My friend Marcia, who would ultimately become a literary agent, found a job as an editor of a chain of magazines. Among the publications were several confession magazines, one of them assigned to Marcia. At the risk of shocking the faithful, I am revealing the fact that confession stories are not written by the confessors but by professional writers. Someone writes the young marrieds, another scribe does the older marrieds, someone else the singles, etc. One day Marcia called me. "We need a writer for our teenage stuff," she said. "I know you can do it. Try one."

I did. It wasn't very difficult. After all, I was surrounded by my teenage students all day. Marcia called again. "Great. Everybody loved it. Other writers, writing in the first person, use the language spoken when they were teenagers. You've got the language down pat."

"The bathing suit picture."

Why not? I heard it all the time.

"We want you to hand in a story every month," Marcia said calmly.

I kept a copy of my first writing check. I bought myself an expensive velvet shirt in a fancy New York store as a special treat. And I continued to pen such classics as Little Miss Innocence. With my other hand, I tried to sell more literary works. Now, I was relieved of my library duties and given a position as an English teacher. With my third hand, I wrote lesson plans, marked papers, and read essays. Teaching English entailed lots of after-school time that I wanted to devote to writing. There had to be another way to earn a living. There was.

A friend of a friend was a principal at P.S. 44 in the Bedford-Stuyvesant section of Brooklyn. Bed-Stuy, as it is known, is a primarily African American area. Being a minority school and an area below the poverty level, the school qualified for special funding.

"I have a prekindergarten class," Mrs. Starr told me. "It's funded as part of the Head Start program. I need a teacher. The job is yours if you want it."

I went to check out the school and the program. It was great. The kids were four years old, and the program was wonderfully worthwhile. "I want the job," I told Mrs. Starr. "When does it start?"

Miss Blue became the prekindergarten teacher at P.S. 44. I had paraprofessionals helping with the children—women in the neighborhood who otherwise would have been on welfare. The program provided people with jobs and provided the kids with a great learning opportunity. I bought toys, books, and games above and beyond what was provided and took the kids on trips and outings. I loved the job. As I told Mrs. Corbett, a great assistant, we had a class to rival any fancy, expensive private school in New York. Doing something of social value and having great fun at the same time was enviable work.

In order to keep my job, I needed a license in early childhood education. Having majored in English, I lacked the necessary education courses for such a license. I decided to take graduate studies at the Bank Street College of Education, a very special institution of higher learning. Now there are classes for kids intermingled with classes for teachers. It is truly a learning lab. There is a sensational children's bookstore and a terrific library. I keep in touch, and I regularly attended a writers group there, led by my acclaimed colleague Bill Hooks, until his recent move from the city.

Having decided upon Bank Street for my graduate work, I further decided to attend summers when school was closed. That first summer I enrolled in a children's literature course.

The professor was a brilliant scholar. She was a prestigious writer on the topic of children's books. She gave a fascinating course and a tremendous amount of work. I enjoyed speaking with her, and one day after class, we chatted a while. "I enjoy your course very much," I told her. "But tell me. When are we going to get to the really good books? You know, realistic stuff. Books that the kids I teach can identify with."

She looked at me strangely. "Rose," she said patiently, "you've now read nearly every children's book ever written."

"But that can't be," I said. "There's nothing about day-to-day life in the city. Nothing for my kids."

"That's it," she repeated.

"I can do better than that."

She shrugged. "What's stopping you? Go ahead."

And I did. After summer school ended, I sat down and wrote *A Quiet Place.* It was about an African-American foster child whose beloved library was being remodeled. He goes in search of a quiet place to read the books he borrows from a temporary bookmobile.

By summer's end, I had a complete manuscript and not the vaguest idea of what to do with it. I wrote the professor asking if she would like to see the manuscript and suggest how I might go about getting a publisher. She replied curtly. She had no time to read it. I sent it to two publishers with no foot in either door. One editor sent a form rejection letter. The other replied with a more personal note. It was too quiet. I groaned. I didn't set out to write an adventure, did I? I called it *A Quiet Place,* didn't I?

Discouraged, I told my plight to Marcia. She remembered that Carolyn, who worked as an editor on the confession magazine, had come to New York from another state. A friend of hers, who had also relocated, had found a job with a prestigious children's book publishing house. I contacted Carolyn, who put me in touch with Claudia Cohl at Franklin Watts. She accepted the book.

I was truly in seventh heaven. I had a new niche. The confession stories were not truly great literature, and the chance to write and publish quality work was a dream come true. I jotted a note to the Bank Street professor telling her of my good fortune. I received a lengthy letter inviting me to her home with the book. She included a map. Now she had time. I declined. For my part, she could buy the book herself.

Claudia was a remarkable editor. Her suggestions vastly improved the book. She assigned a marvelous illustrator, the perfect choice. Tom Feelings, now an award-winning illustrator, honored me with his art on my very first book. *A Quiet Place* arrived to great reviews and was a smash. My friends Renee and Al threw a party for me upon publication. Renee had been my friend since high school and became an attorney. She and her husband invited Tom and Claudia to celebrate. It was lovely. Tom presented me with a sketch of the cover, which still hangs on my wall. Through the years I have added gifts of art given to me by illustrators, and my walls are a source of great pleasure to me.

Realistic children's books are to me the core of children's literature. I have no objection to fun, games, and entertainment, but kids raised on the alligator in the tomato or cutesy kitty goes to kindergarten can hardly be expected to become avid, discerning readers of fine literature in adulthood. I consider the publication of *A Quiet Place* a great milestone in my life and career.

Claudia, however, did not permit me to rest on my laurels. I followed up *A Quiet Place* with three picture books for young children. *How Many Blocks Is the World?* was about the expanding horizons of a young child embarking upon school. The dedication read, "To Nonny, who knew it all the time."

Nonny knew that she knew it all the time, and she was thrilled. Next came *Bed-Stuy Beat,* a story about my school neighborhood in rhyme and rhythm, and *I Am Here: Yo*

Rose and her class at P.S. 44.

Estoy Aqui about a Hispanic girl adjusting to life in her new home after moving from the place of her birth.

Then I interrupted my picture-book streak with a middle-grade fiction novel. A friend of mine had recently been divorced, and the two children were devastated at seeing their father only on Sundays. I dedicated the book, *A Month of Sundays,* to them and hoped it helped the many youngsters in the same position as well. *A Month of Sundays* received excellent reviews. This book was illustrated by Ted Lewin, a wonderful artist who continues to enjoy a full workload and has numerous awards to his credit.

Then Claudia invited me to lunch. We sat chatting in a New York City restaurant. "Rose," Claudia said, "I'd like to see a book based on my grandmother. How about doing a book about a kid who adjusts to the senility of a beloved grandmother?"

Nothing like it had ever been done. I had no experience in the matter at that time. But it would be a marvelous step forward in realism in children's literature.

"It's great, Claudia," I replied. "Let's do it."

I researched and outlined the book. Claudia approved. I sat down and wrote *Grandma Didn't Wave Back.* The reviews were phenomenal. A producer contacted us. Tom Robertson did a children's TV series called "The Young People's Special," which aired on NBC at 7:30 P.M., an hour in which families as well as kids comprised the audience.

Tom's goal was to do quality TV, and he thought *Grandma* filled the bill. We collaborated on the script. A number of actresses were sent the script, among them Helen Hayes, who replied, "I don't work with children or dogs." Fortunately, Molly Picon didn't share that view. An actress of world acclaim, Molly loved it. She invited us to her apartment and was a gracious, remarkable lady. She was perfect for the part of Grandma.

The special was shot near the water in Brooklyn. I was overjoyed to be on the set watching such talent. *When Grandma Didn't Wave Back* appeared on TV, it was a

genuine thrill for me. I have the tape and still watch it occasionally. The special won the Red Ribbon Award of the American Film Festival. The award hangs on my wall, joining the illustrations.

Tom produced another one of my books for television and engaged me to do the teleplay as well. *My Mother the Witch* was a historical-fiction piece for youngsters in the eight-through-twelve age group. It concerned a ten-year-old girl in Salem, Massachusetts, during colonial times who believes her mother may be a witch. Ted Lewin illustrated the book, and the production was shot in Salem. I went up for the filming and enjoyed it immensely. The special was well reviewed. One of the reviews was very complimentary: "The book is so realistic, it is clear that the author must be a witch."

For the record, the author is not a witch. Nor is she divorced, senile, or adopted. An author does not need to have direct experience with the topic of his or her book. It is a common misconception that shuts the door on the creativity of many writers. A children's book writer is able to write about what can be read by children—any and all children—and that is what I attempt to do.

After *Grandma Didn't Wave Back,* Claudia wanted some more books written for the middle grades and illustrated by Ted. She signed us up for two more books, and along with *Grandma Didn't Wave Back,* she called it a trilogy. The books *Nikki 108,* about a girl whose beloved older brother dies of a drug overdose, and *The Preacher's Kid,* about a girl whose clergyman father experiences trouble with his job and congregation after he takes a strong stand for school integration. Just as I was to begin work on *The Preacher's Kid,* two things happened: Claudia left Franklin Watts, and I left my job at the Head Start program.

Claudia found a position at Scholastic Press working on their magazines. At about the same time, I decided that the time had come to do something about my dual careers. It was time for a decision. I found myself taking days off from teaching to meet working deadlines and to meet editors for lunch. I found myself writing after school late into the evening, when I was not fresh. It seemed that if I continued along these lines, my writing would suffer. That would be unfair to my editors, my readers, and me. If I continued to take time off from school to pursue my writing, it would be grossly unfair to my children. I decided to take a leave of absence, and I never returned to the program. It was an experience I considered truly rewarding and one I would never have exchanged for anything. I continued to do substitute teaching in the school system. In that way I kept in touch with the language, dress, and demeanor of the kids I was writing about. I believe it's important for a writer to come down from the ivory tower and see the world. It's especially important for a children's book writer to spend time with kids.

When Claudia left the publishing firm, more work came my way. Another editor was assigned to me at Watts. She was to be my editor on *The Preacher's Kid* and subsequent books. We had a great editorial relationship, which was later to expand fortuitously. Her name was Corinne Naden.

The Preacher's Kid was based on a true story. A Brooklyn, New York, rabbi walked out of his synagogue and into a barrage of media. TV cameras and reporters were gathered around a nearby school, at which a school integration battle was raging. One of the reporters spotted the rabbi. "Here is a spiritual leader. Let's find out what he has to say."

The highly principled rabbi had a lot to say. He was in favor of school integration, and everything he had to say wound up on the six o'clock news. This did not sit well with the congregation, and the rabbi was in deep trouble. He would not move from his stand, and his family was shunned. I changed the Brooklyn rabbi to a New England minister, and when the book came out, coincidentally there was trouble of the same kind in Boston. Corinne and I made a fine editor-writer team, and the book enjoyed favorable reviews.

Meanwhile, Claudia called from Scholastic to tell me of a new program for reluctant readers. An editor she had met at her new firm was doing a line of high-interest, low-reading-level books for teens. The plot lines were to be of interest to teens, but the vocabulary was to be lower. Ray Shepard was having difficulty finding authors. We met, and I wound up doing a number of books for this very worthwhile educational series. Among them were *Camp 13, Second Chance,* and *Sabotage Rock.*

Now that I was no longer teaching full-time, more work began to come my way. The transition from teaching to writing full-time was a difficult one. Working at home demands serious self-discipline. There is no time clock, no supervisor to frown and chastise you for being late, nobody waiting for you to arrive. You must get yourself up and running and down to serious work all by yourself. That means no idle phone chats, second cups of coffee, and morning television shows.

Some writers work afternoons. Others prefer late evenings into the night. They say things are quiet then, no phone calls, ringing door bells, family interruptions. That could work, but not for me. I'm an early riser, and my brain shuts down for the night. I need to wake up, get ready for work, and get going bright and early.

Another problem with working at home is loneliness. At school I would sit in the teachers' lounge before class and sip coffee. There was someone to speak with, to exchange good mornings. The conversation may not have been scintillating, but it was human, work-related interaction. The principal, assistant principal, district supervisor said thus and so. There is nothing like that if you write at home. The up side occurs when it snows, when the temperature hovers around zero, or when the TV weathercasters and traffic tragedy reporters give the horrific effects of hurricane whatever. I can get to work without worrying about all that.

The loneliness appears pervasive as an occupational hazard. I remember when Claudia ran a party for an artist whose career she was launching. It took place in a run-down tenement in a less than elegant part of downtown Manhattan. I went because Claudia asked and didn't expect to see people outside of her circle and that of the artist. A gentleman came up to me and said, "How do you do. I'm Jack Keats." I was thrilled. *A Snowy Day, Peter's Chair,* so many classics. I gushed over the pleasure of meeting him and introduced myself. "How wonderful to meet you," he said graciously. "I so admire your work." I believe he would have said that no matter what my name. But it didn't matter. I decided to believe him.

When I went up to other people excitedly saying, "I just met Ezra Jack Keats. What's he doing here?" I got my answer. "Oh, he comes to everything. Just invite him. He's lonely."

I accepted that fact. I adjusted and continued on with my work and occasionally literary outings of such organizations as PEN, the Authors Guild, the Society of Children's Book Writers and Illustrators, and occasional business lunches.

Shortly thereafter, Corinne left Franklin Watts, and the firm, for a time, stopped publishing children's fiction. I did *My Mother the Witch* and *Cold Rain on the Water* for McGraw-Hill. *Cold Rain on the Water* received an award from the National Council of Social Studies. It concerned the influx of Russian Jews into the Brighton Beach area of Brooklyn, fleeing from persecution and anti-Semitism. I continued to do fiction for various publishers, such as *Me and Einstein: Breaking through the Reading Barrier* for Human Sciences Press, *Goodbye Forever Tree* for New American Library, *Heart to Heart* for Tempo, and *The Secret Papers of Camp Get Around* and *Everybody's Evy* for New American Library and Berkley, respectively.

I also did a few recorded pop song lyrics, one of which, "Drama of Love," wound up as the back side of a smash hit. I put my lyrical talents to good use with a book-recording package for Caedmon Records entitled "Sandy's World." It was a picture book series illustrated by Vala Kondo about a child's experiences. They included *First Day of School Blues, Happy Birthday and All That Jazz, Clean Up Your Room Rag,* and *Rock-a-New Baby Rock.* The music for the series was composed by Janet Gari, who hails from an illustrious show-business family, whose patriarch was the late entertainer Eddie Cantor. She was great fun to work with and regaled me with tales of the show-biz world. I enjoyed working with another person rather than solo.

At about that time, I received a call from Corinne. She had left her full-time editing career and decided to work from home and freelance. It would be wonderful, quiet, and

Brooklyn College clock tower and the lily pond.

peaceful, and she watched the deer gamboling on the lawn of her suburban home. I found it stimulating to work at home amidst the comforting sound of city horns, but to each her own I thought. However, shortly thereafter, Corinne began to leave the deer and heed the call of lunch in the city with her former colleagues. I don't quite remember how it came about, but one day at lunch, Corinne and I decided to write a nonfiction book together. I had enjoyed working with Janet on the Caedmon package and relished the idea of working with another writer.

Corinne and I did *Barbara Bush: First Lady* for Enslow. Unfortunately for our venture, the book took so long to come after we had handed it in that its arrival just about coincided with President Bush's departure. The first lady was no longer Barbara; therefore, despite fine reviews, our book was dated before it had a chance to grow in the publishing world. Barbara Bush was a marvelously gracious lady. I requested an interview and was granted one by phone. Her press secretary called me with a time to await the first lady's call. At precisely the appointed time, the phone rang. "Please hold for Mrs. Bush," an efficient voice said. The next voice I heard was that of Barbara Bush. She was pleasant, friendly, and cooperative. I enormously enjoyed our chat. At her suggestion, I taped the conversation. Unfortunately, when I played the tape, it was low and garbled. I had taken notes as a backup, but I wanted the tape as a keepsake. I took the tape to several sound studios with no success and finally to a technician, who had been an FBI agent. He suggested the possibility that Mrs. Bush had unknowingly been speaking from a White House phone that had been scrambled to prevent taping. I could not get a restored tape, but I do have two handwritten, hand-signed letters from Mrs. Bush, one complimenting me on one of my books and the other thanking me for the autographed copy I sent her. I shall always treasure that correspondence.

The best thing to come of that book was my collaboration with Corinne. Everybody asks, "How do you write a book together?" We don't really always know who did what. We just know it gels and works.

After Barbara Bush, we did biographies of such luminaries as Colin Powell, Christa McAuliffe, John Muir, Barbara Jordan, Jerry Rice, and Whoopi Goldberg. We also did compilation bios such as *People of Peace,* minorities in show business and sports, and White House kids. *The White House Kids* was the idea of my cousin Bill's daughter Rachel, who said, "Why don't you write a book about Chelsea Clinton? Kids would love to know how it feels to live in the White House." It's a bit too soon for Chelsea to have enough life experience to warrant a book, but what about all the other young residents? We did *The White House Kids* and included every child to inhabit the home of the presidents. We spoke with Lucy Johnson, Julie Nixon Eisenhower, Susan Ford, and Calvin Coolidge's son, a lovely gentleman, the oldest living White House kid. I wrote a note to Julie Nixon Eisenhower requesting an interview. One Sunday morning, as I was sitting at home doing the *New York Times* crossword puzzle, the phone rang. "Hi," said a charming bubbly voice. "I hope you don't mind my calling on Sunday, but I got your note. This is Julie Nixon Eisenhower." I was floored. Moral of the story—celebrity does not necessarily equal snootiness.

Corinne and I are now completing more on that venerable home, the White House. It's a six-book series

(Left to right, standing) Rose, Cousin Ruth, Cousin Elaine, and (seated) Mom.

called "Who's That in the White House?," about all the presidents and the manner in which their terms in office affected the course of history. We anticipate summer of 1997 publication. That pleasant little lunch gave rise to a prolific, productive, and firm partnership that continues on merrily, and hopefully, on and on.

Regarding fiction, I do that solo, and I do love it. It grows difficult, however, in these days of the bottom line, competing media sources vying for the attention of young people, to write and publish creative and quality literature. I recently embarked upon such a journey.

Some time after the death of my father, I felt the need to assuage my grief through my art. I felt that I wished to establish a memorial to him by writing a book based upon the core philosophy of his life. Since I am a children's book writer, I decided to do a novel about a ten-year-old girl who has lost her father. I patterned the father after my own, a pharmacist with great standing in the community.

Although, as I stated, I receive many letters and reviews assuming I have experienced all the lives of my fictional protagonists, this is the very first semiautobiographical book I have ever done. Generally, once we are established writers, we sell our work by means of an outline and sample chapter. When we elicit interest from a publisher, we receive a contract and partial advance and complete the book. Otherwise we would be amassing manuscripts that never get published and working forever on material that does not earn us a cent.

However, in this instance I elected to sit down and write a complete book. I really wanted to do it, and do it my way, with no input or suggestions from editors along the way. It was a literary labor of love, and I did it in a special style with no view to the commercial aspect of the work. After my father died, each time I met members of the community, they would share with me memories of him. I found it very comforting, and when I met people who expressed their sympathy, I asked, "Can you tell me something you remember?" With this in mind, I entitled my manuscript *Bring Me a Memory*.

I sent the manuscript to a very fine editor at a large publishing house. She replied that she would publish it if I made extensive revisions with a view to making the book more commercial and saleable. I didn't really want to do that, and I told her so. I am not a very temperamental writer and normally am willing to do revisions when suggested by an editor if they are valid. In this instance, they were valid, since an editor needs to publish a book he or she thinks is commercial in order to keep on working in the firm. The editor was very understanding. She knew how much the book meant to me, and she said, "Try to sell it as it is elsewhere and if you can't, then come back to me." She also made an extremely valuable suggestion. She advised me to go to the small presses, since they were in a position wherein they did not have to worry about the bottom line and could do more quality literature.

Just about that time my phone rang. A small publisher in Oklahoma called requesting permission to use part of one of my books in an anthology. We got to chatting, and the editor asked what I was doing now. They wanted to branch out into fiction. It was serendipity. I told her about *Bring Me a Memory*. She asked to see it, loved it, and sent me a contract. She also engaged a very talented Oklahoma artist, Suzanne Olah, to illustrate the book. The illustrations were well underway when disaster struck. I was informed that the company could not afford to publish my book and in fact was shortly closing down. I kept in touch; happily, they are now back in publishing. At the time, however, I had no way of knowing that the firm would survive, and I had no choice but to return to the drawing board and find another publisher.

I went to the library and did very careful and methodical research. I narrowed my choices down to two publishers I thought would best be able to provide a home for *Bring Me a Memory*. I sent the manuscript to them and

Cousin Bill and his daughter Rachel.

took the liberty of including Suzanne Olah's illustrations. One of them accepted the book and hired Suzanne as well. *Bring Me a Memory* was published by DIMI Press in Salem, Oregon. I received a gift of a lovely oil painting from the artist, and it hangs on my wall. When I brought it to be framed, the shop's artist—I believe he was Russian—was simply thrilled. He was accustomed to framing photographs, and the oil painting was a thrill. He asked if I was the artist. I said no and explained the situation. He replied, "You are an artist. You artist with words, not pictures." He did a lovely job and refused to charge me. "A gift from one artist to another," he said. It was a lovely gesture and underscored the importance of art to those of us who make it our life's work. *Bring Me a Memory* was well reviewed but did not receive the attention and sales it might have had it been published by a large house able to publicize and market it easily. Still, the small presses perform a wonderful function, and I would not have taken *Bring Me a Memory* any other route. The painting on my wall and the words of the Russian artist who framed it serve as a constant reminder of my literary journey.

Dad is gone, but in many ways he is still with me through *Bring Me a Memory* and through my memories. Nonny is gone now as well, and I miss her terribly, but she too is with me in spirit. My mother is quite ill, and I am doing my best to see that she is comfortable and content during these difficult times. I am glad to have my cousins, although it would be nice if we were nearer. Bill is in Kansas and we are in touch and close, but geographically close would be better still. My cousins Bernie and Claire, are in the area and we try to get together and keep in touch. My other cousins are in different states, and we call and write.

Friends, too, are very important and form an extended family. I have had many of my friends as part of my life since childhood, high school, and college. Old friends are the historians of one's life, and my friendships appear to have staying power.

There is no lack of things to do in New York City. Art museums, theaters, restaurants, and shopping areas are everywhere you turn. I doubt I will ever wish to leave this town or retire. As Ted Lewin told me recently, "I plan to die at my desk and I'm sure you plan to do the same." Thanks, Ted.

It is necessary for someone who writes for young people to keep a finger on the pulse of youth. I've been trying to do that. I help some youngsters with schoolwork, particularly Katie. Her mother helps care for my mom. The family came from Russia six years ago, and Katie struggled with her studies in the new land. She is bright and delightful, and I help her. I continue to do so now that she is in the high-school honors program! She says I am her second mother—the American one—and brings me flowers and a card on Mother's Day.

Since I continue to love Brooklyn College, I seize upon every opportunity to go back. Thomas Wolfe said you can't go home again, but I do and enjoy every moment. I served as writing consultant on several occasions for the education and speech and hearing departments at my alma mater. The speech and hearing department was funded for material geared to the reading pleasure of adults who had suffered strokes and other impairments. These people required books on a low-reading level containing material

Katie's gift of a picture to her "American mother."

of interest to them. That was a highly challenging task and worthwhile reason to go home again.

I also did consulting for the education department creating training materials for future paraprofessionals in early childhood education. People in training to work with youngsters in prekindergarten programs and nursery schools needed simply and interestingly written texts to help them in their future careers. I was honored to be a part of that program.

Recently I was invited by Brooklyn College to give a seminar to young people enrolled in a marvelous enterprise called the Teachers Opportunity Program (TOP). The students are primarily young adults who have struggled with the problems of life and have now resumed their educations. The focus of TOP is to train minority people for teaching positions in the inner-city schools, a most promising idea both for the college students and the youngsters who they will one day teach.

I eagerly accepted the professor's invitation, yet another opportunity to return to BC, the rose garden, the lily pond, and the clock tower. I prepared carefully, doing an amusing speech. I felt it was important to capture the interest of the members of the program. Then, Mom fell and was hospitalized with a broken hip. She was scheduled for surgery on the day of my guest appearance. I really wanted to cancel and be with Mom. But prepublicity had been painstakingly and caringly prepared by the staff. Flyers had been composed and distributed. And the TOP members had prepared lunch, with everyone cooking

something for the potluck repast. There was no way I could disappoint everyone.

I didn't think I could do it under the circumstances. But the show must go on. And go on it did. I did a stand-up comedy routine that rocked the house. I was a smash hit. I looked into the eyes of the audience, and I knew I had to come through for them. They knew I was a Brooklyn College graduate and that I had achieved some success. They wanted to hear it. They wanted me to tell them: It's rough. But I sat where you're sitting and I made it. If I can do it, you will do it too. I delivered the message with humor and sincerity. I answered all their thoughtful questions. I had one of the loveliest lunches I can remember. Then I promised to return again to work with the TOP group, left, and went to Mom.

It's often said that giving back to the community is a requirement. It's a moral obligation. A payback. A noble deed. Maybe so. But you must keep on giving back to the community because as you do so the community keeps right on giving to you, over and over. I was so grateful to the TOP program members. They showed me that when you need to do something, no matter how difficult the circumstances, you can summon up the courage to do the best possible job. Maybe it appeared that I was giving that message to the youngsters, but they were giving it to me and beautifully.

From your students shall you learn, and that's what it's all about. Keeping in touch with young people and helping at every opportunity are more than noble gestures. They are tonic for the soul. It's an entry into the ever changing world of youth. It's an absolute necessity for anyone in any way involved with young people, and children's book writers are certainly included in that group.

From here to where? Where do I go from the here and now? What are my plans for the future? If I have any say in the matter, more of the same.

There are still children to write books for. There will always be. They keep coming. And so too I hope will my books. Corinne and I hope to continue our partnership in

Rose relaxing at a friend's home.

the creation of nonfiction for many many years to come. We are completing projects now and have proposals out for more.

We are enjoying our work together tremendously and feel we are contributing to an important part of children's literature. I am moving along with children's fiction, planning some picture books and children's middle-grade fiction. It is always new and exciting, each project is a fascinating beginning and a challenge. Like Ted Lewin, I hope to die at my desk—sometime. The rewards of writing children's books are not great financially, but they are great in so many other ways. The letters from kids alone would make it all worthwhile. The knowledge that you have changed young lives for the better is priceless. I really can't conceive of writing anything but children's books. After all, I haven't grown up yet. And really, why would I want to?

———————————

Writings

FOR CHILDREN; FICTION

A Quiet Place, illustrated by Tom Feelings, F. Watts, 1969.

Black, Black, Beautiful Black, illustrations by Emmett Wigglesworth, F. Watts, 1969.

How Many Blocks Is the World?, illustrated by Harold James, F. Watts, 1970.

Bed-Stuy Beat, illustrated by Harold James, F. Watts, 1970.

I Am Here: Yo Estoy Aqui, illustrated by Moneta Barnett, F. Watts, 1971.

Grandma Didn't Wave Back, illustrated by Ted Lewin, F. Watts, 1972.

A Month of Sundays, illustrated by Ted Lewin, F. Watts, 1972.

Nikki 108, illustrated by Ted Lewin, F. Watts, 1973.

We Are Chicano, illustrated by Bob Alcorn, F. Watts, 1973.

The Preacher's Kid, illustrated by Ted Lewin, F. Watts, 1975.

Seven Years from Home, illustrated by Barbara Ericksen, Raintree, 1976.

The Yo-Yo Kid, illustrated by Barbara Ericksen, Raintree, 1976.

The Thirteenth Year: A Bar Mitzvah Story, F. Watts, 1977.

Cold Rain on the Water, McGraw-Hill, 1979.

Me and Einstein: Breaking through the Reading Barrier, illustrated by Peggy Luks, Human Sciences Press, 1979.

Wishful Lying, illustrated by Laura Hartman, Human Sciences Press, 1980.

My Mother the Witch, illustrated by Ted Lewin, McGraw-Hill, 1981.

Everybody's Evy, Berkley, 1983.

Bring Me a Memory, illustrated by Suzanne Olah, DIMI Press (Salem, OR), 1995.

Good Yontif: A Picture Book of the Jewish Year, illustrated by Lynne Feldman, Millbrook Press, 1997.

Staying Out of Trouble in a Troubled Family, Twenty First Century Books, 1998.

"SANDY'S WORLD" SERIES; INCLUDES RECORDINGS

First Day of School Blues, illustrated by Vala Kondo, Caedmon, 1986.

Happy Birthday and All That Jazz, illustrated by Vala Kondo, Caedmon, 1986.

Clean Up Your Room Rag, illustrated by Vala Kondo, Caedmon, 1986.

Rock-a-New Baby Rock, illustrated by Vala Kondo, Caedmon, 1986.

TELEPLAYS

Grandma Didn't Wave Back (first broadcast on NBC-TV, 1982), Multimedia Entertainment, 1982.

My Mother the Witch, first broadcast on NBC-TV, 1984.

NONFICTION

(With Corinne J. Naden) *The U.S. Air Force,* Millbrook, 1993.

(With Corinne J. Naden) *The U.S. Coast Guard,* Millbrook, 1993.

(With Corinne J. Naden) *The U.S. Navy,* Millbrook, 1993.

(With Corinne J. Naden) *Working Together against Hate Groups,* Rosen, 1994.

(With Corinne J. Naden) *Black Sea,* Raintree, 1995.

(With Corinne J. Naden) *Andes Mountains,* Raintree Steck-Vaughn, 1995.

"WHO'S THAT IN THE WHITE HOUSE" SERIES

(With Corinne J. Naden) *The Expansion Years: 1857 to 1901,* Raintree Steck-Vaughn, 1997.

(With Corinne J. Naden) *The Formative Years: 1829-1857* Raintree Steck-Vaughn, 1998.

(With Corinne J. Naden) *The Founding Years: 1789-1829,* Raintree Steck-Vaughn, 1998.

(With Corinne J. Naden) *The Modern Years: 1969-2001,* Raintree Steck-Vaughn, 1998.

(With Corinne J. Naden) *The Progressive Years: 1901-1933,* Raintree Steck-Vaughn, 1998.

(With Corinne J. Naden) *The Turbulent Years: F.D. Roosevelt to L. Johnson, 1933-1969,* Raintree Steck Vaughn, 1998.

"THE HOUSE DIVIDED (THE CIVIL WAR)" SERIES

(With Corinne J. Naden) *Chancellorsville to Appomattox: The Battles of 1863-1865,* Raintree Steck-Vaughn, 1999.

(With Corinne J. Naden) *Civil War Ends: Assassination, Reconstruction, and the Aftermath,* Raintree Steck-Vaughn, 1999.

"CRIME, JUSTICE AND PUNISHMENT" SERIES

(With Corinne J. Naden, et al) *Duty to Rescue,* Chelsea House, 1999.

(With B. Marvis) *Punishment and Rehabilitation,* Chelsea House, 2000.

BIOGRAPHIES

(With Joanne E. Bernstein) *Diane Sawyer: Super Newswoman,* Enslow (Hillside, NJ), 1990.

(With Joanne E. Bernstein and Alan Jay Gerber) *Judith Resnik: Challenger Astronaut,* Lodestar Books, 1990.

(With Corinne J. Naden) *Christa McAuliffe: Teacher in Space,* Millbrook, 1991.

(With Corinne J. Naden) *Barbara Bush: First Lady,* Enslow, 1991.

(With Corinne J. Naden) *Colin Powell: Straight to the Top,* Millbrook (Brookfield, CT), 1991.

(With Corinne J. Naden) *Barbara Jordan,* Chelsea House, 1992.

(With Corinne J. Naden) *John Muir: Saving the Wilderness,* Millbrook, 1992.

(With Corinne J. Naden) *People of Peace,* Millbrook, 1994.

(With Corinne J. Naden) *Jerry Rice,* Chelsea House, 1994.

(With Corinne J. Naden) *Whoopi Goldberg: Entertainer,* Chelsea House, 1994.

(With Corinne J. Naden) *The White House Kids,* Millbrook, 1995.

(With Corinne J. Naden) *Madeleine Albright: U.S. Secretary of State,* Blackbirch, 1998.

(With Corinne J. Naden) *Chris Rock,* Chelsea House, 2000.

OTHER

Also author (with Corinne J. Naden) of *Heroes Just Don't Happen* (five volumes), 1996; author of five books for high-interest, low-reading level series for Scholastic; five workbooks and twenty-five leaflets for day-care center personnel at Brooklyn College School of Education; *Bright Tomorrow,* for Communications Skill Builders; *Goodbye Forever Tree,* New American Library; *Heart to Heart,* Tempo; *The Secret Papers of Camp Get Around,* New American Library; and the "Honey Bear" series, includes recording, Modern Publishing. Author of lyrics for published and recorded songs, including "Drama of Love," "Let's Face It," "My Heartstrings Keep Me Tied to You," "Give Me a Break," and "Homecoming Party," for artists including Damita Jo, Jodie Sands, and the Exciters.

BONE, Ian 1956-

Personal

Born October 11, 1956, in Geelong, Australia; son of Max (a factory foreman) and Val (a secretary; maiden name, Craven) Bone; married Elizabeth Hetzel (a community artist), February, 1985; children: Jack, Elinor, Bridget. *Education:* Attended Rusden State College, 1975-78; Australian Film and Television School, diploma of art, 1981. *Politics:* "The politics of tolerance and reason."

Addresses

Home—116 Fifth Ave., Royston Park, South Australia 5070. *E-mail*—ianbone@senet.com.au. *Agent*—Franny Kelly, 25 Panorama Cres., Toowoomba, Queensland 4350, Australia.

Career

Australian Broadcasting Corp., producer and director of children's television programs (including *Play School, Swap Shop,* and *Finders Keepers*) in Sydney and Adelaide, Australia, 1983-93; freelance writer, 1993—.

Awards, Honors

Certificate of special recognition, Television Society of Australia, 1985, for "Hats," an episode of the series *Play School;* award for best children's program, Asia Broadcasting Union, 1989, for "Moo," an episode of the television series *Swap Shop;* short-listed for Ned Kelly Award for Crime Fiction, 1997, for *The Ghost of Johnny Savage;* "notable book" citation, Children's Book Council of Australia, 1999, for *Fat Boy Saves World;*

certificate of commendation, Television Society of Australia, for a training film, *The Added Dimension.*

Writings

The Ghost of Johnny Savage, Reed Books, 1996.

Fat Boy Saves World, Thomas C. Lothian (Port Melbourne, Australia), 1998.

The Puppet, Thomas C. Lothian, 1999.

Winning Back Dad, illustrated by Craig, Walker Books (London, England), 1999.

"THE WIGGLES" SERIES; PHOTOGRAPH BOOKS

Dorothy's Adventure, Read for Kids, 1998.

D.O.R.O.T.H.Y., Read for Kids, 1998.

Wake Up Jeff, Read for Kids, 1998.

A Day Out with the Wiggles, Read Books, 1998.

"BANANAS IN PYJAMAS" SERIES

Three Legged Bananas, Read for Kids, 1998.

The Hiding Tree, Read for Kids, 1999.

Rat's Birthday Present, Read for Kids, 1999.

The Hat Mystery, Read for Kids, 1999.

Work in Progress

A young adult novel, *Tin Soldiers.*

Sidelights

Ian Bone told *SATA:* "I was born in Geelong, a coastal and industrial town in Australia where the Ford motor car is manufactured. Geelong is also the gateway to the southern surf beaches of Victoria; hence, there is a schizophrenic feel about the place—heavy industry mixed with sun and surf.

Ian Bone

"During my misspent youth, I watched the cars burn 'round the 'Golden Mile' in the middle of town, hoping one day that I could own one of these noisy machines. As I grew older, my passion changed direction, and I turned to cameras and photography. It was a logical step for me to attend teacher's college in Melbourne, where I studied the media (including photography). It was during this time that I discovered a new passion: filmmaking.

"After four years of teacher's college, I enrolled in the Australian Film and Television School. This was quite a prestigious place at the time (and it probably still is). It has pumped out many Australian film directors who have 'made it big' in the United States. I was never one of the 'big fish' at film school. One look at the amount of energy, time, and effort it took to be successful in the film industry put me off.

"After graduating I joined the Australian Broadcasting Corporation and began producing and directing children's television programs. I found a happy niche, and my passion changed again. Children's television gave me a great outlet for my stupid sense of humor. I produced and developed many programs, such as *Play School, Swap Shop,* and *Finders Keepers.* Some of these went on to win national and international awards.

"After many years of producing for children's television, my passion changed yet again. I started writing stories for one of my programs, something I found I enjoyed immensely. So, I mixed story writing at night with television producing during the day for a year or two, until I realized that one had to go.

"I left the Australian Broadcasting Corporation in 1993 with the romantic notion that I would be an 'author' in the not-too-distant future. After many years of hard work and freelance jobs, I finally achieved this ambition. Let's just hope my passion doesn't change again—not for a while, at least."

For More Information See

PERIODICALS

Australian Book Review, February-March, 1999.
Australian Bookseller and Publisher, October, 1998.
Brisbane Courier Mail, February 9, 1999.
Magpies, March, 1999, p., 37.
React, November, 1998.
Viewpoint, winter, 1999.*

*   *   *

BOUCHARD, David 1952-

Personal

Born in 1952; married, wife's name, Vicki; children: Todd and Ashleigh (stepchildren); Adrien and Etienne (first marriage); Victoria Patricia. *Hobbies and other interests:* Collecting art, toys, and books.

Career

Poet and author; teacher and school administrator, beginning c. 1971. Frequent public speaker.

Awards, Honors

Lee Bennett Hopkins Poetry Award, 1996, Silver Birch Award nomination, and Canadian Children's Book Centre Our Choice Award, all for *Voices from the Wild;* Silver Birch Award nomination and Sheila A. Egoff Children's Prize, both for *If You're Not from the Prairie;* Governor-General's Award shortlist, 1998, Mr. Christie Award shortlist, Amelia Frances Howard-Gibbon Award shortlist, and Red Cedar Award, 2000, all for *The Great Race;* Silver Birch Award nomination, 1999, and Canadian Children's Book Centre Our Choice Award, both for *If Sarah Will Take Me;* Governor-General's Award for illustration nomination and Amelia Frances Howard-Gibbon Award, both for *The Dragon New Year.*

Writings

White Tail Don't Live in the City, Blue Frog Books (Winnipeg), 1989.
The Elders Are Watching, Raincoast Book Publishers (Vancouver), 1990.
My Little Pigs, Blue Frog Books, 1991.
Koko, Blue Frog Books, 1992.
If You're Not from the Prairie, illustrated by Henry Ripplinger, Raincoast Book Publishers, 1992, Atheneum, 1995.
The Meaning of Respect, Pemmican Book Publishers (Winnipeg), 1994.

David Bouchard

The Colours of British Columbia, Raincoast Book Publishers, 1995.

Voices from the Wild: An Animal Sensagoria, illustrated by Ron Parker, Chronicle, 1996.

If Sarah Will Take Me, illustrated by Robb Terrence Dunfield, Orca Book Publishers (Victoria), 1997.

Prairie Born, illustrated by Peter Shostak, Orca Book Publishers, 1997.

The Great Race, illustrated by Zhong-Yang Huang, Millbrook, 1997.

The Journal of Etienne Mercier, illustrated by Gordon Miller, Orca Book Publishers, 1998.

The Dragon New Year, illustrated by Zhong-Yang Huang, Peachtree, 1999.

The Barnyard Bestiary, illustrated by Kimball Allen, Orca Book Publishers, 1999.

The Mermaid's Muse: The Legend of the Dragon Boats, illustrated by Zhong-Yang Huang, Raincoast Book Publishers, 1999.

Fairy, Orca Book Publishers, 2000.

Buddha in the Garden, illustrated by Huang, Raincoast, 2001.

Dragon of Heaven, illustrated by Huang, Raincoast, 2001.

The Elders Are Watching has been translated into four languages.

Sidelights

"I am blessed," David Bouchard told *SATA* in 1999. "I am blessed by those with whom I share my life and by the numerous, incredible experiences that I have had throughout my life. "I live in what must be the most beautiful spot in the world. Ours is an eighty-year-old French country house situated in quaint Victoria, British Columbia. As of yet, we have no garden (we've just moved in and Vicki is working on it now). We, of course, have numerous animals. We drive a solid-silver Durango and a red, 1977 Land Cruiser. Together, Vicki and I share five children; Vicki's two: Todd (17) and Ashleigh (15) and my two sons, Adrien (22) and Etienne (18). On August 14, 1998, we were blessed with our own baby girl, Victoria Patricia. I could write pages about each of the kids; suffice to say that on most weekdays, I am blessed.

"As a writer, I have been blessed with incredible artists with whom to work on each of my books.... *MY BOOKS!* Who would have believed that I would ever be talking about '*my books*'? In 1952 I was born a non-reader. I was a reluctant reader until the age of twenty-seven. I rarely read and I never wrote. It wasn't that I didn't have ideas! I just didn't write. One day (I think it was in the spring of 1988), I came up with an idea that I thought might interest others. I first thought of one idea, then another and then another and then.... Through

Bouchard combines fact and folklore as a grandmother explains to her granddaughter the origins of the Chinese New Year celebration in this second book of the "Chinese Legends" series. (Cover illustration by Zhong-Yang Huang.)

If you're not from the prairie...

Over 100,000 Sold

DAVID BOUCHARD
Story

HENRY RIPPLINGER
Images

Bouchard's picture book is a nostalgic, poetic look at the bittersweet experience of being raised on the prairies. *(Cover illustration by Henry Ripplinger.)*

writing, I've learned to read. Can you imagine learning to read through writing? Novel thought, no doubt!

"Today, at the age of forty-seven, I read children's books. My favorite authors are children's authors, and how not? I love Avi, Gary Paulsen, Cynthia Rylant, and Roch Carrier. I have developed a love for reading and writing, and I am always working on a new book (that I dare not get into because I so love talking about my next book). If I failed to mention it earlier, I've been a teacher and a principal for twenty-nine years. I ran for Canada's parliament twice and for the Saskatchewan legislature once (I obviously grew up on the Prairie). I am a collector of art, toys, and books.

"It has taken me some time I admit, but I've finally come to know who and what I am. I am David Bouchard and I am blessed."

David Bouchard has written several children's books that celebrate the landscape and rural lifestyle of the author's childhood on the Canadian prairie. In *If You're Not from the Prairie,* for example, a series of poems describes windswept prairies in all seasons, while Henry Ripplinger's illustrations show a boy throwing snowballs with friends, walking a creek bed alone, and boarding a school bus during a snowstorm. The poems directly address the reader, and challenge the audience to learn about the prairie in order to learn about the speaker. "The dialogue style works well rhythmically and makes for a possible story hour or program read-aloud," observed Susannah Price in *School Library Journal.* "The book affectionately shows farm life on flat land, wherever the land is," remarked Mary Harris Veeder in *Booklist.* A later book, *Prairie Born,* is another paean to Bouchard's childhood, as the narrator recounts memories of a simpler, rural time gone by in a voice that is "folksy and familiar," according to a reviewer for *Publishers Weekly.*

In *Voices from the Wild,* Bouchard presents what his subtitle calls a "sensagoria," that is, a catalogue of the senses—touch, taste, sight, smell, and hearing—each illustrated by five wild animals whose reliance on the particular sense aids in finding food, evading predators, and protecting the young. Like his earlier books, the text of *Voices from the Wild* is a series of first-person poems, here, each is in the voice of the animal showcased, who urges an unseen painter to depict accurately the animal's effective use of one of the senses. "But while Bouchard casts the painter as mediator between wildlife and humans, it is the poet's rhythmic, quietly urging voice that empowers the art," remarked a reviewer for *Publishers Weekly. Booklist* reviewer Lauren Peterson praised Bouchard's "effective" use of the first person in his poems and predicted that, because the author relies upon concrete images over abstract language to describe the animals' activities, "this attractive, well-designed volume will be useful in science instruction as well as in many areas of language arts." Patty Lawlor, a reviewer for *Quill & Quire,* similarly called *Voices from the Wild* "an enjoyable marriage between language, natural history, and Ron Parker's outstanding wildlife paintings."

Bouchard has published a trilogy of books on Chinese culture. In the first, *The Great Race,* the author devises a fictional scenario that explains how ancient Chinese astronomers created the zodiac. A grandmother tells her small granddaughter the legend of a race around the world conceived by Buddha between the rat, pig, tiger, ox, and the other animals of the traditional Chinese zodiac. Bouchard's version of this legend celebrates "friendship, cooperation, and self-sacrifice among the animals who finish the race behind the conniving rat," observed a reviewer in *School Library Journal. Booklist* reviewer Shelle Rosenfeld celebrated *The Great Race* as "not only an interesting story but also a fine introduction to the Chinese zodiac." In *The Dragon New Year,* Bouchard utilizes a similar scenario between a grand-mother and her granddaughter to tell the legend of how the traditional Chinese celebration of the new year began. Here, Bouchard creates "a dramatic story told in strong, spare prose," according to Joanne Findon in *Quill & Quire.* In *The Mermaid's Muse,* Bouchard devises a legend that explains the origins of the dragon-boat races. Here again, the author's writing was de-scribed as "economical and dramatic," in the words of a reviewer for *Maclean's.* All three books are illustrated by Zhong-Yang Huang in a fashion that emphasizes the emotions of the easily frightened little girl in *The Dragon New Year,* and the various characteristics of the animals in *The Great Race.*

Through all my life I've tried to please
my king and serve my country.
I have never sought for my own gain,
I've never thirsted for wealth nor fame

And yet I've somehow come to find
a friend unlike all others —
One who has made me feel alive and dear,
who makes me feel I'm special.

In the third book of the "Chinese Legends" series, Bouchard retells the story of Chinese poet Qu Yuan and his friendship with a sea dragon disguised as a mermaid. *(Cover illustration by Zhong-Yang Huang.)*

The Journal of Etienne Mercier both carries on the strengths of Bouchard's earlier books and pushes at the limits of the picture book genre, according to *Quill & Quire* reviewer Patty Lawlor. In this fictionalized diary account of explorer Etienne Mercier's journey to the Queen Charlotte Islands in 1853, the author first establishes the character of his narrator as good-natured, friendly, and curious, then, through subsequent entries "delivers an amazingly effective introduction to the people, customs, languages, and wildlife of the time," Lawlor averred. The book also prints the verses of ten French-Canadian folk songs of the era, and a companion CD features Bouchard's reading of the story and rendition of the songs. The result is an "innovative glimpse of Canadian history," concluded Lawlor.

Works Cited

Review of *The Dragon New Year* and *The Mermaid's Muse, Maclean's,* November 22, 1999, p. 98.

Findon, Joanne, review of *The Dragon New Year, Quill & Quire,* March, 1999, p. 68.

Review of *The Great Race, School Library Journal,* January, 1998, p. 96.

Lawlor, Patty, review of *The Journal of Etienne Mercier, Quill & Quire,* July, 1998, pp. 42-43.

Lawlor, Patty, review of *Voices from the Wild, Quill & Quire,* November, 1996, pp. 43-44.

Peterson, Lauren, review of *Voices from the Wild, Booklist,* December 1, 1996, p. 658.

Review of *Prairie Born, Publishers Weekly,* December 22, 1997, p. 58.

Price, Susannah, review of *If You're Not from the Prairie, School Library Journal,* September, 1995, p. 190.

Rosenfeld, Shelle, review of *The Great Race, Booklist,* February 1, 1998, p. 912.

Veeder, Mary Harris, review of *If You're Not from the Prairie, Booklist,* June 1, 1995, p. 1758.

Review of *Voices from the Wild, Publishers Weekly,* November 4, 1996, p. 76.

For More Information See

PERIODICALS

Booklist, September 1, 1999, p. 137.
Canadian Children's Literature, spring, 1998, p. 76.
Kirkus Reviews, April 15, 1995, p. 553.
School Library Journal, August, 1997, pp. 163-64; July, 1998, p. 86.
Skipping Stones, January, 2000, p. 22.

* * *

BUCKLESS, Andrea K. 1968-

Personal

Born April 11, 1968, in Minot, ND; daughter of Leo J. (an athletic director) and Pamela (a secretary; maiden name, Parker) Kinsella; married Bruce E. M. Buckless (a manager of a mortgage company), September 1, 1990. *Education:* Michigan State University, B.A., 1990; North Carolina State University, M.Ed. *Religion:* Roman Catholic.

Addresses

Home—37 Summer Glen Dr., Simpsonville, SC 29681. *Office*—Woodruff Primary School, 1100 Lucy P. Edwards Dr., Woodruff, SC. *E-mail*—andibuckless@yahoo.com.

Career

Reading specialist and "reading recovery" teacher at public schools in Durham, NC, 1992-97; Woodruff Primary School, Woodruff, SC, reading specialist, 1997—. Volunteer for Junior League of Greenville and Greenville Literacy Association. *Member:* International Reading Association (president of Durham chapter, 1995-97), Reading Recovery Council, Society of Children's Writers and Illustrators, South Carolina Writers Workshop, Greenville Writers Guild.

Awards, Honors

Oppenheim Toy Gold Award, 1999, for *Class Picture Day.*

"When the photographer says 'Cheese!' stick out your tongue," said Amy.
"Okay," said Richard.
"Okay," I said.

A student sticks out her tongue for the class picture and has to fix her mistake in Class Picture Day, a reader for ages five to seven written by Andrea K. Buckless and illustrated by Patti Goodnow.

Writings

I Hate Peas, Addison-Wesley (Reading, MA), 1998.
Drawing, Addison-Wesley, 1998.
Class Picture Day, illustrated by Patti Goodnow, Scholastic Inc. (New York City), 1998.
Too Many Cooks, illustrated by Kayne Jacobs, mathematics activities by Marilyn Burns, Scholastic Inc., 2000.

* * *

BURDETT, Lois

Personal

Education: University of Western Ontario, B.A.; London Teachers College.

Addresses

Home—77 Delamere Ave., Stratford, Ontario, Canada N5A 4Z6. *Office*—Hamlet Public School, 315 West Gore St., Stratford, Ontario, Canada N5A 7N4.

Career

Oakwood Public School, Sarnia, Ontario, teacher, 1972-75; Hamlet Public School, Stratford, Ontario, teacher, 1975—. Has given numerous keynote or featured speaker presentations throughout the United States, Canada, Europe, and Australia.

Awards, Honors

Child Psychology Award, University of Western Ontario, 1971; World Book Scholarship and Muriel Lancaster Award, University of Western Ontario, 1972; Hilroy Fellowship Award, Canadian Teachers' Federation, 1986; Honorary Citizen of Texas, 1986; Award of Merit, Southwest Texas State University, 1986; Encyclopedia Brittanica National Award, Canadian College of Teachers, 1990; Meritorious Service Medal, Canadian government, 1996; Writer's Award, Federation of Women Teachers' Association of Ontario, 1985, and 1996, for *A Child's Portrait of Shakespeare* and *Macbeth for Kids;* District Choice Award, Curriculum Administrator, 1996, for *Macbeth for Kids,* and 1998, for *A Midsummer Night's Dream for Kids;* Information Book Award nomination, 1996, for *A Child's Portrait of Shakespeare;* Plays, Skits and Musicals for Children Award, amazon.com, 1998, for *A Midsummer Night's Dream for Kids;* Fred Bartlett Memorial Award, Ontario Public School Boards Association, 1999.

Lois Burdett

Writings

(With Christine Coburn) *Twelfth Night for Kids: Shakespeare Can Be Fun!,* Firefly (Willowdale, Ontario), 1994.
A Child's Portrait of Shakespeare, Firefly, 1995.
Macbeth for Kids, Firefly, 1996.
A Midsummer Night's Dream for Kids, Firefly, 1997.
Romeo and Juliet for Kids, Firefly, 1998.
The Tempest for Kids, Firefly, 1999.
Hamlet for Kids, Firefly, 2000.

Contributor to periodicals, including *Cambridge University Journal, F.W.T.A.O. Magazine,* and *Stratford Festival Newsletter.*

Work in Progress

A documentary video, *The Secret of Will: A Child's Portrait of Shakespeare,* for Northwest Passage Communications, and *Much Ado about Nothing for Kids* for Firefly Books.

Sidelights

Lois Burdett told *SATA,* "Most students will be exposed to the works of Shakespeare at some point in their educational careers. Traditionally, this initial exposure has been delayed until their high school years, presumably on the theory that the language and content of Shakespeare's plays are too difficult for younger children to understand. Indeed, some adults may well recall struggling as students to decipher seemingly incomprehensible passages of a play. However, too often primary children are underestimated as to what they can accomplish given the challenge. The study of Shakespeare has become a tremendously powerful medium and an integral part of my grade two program at Hamlet School, in Stratford, Ontario, Canada.

This was not always the case. When I first moved to Stratford, over twenty-five years ago, I had no intention of teaching Shakespeare to seven and eight year olds. Stratford is a beautiful city noted worldwide for its Shakespearean theatre, and I was interested to find that the schools were all named after Shakespearean characters. I asked my class, 'Who is William Shakespeare?' and 'Why is our school called Hamlet?' Their answers were surprising. One thought he was a famous boxer. Another believed he was the president of Canada. A third student responded, 'I don't know who William Shakespeare is. I don't know any of the big kids.' It was the children's enthusiasm and excitement on making the connection between an historical figure and the name of their school that led me to continue. The project evolved into a learning experience of a lifetime.

"I have endeavored in my books to share with others the excitement of exploring with children the timeless emotions and ideas of Shakespeare. The comments of two of my children, written at various times in their daily journals, show the lasting impression Shakespeare has had on them. 'Shakespeare is like a big piece of chocolate cake. Once you've started you wish you could go on and on forever, in a non-stopping dream' (Anika, age seven). 'I think Shakespeare had a brain from God. His brain was as smart as life and is for always' (Devon, age seven)."

Lois Burdett is an educator whose book publications have grown out of her experience teaching Shakespeare to her second grade classes. In her first book, for example, *Twelfth Night for Kids: Shakespeare Can Be Fun!,* Burdett rewrites Shakespeare's comedy in rhyming couplets. The book is illustrated with selected drawings from her students. Also included are students' writings, including diary entries and letters by the characters in the play. Arlene Perly Rae, writing in the *Toronto Star,* judged the book to be "captivating" and "upbeat."

Burdett's second book, *A Child's Portrait of Shakespeare,* follows the format established by her first, including a text written in rhyming couplets and contemporary language surrounded by artwork and classroom assignments by the author's students. In a review for *Books in Canada,* Diane Schoemperlen termed the work "a charming and intelligent book" not only for children, but for "readers of all ages." Philippa Sheppard commented in *Quill & Quire* that the children's drawings, similar to those in her previous book, "burst with life and innocence."

Other Shakespearean titles that Burdett has adapted include *Romeo and Juliet for Kids, A Midsummer Night's Dream for Kids,* and *The Tempest for Kids.* The characters in *Romeo and Juliet for Kids* "speak out with warmth," testified Diedre Baker in the *Toronto Star.* Sheppard, in *Quill & Quire,* deemed Burdett's idea a success, observing that "her students have developed a burning love of Shakespeare that infuses their writing, their drawing, and their performances."

Works Cited

Baker, Deidre, review of *Romeo and Juliet for Kids, Toronto Star,* July 11, 1998, p. 7.

Rae, Arlene Perly, review of *Twelfth Night for Kids, Toronto Star,* June 4, 1994. p. L11.

Schoemperlen, Diane, "Fringe Benefits," *Books in Canada,* October, 1995, pp. 47-48.

Sheppard, Philippa, "Bardolatry for Beginners," *Quill & Quire,* June, 1996, pp. 53-54.

For More Information See

PERIODICALS

Canadian Children's Literature, May, 1997, p. 41.
Teach Magazine, May 1997, p. 22.
The Writing Teacher, May-June, 1997, p. 3.

C

CARWELL, L'Ann
See McKISSACK, Patricia C.

* * *

CHICHESTER CLARK, Emma 1955-

Personal

Born October 15, 1955, in London, England; daughter of Robin Chichester Clark (a company director) and Jane Helen (Goddard; present surname, Falloon); married Lucas van Praag (a management consultant). *Education:* Chelsea School of Art, B.A. (with honors), 1978; Royal College of Art, M.A. (with honors), 1983.

Addresses

Home—47 Richford St., London W12 8BU, England. *Agent*—Laura Cecil, 17 Alwyne Villas, London N1, England.

Career

Author, illustrator, and editor of children's books, 1983—. Worked in a design studio and as a freelance illustrator of newspapers, periodicals, and book jackets. Visiting lecturer at Middlesex Polytechnic and City and Guilds School of Art, 1984-86. *Exhibitions:* Exhibitor at the Thumb Gallery, England, 1984 and 1987. *Member:* Chelsea Arts Club.

Awards, Honors

Mother Goose Award, 1988, for *Listen to This;* Golden Duck Award, 1999, for *Noah and the Space Ark;* shortlisted for the Kate Greenaway Medal, 1999, for *I Love You, Blue Kangaroo!;* shortlisted for the Kurt Maschler Award, 1999, for *Elf Hill.*

Writings

SELF-ILLUSTRATED PICTURE BOOKS

Catch That Hat!, Bodley Head (London), 1988, Little, Brown (Boston), 1990.
The Story of Horrible Hilda and Henry, Little, Brown, 1988.
Myrtle, Tertle, and Gertle, Bodley Head, 1989.
The Bouncing Dinosaur, Farrar, Straus (New York), 1990.
Tea with Aunt Augusta, Methuen, 1991, published as *Lunch with Aunt Augusta,* Dial (New York), 1992.
Miss Bilberry's New House, Methuen, 1993, published as *Across the Blue Mountains,* Harcourt (San Diego), 1993.
Little Miss Muffet Counts to Ten, Andersen (London), 1997, published as *Little Miss Muffet's Count-Along Surprise,* Bantam (New York), 1997.
More!, Andersen, 1998, Bantam, 1999.
I Love You, Blue Kangaroo! Bantam, 1999.
Follow My Leader, Andersen, 1999.

ILLUSTRATOR

Laura Cecil, compiler, *Listen to This,* Greenwillow (New York), 1987.
Janet Lunn, *Shadow in Hawthorn Bay,* Walker, 1988.
Laura Cecil, compiler, *Stuff and Nonsense,* Greenwillow, 1989.
Primrose Lockwood, *Cissy Lavender,* Little, Brown, 1989.
James Reeves, *Ragged Robin: Poems from A to Z,* Little, Brown, 1990.
Margaret Ryan, *Fat Witch Rides Again,* Methuen, 1990.
Laura Cecil, compiler, *Boo! Stories to Make You Jump,* Greenwillow, 1990.
Roald Dahl, *James and the Giant Peach,* Unwin Hyman (London), 1990.
(And editor) *I Never Saw a Purple Cow and Other Nonsense Rhymes* (anthology), Little, Brown, 1990.
Pat Thomson, *Beware of the Aunts!,* McElderry Books (New York), 1991.
Margaret Mahy, *The Queen's Goat,* Dial, 1991.
Diana Wynne Jones, *Wild Robert,* Mammoth, 1991, Chivers North America, 1992.
Diana Wynne Jones, *Castle in the Air,* Mammoth, 1991.

Little Miss Muffet's animal friends bring gifts, decorations, and treats for a special event in Emma Chichester Clark's self-illustrated **Little Miss Muffet's Count-Along Surprise.**

Jenny Nimmo, *Delilah and the Dogspell,* Methuen, 1991.

Laura Cecil, compiler, *A Thousand Yards of the Sea,* Methuen, 1992, published as *A Thousand Yards of Sea,* Greenwillow, 1993.

D. J. Enright, *The Way of the Cat,* HarperCollins (New York), 1992.

Anne Fine, *The Haunting of Pip Parker,* Walker (London), 1992.

Ben Frankel, *Tertius and Plinty,* Harcourt (San Diego), 1992.

Geraldine McCaughrean, reteller, *The Orchard Book of Greek Myths,* Orchard (London), 1992, published as *Greek Myths,* McElderry Books, 1993.

Peter Dickinson, *Time and the Clockmice, et cetera,* Doubleday (London), 1993, Delacorte (New York), 1994.

Rosemary Sutcliff, *The Princess and the Dragon Pup,* Walker, 1993, Candlewick, 1996.

Ann Turnbull, *Too Tired,* Hamish Hamilton, 1993, Harcourt, 1994.

Laura Cecil, *The Frog Princess,* Cape (London), 1994, Greenwillow, 1995.

Laura Cecil, compiler, *Preposterous Pets,* Hamish Hamilton, 1994, Greenwillow, 1995.

Charles Ashton, *Ruth and the Blue Horse,* Walker, 1994.

Kate McMullan, *Good Night, Stella,* Candlewick, 1994.

Sir Arthur Sullivan, *I Have a Song to Sing, O!: An Introduction to the Songs of Gilbert and Sullivan,* selected and edited by John Langstaff, McElderry Books, 1994.

Laura Cecil, *Piper,* Cape, 1995.

William Shakespeare, *Something Rich and Strange: A Treasury of Shakespeare's Verse,* compiled by Gina Pollinger, Larousse Kingfisher Chambers (New York), 1995.

Allan Ahlberg, *Mrs. Vole the Vet,* Puffin (London), 1996.

(And editor with Catherine Asholt and Quentin Blake) *The Candlewick Book of First Rhymes* (anthology), Candlewick (Cambridge, MA), 1996.

Henrietta Branford, *Dimanche Diller at Sea,* Collins (London), 1996.

Ian Whybrow, *Miss Wire and the Three Kind Mice,* Kingfisher, 1996.

Laura Cecil, *Noah and the Space Ark,* Hamish Hamilton (London), 1997, Lerner (New York), 1998.

Geraldine McCaughrean, reteller, *The Orchard Book of Greek Gods and Goddesses,* Orchard, 1997.

Jane Falloon, reteller, *Thumbelina,* Pavilion (London), 1997.

William Shakespeare, *The Little Book of Shakespeare,* compiled by Gina Pollinger, Kingfisher, 1997.

John Yeoman, *The Glove Puppet Man,* Collins, 1997.

Adrian Mitchell, reteller, *The Adventures of Robin Hood and Marian,* Orchard, 1998.

Matthew Price, *Where's Alfie?,* Orchard, 1999.

Matthew Price, *Don't Worry, Alfie,* Orchard, 1999.

Naomi Lewis, *Elf Hill: Tales from Hans Christian Andersen,* Star Bright Books, 1999.

Contributor to *Tom's Pirate Ship and Other Stories* and *Mostly Animal Poetry,* both Heinemann (Oxford), 1997, and *Alphabet Gallery,* Mammoth, 1999; the latter is an alphabet book illustrated by twenty-six prominent English artists and published to benefit the United Kingdom's Dyslexic Institute. Illustrator of *Rock-a-Bye Baby* by Jane Rohmer, 1990; *Little Red Riding Hood,* edited by Sam McBratney, 1996; *Sinan* by Emma Alcock, 1996; and *Mehmet the Conqueror* by Laura Mare, 1997. Chichester Clark's illustrations have also appeared in newspapers and periodicals, including the *Sunday Times* (London), *Cosmopolitan,* and *New Scientist.*

Work in Progress

A second picture book about Blue Kangaroo; illustrations for *Roman Myths* by Geraldine McCaughrean, for McElderry Books.

Sidelights

A popular and prolific author, illustrator, and anthologist, Emma Chichester Clark is considered one of the most accomplished contemporary creators of children's literature, as well as one of England's most distinguished book artists. Compared to Beatrix Potter and Edward Ardizzone, as well as to more recent figures such as Tony Ross and her former teacher Quentin Blake, she has written and illustrated picture books and has provided the pictures for more than forty stories, picture books, anthologies, and retellings by other writers. Chichester Clark's illustrations have graced works by a number of prominent authors, editors, and retellers, including Roald Dahl, Anne Fine, Peter Dickinson,

Allan Ahlberg, Rosemary Sutcliff, Sam McBratney, Diana Wynne Jones, John Yeoman, Naomi Lewis, Matthew Price, Janet Lunn, Jenny Nimmo, and Geraldine McCaughrean. In addition, the artist has contributed pictures to works by her mother, Jane Falloon, and her editor, Laura Cecil, as well as to anthologies of Shakespearean poetry and the songs of Gilbert and Sullivan.

As an author/illustrator, Chichester Clark features child, adult, and animal characters in picture books that, although usually humorous and fantastic, provide realistic portrayals of human feelings and foibles. Gwyneth Evans noted in the *St. James Guide to Children's Writers* that her stories "are reassuring, but have an underlying toughness." Chichester Clark's protagonists—boys and girls, older women, and a variety of anthropomorphic animals, including donkeys and lemurs—are not perfect: they fight, tease, overeat, and are greedy and absent-minded, qualities that lead them into danger or cause them to face alarming or surprising situations. However, the characters make positive choices and are supported by family, friends, and strangers; at the end of their adventures, the protagonists return home, satisfied with their lives.

As a literary stylist, Chichester Clark uses both prose and verse to tell her stories, which she writes as fables, cautionary tales, and concept books, as well as straight narratives. As an artist, she is praised for the distinctiveness and recognizability of her style and for her use of color and her ability to evoke action and emotion. Chichester Clark generally works in watercolor and line; her pictures range from bucolic scenes in gentle pastels to luminous, vivid paintings teeming with activity. The artist often pictures her characters in a semi-Edwardian world and outfits them with broad-brimmed hats. In addition, she is noted for drawing the people and animals in her books with wide eyes made with large circles and dots. Chichester Clark is generally considered a talented writer and artist whose works reflect her understanding of human nature while providing children with entertaining, satisfying stories and expressive, appealing pictures. "While her illustrations often suggest the serenity and charm of a timeless world," stated Evans, "her work has a vitality and a multicultural perspective which also makes it contemporary." Quoted in an online biography, Quentin Blake concluded, "Among the many flavours of children's books, that of Emma Chichester Clark's—funny, elegant, and delicious—is unique."

Born in London, England, Chichester Clark was brought to Ireland at the age of three and grew up in an old, white farmhouse surrounded by fields. Her family kept many pets, including dogs, roosters, mice, rabbits, and, as the artist wrote in *Ladybug,* "a very old pony who was pretty vicious." Because she lived a long way from any other children, Chichester Clark said she and her siblings "had to entertain ourselves, which was easy there. I used to draw a lot, houses with windows jammed into the four corners and people with no necks." She also made her own small books, "with proper spines that my mother sewed up for me." She added, "All the way through school, it didn't ever occur to me that I would do anything other than illustrate books when I was 'grown up.'"

In 1975, Chichester Clark left Ireland to attend the Chelsea School of Art in London. After graduating with honors, she began to submit original picture books to publishers. When two of them were rejected, she suspended her quest to work in a design studio. Instead, Chichester Clark designed book jackets and submitted illustrations to newspapers and magazines. A few years later, she decided to go back to school and attend the Royal College of Art, where she was taught by Quentin Blake and prominent author/illustrator Michael Foreman. After receiving her master's degree, once again graduating with honors, Chichester Clark received a phone call from an editor at Bodley Head, a publishing house in London. The editor had been looking through some old photocopies and, according to Chichester Clark in *Ladybug,* "had found something of mine that she liked. . . . The photocopies of my drawings that the publisher had been looking at were from the very book that they had first rejected!" She was asked to illustrate *Listen to This,* a collection of stories for children compiled by Laura Cecil. The artist began a fruitful collaboration with Cecil, who also became Chichester Clark's literary agent.

Listen to This is a compilation of thirteen stories that Cecil chose for their read-aloud quality. The collection includes works by such authors as Rudyard Kipling, Philippa Pearce, Virginia Hamilton, and Margaret Mahy, as well as familiar folktales from sources such as the Brothers Grimm. Writing in the *Times Educational Supplement,* Jenny Marshall noted that Chichester Clark's colorful illustrations "have verve and wit," while Lesley Chamberlain concluded in the *Times Literary Supplement* that the artist "has brought an energetic and unsentimental streak to very varied material." She received the Mother Goose Award in 1988 as the most exciting newcomer to British children's book illustration for her pictures in *Listen to This.* Reflecting in *Ladybug* on how her first book led to her success, Chichester Clark stated, "I guess one shouldn't always take rejection too badly—it might lead somewhere eventually."

Chichester Clark and Cecil have continued their collaboration on several well-received volumes, both compilations and original stories. One of the latter, *Noah and the Space Ark,* is a picture book with an environmental theme that places the Biblical character in a future in which the earth is so polluted that people and animals are in danger of extinction. Noah builds a rocket ship and takes the small animals—the larger ones have already died out—into space to find a new home. After they find a planet that resembles Earth, they disembark and vow to take better care of it than the stewards of Earth had done.

Chichester Clark published her first original work, the picture book *Catch That Hat!,* in 1988. In this work, which is written in verse, small Rose loses her pink hat to the wind as she chases a cat. As she retrieves and then again loses her hat, Rose is aided by animals such as a cow, a rabbit, and a kangaroo, as well as by a boy. Her hat finally lands in a monkey puzzle tree that no one can climb. A cockatoo lands on the hat and makes a nest, which pleases Rose even as she sheds a tear for her lost chapeau. At the end of the story, Rose's friends give her a new hat, complete with a ribbon to tie under her chin, that is even better than the old one. *Booklist* contributor Barbara Elleman predicted that children "will enjoy the whimsy of this airy, light-as-a-breeze tale."

Chichester Clark's next book, *The Story of Horrible Hilda and Henry,* is a cautionary tale in picture book form about a brother and sister who like to misbehave: They trash their house, squirt their parents with a hose, have food fights, and tease each other unmercifully. Finally, the children's parents send them to the zoo. After annoying the animals, Hilda and Henry are placed in a cage with Brian, a bad-tempered lion. Brian frightens the siblings so much that they become model children. Their parents take Hilda and Henry home with Brian, who is supposed to act as insurance. However, Clark's last picture shows that the children are about to revert back to form. Writing in *Booklist,* Ilene Cooper said, "Clark uses comic-book strips, full-page pictures, and two-page spreads to tell this amusing story, all to good effect." A critic for *Kirkus Reviews* claimed that young readers will enjoy the "gleefully exaggerated pranks here, which [Chichester] Clark illustrates with her usual zest."

Chichester Clark produced the verse compilation *I Never Saw a Purple Cow and Other Nonsense Rhymes* in 1990. A collection of over one hundred poems by such writers as Edward Lear, Lewis Carroll, and Hilaire Belloc, plus traditional rhymes, riddles, limericks, and ballads, the book is arranged according to animal species and behavior. A *Kirkus Review* critic said that Chichester Clark's witty illustrations are "just right" before calling *I Never Saw a Purple Cow* a "delightful compilation, handsomely presented." Writing in *School Librarian,* Joan Nellist claimed that Chichester Clark matches the rhymes and poems "with a beautiful simplicity which is sure to please young and old alike."

Tea with Aunt Augusta (published in the United States as *Lunch with Aunt Augusta*) is one of Chichester Clark's most popular works. The story outlines what happens when Jemima, a ring-tailed lemur who is the youngest in her family, goes with her two older brothers to visit their beloved Aunt Augusta. After Jemima gorges herself on the lavish variety of mixed fruits provided by Aunt Augusta, the little lemur cannot keep up with her older brothers on their way home. Lost in the dark, she is rescued by a group of friendly fruit bats, who carry her home in a leaf sling. Jemima is lectured by her parents on overeating, but they welcome her with hugs and kisses. Her brothers, on the other hand, are sent to bed without supper for abandoning their sister in the jungle. Calling Chichester Clark's illustrations "delightfully vivid, witty, and tender," *Times Educational Supplement*

That night, as Lily got ready for bed, she said, "I love Yellow Cotton Rabbit . . . "

Blue Kangaroo feels left out when other stuffed animals appear on Lily's bed in Chichester Clark's self-illustrated **I Love You, Blue Kangaroo.**

reviewer Andrew Davies concluded, "I've never given ring-tailed lemurs much thought before. Now I wish I owned one. In fact I wish I was one." Roberta Palmer stated in *BPI Entertainment News Wire* that Chichester Clark writes about "youthful indulgence, fear and punishment with a comic and understanding hand," while a *Publisher Weekly* reviewer, noting the "unique and captivating cast," commented that the "playful artwork calls to mind a cartoony Rousseau." Writing in *Booklist,* Hazel Rochman concluded, "[W]ith all its nonsense . . . this satisfying story combines the small child's fear of being lost with the dream of adventure."

With *Little Miss Muffet Counts to Ten* (published in the United States as *Little Miss Muffet's Count-Along Surprise*), Chichester Clark extends the traditional nursery rhyme in a concept book written in rhyme that teaches basic mathematics. Instead of frightening Miss Muffet away, the spider asks her politely to stay. She is pleased when her animal friends—such as bears with chairs and puffins with muffins—arrive to give her a surprise birthday party. When two crocodiles with greedy smiles show up, things get tense; however, they are just bringing the cake. Writing in *School Librarian,* Sarah Reed termed the book a "successful combination of a counting book, traditional rhyme, repetition, a chain story, all beautifully illustrated," while *FamilyFun*

There were running races, leaping races,

bouncing and balancing,

hopping and jumping and prizes for winning.

Billy's friend the lion takes him to a fantasy land of amusement when Billy can't get enough entertainment in the real world. (From More!, *written and illustrated by Chichester Clark.)*

reviewer Sandy MacDonald added, "The rhymes are tightly sprung, the imagery deliciously imaginative." A critic for *Kirkus Reviews* concluded by calling the book "a wonderful variation on the nursery rhyme that for once will frighten no one away."

In *More!*, little Billy wants one more story, one more ice cream, one more game, et cetera, at bedtime. When his mother refuses, Billy stomps off to his room, gathers his stuffed toys and the life-size lion that lives behind the curtain, and goes off to the center of the Earth, where he gets more rides, more spins, and more lollipops than he could ever want. Billy becomes over-saturated and finally realizes that all he wants to do is to go home to bed, which he does. *School Librarian* critic Jane Doonan raved that, with *More!*, "she succeeds in picturing the indescribable"; the critic concluded, "Please, Miss Chichester Clark, MORE! MORE! MORE!" Writing in the *Independent—London*, Sally Williams noted, "The illustrations are stunning." The critic further urges readers to "marvel" at the vivid, colorful illustrations.

I Love You, Blue Kangaroo! is among Chichester Clark's most well-received books. Small Lily loves her stuffed blue kangaroo more than any of her other toys. When she begins to receive some new stuffed animals, Blue Kangaroo is pushed to the side. When he makes his

way to the crib of Lily's baby brother, Blue Kangaroo is welcomed joyfully. The next day, Lily sees Blue Kangaroo in her brother's arms. She is devastated until she comes up with a mutually beneficial plan: Lily gives all of her other toys to her brother in exchange for Blue Kangaroo. Writing in the *Times Educational Supplement*, William Feaver stated that Chichester Clark "has perfect pitch as an author/illustrator . . . . Graphically, *Blue Kangaroo* is a winner." Stephanie Zvirin of *Booklist* praised the book's illustrations, noting that they "can open the way to parent-child discussions of selfishness and generosity." A reviewer for *School Library Journal* called *I Love You, Blue Kangaroo!* a "heartwarming story . . . wholly satisfactory." Writing online on the website *Emma Clark Talkback*, Chichester Clark noted that her nephew Finn has a worn and grubby kangaroo, the first stuffed animal that he was given, that he cannot go to sleep without. She also recalled that her first stuffed animal was a bear called William: "He went everywhere with me. I used to worry about hurting his feelings and I tried not to let him get jealous when I was given new toys, but sometimes I forgot, and sometimes he must have felt quite unloved . . . . I still have him, and still sometimes talk to him." In 1999, Chichester Clark was shortlisted for the Kate Greenaway Medal for her illustrations for *I Love You, Blue Kangaroo!*.

Works Cited

Blake, Quentin, quoted in *Emma Clark Biography:* http://www.la-hq.org.uk/directory/medals-awards/shadow/shortlists/emclark.htm.

Chamberlain, Lesley, "Igniting the Imagination," *Times Literary Supplement,* December 4, 1989, p. 1361.

Chichester Clark, Emma, *Emma Clark Talkback:* http://www.la-hq.org.uk/directory/. . .ards/shadow/shortlists/kang/fee.htm.

Chichester Clark, "Meet the Artist: Emma Chichester Clark," *Ladybug,* March, 1997, p. 39.

Cooper, Ilene, review of *The Story of Horrible Hilda and Henry, Booklist,* April 15, 1989, p. 1464.

Davies, Andrew, "Having a Good Time," *Times Educational Supplement,* February 14, 1992, p. 27.

Doonan, Jane, review of *More!, School Librarian,* autumn, 1998, p. 129.

Elleman, Barbara, review of *Catch That Hat!, Booklist,* May 15, 1990, pp. 1797-98.

Evans, Gwyneth, entry in *St. James Guide to Children's Writers,* edited by Sara and Tom Pendergast, St. James, 1999, pp. 230-32.

Feaver, William, "Leap of Imagination," *Times Educational Supplement,* December 11, 1998, p. 37.

Review of *I Love You, Blue Kangaroo!, School Library Journal,* April, 1999.

Review of *I Never Saw a Purple Cow and Other Nonsense Rhymes, Kirkus Reviews,* April 15, 1991.

Review of *Little Miss Muffet's Count-Along Surprise, Kirkus Reviews,* September 15, 1997, p. 1454.

Review of *Lunch with Aunt Augusta, Publishers Weekly,* January 6, 1992, p. 65.

MacDonald, Sandy, review of *Little Miss Muffet's Count-Along Surprise, FamilyFun,* November, 1997.

Marshall, Jenny, "Storybook Worlds," *Times Educational Supplement,* November 6, 1987, p. 27.

Nellist, Joan, review of *I Never Saw a Purple Cow and Other Nonsense Rhymes, School Librarian,* May, 1991, pp. 681-82.

Palmer, Roberta, review of *Lunch with Aunt Augusta, BPI Entertainment News Wire,* June, 1992.

Reed, Sarah, review of *Little Miss Muffet Counts to Ten, School Librarian,* August, 1987, p. 130.

Rochman, Hazel, review of *Lunch with Aunt Augusta, Booklist,* May 1, 1992, p. 1606.

Review of *The Story of Horrible Hilda and Henry, Kirkus Reviews,* April 15, 1989, p. 622.

Williams, Sally, review of *More!, Independent—London,* May 14, 1998.

Zvirin, Stephanie, review of *I Love You, Blue Kangaroo!, Booklist,* January 1, 1999, p. 886.

For More Information See

PERIODICALS

Books for Keeps, January, 1998, p. 18.
Junior Bookshelf, April, 1996, p. 56.
Magpies, September, 1998, p. 28; November, 1998, p. 26.*

*   *   *

CLARK, Emma Chichester
See CHICHESTER CLARK, Emma

*   *   *

CLARK, Patricia Denise 1921-
(Patricia Robins, Claire Lorrimer, Susan Patrick)

Personal

Born February 1, 1921, in Hove, Sussex, England; daughter of Arthur and Denise (a writer; maiden name, Klein) Robins; married D. C. Clark, 1948 (divorced); children: two sons, one daughter. *Education:* Attended schools in Sussex, England, in Switzerland, and in Munich, Germany.

Addresses

Home—Chiswell Barn, Christmas Mill Lane, Marsh Green, Edenbridge, Kent TN8 5PR, England. *Agent*—Anthea Morton-Saner, Curtis Brown, 162-168 Regent St., London W1R 5TB, England.

Career

Writer. *Woman's Illustrated,* London, England, subeditor, 1938-40. *Military service:* Royal Air Force, Women's Auxiliary Air Force, worked in a radar filter room, 1940-45; became flight officer.

Writings

NOVELS; AS PATRICIA ROBINS

To the Stars, Hutchinson (London, England), 1944.
See No Evil, Hutchinson, 1945.
Statues of Snow, Hutchinson, 1947.
Three Loves, Hutchinson, 1949, updated and reprinted under name Claire Lorrimer as *The Reunion,* Severn, 1997.
Awake My Heart, Hutchinson, 1950.
Beneath the Moon, Hutchinson, 1951.
Leave My Heart Alone, Hutchinson, 1951, updated and reprinted under name Claire Lorrimer as *An Open Door,* Severn, 1999.
The Fair Deal, Hutchinson, 1952.
Heart's Desire, Hutchinson, 1953, updated and reprinted under name Claire Lorrimer as *The Reckoning,* Severn, 1998.
So This Is Love, Hutchinson, 1953.
Heaven in Our Hearts, Hutchinson, 1954.
One Who Cares, Hutchinson, 1954.
Love Cannot Die, Hutchinson, 1955, updated and reprinted under name Claire Lorrimer as *Never Say Goodbye,* Severn, 2000.
The Foolish Heart, Hutchinson, 1956.
Give All to Love, Hutchinson, 1956.
Where Duty Lies, Hutchinson, 1957.
He Is Mine, Hurst & Blackett (London, England), 1957.
Love Must Wait, Hurst & Blackett, 1958.
Lonely Quest, Hurst & Blackett, 1959, updated and reprinted under name Claire Lorrimer as *Search for Love,* Severn, 2000.
Lady Chatterley's Daughter, Ace, 1961, updated and reprinted under name Claire Lorrimer as *Connie's Daughter,* Severn, 1995.
The Last Chance, Hurst & Blackett, 1961.
The Long Wait, Hurst & Blackett, 1962.
The Runaways, Hurst & Blackett, 1962.
Seven Loves, Consul (London, England), 1962.
With All My Love, Hurst & Blackett, 1963.
The Constant Heart, Hurst & Blackett, 1964.
Second Love, Hurst & Blackett, 1964, updated and reprinted under name Claire Lorrimer as *Second Chance,* Severn, 1998.
The Night Is Thine, Consul, 1964.
There Is But One, Hurst & Blackett, 1965.
No More Loving, Consul, 1965.
Topaz Island, Hurst & Blackett, 1965.
Love Me Tomorrow, Hurst & Blackett, 1966.
The Uncertain Joy, Hurst & Blackett, 1966.
Forbidden, Mayflower, 1967.
The Man behind the Mask, Sphere (London, England), 1967.
Return to Love, Hurst & Blackett, 1968.
Sapphire in the Sand, Arrow (London, England), 1968.
Laugh on Friday, Hurst & Blackett, 1969.
No Stone Unturned, Hurst & Blackett, 1969.
Cinnabar House, Hurst & Blackett, 1970.
Under the Sky, Hurst & Blackett, 1970, Atlantic Monthly Press (New York City), 1988, updated and reprinted under name Claire Lorrimer as *Beneath the Sun,* Severn, 1996.

The Crimson Tapestry, Hurst & Blackett, 1971, Atlantic Monthly Press, 1988, updated and reprinted under name Claire Lorrimer as *The Woven Thread,* Severn, 1997.

Play Fair with Love, Hurst & Blackett, 1972, Atlantic Monthly Press, 1988.

None But He, Hurst & Blackett, 1973.

Forever, Severn (London, England), 1991.

Fulfilment, Severn, 1993.

Forsaken, Severn, 1993.

FOR CHILDREN; AS PATRICIA ROBINS

The Adventures of Three Baby Bunnies, Nicholson & Watson (London, England), 1934.

Tree Fairies, Hutchinson, 1945.

Sea Magic, Hutchinson, 1946.

The Heart of a Rose, Hutchinson, 1947.

The 100-Pounds Reward, Wheaton (Exeter, England), 1966.

NOVELS; UNDER PSEUDONYM CLAIRE LORRIMER

A Voice in the Dark, Souvenir (London, England), 1967, Avon, 1968.

The Shadow Falls, Avon, 1974.

Relentless Storm, Avon, 1975.

The Secret of Quarry House, Avon, 1976.

Mavreen, Arlington (London, England), 1976, Bantam, 1977.

Tamarisk, Arlington, 1978, Bantam, 1979.

The Garden, Arlington, 1980.

Chantal, Arlington, 1980, Bantam, 1981.

The Chatelaine, Arlington, 1981, Ballantine, 1982.

The Wilderling, Arlington, 1982, Ballantine, 1983.

Last Year's Nightingale, Century (London, England), 1984.

Frost in the Sun, Century, 1986.

House of Tomorrow, Corgi (London, England), 1987.

Ortolans, Bantam, 1990.

The Calverly Inheritance, Doubleday (London, England), 1990.

The Spinning Wheel, Bantam, 1991.

The Silver Link, Bantam, 1993.

Fool's Curtain, Bantam, 1994.

OTHER

(As Patricia Robins) *Seven Days Leave* (poems), Hutchinson, 1943.

(Under pseudonym Claire Lorrimer) *Variations* (short stories), Bantam (London, England), 1991.

Sidelights

Patricia Denise Clark has achieved success in two distinct areas of romance fiction. As Patricia Robins, she has published nearly fifty novels that have been characterized as traditional romances. As Claire Lorrimer, she has attracted critical notice for nearly twenty novels that fall into the category of epic, historical romance.

For the first thirty years of her career, Clark produced novels under the name Patricia Robins that, according to Geoffrey Sadler in *Twentieth-Century Romance and Historical Writers,* "use controversial subjects as themes" and "[display] a refreshing honesty in her treatment of physical passion, neither over-glamorizing nor sensationalizing what is a basic fact of life." Sadler cited the example of *Forever,* in which "the heroine is forced to resolve the conflict of adulterous passion with pity for a husband who has recently gone blind. The unsentimental presentation of the dilemma, and the complex personalities of the characters themselves, lend added interest to an otherwise conventional love story."

The pseudonym Claire Lorrimer emerged in the late 1960s, allowing the author to explore a variety of sub-genres, including gothic and suspense novels. Eventually Clark settled on using the Lorrimer name for the epic, historical romance, as evidenced by *Mavreen,* which features a "tempestuous and striking [heroine] against a strongly drawn historical background," according to Sadler. Other similar novels followed, in steady succession.

The Chatelaine, a novel of the popular "Rochford" series, follows the story of Willow, an American heiress who marries an English nobleman, Rowell Rochford, unaware that he is the bankrupt head of a family riddled with ominous secrets. Sadler declared: "*The Chatelaine* is one of the most impressive of Lorrimer's novels to date, compact and well crafted. Willow, in her gradual assertion of independence from Rowell and his dragon of a mother, is at once interesting and credible." The critic suggested that, as Clark's popularity grew, her writing matured along with it. He pointed especially to *The Spinning Wheel,* which he ranked among the author's "finest novels.... The involved tale ... [shows] the author working at the peak of her form. Her depiction of rural Sussex life in the period before World War I is superb, equaled only by her convincing presentation of [the heroine's] career as a fashion designer in Paris. Mastery of characters and plot is matched by a strength of period detail and atmosphere."

Works Cited

Sadler, Geoffrey, "Lorrimer, Claire," *Twentieth-Century Romance and Historical Writers,* 3rd edition, St. James, 1994, pp. 404-06.

For More Information See

PERIODICALS

Best Sellers, August 15, 1970.

Books and Bookmen, February, 1968.

West Coast Review of Books, May, 1977.

*   *   *

COMBS, Lisa M.
See McCOURT, Lisa

COOKE, Arthur
See LOWNDES, Robert A(ugustine) W(ard)

* * *

COOPER, Michael L. 1950-

Personal

Born July 6, 1950. *Education:* University of Kentucky, B.A. (English), 1974; City University of New York, M.A. (history), 1989.

Addresses

Home—411 West 21st St., New York, NY 10011.

Career

Writer. *Member:* Authors Guild, Authors League of America, PEN American Center, Society of Children's Book Writers and Illustrators, Society of American Historians.

Writings

Racing Sled Dogs, Clarion (New York), 1988.
Klondike Fever: The Famous Gold Rush of 1898, Clarion, 1989.
Playing America's Game: The Story of Negro League Baseball, Lodestar (New York), 1993.
From Slave to Civil War Hero: The Life and Times of Robert Smalls, Lodestar, 1994.
Bound for the Promised Land: The Great Black Migration, Lodestar, 1995.
Hell Fighters: African American Soldiers in World War I, Lodestar, 1997.
The Double V Campaign: African Americans and World War II, Lodestar, 1998.
Indian School: Teaching the White Man's Way, Clarion, 1999.

Sidelights

Michael L. Cooper told *SATA:* "Books were very important to me as a child. I was one of those kids who seemed unable to do anything very well except read. I loved books of all kinds. I hoarded them the way other boys hoarded baseball cards. Every day when I sit down to work my inspiration my hope is that my writing will nurture a similar love of books among young readers."

Cooper has established a reputation as a writer of African-American histories for young adults. In *Bound for the Promised Land: The Great Black Migration* the author examines the era of 1915 to 1930 when more than a million African Americans emigrated from rural Southern states to urban Northern and Midwestern states in pursuit of factory work and larger opportunities. Cooper pieces the story together out of first-person accounts, newspaper stories, and contemporary photographs, emphasizing life conditions in the South prior to migration, what neighborhoods and jobs blacks found in the North, and how this new population influenced urban culture of the early twentieth century, particularly in the Harlem Renaissance.

Bound for the Promised Land "is an important title because of the sensitive and thorough manner in which Cooper treats his subject," averred Carol Jones Collins in *School Library Journal,* a judgment echoed in the reviews of other critics. In *Bulletin of the Center for Children's Books,* Elizabeth Bush dubbed *Bound for the Promised Land* a "cogent, eminently readable history." Bush added praise for Cooper's "balanced" presentation of the Great Migration, which he achieves by noting the discrimination and violence that blacks met in the North (as well as in the South) and deepens by presenting the conflicting voices of African-American leaders on the subject of migration. Furthermore, according to this critic, Cooper sets the migration against the backdrop of contemporary national and international events such as World War I and the Great Depression. *Voice of Youth Advocates* reviewer Laura L. Lent attested to the scarcity of books on the Great Migration, and called Cooper's book "indispensable for its historical value." "Cooper's work is superbly written and should be nominated for a young adult best book award," Lent concluded.

Cooper focuses on African-American participation in World War I in *Hell Fighters: African American Soldiers in World War I.* In this account of the Fifteenth New York Voluntary Infantry of the National Guard, formed in Harlem in 1916, which became the 369th Regiment of the U.S. Army during the war, Cooper resurrects an important moment in the early civil rights movement, noted David A. Lindsey in *School Library Journal.* The troop, composed mostly of African Americans, began as poorly equipped and poorly trained volunteers in the National Guard who found little recognition from the U.S. Army for their fighting in the trenches, until the French awarded them the Croix de Guerre in 1918. Still, though the Harlem press termed them "hell fighters" and they returned to the states to participate in a triumphant ticker-tape parade in New York City, the 369th was nonetheless targeted for discriminatory acts within the military after the end of the conflict in order to make sure that black soldiers would not mistakenly think they were entitled to the respect accorded white soldiers. Bush commented in another *Bulletin of the Center for Children's Books* article, "Cooper packs a lot into a little space in this account of the 369th Regiment."

Works Cited

Bush, Elizabeth, review of *Bound for the Promised Land, Bulletin of the Center for Children's Books,* December, 1995, p. 124.
Bush, Elizabeth, review of *Hell Fighters, Bulletin of the Center for Children's Books,* February, 1997, p. 201.

Collins, Carol Jones, review of *Bound for the Promised Land, School Library Journal,* December, 1995, p. 114.

Lent, Laura L., review of *Bound for the Promised Land, Voice of Youth Advocates,* April, 1996, p. 52.

Lindsey, David A., review of *Hell Fighters, School Library Journal,* February, 1997, pp. 111-12.

For More Information See

PERIODICALS

Kansas City Star, March 28, 1993, p. J9.
School Library Journal, April, 1993.*

* * *

COX, Judy 1954-

Personal

Born November 25, 1954, in San Francisco, CA; daughter of Walter Alan (a photographer) and Carol (a nurse; maiden name, Dam) Houde; married Tim Cox (a school counselor), June 7, 1974; children: Christopher. *Education:* Lewis & Clark State College, B.A., 1979; Northern Arizona University, M.A., 1984. *Politics:* Democrat. *Religion:* Presbyterian. *Hobbies and other interests:* Music, bird watching, reading, playing bass guitar.

Addresses

Home—2478 Southslope Way, West Linn, OR 97068.

Career

Welches School District, Welches, OR, teacher, 1985-92; West Linn-Wilsonville School District, West Linn, OR, teacher, 1996—. *Member:* Society of Children's Book Writers and Illustrators.

Awards, Honors

First place, Oregon Association of American Mothers Short Story Contest, 1993, for "When the Meadowlark Sings"; Kid's Pick of the List selection, 2000, for *Weird Stories from the Lonesome Cafe.*

Writings

Now We Can Have a Wedding!, illustrated by DyAnne DiSalvo-Ryan, Holiday House (New York), 1998.
The West Texas Chili Monster, illustrated by John O'Brien, Bridgewater Books, 1998.
Third Grade Pet, illustrated by Cynthia Fisher, Holiday House, 1998.
Rabbit Pirates: A Tale of the Spinach Main, illustrated by Emily Arnold McCully, Harcourt/Browndeer Press (San Diego, CA), 1999.
Mean, Mean Maureen Green, illustrated by Cynthia Fisher, Holiday House, 2000.
Weird Stories from the Lonesome Cafe, illustrated by Diane Kidd, Harcourt (San Diego, CA), 2000.

Judy Cox

My Family Plays Music, illustrated by Elbrite Brown, Holiday House, 2001.

Also contributor of short stories, articles, poems, and essays to *Cricket, Spider, Highlights for Children, Children's Playmate, Instructor, Learning, Family Times, Single Parent, Family Fun, Hopscotch,* and *Poem Train.* Short stories have appeared in *Stories from Highlights,* an anthology series published by Boyds Mill Press.

Sidelights

Judy Cox told *SATA,* "I am the oldest of five children. We grew up near San Francisco. Even when I was young, I loved to tell stories to my brother and sisters. As soon as I learned to read, reading became my favorite thing to do. I love books, the way they look, the way they feel, the way they smell. I wanted to be a part of that. I wrote my first story in third grade. In those days, students didn't have much chance to write stories in school. We only had 'creative writing' every other Friday. By the time I was eleven, I knew I wanted to be a writer when I grew up. I started a novel about six girls who had a club in a treehouse. I wrote long descriptions and drew pictures of each of them. I got so involved planning my characters that I never finished the first chapter!

"In the sixth grade, a poem I wrote was published in the local newspaper. My grandmother was so proud of it, she framed it. It hung in her house for the rest of her life. I wrote without getting published again for many, many years! I wrote journals, essays, poems, short stories, picture books. I started several novels. I read somewhere that you have to write a million words before you write anything worth reading and I thought, 'I'd better get busy.' I wrote on an old refurbished manual typewriter my parents gave me when I graduated from high school. I wrote in longhand on yellow, lined tablets.

"After I married, my husband bought me an electric typewriter for Christmas because he liked one of my science-fiction stories, and I wrote on that. I sat on the screened sun porch of the old farmhouse we rented in Idaho, and I wrote my first children's novel, a mystery, on the backs of old dittos he brought home from his teaching job. I wrote in pencil and ink and marker. But I couldn't sell anything. I got discouraged, not realizing that all this practice was leading somewhere. I dreamed of being published. But it seemed as if my dreams would never come true.

"Finally, years and years later, I wrote an article about dinosaurs. I mailed it to *Instructor* magazine. They bought it! I was so excited! My husband and I went out for pizza to celebrate. But I didn't really start to write seriously again until I left teaching to stay home with my baby. I began to write every day. I'd turn on *Sesame*

THIRD GRADE PET

We don't need a rat at all, thought Rosemary. Please no. Not a dirty, flea-bitten rat. Anything but a rat.

Despite her initial disgust, Rosemary tries to hide the class pet rat in her home to save his life, thereby creating chaos in Cox's chapter book **Third Grade Pet.** *(Illustrated by Cynthia Fisher.)*

Street and write straight through until *Mr. Roger's Neighborhood* was over. When I heard Mr. Rogers sing his closing song, I knew it was time to stop.

"I started keeping a journal. I used to think nothing interesting ever happened to me. But I discovered the interesting stuff in the stuff in your head. Your dreams. Your fantasies. Your pretends, and wishes, and ideas. Once I knew that, I had lots to say after all. I use big spiral-bound notebooks and write my journal on one side of each page. The other side I use for story ideas. I started to send things out to magazines and book publishers. My husband calls me 'The Queen of Persistence' because I have more than 350 rejection slips. I have written seven books and more than thirty short stories for magazines such as *Cricket, Spider,* and *Highlights for Children.* Not everything I write gets published. But writing is like piano practice. You do it every day to keep in shape."

Cox writes picture books and chapter stories that are noted for their jovial characters and humorous scenarios. In her first book, *Now We Can Have a Wedding!,* the young narrator goes from kitchen to kitchen in the apartment house where she lives, helping out or merely observing as the residents prepare a special addition to the wedding feast for her sister and Roberto Gonzales, who lives in 4B. "Without being didactic, the book is a showcase for ethnic diversity through gastronomy," contended Ilene Cooper in *Booklist.* Other critics voiced similar observations. "Cox cleverly combines the meanings of the terms 'melting pot' and 'pot luck,'" observed a reviewer for *Publishers Weekly,* noting that the story is strengthened by the author's use of repetition and by emphasizing what the neighbors have in common: "their pleasure in preparing for a wedding and in sharing their traditions." Aided by DyAnne DiSalvo-Ryan's welcoming watercolor renditions of the various kitchens, the result is "a sweet and joyful twist on weddings," Patricia Pearl Dole concluded in *School Library Journal.*

Cox's next book, *The West Texas Chili Monster,* is a "goofy story about a chili cook-off that produces smells powerful enough to attract the attention of a roving space creature," wrote John Sigwald in *School Library Journal.* Cox employs the same brand of whimsical humor in her next picture book, *Rabbit Pirates: A Tale of the Spinach Main,* in which two old friends retire from pirating and open a restaurant in the Provence region of France. Though Monsieur Lapin and Monsieur Blanc wax nostalgic about their days on the open sea, they seem content enough to argue over old times, and prepare and serve food at the Spinach Main, their restaurant. Then a fox comes in one day and expresses the desire to see the cooks featured on the menu. Though Cox's scenario may have more appeal for adult readers than for the children to whom they read *Rabbit Pirates,* Hazel Rochman nevertheless remarked in *Booklist* that many children will "recognize the tough-guy talk and enjoy the clever tricks the rabbits use to get rid of" the fox. A reviewer for *Publishers Weekly* described Cox's book as "a wonderful mix of humor, food and friendship, with just the right touch of je ne sais quoi."

"The fish of happiness," she tells me. "For luck."

Mrs. Haru lays them out. Their heads are still on. I don't like the way they look, but they will taste very good. We rub the fish with salt and Mrs. Haru grills it over a charcoal fire.

"There," says Mrs. Haru. "The tai is ready. Now we can have a wedding!"

Cox pays tribute to wedding customs from around the world in **Now We Can Have a Wedding!** *(Illustrated by DyAnne DiSalvo-Ryan.)*

In *Third Grade Pet* Cox tried her hand at writing a chapter book. Rosemary is at the center of this comic rendition of the adventures that follow when the third-grade class votes to adopt a pet rat, and Rosemary, despite her disgust, is selected to be one of the animal's first caretakers. Critics applauded Cox's descriptions of her protagonist's initial fear of the rat and "how creepiness gives way to cuddly affection," as Hazel Rochman put it in *Booklist.* Rosemary becomes so attached to Cheese the rat that when a boy she does not trust is assigned to take him home for the weekend, Rosemary kidnaps the pet and tries to hide him in her

home. The humorous incidents that ensue will delight young readers, critics predicted, but Cox's "writing has a clarity and an energetic freshness that keeps the roden-tial hijinks . . . realistic rather than corny and contrived," *Bulletin of the Center for Children's Books* reviewer Deborah Stevenson stated. Similarly, a critic for *Publishers Weekly* averred that Cox properly keeps her focus on her human rather than rodent characters, and their "fresh and credible voices . . . give this brief, quick-moving novel plenty of life." Lisa Gangemi Krapp, writing in *School Library Journal,* compared *Third Grade Pet* to chapter books by Suzy Kline and Betsy

Word of the excellent cuisine at the Spinach Main has spread throughout Provence. Business is good.

Two retired pirate rabbits defend their restaurant from a fox who is ruining business in Cox's **Rabbit Pirates.** *(Illustrated by Emily Arnold McCully.)*

Duffey, concluding that readers who enjoy those books "will feel right at home with this light and breezy story." Cox's second chapter book, *Mean, Mean Maureen Green,* is a story of third-grader Lilley, who learns to conquer her fear of a neighborhood bully, a ferocious dog, and riding her two-wheeler bike with the help of a friend and her father. The result is a "solid, well-paced chapter book," according to Gillian Engberg in *Booklist.*

Works Cited

Cooper, Ilene, review of *Now We Can Have a Wedding!,* *Booklist,* February 15, 1998, p. 1019.

Dole, Patricia Pearl, review of *Now We Can Have a Wedding!, School Library Journal,* March, 1998, p. 168.

Engberg, Gillian, review of *Mean, Mean Maureen Green, Booklist,* December 1, 1999, p. 703.

Krapp, Lisa Gangemi, review of *Third Grade Pet, School Library Journal,* February, 1999, p. 83.

Review of *Now We Can Have a Wedding!, Publishers Weekly,* February 9, 1998, p. 94.

Review of *Rabbit Pirates: A Tale of the Spinach Main, Publishers Weekly,* August 2, 1999, p. 83.

Rochman, Hazel, review of *Third Grade Pet, Booklist,* December 15, 1998, p. 749.

Rochman, Hazel, review of *Rabbit Pirates: A Tale of the Spinach Main, Booklist,* October 15, 1999, p. 451.

Sigwald, John, review of *The West Texas Chili Monster, School Library Journal,* June, 1998, p. 103.

Stevenson, Deborah, review of *Third Grade Pet, Bulletin of the Center for Children's Books,* February, 1999, p. 198.

Review of *Third Grade Pet, Publishers Weekly,* December 14, 1998, p. 76.

D

DILLON, Jana (a pseudonym) 1952-

Personal

Born November 9, 1952, in Norwood, MA; daughter of Frank (an artist) and Mary (a homemaker; maiden name, Byrne) Gerulskis; married Michael Doherty, July 21, 1979 (divorced, 1988); children: Brian, Alison. *Education:* Massachusetts College of Art, B.F.A., 1974. *Politics:* Independent. *Religion:* Unitarian-Universalist. *Hobbies and other interests:* Reading, historic sites, geological sites, museums.

Addresses

Home—285 Washington St., Canton, MA 02021.

Career

Art teacher at elementary and middle schools in Scituate, MA, 1974-82; painter in Canton, MA, 1982-92; writer and illustrator, 1992—. Conference speaker; volunteer chairperson of local preschool, 1994-97; visiting author and illustrator to schools, 1992—. *Member:* Society of Children's Book Writers and Illustrators, Northeast Society of Children's Book Writers and Illustrators, Massachusetts Teachers Association.

Writings

Jeb Scarecrow's Pumpkin Patch, self-illustrated, Houghton Mifflin (Boston, MA), 1992.
Lucky O'Leprechaun, self-illustrated, Pelican Publishing (Gretna, LA), 1998.
(Illustrator) Wanda Dionne, *Little Thumb,* Pelican Publishing, 2000.

Work in Progress

Tasha's Matrioska Dolls, illustrated by Robert Rayevsky, for Farrar, Straus (New York City) expected in 2001; *Lucky O'Leprechaun Comes to America,* self-illustrated, for Pelican Publishing, 2001; *Ms. Goody's School for Little Witches,* for Troll, 2001

Sidelights

Jana Dillon told *SATA:* "I enjoy making school visits, where I combine techniques of acting and storytelling to explain to the children how a book is made, from the original daydreaming to the finished hardcover edition. I love building an emotional crescendo of intense enthusiasm in the students for writing and reading.

"I decided to become an author and illustrator of children's books in second grade, when I peeked at the expressions on the faces of my fellow students while Mrs. Talanian read to us. They were enraptured and transported. I thought, what could be a better job than one that brought such interest and pleasure?"

For More Information See

PERIODICALS

Booklist, October 1, 1992, p. 329.

*   *   *

DOBSON, Mary 1954-

Personal

Born December 27, 1954, in Surrey, England; married Christopher Dobson (a professor of chemistry), September 3, 1977; children: Richard, William. *Education:* University of Oxford, B.A. (geography; with honors), 1976, M.A., 1980, D.Phil., 1982; Harvard University, A.M. (history of science), 1980.

Jana Dillon

Addresses

Office—c/o Publicity Director, Oxford University Press, 2001 Evans Rd., Cary, NC2 7513, England. *E-mail*—mary.dobson@wuhmo.ox.ac.uk

Career

Oxford University, Oxford, England, researcher and lecturer in the history of medicine, 1982—. Frequent speaker at professional conferences; has been interviewed and made presentations on radio, television, and in newspapers and magazines. Member of the Romney Marsh Research Trust and the National Meningitis Trust. *Member:* Historical Geography Research Group (Institute of British Geographers), Local Population Studies Group, Society for the Social History of Medicine, International Union of Scientific Studies of Population, British Society of Population, International Network for the History of Malaria, Society of Authors, Historical Novel Society, Royal Society of Tropical Medicine and Hygiene.

Awards, Honors

Old Students' Exhibition, St. Hugh's College, Oxford University, 1973-76; Hurry Prize, St. Hugh's College, and Herbertson Memorial Prize, School of Geography, Oxford, both 1976; postgraduate research studentship, Nuffield College, Oxford, 1976-78, 1980-81; Social Science Research Council postgraduate award, 1976-78, 1980-81; Harkness Fellow, Harvard University, 1978-80; Institute of Historical Research Twenty-Seven Foundation Award, 1981; E. P. Abraham Prize research fellow, Nuffield College, 1981-82; Open Prize research fellow, Nuffield College, 1982-84.

Writings

JUVENILE NONFICTION

Tudor Odours, illustrated by Vince Reid and Martin Cottam, Oxford University Press, 1997.

Victorian Vapours, illustrated by Reid and Mark Robertson, Oxford University Press, 1997.

Roman Aromas, illustrated by Reid and Victor Ambrus, Oxford University Press, 1997.

Reeking Royals, illustrated by Reid, Oxford University Press, 1998.

Mouldy Mummies, Oxford University Press, 1998.

Vile Vikings, illustrated by Reid, Oxford University Press, 1998.

Wartime Whiffs, Oxford University Press, 1998.

Greek Grime, Oxford University Press, 1998.

Medieval Muck, Oxford University Press, 1998.

Messy Medicine, illustrated by Reid, Oxford University Press, 1999.

Dobson's children's books have been translated into twenty languages.

OTHER

Contours of Death and Disease in Early Modern England (adult nonfiction), Cambridge University Press, 1997.

Contributor to books, including *A Chronology of Epidemic Disease and Mortality in Southeast England, 1600-1800,* Historical Geography Research Group, 1987; *A Dictionary of Eighteenth-Century World History,* Blackwell, 1994; *Readers Guide to the History of Science,* Fitzroy Dearborn, 1996; *The Economy of Kent, 1640-1914,* Boydell Press and Kent County Council, 1996; *Western Medicine: An Illustrated History,* Oxford University Press, 1997; *Environmental Change and Human Occupation in a Coastal Lowland,* Oxbow Books, 1998; and *The Malaria Challenge after One Hundred Years of Malariology,* Accademia Nationale dei Lincei, 1999. Contributor to journals, including *Journal of Historical Geography, Geographical Magazine, Continuity and Change, Society History of Medicine, Journal of the Royal Society of Medicine, Wellcome Trust Review, Health Transition Review, Parassitologia, British Medical Journal, Transactions of the Royal Society for Tropical Medicine and Hygiene,* and *East African Medical Journal.*

Work in Progress

Fatal Moves: The British Experience of Malaria, with E. Coleman; editing, with P. Schofield, *A Place to Die: The Geography of Mortality from Medieval to Modern Times; A History of Malaria and Its Control in Twentieth Century East Africa,* with R. W. Snow and M. Malowany; and the textbook *The Management, Control and Eradication of Tropical Diseases, c. 1850-2000,* with M. Malowany. Research on the history of malaria.

Sidelights

Mary Dobson told *SATA:* "I have spent the past twenty years conducting academic research and lecturing at the University of Oxford. The main focus of my academic studies is the history of disease, particularly the history of malaria. As part of this research, I became fascinated by the history of smells, which played a powerful role in the historical understanding of factors causing disease. While writing an academic monograph, *Contours of Death and Disease in Early Modern England,* I decided to use some of the rich material on smells to produce a series of children's books. I have published nine children's books in a series entitled 'Smelly Old History' and one in a series 'Smelly Science,' published by Oxford University Press. I continue to combine my interest in the history of medicine with children's books."

Mary Dobson is an historian of disease at Oxford University in England. She is also the author of ten books for children that bring some of the interesting or gruesome aspects of ancient (and not-so-ancient) history to life for young readers. In *Victorian Vapours, Greek Grime, Vile Vikings,* and her other books for children, Dobson presents a peculiarly intimate glimpse of an era through descriptions of how people lived and died during that time, accompanied by scratch-and-sniff panels that approximate the smells of these eras. "The books ... are littered with fascinating historical facts," contended Andrew Kidd in *Books for Keeps,* citing the vats of urine in which the Romans laundered their clothing, and the concoction of apples and puppy fat favored by Queen Elizabeth I for her hair. In *Reeking Royals,* Dobson presents the scent of rotting corpses alongside the aroma of spices imported from the Holy Land in order to give a uniquely confrontational sense of the medieval era. Because the scratch-and-sniff panels really do smell, a *Publishers Weekly* reviewer advised readers to "keep these in a drawer or other enclosed place." Todd Morning, writing in *School Library Journal,* noted that while the series does not attempt to give an in-depth portrait of the societies it presents, it nonetheless "may give students enough of a whiff to want to read further."

Works Cited

Kidd, Andrew, review of *Victorian Vapours, Books for Keeps,* July, 1997, p. 24.

Review of *Medieval Muck, Reeking Royals,* and *Wartime Whiffs, Publishers Weekly,* February 8, 1999, p. 216.

Morning, Todd, review of *Greek Grime* and *Vile Vikings, School Library Journal,* January, 1999, pp. 137-38.

For More Information See

PERIODICALS

Publishers Weekly, October 26, 1998, p. 68.*

DUDER, Tessa 1940-

Personal

Born November 13, 1940, in Auckland, New Zealand; daughter of John (a physician) and Elvira (a homemaker; maiden name, Wycherley) Staveley; married John Nelson Duder (a civil engineer), April 23, 1964; children: Lisa, Alexandra Clare, Joanna, Georgia. *Education:* Attended University of Auckland, 1958-59, 1982-84. *Hobbies and other interests:* Reading, sailing, music, opera, theater.

Addresses

Home—Unit 6, 169 Jervois Rd., Herne Bay, Auckland, New Zealand. *Agent*—Ray Richards, Richards Literary Agency, P.O. Box 31240, Milford, Auckland, New Zealand.

Career

Novelist, 1982—. *Auckland Star,* Auckland, New Zealand, reporter, 1959-64; *Daily Express,* London, England, reporter, 1964-66; freelance journalist and editor, 1976—; *Dominion Sunday Times,* Wellington, New Zealand, book reviewer, 1989-93; actor, appearing in own plays and in *Shortland Street,* a New Zealand soap opera. Queen Elizabeth II Arts Council Literature Programme, member of children's writing panel, 1986-93; University of Waikato, writer in residence, 1991; judge for literary competitions, including young writers' sections of Bank of New Zealand short story awards and *Dominion Sunday Times*/Mobil short story awards, 1991, and Goodman Fielder Wattie Book Awards, 1992; script consultant for film *Alex,* 1993. Speaker at conferences on children's literature in New Zealand, Australia, United States, and Sweden. Spirit of Adventure Trust, trustee, 1993. *Member:* PEN (New Zealand Society of Authors, national vice-chair, 1992; president, 1996-98), New Zealand Children's Book Foundation (vice-chair, 1990-91; national committee member, 1990—).

Awards, Honors

Choysa Bursary for Children's Writers, 1985; American Library Association Notable Book, 1986, for *Jellybean,* and 1989, for *In Lane Three, Alex Archer;* New Zealand Book of the Year, 1988, for *Alex;* Esther Glen Medal, New Zealand Library Association, 1989, for *Alex,* 1990, for *Alex in Winter,* and 1992, for *Alessandra: Alex in Rome,* and shortlisted, 1993, for *Songs for Alex;* Queen Elizabeth II Arts Council travel grant, 1989; AIM Children's Book of the Year, 1990, for *Alex in Winter,* and 1993, for *Songs for Alex;* New Zealand Commemorative Medal, 1990; Queen Elizabeth II Arts Council Special Writing Bursary, 1990; Australia-New Zealand Literary Exchange fellow, 1993; member of the Order of the British Empire (O.B.E.), 1994; Margaret Mahy Award, New Zealand Children's Book Foundation, 1996; New Zealand Post Senior Fiction award, 2000, for *The Tiggie Tompson Show.* Silver medal for swimming,

Tessa Duder

British Empire Games, 1958; national butterfly and medley swimming championship, New Zealand; twice Swimmer of the Year, New Zealand.

Writings

NOVELS; FOR CHILDREN

Night Race to Kawau, Oxford University Press, 1982.
Jellybean, Oxford University Press, 1985, Viking Kestrel, 1986.
Mercury Beach, Penguin, 1997.
The Tiggie Tompson Show, Penguin, 1999.
(With William Taylor) *Hot Mail,* Penguin, 2000.

"ALEX QUARTET" SERIES; FOR YOUNG ADULTS

Alex, Oxford University Press, 1987, published as *In Lane Three, Alex Archer,* Houghton, 1989.
Alex in Winter, Oxford University Press, 1988.
Alessandra: Alex in Rome, Oxford University Press, 1991, published as *Alex in Rome,* Houghton, 1992.
Songs for Alex, Oxford University Press, 1992.

NONFICTION

Kawau: The Governor's Gift, Bush Press, 1980, revised edition published as *Discover Kawau,* 1984.
Spirit of Adventure: The Story of New Zealand's Sail Training Ship, Century Hutchinson, 1985.
The Book of Auckland, Oxford University of Press, 1985.

Waitemata: Auckland's Harbour of Sail, Century Hutchinson, 1989.

Journey to Olympia: The Story of the Ancient Olympics, Ashton Scholastic, 1992.

The Making of Alex: The Movie, Ashton Scholastic, 1993.

OTHER

Play It Again Sam (educational reader), illustrated by Kelvin Hawley, Shortland, 1987.

Dragons (educational reader), illustrated by Kelvin Hawley, Shortland, 1987.

Simply Messing About in Boats (educational reader), Shortland, 1988.

(Editor and contributor) *Nearly Seventeen* (anthology of short stories and plays; includes Duder's one-act play *The Runaway*), Penguin, 1993.

(Editor and contributor) *Falling in Love* (short stories), Penguin, 1995.

(Editor, with Agnes Nieuwenhuizen, and contributor) *Crossing* (short stories), Reeds, 1995.

(Editor, with Peter McFarlane, and contributor) *Personal Best* (short stories), Reed, 1997.

Salt beneath the Skin (anthology), HarperCollins, 1999.

Contributor to books, including *Through the Looking Glass,* edited by Michael Gifkins, Century Hutchinson, 1989; and *My Father and Me,* edited by Penny Hansen, Tandem Press, 1992. Also author of plays, including *Foreign Rites, Five Go to the Dogs, Ghost Writers, Freeze Frame,* and *The Warrior Virgin,* Heinemann, all with Martin Baynton. Short stories represented in anthologies, including *The Magpies Said,* edited by Dorothy Butler, Viking Kestrel, 1981; *Ice Cream and Tabasco Sauce,* edited by Lydia Weavers, Macmillan, 1990; *Zig Zag,* edited by William Taylor, Penguin, 1993; *Ultimate Sports,* edited by Donald R. Gallo, Delacorte, 1995; and *The First Time, Volume 1,* edited by Charles Montpetit, Hodder Headline, 1996. Contributor to periodicals, including *Auckland Star, Listener,* and *Metro.* Editor, *Spirit,* 1986-90, 1999—.

Adaptations

Alex was adapted for film by Isambard Productions and Total Film, 1993.

Sidelights

Tessa Duder, novelist, short story writer, playwright, editor, columnist, public speaker, and actor with television and stage credits in her native New Zealand, is best known in America as the author of the popular "Alex" novels. That quartet of young adult books features fifteen-year-old Alex Archer, a star swimmer who learns to balance the demands of her athletic aspirations with those of her private life. "Far and away the best-selling children's novel ever produced in New Zealand," is how Duder herself has described the lead novel in the series, *In Lane Three, Alex Archer,* in the *St. James Guide to Young Adults Writers.* All four books remain in print in the English-speaking world more than a decade after publication, and a film was made of the first book. Since the mid-1990s, however, Duder's energies have been

placed increasingly in the theater, both writing plays and acting; she has also edited several popular volumes of short stories for young readers. In 1997 her first novel in five years, *Mercury Beach,* appeared; it was well received in New Zealand but was less well known in the United States. *The Tiggie Tompson Show,* first in a new series for Penguin, won the Senior Fiction award at the 2000 New Zealand Post book awards.

Duder once told *Something about the Author (SATA),* "I'm passionate about New Zealand, my country. Raising four daughters in the seventies made me aware of how much our children were exposed, through books and the moving image, to other country's cultures, and how relatively few local writers were publishing fiction which reflected our own unique way of life." To remedy this situation, Duder has focused her writing efforts on New Zealand. From the sailing adventure *Night Race to Kawau* to the "Alex" books, Duder has fashioned an image of life in New Zealand that is intimately related to both the geography and culture of the country.

Born in Auckland, New Zealand, in 1940, Duder spent the first five years of her life in a fatherless family, for he was in the army during World War II. She and her mother, who had given up a music scholarship to London to marry, spent much of this time with the maternal grandparents until the family was reunited at war's end. Then they packed up for a year in England while the father took pathology exams. Young Duder spent several months in a boarding school on England's south coast at this time. Here she learned, as she recounted in the *Something about the Author Autobiography Series (SAAS),* "what it was to be an outsider, bullied and humiliated by adults." After this brief interlude, the family moved back to Auckland, where for the next decade "all I remember is years of Auckland's sunshine and rain, good food, achievement at school, and order and security typical of professional families in the fifties." A younger brother was added to the family, but Duder was more attracted to books than his adventures. "As a child I read endlessly and compulsively," she wrote in *SAAS,* "armfuls of classics and imported horsey books from the local libraries." At age twelve she determined she would become a writer, but there were few female New Zealand role models for her to follow, so she set her sights on becoming a journalist—after, that is, she had had a successful career as a swimmer, something for which there were plenty of role models in New Zealand.

Duder began her swimming career at age eleven, and though she also participated in hockey, school dramatics, and piano and ballet, it was competitive swimming that formed the core of her life for years. She became New Zealand's national champion in butterfly and medley and set the medley record for her country. She competed in the Commonwealth Games at eighteen and won a silver medal; she was also a medal winner in the British Empire Games in the same year. After successively winning, losing, and then recapturing the title of New Zealand Swimmer of the Year, Duder retired from

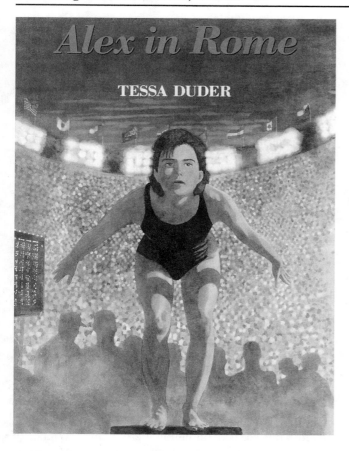

Alexandra meets a fellow New Zealander while participating in the Olympic Games in Rome in the third book in Duder's "Alex Quartet." (Cover illustration by Peter Catalanotto.)

swimming at age eighteen. She was ready to start her career as a journalist with the *Auckland Star.*

She worked for the next five years as a beginning reporter, covering swimming and the women's page as well as general reporting. She also studied singing and became a chorus member of the Auckland Operatic Society. In 1964 she married and went to England with her engineer husband, where she worked for a couple of years for the *Daily Express.* Her first daughter was born in 1966, and shortly thereafter the family moved for five years to Pakistan, where her husband worked on hydroelectric projects. More children followed, all girls, and then in 1971 they returned to their native New Zealand to an isolated life in the central North Island. Finally, in 1973, Duder was back in her hometown of Auckland, a busy mother of four.

When her fourth child entered school, Duder had her first breathing space in over a decade. Influenced somewhat by the wave of feminist literature just then hitting New Zealand, Duder experienced what she termed in *SAAS* "a midlife crisis," and decided to write a novel. She began a story about a young family's participation in a sailing race that goes wrong. Within two years she had the manuscript to her fist book, *Night Race to Kawau.* Then came another year-long stint

following her husband's work, this time in Malaysia. When Duder returned to New Zealand, she found that Oxford University Press, the first publisher to see her novel, had taken it on.

Night Race to Kawau recreates the heroic exploits of Sam, a twelve-year-old girl who must take charge of her family's sailboat during an annual race across the Hauraki Gulf, north of Auckland. After Sam's father is knocked unconscious by the boat's boom, and her mother is incapacitated by seasickness, Sam takes the helm and sails the boat safely through the night. A *Growing Point* reviewer found the book uncompromisingly realistic. "Sam is afraid but she is also, at times, angry with the discomfort of cold and fatigue and even bored." The reviewer went on to declare *Night Race to Kawau* a "small triumph" among adventure books.

Duder now began to think of herself as a professional writer, and in addition to adult titles on New Zealand and sailing, she also continued to write children's novels. In 1985 she brought out her second novel, *Jellybean,* in which she explored decidedly less adventurous situations than in her first novel. Geraldine, whose nickname is Jellybean, struggles to deal with her mother's career as a cellist, which often interferes with their relationship. As Geraldine's frustration mounts, a boyfriend and musician from her mother's past appears and attempts to renew their relationship. With abundant potential to further alienate Geraldine from her mother, the boyfriend actually helps Geraldine come to terms with her mother's profession and her own musical ambitions, which lie in conducting. As a result of the relationship that emerges between Geraldine and her mother's former romantic interest, Geraldine finds herself in a position to appreciate her mother's career and tolerate the inconveniences that accompany it.

"Particularly vivid are the passages of Geraldine experiencing certain pieces of music," declared Betsy Hearne in a *Bulletin of the Center for Children's Books* review. The book "is a commentary on the dedication and single-mindedness that a musician must have in order to succeed," Donna Rodda noted in *School Library Journal.* Margery Fisher, writing in *Growing Point,* remarked that the mother-daughter relationship in *Jellybean* was described "not in a portentous style but with speed and grace in the writing, with conversations that go far to suggest personal feelings and readjustments." Fisher went on to conclude, "Humour and good humour combine in a tale told with sympathy for the young."

In late 1985 Duder became the recipient of a fellowship that enabled her to write a book long in her imagination, one that dealt with her own experiences as a teenage swimmer. These came into play as the backdrop to the novel *Alex,* published in the United States as *In Lane Three, Alex Archer.* Fifteen year old Alexandra Archer's story focuses on her struggle to become a member of the 1960 New Zealand Olympic swimming team. Her main rival is Maggie, another young star, whose wealthy family attempts to provide her every advantage she will need to make the team. Accounts of actual meets are periodically isolated from the main body of the text by flashbacks, and the story brings in the details of Alex's life outside swimming. The untimely death of a close friend forces Alex to mature in a manner that her sporting rival could not. The novel does not disclose whether or not Alex makes the Olympic team, leaving audiences to admire the more profound changes in Alex's character.

Critical appraisals were favorable both in Duder's native New Zealand and in the United States and England. "Readers will not fail to be uplifted" by this novel, wrote a *Publishers Weekly* reviewer. In *Junior Bookshelf* another critic observed that "the authentic detail unfolds absolutely naturally, without distracting," and concluded that the book successfully addresses a wide range of adolescent experiences. Writing in *Voice of Youth Advocates,* JoEllen Broome remarked, "This is a tightly crafted novel where all of the hormonal and psychological stresses that fall on a young champion are looked upon with honesty and occasional humor." Linda Newbery, reviewing the title in *Books for Keeps,* felt that with her understated climax to the book Duder provided "a satisfying end to a moving and engrossing book."

Duder returned to Alex in three later novels, all of which focus on her success as a swimmer. In the second novel, *Alex in Winter,* the young swimmer competes for the chance to swim in the Rome Olympics, having to negotiate not only the waters of the swimming pool, but also those of the selection committees. Julia Wright, reviewing the novel in *School Librarian,* called it an "impressive book which is intellectually demanding but well worth the effort." In the third novel, *Alessandra: Alex in Rome,* the reader follows Alex to the Olympic Games in Rome, where Alex meets a young New Zealander who is studying music. They have a brief relationship, which ends when Alex returns to New Zealand. In the meantime Alex enjoys encouraging success in the Games. "The feeling of place and time and situation is wonderful" in this book, wrote Janet R. Mura in a *Voice of Youth Advocates* review. A writer for *Kirkus Reviews* commented, "Duder re-creates the 1960s, the Roman ambience, and the Olympic experience in vivid, authentic detail." *Booklist's* Stephanie Zvirin felt this third title "won't grab as many readers as its predecessor," but concluded that "The story is about the kind of teenage character that appears too infrequently in YA novels these days, and Duder's artful probing yields a vision of a confident, determined young woman who validates her already strong sense of herself." With *Songs for Alex,* Duder rounded out her quartet with Alex's return to New Zealand after her Olympic success and learning to deal with day-to-day life. She does not want the life of a sports celebrity; rather, the theater draws Alex in this culminating volume. Monica Dart called the fourth novel "a worthy successor" in a *School Librarian* review.

"I'm often asked if I'll write more about the tall and talented Alex, to which I firmly reply no," Duder commented for *SATA.* "I'm branching out now into other challenges: monologues for performance, play writing, writing for television, for theatre." Since the final novel in the "Alex" series, Duder has published the novel, *Mercury Beach,* "a lighthearted romp for the eleven-plus age group," as Duder described it in *SAAS,* featuring a plump Maori boy named Freddie Bone. As Duder noted in *SAAS:* "Much of our children's literature has portrayed Maori children as disadvantaged loners, on the edge of crime and abuse, so Freddie is an archetype less often seen: middle-class, supported by a loving mother, very bright, ambitious and purposeful with it." Freddie first made an appearance in *Personal Best,* a collection of stories that Duder co-edited with Peter McFarlane, and to which she contributed one story. There, the overweight Maori swimmer "triumphs as the greater skilled fall by the wayside," according to Jane Connolly in *Magpies,* because of his "courage and perseverance."

The early 1990s were turbulent years for Duder. She was working as a script advisor to the filming of *Alex;* then in the summer of 1992 her mother and one of her four daughters died within two weeks of each other. Her marriage later unraveled, and she began looking at other possibilities for her life, including collaboration with Martin Baynton on several plays, one of which, *The Warrior Virgin,* is about Joan of Arc. She also began her own acting career, appearing on a popular New Zealand soap opera.

A woman of many talents, Duder continues to be a sought-after speaker on children's literature. Winner of the prestigious Margaret Mahy Award in 1996, she is also at work on a more somber, edgy young adult novel. "Wherever I am," Duder concluded in *SAAS,* "I can't imagine a future without writing."

Works Cited

Review of *Alex, Junior Bookshelf,* February, 1989, p. 27.

Review of *Alex in Rome, Kirkus Reviews,* August 1, 1992, p. 988.

Broome, JoEllen, review of *In Lane Three, Alex Archer, Voice of Youth Advocates,* February, 1993, pp. 342-43.

Connolly, Jane, review of *Personal Best, Magpies,* March, 1998, pp. 37-38.

Dart, Monica, review of *Songs for Alex, School Librarian,* June, 1993, p. 108.

Duder, Tessa, essay in *Something about the Author Autobiography Series,* Volume 23, Gale, 1997, pp. 63-77.

Fisher, Margery, review of *Jellybean, Growing Point,* May, 1985, p. 4625.

Hearne, Betsy, review of *Jellybean, Bulletin of the Center for Children's Books,* November, 1986, p. 47.

Review of *In Lane Three, Alex Archer, Publishers Weekly,* October 13, 1989, p. 54.

Mura, Janet R., review of *Alex in Rome, Voice of Youth Advocates,* December, 1992, p. 276.

Newbery, Linda, review of *Alex, Books for Keeps,* May, 1990, p. 19.

Review of *Night Race to Kawau, Growing Point,* September, 1985, pp. 4490-91.

Rodda, Donna, review of *Jellybean, School Library Journal,* January, 1987, p. 73.

St. James Guide to Young Adult Writers, second edition, edited by Tom Pendergast and Sara Pendergast, St. James, 1999, pp. 250-52.

Wright, Julia, review of *Alex in Winter, School Librarian,* August, 1990, p. 120.

Zvirin, Stephanie, review of *Alex in Rome, Booklist,* October 15, 1992, p. 417.

For More Information See

BOOKS

Children's Literature Review, Volume 43, Gale, 1997.

Fitzgibbon, Tom, and Barbara Spiers, *Beneath Southern Skies,* Ashton Scholastic (Auckland), 1993.

Twentieth-Century Children's Writers, third edition, St. James, 1989.

PERIODICALS

Bulletin of the Center for Children's Books, November, 1989, p. 54; September, 1992, p. 9.

Horn Book, January-February, 1990, p. 68; November-December, 1992, p. 727.

Junior Bookshelf, June, 1993, p. 108.

Kliatt, September, 1996, p. 5.

Magpies, July, 1996, p. 33; September, 1998, p. 10.

Publishers Weekly, August 3, 1992, pp. 72-73.

School Library Journal, January, 1990, p. 120; October, 1992, p. 140.

Viewpoint, summer, 1993.

ON-LINE

New Zealand Book Council Web site, located at http://www.vuw.ac.nz/nzbookcouncil.

F

FARMER, Nancy 1941-

Personal

Born July 9, 1941, in Phoenix, AZ; daughter of Elmon Frank and Sarah (Marimon) Coe; married Harold Farmer (a literature teacher and poet), 1976; children: Daniel. *Education:* Phoenix College, Arizona, A.A., 1961; Reed College, B.A., 1963; attended Merrit College and University of California at Berkeley, 1969-71. *Politics:* "None whatsoever." *Religion:* Animism. *Hobbies and other interests:* Ethnology, criminology, marine biology, African culture and history.

Addresses

Agent—c/o Orchard Books, 95 Madison Ave., New York, NY 10016.

Nancy Farmer

Career

Worked in the Peace Corps in India, 1963-65; University of California, Berkeley, CA, lab technician, 1969-72; Loxton, Hunting and Associates, Songo, Mozambique, chemist and entomologist, 1972-74; University of Zimbabwe, Rukomeche, Zimbabwe, lab technician and entomologist, 1975-78; freelance scientist and writer in Harare, Zimbabwe, 1978-88; Stanford University Medical School, Palo Alto, CA, lab technician, 1991-92. Freelance writer, 1992—. *Member:* Society of Children's Book Writers and Illustrators, Science Fiction and Fantasy Writers of America.

Awards, Honors

Writers of the Future Gold Award, Bridge Publications, 1988; National Endowment for the Arts grant, 1992; Newbery Honor Book, 1995, Notable Children's Book, American Library Association, 1995, and Golden Kite Honor, Society of Children's Book Writers and Illustrators, all for *The Ear, the Eye, and the Arm;* Best Children's Book, Zimbabwe International Book Fair, 1996, for *The Warm Place;* National Book Award finalist for Children's Literature, 1996, Silver Medal, Commonwealth Club of California, 1996, Top Ten Best Book for Young Adults, American Library Association, 1997, and Newbery Honor Book, 1997, all for *A Girl Named Disaster.*

Writings

NOVELS; FOR YOUNG READERS

Lorelei: The Story of a Bad Cat, College Press (Zimbabwe), 1987, Orchard Books (New York), 1994.
The Ear, the Eye, and the Arm (science fiction), College Press, 1989, Orchard Books, 1994.
Tapiwa's Uncle, College Press, 1993.
Do You Know Me?, illustrated by Shelley Jackson, Orchard Books, 1993.
The Warm Place, Orchard Books, 1995.
A Girl Named Disaster, Orchard Books, 1996.

PICTURE BOOKS

Tsitsi's Skirt, College Press (Zimbabwe), 1988.
Runnery Granary, illustrated by Jos. A. Smith, Greenwillow Books (New York), 1996.
Casey Jones's Fireman: The Story of Sim Webb, illustrated by James Bernardin, Phyllis Fogelman Books (New York City), 1998.

OTHER

Contributor to *Writers of the Future Anthology, #4,* Bridge Publications, 1988, and *Best Horror and Fantasy of 1992,* St. Martin's, 1993. *The Ear, the Eye, and the Arm* has been published in German and Italian; *A Girl Named Disaster* has been published in Dutch.

Adaptations

"Tapiwa's Uncle," a play adapted by Aaron Shepard and published in *Stories on Stage,* Wilson, 1993; *The Ear, the Eye, and the Arm* and *A Girl Named Disaster* were recorded by Recorded Books, 1995 and 1996, respectively; "Resthaven," a play adapted by Aaron Shepard and published in *Aaron Shegard's Reader's Theatre,* http://www.aaronshep.com/rt, March, 1998.

Work in Progress

An adult science fiction novel entitled *VaiDoSol.*

Sidelights

Award-winning novelist Nancy Farmer is the author of juvenile novels and picture books that demonstrate her talent as a storyteller and her interest in African culture. The seventeen years Farmer spent in central Africa proved to be critical to her writing career. "The character, viewpoint and zany sense of humor of the people I met there have had a major effect on my writing," she recounted for *SATA.* Indeed, many critics have applauded her work for her characterizations, humor, and depiction of locale. A sure measure of her success is that *The Ear, the Eye, and the Arm* and *A Girl Named Disaster* were both named Newbery Honor books and have been translated into other languages.

Farmer grew up during the 1950s in a small town on the Arizona-Mexico border, where she lived in the hotel her father managed. Although her school friends were not allowed to visit her in the rough neighborhood in which the hotel was located, "life at the hotel was a wonderful preparation for writing," Farmer remembered in the *St. James Guide to Young Adult Writers.* "I worked at the desk from age nine, renting rooms and listening to the stories the patrons told each other in the lobby." Among the colorful characters at the hotel were cowboys, railroad men, rodeo riders, and circus performers. "My father took me to the American Legion hall on bingo nights, and I heard a lot more stories there," she told *SATA.* "People were able to spin tales back then, and they taught me a lot."

Although she was not interested in school and often played hooky, Farmer eventually earned a Bachelor of Arts degree from Reed College in Portland, Oregon. In search of adventure, she spent two years in India as a Peace Corps volunteer. Then Farmer traveled for two more years before returning to California, where she studied at Merrit College and the University of California at Berkeley. Again she was seized with the desire to travel, and in 1971 she and a friend sailed to Africa on a freighter. "We planned to sail from port to port, get jobs when we ran out of money, and hopefully meet a lonely Greek shipping tycoon," Farmer remembered to *SATA.* "We arranged passage on a yacht that was actually in the process of being stolen. We didn't know this. The coast guard arrested the 'captain' as he sailed out under the Golden Gate. We were upset, but they probably saved us from being dumped overboard somewhere."

From 1972 to 1988, Farmer worked at a variety of jobs in Mozambique and Zimbabwe (formerly called Rhodesia). While in Zimbabwe, Farmer met her future husband, Harold Farmer, an English professor at the University of Zimbabwe. They married in 1976, and it was when their son was about four years old that Farmer was inspired to start writing. "I had been reading a novel by Margaret Forster and thought: *I could do that.* Three hours later I emerged with a complete story. The experience was so surprising and pleasant I did it again the next day." In the following four years, Farmer refined her craft. She studied works by Roald Dahl, J. R. R. Tolkien, C. S. Lewis, P. D. James, Ruth Rendell, and Stephen King. According to Farmer, it takes a minimum of four years to learn to write. "The horrible truth is that one's first efforts are amateurish," she once commented. "It takes time, practice, and objectivity to correct this problem. I have never understood why people think they can write well without effort. No one expects a first-year medical student to transplant a kidney."

After publishing several novels and a picture book with a Zimbabwean press, Farmer found her writing stalled. For the sake of their son, Daniel, the Farmers decided to move to the United States, and for a time after the move Farmer was unable to write. Finally, Farmer made her American debut with *Do You Know Me?,* a novel that is set in Zimbabwe and revolves around Tapiwa and her Uncle Zeka, who moves from the country to the city. Reviewers praised the novel for its characterizations and humor. Remarking on the universal theme, "carefully drawn" characters, and humorous outcome, *Horn Book* contributor Lois F. Anderson asserted that Farmer "manages to deal with serious issues and at the same time provoke laughter." Calling Farmer a "born storyteller," a *Publishers Weekly* critic applauded her "astute ear for dialogue,... deft hand with plot twists and ... keen, dry wit."

Farmer further demonstrated her storytelling talent with the science fiction tale *The Ear, the Eye, and the Arm.* Although she originally published this young adult novel in Zimbabwe in 1989, she revised it for republication by Orchard in 1994. Taking place in a futuristic Zimbabwean society in the year 2194, the novel follows the adventures of three children of the country's security

Imprisoned in a San Francisco zoo, Ruva the giraffe gets help from a rat, a chameleon, and a runaway boy to escape and return home to Africa. (Cover illustration by Matthew Henry.)

chief. Because they have always been highly sheltered, the children do not anticipate the dangers they will encounter when they decide to secretly leave their safe compound and venture through the city of Harare. In no time the children are kidnapped by criminals, and soon the Ear, the Eye, and the Arm—three mutant detectives—are on their trail. For this "intriguing, multivalent novel," to quote Anne Deifendeifer in *Horn Book,* Farmer won kudos from critics. "Farmer is emerging as one of the best and brightest authors for the YA audience," enthused a *Publishers Weekly* reviewer. As well as judging the author's "impeccable creation of the futuristic society ... a remarkable achievement," Deifendeifer praised Farmer for her "fully developed, unique characters" and treatment of futuristic social and political issues. Hazel Rochman of *Booklist* predicted that the "thrilling adventures ... will grab readers," as will the many "comic, tender characterizations." In 1995, *The Ear, the Eye, and the Arm* was named a Newbery Honor Book.

For *The Warm Place,* Farmer employed animal characters, in particular Ruva, a young giraffe who escapes

from a San Francisco zoo and, with the help of animal colleagues and one human friend, voyages home. Reviewers applauded Farmer for her creativity in portraying animal characters. "The plot is fresh and fast-moving, and many of the details [are] inventive," praised Ellen Fader in her review for *School Library Journal*. In addition, Roger Sutton asserted in the *Bulletin of the Center for Children's Books,* "Farmer keeps her story fresh through lots of action and snappy dialogue." "With witty, crisp dialog, this novel will be a fine read," seconded Mary Harris Veeder in *Booklist*. Noting that with the possible exception of the villains, Farmer "created highly original events and characters," *Horn Book* critic Sarah Guille judged that reading *The Warm Place* would be both an "entertaining and rewarding experience." Because it is "laced with dry humor and populated by memorable characters," *The Warm Place,* asserted a *Publishers Weekly* reviewer, is "pure delight."

In 1996, Farmer scored a resounding success for the young adult novel *A Girl Named Disaster,* which was named a Newbery Honor Book. Set in modern Zimbabwe and Mozambique, this novel details the journey of Nhamo (her name literally means "disaster") from life in her traditional, isolated village, to life on a series of uninhabited islands, to life in urban Zimbabwe. During her trek, Nhamo faces many challenges and uses traditional survival skills, including communing with spirits, to survive. "The novel is unusual in its scope and setting," remarked Martha V. Parravano in *Horn Book,* "although, as in *The Ear, the Eye, and the Arm,* the author's skill makes the setting real and nonexotic even as the reader learns an amazing amount about survival techniques, Shona culture, and Zimbabwean politics." Likewise, Sheila H. Williams noted in *Kliatt* that "Nhamo's rich character compels the listener to accompany her to the end," despite the occasionally uneven pacing. "Farmer overlays this suspenseful tale with a rich and respectful appreciation of Nhamo's beliefs," averred a critic for *Publishers Weekly,* who also described the character of Nhamo as "stunning" and a "supremely human" creation.

After publishing her initial picture book in Zimbabwe in 1988, it was nearly a decade before Farmer returned to the genre with two well-received works, *Runnery Granary* and *Casey Jones's Fireman: The Story of Sim Webb*. In *Runnery Granary,* Farmer spins the tale of Mrs. Runnery, who discovers that something is eating the grain from her medieval grain storage house. After some investigation, she determines that gnomes are the culprits, and she knows just how to send them packing. *Runnery Granary* fared well with critics; in *Booklist,* Carolyn Phelan praised the work as "an unusual and entertaining picture book," and in *Horn Book,* Lolly Robinson called it "an unusual original trickster tale." "A winsome yarn" is how a *Publishers Weekly* critic described it, while Kathy East, writing in *School Library Journal,* predicted that children at library story hours are "sure to eat up" this "charming tale." Farmer's *Casey Jones's Fireman* met with a similar reaction. Farmer tells this story of the Cannonball Express train disaster from the viewpoint of Sim Webb, who stokes the steam engine's furnace. According to *Booklist* reviewer Shelle Rosenfeld, "Farmer eloquently interweaves history and myth into a suspenseful, engrossing drama, enhanced by well-developed characters." A *Publishers Weekly* reviewer similarly said that Farmer created an "exciting blend of history and imagination" and a "fully realized portrait" of Sim Webb that will "fascinate readers."

Although Farmer does not like to analyze her motivation or career, she once told *SATA:* "According to the Shona, the Africans among whom we lived, I had been visited by a *shave* (pronounced 'shah-vay') or wandering spirit. *Shaves* come from people who haven't received proper burial rites. They drift around until they find a likely host, possess whoever it is, and teach him or her a skill. In my case I got a traditional storyteller. Now I am a full-time professional storyteller myself." She also recommended to would-be writers: "My rules for becoming a successful writer are these: (1) Read as much as possible, (2) write as much as possible for several years, and (3) submit manuscripts to a wide variety of editors. Sooner or later you will find one who loves your particular style. Your B.A. degree in writing is your first book contract."

Works Cited

Anderson, Lois F., review of *Do You Know Me?, Horn Book,* September-October, 1993, pp. 597-98.

Review of *Casey Jones's Fireman, Publishers Weekly,* September 6, 1999, p. 102.

Deifendeifer, Anne, review of *The Ear, the Eye and the Arm, Horn Book,* September-October, 1994, pp. 597-98.

Review of *Do You Know Me?, Publishers Weekly,* March 15, 1993, pp. 88-89.

Review of *The Ear, the Eye and the Arm, Publishers Weekly,* April 11, 1994, p. 66.

East, Kathy, review of *Runnery Granary, School Library Journal,* August, 1996, p. 122.

Fader, Ellen, review of *The Warm Place, School Library Journal,* March, 1995, p. 204.

Farmer, Nancy, *St. James Guide to Young Adult Writers,* second edition, St. James, 1999, pp. 272-74.

Review of *A Girl Named Disaster, Publishers Weekly,* October 28, 1996, p. 82.

Guille, Sarah, review of *The Warm Place, Horn Book,* September-October, 1995, pp. 597-98.

Parravano, Martha V., review of *A Girl Named Disaster, Horn Book,* November-December, 1996, pp. 734-35.

Phelan, Carolyn, review of *Runnery Granary, Booklist,* June 1, 1996, p. 1731.

Robinson, Lolly, review of *Runnery Granary, Horn Book,* September-October, 1996, p. 575.

Rochman, Hazel, review of *The Ear, the Eye, and the Arm, Booklist,* April 1, 1994, p. 1436.

Rosenfeld, Shelle, review of *Casey Jones's Fireman, Booklist,* September 15, 1999, p. 259.

Review of *Runnery Granary, Publishers Weekly,* May 20, 1996, p. 259.

Sutton, Roger, review of *The Warm Place, Bulletin of the Center for Children's Books,* May, 1995, p. 304.

Veeder, Mary Harris, review of *The Warm Place, Booklist,* April 1, 1995, p. 1391.

Review of *The Warm Place, Publishers Weekly,* March 20, 1995, p. 62.

Williams, Sheila H., review of *A Girl Named Disaster, Kliatt,* July, 1998, p. 46.

For More Information See

PERIODICALS

Booklist, April 1, 1993, p. 1431; August, 1998, p. 2029; September 15, 1998, p. 219.

Kliatt, July, 1996, pp. 46-47.

School Library Journal, April, 1993, p. 118; October, 1999, pp. 136-37.

Voice of Youth Advocates, June, 1997, p. 85.

Wilson Library Bulletin, June, 1995, p. 134.

*   *   *

FLEAGLE, Gail S(hatto) 1940-

Personal

Born February 21, 1940, in Harrisburg, PA; daughter of Benjamin (an insurance agent) and Dolores (an auditor for government programs; maiden name, Seewald) Shatto; married Jan Ruhl Fleagle (a systems analyst), June 18, 1960; children: Jeff, Scott. *Education:* University of North Carolina at Greensboro, B.A. and M.A; attended Education Center Writing Institute.

Addresses

Home and office—3419 Cotswold Terr., Greensboro, NC 27455. *E-mail*—jgfleagle@earthlink.net and http:// home.earthlink.net/~jgfleagle.

Career

Elementary schoolteacher for more than twenty years; Guilford County Schools, Greensboro, NC, substitute teacher. Storyteller, writer, and illustrator. *Member:* Society of Children's Book Writers and Illustrators, North Carolina Science Teachers Association, NSTA, GGIRA, NCWN, WGOT.

Awards, Honors

Contest winner, *Instructor,* 1981, for "Entering Space Shuttle Camp," and *Greensboro News and Record,* 1996, for "Most Exotic Trip;" Silver Arts essay winner, 1996, for "Can I Change My Mind Now?"

Writings

Play Ball!, illustrated by Marilyn Henry, Richard C. Owen (Katonah, NY), 1998.

Author of "Best of the Bunch," a quarterly interview column in *Reflector,* 1999. Contributor of articles and reviews to periodicals, including *Science and Children, Pennsylvania, Instructor,* and *Greensboro News and*

Record. Contributing coeditor of science newsletter for Greensboro and Guilford County Science Teachers, 1987-90.

Work in Progress

The Great Giving Shaman, with Helen Cook, with illustrations by Fleagle, expected 2001; *The Great Green Medicine Man; Gertrude Giraffe,* a humorous illustrated story based on a true event, for early primary grades; *Gallant Gillies,* a true story about a fourteen-year-old boy; "The Creepy Crawly Swamp," a poem.

Sidelights

Gail S. Fleagle told *SATA:* "Many years ago I began storytelling for my two younger sisters in our room at bedtime. In school I received praise for reports and essays I wrote. Years later writing was my therapy during an illness.

"Now I write or read daily, sometimes for only one hour and sometimes nearly all day. Ideas come from the children I teach, my grandchildren's needs, or my experiences observing people while traveling. Sometimes I envision an entire story before putting it on paper. I love writing what I dream, and I love reading!

"Research is time-consuming, but important to all of my stories. I have completed much of the research by actively viewing the characters, places, and events. I interviewed one shaman in a Peruvian garden and another in Ecuador, toured a home built in 1740, traveled to Alaska and Africa, and read historic first-account records at historical societies and the museums of national parks. This method produces accurate, honest stories that are historically or scientifically based.

"Children's book authors William Hooks, Lynne Cherry, Gary Paulsen, Jean Craighead George, Harold Underwood, Lois Lowry, Vicki Cobb, and so many more provide vicarious adventures I enjoy. I learn something every time I read many of today's authors. Their books have fresh voices, unique stories that thrill children—and me! They are storytellers first and writers second. Barbara Lavallee, Lynne Cherry, and Uri Shulevitz provide appealing art work, attracting my attention like the positive end of a magnet pulls the negative end toward it.

"My first published book *Play Ball!* is a success story for me and its national and international readers. Illustrator Marilyn Henry provides subtle clues that the ball Ox pushes is something different from what is first perceived by the readers. It is to the credit of editor Janice Boland of Richard C. Owen Publishers, Inc. that we have such a successful book.

"My language is English only, yet the book was translated into Spanish. I taught a second-grade class that included six immigrants. Two children were Spanish-speaking. One of the two children sat expressionless, with sad brown eyes, because she could not speak or read English. When she read the Spanish version of *Play Ball!* to the class, her eyes gleamed and her face beamed as her classmates clapped and cheered for her. And she now understood what I had just read in English!

"The Spanish version of *Play Ball!* has traveled with me as far south as Peru. In a village off the Napo River, a tributary of the Amazon River, the people of all ages came to gawk at the visiting teachers from America. We all walked to their one-room school. I observed the only books were a few manuals used by the teacher. Teaching was by rote or writing on a chalkboard. As I waited to present *Play Ball!* to the teacher, my book disappeared. How could I present the book when I did not have it? I had already given away all the other copies to children and a school in another village. I searched frantically. As I walked around the small, crowded room of the school house, I saw someone almost hidden behind the people standing. A mother sat on the dirt floor reading to a small child—reading *Play Ball!*

"The English version has been successful, too. After one or two times of reading to a child, the child reads the story himself and laughs at the odd ball. A new reader is born! That is success.

"The teacher in me writes stories for learning, and my writer self makes the stories fun to read."

*   *   *

FORRESTAL, Elaine 1941-

Personal

Born October 9, 1941, in Perth, Western Australia; daughter of Russell Alfred (a bank officer) and Emily Annie "Bonnie" (a secretary; maiden name, Ives) Chandler; married Barry Edmonds, November 17, 1962 (marriage ended February 28, 1980); married Peter Forrestal (a wine and food writer), January 10, 1981; children: Lee Anne Beet, Carmel Jane Keylock. *Hobbies and other interests:* Swimming, walking, gardening.

Addresses

Home and office—1 Cobb Street, Scarborough, 6019, Western Australia. *Agent*—Peter Forrestal, 1 Cobb Street, Scarborough, 6019, Western Australia. *E-mail*—forrie@iinet.net.au, or forrie@attglobal.net.

Career

Bank of New South Wales, secretary, 1958-62; Education Dept. of Western Australia, teacher, 1970-81, early childhood specialist, 1984-99. Lecturer; writer-in-residence at Claremont Library, Claremont, Western Australia; Kununurra Library, Kununurra, Western Australia; Abercorn Primary School, Banbridge, Northern Ireland, Manjimup Library, Manjimup, Western Australia; and South Hedland Library, Hedland, Western Australia. *Member:* Early Childhood Teachers Association, Aus-

Elaine Forrestal

tralian Literary Educators Association, Australian Children's Book Council.

Awards, Honors

Shortlisted for the Western Australian Premier's Book Awards, 1991, and named a Children's Book Council Notable Book, 1992, both for *The Watching Lake;* Highly Commended, NASEN Children's Book Award, 1997, Book of the Year, Australian Children's Book Council, 1998, winner, WAYRBA Hoffman Award, Younger Readers category, 1998, and shortlisted for the YABA Awards, 1999 and 2000, all for *Someone Like Me;* shortlisted for Western Australia Premier's Book Awards, 1999, for *Straggler's Reef;* shortlisted for Book of the Year, Younger Readers, Australian Children's Book Council, 2000, for *Graffiti on the Fence.*

Writings

The Watching Lake, Puffin (Melbourne), 1991.
Someone Like Me, Puffin, 1996.
Straggler's Reef, Fremantle Arts Centre Press (Fremantle), 1999.
Graffiti on the Fence, Puffin, 1999.

Someone Like Me is being translated into Italian. Stories have appeared on Australian television channel 10,

Mulligrubs; in the magazine *Highlights for Children* and *Highlights for Children Pre-Reader's Supplement* (cd-rom); and in the anthologies, *Creepy-Crawly Stories,* edited by Barbara Ireson, Century Hutchinson (London), 1986, and *Stories to Share,* edited by Jean Chapman, Hodder and Stoughton (Sydney), 1983.

Work in Progress

Novel for children, *Leaving No Footprints,* expected completion 2000-01.

Sidelights

Elaine Forrestal told *SATA:* "Children are not as easily fooled as some people seem to think. They will not tolerate anything but the highest degree of honesty and transparency from their authors. And they demand relevance in what they read, which means that the children's author must keep up to date with what kids are watching on TV, the games they are playing, and the music they are listening to. In this regard, access to kids in a school playground is a very useful thing.

"Until recently, teaching and writing have been complementary careers for me. I began writing stories to use with my class when I became frustrated with the lack of suitable commercially available material. And many of my stories are based on incidents or characters I have encountered at school.

"But since I won the Australian Children's Book Council Book of the Year Award in 1998 my writing career has really taken off. I find that I am doing more and more lectures, workshops, meet-the-author sessions, and writer-in-residencies and have little time left for teaching my class!"

Elaine Forrestal's first novel, *The Watching Lake,* is a mystery with an inherent warning about the ecological damage that may result from tampering with nature. In her second novel, *Someone Like Me,* the life of an ordinary sixth-grade boy is changed in many ways when he gets a new neighbor with a troubling mystery in her past. The story is "bursting with lovely images of the Australian countryside and lifestyle," according to Cecile Grumelart in *Magpies.* Ten-year-old Juliana Oliver reviewed *Someone Like Me* for *Books for Keeps,* saying in part: "There is something that the author doesn't reveal until the end. She gives no clues whatsoever in the whole book. I guarantee you a SURPRISE!"

For her third novel for middle-grade readers, Forrestal wrote *Straggler's Reef,* in which the past surfaces in the present of young Australians Karri and Jarrad when they are stranded on the reef while sailing with their father. Karrie is passing the time reading her grandmother's journal when Carrie, a figure from the past, appears on the yacht deck and tells them they are stranded over sunken treasure. "The recount of events in the 1840s is engrossing and evocative, and made this reader long for a straight historical novel," opined Pam Mcintyre in

Australian Book Review. Once the youngsters decide to dive for the treasure the excitement of the plot increases, the reviewer noted; Fran Knight called *Straggler's Reef* "a gripping tale set on the seas off the Western Australian coast," in her review in *Magpies.* Though Forrestal emphasizes the action in her plot, and critics agreed that this aspect may be the most likely to appeal to the author's intended audience, issues of interest raised by the book include "how [language] has changed, family history, children's roles in their families and expectations of how boys and girls should behave," as Kylie Williams noted in *REACT.*

Works Cited

Grumelart, Cecile, review of *Someone Like Me, Magpies,* March, 1997, p. 33.

Knight, Fran, review of *Straggler's Reef, Magpies,* July, 1999.

Macintyre, Pam, review of *Straggler's Reef, Australian Book Review,* July, 1999, p. 43.

Oliver, Juliana, review of *Someone Like Me, Books for Keeps,* May, 1998, p. 18.

Williams, Kylie, review of *Straggler's Reef, REACT,* vol. 99, no. 4, p. 3.

For More Information See

PERIODICALS

Magpies, July, 1992, p. 20.
Reading Time, Vol. 43, no. 4.

G

GIBBONS, Kaye 1960-

Personal

Born in 1960, Nash County, NC; married Frank Ward (an attorney); children: (from previous marriage) three daughters. *Education:* Attended North Carolina State University and the University of North Carolina at Chapel Hill.

Addresses

Home—Raleigh, NC.

Kaye Gibbons

Career

Novelist.

Awards, Honors

Sue Kaufman Prize for First Fiction, American Academy and Institute of Arts and Letters, and citation from Ernest Hemingway Foundation, both for *Ellen Foster;* National Endowment for the Arts fellowship, for *A Virtuous Woman;* Nelson Algren Heartland Award for Fiction, Chicago Tribune, 1991, PEN/Revson Foundation Fellowship, and North Carolina Sir Walter Raleigh Award, all for *A Cure for Dreams;* Chevalier de L'Ordre des Arts et des Lettres, 1997; honorary Ph.D., North Carolina State University, 1998.

Writings

NOVELS

Ellen Foster, Algonquin Books (Chapel Hill, NC), 1987.
A Virtuous Woman, Algonquin Books, 1989.
A Cure for Dreams, Algonquin Books, 1991.
Charms for the Easy Life, Putnam (New York City), 1993.
Sights Unseen, Putnam, 1995.
On the Occasion of My Last Afternoon, Putnam, 1998.

Contributor to the *New York Times Book Review.*

Adaptations

Ellen Foster was adapted for audiocassette by Simon and Schuster in 1996, and for a Hallmark Hall of Fame television movie in 1997; movie rights to *A Virtuous Woman* were bought by the Oprah Winfrey production company.

Sidelights

Kaye Gibbons burst upon the American literary scene at the age of twenty-seven with publication of her Southern coming-of-age novel, *Ellen Foster.* This short novel tells the story of plucky, spirited Ellen, eleven going on thirty, and a survivor who faces the suicide of her abused mother, fends off the drunken advances of her father, and deals with the malignant neglect of aunts and a grandmother to finally find a family for herself. Something of a female Huck Finn, Ellen Foster, both character and novel, won the hearts of readers and earned prestigious literary awards for its young Southern author. The novel became the first in a string of best-sellers for Gibbons, all set in the South and told in the simple vernacular of that region.

Resilient is a word often used to describe a typical Kaye Gibbons character. Her female protagonists are survivors, quiet domestic heroines in the conflict between the sexes. Her male characters are mostly '3-D': the men in a Gibbons novel can usually be counted on to "disappoint, disappear and die," as Stephen McCauley pointed out in a critical appraisal of *A Cure for Dreams* in the *New York Times Book Review*. But her women persevere and more. There is Ellen of course, and then comes Ruby in *A Virtuous Woman,* Lottie in *A Cure for Dreams,* Charlie in *Charms for the Easy Life,* Hattie in *Sights Unseen,* and Emma in Gibbons's sixth novel, *On the Occasion of My Last Afternoon.* Often these narrators are young: Ellen is eleven, Hattie twelve, and Emma an adolescent throughout much of the action of the last-named novel. Gibbons's trademark heroine is, as Kathryn Harrison noted in the *New York Times Book Review,* "a girl who, having lost her mother—having lost all comfort and safety—attacks the chaos of her life with heartbreaking bravery. For this girl, assuming blame is less terrifying than perceiving herself a victim of an impossibly cruel fate. Focused on the frailty or absence of her mother, the vigilant heroine misses out on childhood."

Gibbons's female characters do not go softly into that good night. They fight what others might term fate; they wage quiet wars against sexist inequity, against racism, against buttons that refuse to close properly, for Gibbons's characters do not exist on the abstract plane. One of her great strengths as a writer is her use of concrete detail. "When I talk and when I write," Gibbons told a chat room sponsored by Barnes and Noble, "I try to avoid the abstract. I am drawn to detail in writing as a way of offering density and showing rather than telling. I couldn't imagine something more unbearable than having somebody asking me to write about an abstract like tenderness, with no examples of it, with no examples of chimps picking lice out of a little chimp's head. I would have to show examples of an emotion."

Like her own female protagonists, Gibbons does not beat her own drum too loudly. "Soft-spoken and self-deprecating, Kaye Gibbons is the stealth candidate among Southern writers," James Wolcott remarked in the *New Yorker.* "She has produced a handful of seriocomic studies of female coping and comradeship which may someday lodge on the permanent shelf."

While being lovingly thorough about every aspect of the history of her fictional characters, Gibbons has long maintained a reticence about her own past. In fact, there are parallels in Gibbons's early life and that of the

Gibbons's award-winning first novel is a Southern coming-of-age story of a spirited survivor. (Cover illustration by David Hyman.)

fictional life of her first female protagonist, Ellen Foster. Born in Nash County, North Carolina, in 1960, Gibbons grew up in the South with all its prejudices and pride. Gibbons's own mother committed suicide when the author was ten, and this occasioned the break up of her family, including her alcoholic father. Gibbons thereafter lived with a couple of aunts before finally moving in with an older brother. But of this she has little to say, not wishing it to be the focus of critical analysis or gossip. "I had read enough Thomas Wolfe to know what would happen if that occurred," Gibbons told Bob Summer in an interview for *Publishers Weekly.* "I didn't want the publicity hook to be my miserable childhood." Gibbons went on to say, however, "the years between 10 and 13 were pretty hard." And in the Barnes and Noble chat room, she commented: "I knew as a child that I had a gift that the other children didn't get, and because I was born dirt-poor with a suicidal mother and alcoholic father, I feel like I deserved to have that present in my cradle. I thought I would grow up and teach literature. I didn't think that people made livings at being writers unless they were dead or from Mississippi. But I have always used books as a haven."

An avid reader as a child, Gibbons was a constant patron of the local library, as the books at home consisted mainly of a Bible and a set of encyclopedias. She graduated from Rocky Mount High School and then went on to North Carolina State University on a scholarship, intending, as she noted, to go into teaching. But her interest in writing led her to change schools; attending the University of North Carolina at Chapel Hill, she became fascinated with the writings of James Weldon Johnson, an African-American poet of the turn of the twentieth century. "He seemed to me to be the first poet in the South—not the first writer, since Twain had already done it—to make art out of everyday language," Gibbons told *Summer.* "Inspired by him, I wanted to see if I could have a child use her voice to talk about life, death, art, eternity—big things from a little person."

In 1985, Gibbons began writing a poem from the point of view of a young black girl, Starletta, but soon the poem turned into a novel narrated by a young white girl, Ellen, a friend of Starletta's. Gibbons was still taking classes at Chapel Hill at the time, with Louis Rubin, who founded the Algonquin Press at the university. Rubin looked at the book Gibbons came up with, and showed it to some influential literary friends as well, Walker Percy and Eudora Welty among them, and decided to publish this first novel. For Gibbons, still without a degree, married and with two children, this was a life-altering event.

"When I was little I would think of ways to kill my daddy. I would figure out this way or that way and run it through my head until it got easy.

"The way I liked best was letting go a poisonous spider in his bed, it would bite him and he'd be dead and swollen up and I would shudder to find him ...

"But I did not kill my daddy. He drank his own self to death the year after the County moved me out. I heard how they found him shut up in the house dead and everything. Next thing I know he's in the ground and the house is rented out to a family of four."

So begins Gibbons's first novel, *Ellen Foster,* and the reader is immediately presented with a narrator who is a female equivalent of Holden Caulfield and Huck Finn. The book that follows is a narrative mix of flashback memories of Ellen's abused childhood and current scenes of her life in a foster family. Ellen's mother is the daughter of a well-to-do family who never forgave her for marrying beneath herself. Sickly, she still must take care of her brutish husband. Young Ellen tries to protect her mother from her father, but finally her mother opts out by taking an overdose of pills. Ellen's father refuses to allow her to get help for her dying mother. After Ellen's mother dies, her drunken father becomes even worse, signing over the farm for a monthly remittance which he promptly drinks up. Ellen's only friends are a black family and their mute daughter Starletta who live nearby. Despite her liking for these people, Ellen is still

stuck with blind prejudice, a result of her Southern upbringing.

When Ellen's father makes drunken advances toward her, she runs off to Starletta's house and then to an aunt's. However, when the aunt learns that Ellen hopes to make the move permanent, she sends the girl back to her abusive parent. Finally, discovering bruises on the young girl, a teacher intervenes and takes Ellen in for a time, until the court awards custody to her maternal grandmother, a woman still bitter about her daughter's marriage. Ellen is put to work in the fields where the work is hard, but where she begins to learn about the realities of her family, and families in general, from some of the field hands. Ellen's father drinks himself to death and then her grandmother too falls ill. When she dies, Ellen is sent to other aunts, and while in their reluctant care, she spies a single woman at church with a bevy of children and is informed this is the local foster family. Ellen decides she wants to be part of Mrs. Foster's family, confusing the adjective for a name, and offers the woman all the money she has saved if she can only be part of her family. Refusing the money, the woman happily takes the love-starved youth in. Ellen has finally found a home.

Baldly told, the novel has melodramatic overtones. A *Publishers Weekly* contributor noted, "this slim first novel ... [does] resemble a Victorian tearjerker, transplanted to the South." But as Alice Hoffman commented in *New York Times Book Review,* "What might have been grim, melodramatic material in the hands of a less talented author is instead filled with lively humor ... compassion and intimacy. This short novel focuses on Ellen's strengths rather than her victimization, presenting a memorable heroine who rescues herself." *Booklist*'s Brad Hooper noted that this "commendable first novel" is "humorous and unsentimental ... never weepy or grim, despite the subject matter."

Other reviewers commended Gibbons's use of language and her willingness to tackle large themes. A *Kirkus Reviews* contributor drew attention to the "laconic and telegraph-style voice" of the youthful narrator, while Pearl K. Bell, writing in *New Republic,* noted that "Gibbons never allows us to feel the slightest doubt that [Ellen] is only 11. Nor does she ever lapse into the condescending cuteness that afflicts so many stories about precocious children." Bell went on to note that "the voice of this resourceful child is mesmerizing because we are right inside her head. The words are always flawlessly right." Bell also praised Gibbons for the fact that she "doesn't evade the racism of Southern life, which she subtly reveals through the tenacious child's mind." Linda Taylor, reviewing the novel in *Sunday Times,* felt that *Ellen Foster* "is one of those novels that you feel compelled to read from cover to cover in one sitting.... [I]t is a novel about sexism, racism, family rancor and child abuse, issues that are dealt with through revelation rather than moral axe-grinding."

Still other reviewers remarked on the literary tradition into which *Ellen Foster* fits, drawing comparisons to both *Huck Finn* and *Catcher in the Rye. Kirkus Reviews* noted that "Ellen Foster is a kind of Huck Finn," while her father, "like Huck's Pap, is a piece of mean, worthless, lecherous, drunken white trash." Expanding on this theme, Veronica Makowsky commented in *Southern Quarterly* that "*Ellen Foster* is Gibbons's attempt to rewrite the saga of the American hero by changing 'him' to 'her' and to rewrite the southern female *bildungsroman* by changing its privileged, sheltered, upper-class heroine to a poor, abused outcast." But Makowsky further noted that "although [Ellen's] gutsy, vernacular voice recalls Huck Finn, she does not light out for the territories" as did Huck. Rather, Ellen finds strength in "the female tradition of community and nurturance."

Awards committees agreed with the reviewers: Gibbons's debut novel won the Sue Kaufman Prize for First Fiction from the American Academy and Institute of Arts and Letters as well as a citation from the Ernest Hemingway Foundation. Gibbons's literary career was solidly launched.

Gibbons is best known for her strong female characters, and in her second novel, *A Virtuous Woman,* she presents Ruby, a woman who never made headlines but whose quiet, determined, virtuous life resounds in the telling. Set again in the rural South and employing the idiomatic vernacular of the region, *A Virtuous Woman* is told from the dual viewpoints of Ruby, as she lays dying from lung cancer, and from that of her second husband, Jack Stokes, several months after Ruby's death. By this time Jack has worked through all the meals in the freezer that Ruby has lovingly prepared for him before dying. The novel has little plot; its strength lies in the retelling of an ordinary life made extraordinary by such details. And it is also the story of how Jack finally must get on with his life after losing Ruby.

"The story, which is a pleasure to read," wrote Deanna D'Errico in *Belles Lettres,* "evokes subtly and lovingly the bond that has united Jack and Ruby through life and beyond." Roz Kavaney, writing in *Times Literary Supplement,* also remarked on the novel's readability: "Kaye Gibbons's second novel ... has the simplicity of a good Country-and-Western song ... here she shows us two adults for whom extremity has revealed the bare bones of life." Kavaney concluded, "*A Virtuous Woman* dares to do the ordinary thing, to transfigure the commonplace into a plain language that speaks with as much complexity as the rococo might, but with more appropriateness." Not all reviewers agreed with such an assessment on Gibbons's use of the vernacular, however.

With her third novel, *A Cure for Dreams,* and fourth, *Charms for the Easy Life,* Gibbons wrote a pair of multigenerational family sagas. *Charms,* in fact, was initially intended as a sequel to *A Cure for Dreams,* but Gibbons later decided against such a course. In *A Cure for Dreams,* the main characters are Lottie, her daughter Betty, and granddaughter Marjorie. While Lottie is the focus protagonist, much of the story is told through the narrative voice of Betty; this technique, as Gibbons has pointed out, prevents strong characters from completely running away with the story. Betty tells the story of her mother, Lottie, and her difficult life in rural Kentucky in the late nineteenth century. Lottie finally escaped such a life by marrying and moving to North Carolina, though such an escape proved only another imprisonment as her workaholic husband kept her emotionally isolated. This changed, however, with the birth of Betty. Betty becomes Lottie's focus and begins to alarm her as she grows up and is in turn attracted to the wrong kind of men. Lottie, settled in North Carolina, becomes something of the leader of the local women, organizing card parties, imparting wisdom, and even helping a friend who shoots her abusive husband.

"That's about all," noted Rhoda Koenig in *New York* magazine, "but a lot goes on in this little mill town of neglected women and taciturn, sometimes brutal men." Koenig called Gibbons's story an "absolutely darling novel," without meaning to belittle the novel. "I suppose if there is a platonic perky, plucky, and dear, though—ones that have resisted the gunky accretions of self-dramatizing cuteness—it's here that they apply." Benedict Cosgrove, writing in *San Francisco Review of Books,* called the novel "a celebration of the spoken word, of family history verbally constructed and passed on," while *New York Times Book Review* critic James Wilcox pointed to the well chosen details "like the proverbial picture worth a thousand words." Josephine Humphreys, writing in the *Los Angeles Times Book Review,* declared: "Full of unforgettable scenes and observations, characters drawn surely and sharply, and writing that is both lyrical [and] lightning-keen, this is a novel of vision and grace. It shines."

Three generations of women are also at the heart of *Charms for the Easy Life,* the story of Charlie (Clarissa) Kate, a midwife with a charismatic personality, her daughter, Sophie, and Sophie's daughter, Margaret, who narrates the novel. Spanning forty years, the novel takes its name from a rabbit's foot "easy-life charm" given to Charlie Kate by a black man whom she saves from a lynching. The novel focuses on the activities of Charlie Kate, a folk healer with subscriptions to magazines such as the *New England Journal of Medicine* and *Saturday Review of Literature* which enable her to keep up with the intellectual and medical world from her home in rural North Carolina. The character of Charlie Kate originally took form in *A Cure for Dreams* as the African-American midwife who was Lottie's best friend. Initially intended as a sequel to that novel, *Charms for the Easy Life* soon took on its own life, and Charlie Kate outgrew the constraints of the former character.

Charlie Kate is abandoned by her husband; her daughter is, as well. The three generations of women ultimately live together; only at the end of the novel does it appear Margaret may have a happy relationship with Tom Hawkins, a sympathetically drawn male character. Set partly during World War Two, the novel owes a debt to two other writers, according to Gibbons: Studs Terkel, whose writings about the Second World War allowed Gibbons to understand the common people during that conflict, and Gabriel Garcia Marquez, whose *One Hundred Years of Solitude* showed her how to include history in the narrative.

Writing about Charlie Kate in *New York Times Book Review,* Stephen McCauley called her "an implacable force of nature, a pillar of intellect, with insight and powers of intuition so acute as to seem nearly supernatural." Reviewing the novel in *Time* magazine, Amelia Weiss also commented on Charlie Kate's character, noting that "her best healing power lies in her self . . . . and it is her 'winning streak' of a life that she passes on to her daughter Sophie and to Margaret." Weiss also noted that "[s]ome people might give up their second-born to write as well as Kaye Gibbons, so graceful and spirited are her fictional histories of North Carolina women."

Gibbons's fifth novel, *Sights Unseen,* published in 1995, went through seven rewrites before the author was satisfied. *Sights Unseen* tells the story of a girl who nearly loses her mother to insanity. Writing it, Gibbons was in part exorcising her fears of her own manic-depression, a condition she was diagnosed with in 1980.

Betty tells her daughter of her own and her mother's lives in Kentucky and North Carolina in Gibbons's multi-generational story.

Hattie, twelve years old, is another youthful narrator like Ellen Foster, which attracts young readers to Gibbons's ranks of loyal fans. Through Hattie's observations the reader follows the roller coaster ride of the mother's battle with mental illness and its effects on her family.

Hattie states at the outset: "Had I known my mother was being given electroconvulsive therapy while I was dressing for school on eight consecutive Monday mornings, I do not think I could have buttoned my blouses or tied my shoes or located my homework." From there, the narrative takes off to explore the mostly painful but sometimes humorous world in which Hattie is growing up. Gibbons's subject matter here is, as Jacqueline Carey pointed out in *New York Times Book Review,* "a manic-depressive mother and the havoc she wreaks in her family." Carey went on to comment, "Hattie's sights are always set at a delicate intersection of the ordinary and the horrific." Carey concluded that she found *Sights Unseen* "even better" than *Charms for the Easy Life.* "It is more intense, more vibrant, both richer and stranger." *Booklist*'s Donna Seaman remarked that "Gibbons writes seamless and resonant novels, the sort of fiction that wins hearts as well as awards," and further noted that *Sights Unseen* "is a novel that deserves unwavering attention from start to finish, like a symphony or a sunset." And Rebecca Ascher-Walsh concluded in *Entertainment Weekly,* this "is another chance to read what is surely one of the most lyrical voices writing today."

Gibbon's career was given a huge boost in 1997 with production of her first novel, *Ellen Foster,* as a television movie, and the selection of both that novel and *A Virtuous Woman* for Oprah's Book Club. The first novel to appear after these life-changing events mapped new fictional territory for the North Carolina author, *On the Occasion of My Last Afternoon* is the story of another strong female protagonist, but this time with a historical perspective. Emma Garnet Tate Lowell is a Southerner who comes of age in the years leading up to the Civil War. Using the occasion of her seventieth birthday, Emma makes a clean breast of her life. She was born to privilege on a Southern plantation, but grows up with an increasing awareness of the inequity inherent in the slave system that supports her life and that of others in the South. The book, indeed, opens with her witnessing the aftermath of a senseless killing of a slave by her brutish father. Emma ultimately flees the family home and sets up house in Raleigh, North Carolina, with her new husband, Quincy Lowell, a product of the Boston Lowells and a skilled surgeon. With the coming of war, Emma works alongside her husband, treats wounded soldiers, and sees firsthand the horrors of the conflict. Throw in an indomitable family servant, Clarice, and a guilty family secret, and there are the makings of a Southern epic on a grand scale.

Writing in *School Library Journal,* Molly Connally noted, "YAs will find Emma ... and Quincy to be fascinating and endearing characters whose flaws as well as strengths are revealed as the story unfolds." Connally also mentioned that the "author's picture of life in the

Civil War South is vivid and unsentimental, and her characters are drawn with clarity and sympathy." Other critics were less enthusiastic about this new direction in Gibbons's fiction, however. The reviewer for *People* praised Gibbons's efforts at telling two stories at once, both Emma's personal history as well as the larger story of the antebellum South. However, this reviewer felt that the author's attempt "to find an authentic historical tone results in a vocabulary and style ... [that is] stilted and eccentric." Despite this drawback, the *People* reviewer concluded that Gibbons's sixth novel was "a nicely detailed portrait of the Old South."

Gibbons, who was knighted by the French government in 1996 for her contributions to literature, takes criticism of her work in stride. This author, for whom "writing is a metaphor for life," as she told the Barnes and Noble chat room, is content to work on her novels, producing one every two years or so, and leave the reviewing to others. As she told Summer in a *Publisher Weekly* interview: "Nobody ever told me [the writing life] was going to be easy.... I wouldn't want to do anything easy, and I chose to be a writer.... It's working with that element of fear that keeps a book going." And fans hope Gibbons keeps going.

Works Cited

Ascher-Walsh, Rebecca, review of *Sights Unseen, Entertainment Weekly,* April 4, 1995, p. 53.

Bell, Pearl K., "Southern Discomfort," *New Republic,* February 29, 1988, pp. 38-41.

Carey, Jacqueline, "Mommy Direst," *New York Times Book Review,* September 24, 1995, p. 30.

Connally, Molly, review of *On the Occasion of My Last Afternoon, School Library Journal,* September, 1998, p. 229.

Cosgrove, Benedict, review of *A Cure for Dreams, San Francisco Review of Books,* spring, 1991, pp. 31-32.

D'Errico, Deanna, "Two Timers," *Belles Lettres,* summer, 1989, p. 7.

Review of *Ellen Foster, Kirkus Reviews,* March 15, 1987, p. 404.

Review of *Ellen Foster, Publishers Weekly,* March 20, 1987, p. 70.

Gibbons, Kaye, "Author Interview," Barnes and Noble chat room, http://shop.barnesandnoble.com.

Gibbons, Kaye, *Ellen Foster,* Algonquin Books, 1987.

Gibbons, Kaye, *Sights Unseen,* Putnam, 1995.

Harrison, Kathryn, "Tara It Ain't," *New York Times Book Review,* July 19, 1988, p. 12.

Hoffman, Alice, "Shopping for a New Family," *New York Times Book Review,* May 31, 1987, p. 13.

Hooper, Brad, review of *Ellen Foster, Booklist,* September 1, 1987, p. 27.

Humphreys, Josephine, review of *A Cure for Dreams, Los Angeles Times Book Review,* May 19, 1991, p. 13.

Kavaney, Roz, "Making Themselves Over," *Times Literary Supplement,* September 15, 1989, p. 998.

Koenig, Rhoda, "Southern Comfort," *New York,* April 1, 1991, p. 63.

Makowsky, Veronica, "The Only Hard Part Was the Food: Recipes for Self-Nurture in Kaye Gibbons's Novels," *Southern Quarterly,* winter-spring, 1992, pp. 103-12.

McCauley, Stephen, "He's Gone, Go Start the Coffee," *New York Times Book Review,* April 11, 1993, pp. 9-10.

Review of *On the Occasion of My Last Afternoon, People,* June 15, 1998, p. 49.

Review of *On the Occasion of My Last Afternoon, Publishers Weekly,* April 20, 1998, p. 43.

Seaman, Donna, review of *Sights Unseen, Booklist,* June 1, 1995, p. 1683.

Summer, Bob, "Kaye Gibbons," *Publishers Weekly,* February 8, 1993, pp. 60-61.

Taylor, Linda, "A Kind of Primitive Charm," *Sunday Times,* May 8, 1988, p. G6.

Weiss, Amelia, "Medicine Woman," *Time,* April 12, 1993, pp. 77-78.

Wilcox, James, review of *A Cure for Dreams, New York Times Book Review,* May 12, 1991, pp. 13-14.

Wolcott, James, "Crazy for You," *New Yorker,* August 24, 1995, pp. 115-116.

For More Information See

BOOKS

Contemporary Fiction Writers of the South: A Bio-bibliographical Sourcebook, edited by Joseph M. Flora and Robert Bain, Greenwood Press, 1993.

Novels for Students, Volume 3, edited by Diane Telgen and Kevin Hile, Gale, 1998.

Sternburg, Janet, editor, *The Writer and Her Work,* Volume II, Norton, 1991.

Watkins, James, editor, *Southern Selves, from Mark Twain and Eudora Welty to Maya Angelou and Kaye Gibbons: A Collection of Autobiographical Writing,* Vintage, 1998.

PERIODICALS

Belles Lettres, winter, 1993-94, pp. 16-18.

Kliatt, September, 1997, p. 4; September, 1998, pp. 4, 61.

Library Journal, June 1, 1998, p. 150; September 15, 1998, p. 129.

Los Angeles Times Book Review, June 11, 1989, p. 15.

New Yorker, June 21, 1993, p. 101.

Publishers Weekly, June 5, 1995, p. 48.

School Library Journal, September, 1993, p. 260; December, 1993, p. 29.

Tribune Books (Chicago), September 15, 1991, p. 7.

Washington Post Book World, July 12, 1998, p. 9.

—*Sketch by J. Sydney Jones*

*   *   *

GOODWIN, William 1943-

Personal

Born October 25, 1943, in Tyler, TX; son of William Thad (a manager) and Olga Francis (an accountant) Goodwin; married; wife's name, Donna (a physical therapist), November, 1999; children: Gideon, Marilyn.

Education: University of California, Los Angeles, B.S. (biochemistry; departmental honors), 1967; University of California, Santa Barbara, M.S., 1969; also studied English and education at University of California, San Diego. *Politics:* "Eclectic." *Religion:* "Ditto."

Addresses

E-mail—wgg37@aol.com.

Career

High school science teacher in private American overseas schools in Brazil, Kuwait, and Iran, 1969-73; Southwest Yachts, San Diego, CA, captain, navigator, and marine consultant, 1974-94; founder and director of Sailing Solutions, Inc., 1986-92; reporter for San Diego Independent Community Newspaper Group, 1992-95; Spectrum Business Communications, Wisconsin, contributing editor, 1996-98; Lucent Publications, San Diego, author of middle-school resource books, 1996—; Ola Grimsby Physical Therapy Institute, San Diego, writing consultant, 1996—; curriculum development author for Allegra Learning Solutions, 1998—; Heritage Media Corp., Carlsbad, CA, business profile writer, 1998—; Strategene Corp, San Diego, marketing/communications writer, 1998—. Has also worked as a freelance author of educational, business, and technical articles, manuals, brochures, and press releases.

Writings

JUVENILE

Teen Violence, Lucent Books, 1998.
Mexico, Lucent Books, 1999.
India, Lucent Books, 2000.

OTHER

Introduction to Management—Workbook, Apollo (Phoenix, AZ), 1991.
(With Peggy Morrison) *Touchstones for a New Millennium: Ground Rules for Working Relationships,* Wind 'n' Sea Books (San Diego, CA), 1997.

Articles have been published in *Progressive MRO Distributor, Maintenance Repair Operations Today, San Diego North County Magazine,* and *Western Boatman.* Also author of script for educational video, *Bareboat Charter Checklist,* Bennett Marine and American Sailing Association, 1991. Columnist, contributor, and field editor for *Western Boatman Magazine, SAILING Magazine, SANTANA Magazine, H20 Magazine, San Diego North County Magazine,* 1991-96.

Work in Progress

Nonfiction on Saudi Arabia; a children's book, *The Mystery of Phaat Bhat Island.*

Sidelights

William Goodwin has had an eclectic career as a teacher, yacht captain, journalist, and freelance writer.

William Goodwin gives an overview of the causes and prevention of teen violence and the workings of the juvenile justice system in this title from the "Teen Issues" series.

As an author, he has written several nonfiction, informational books for young adults and for adult audiences. In *Teen Violence,* Goodwin's contribution to the "Overview" series published by Lucent Books, the author "provides solid information on the scope, causes, and prevention of teen violence," contended Chris Sherman in *Booklist.* Sherman is an admirer of Lucent's series for young adults, which, the critic claimed, is not only readable but thorough in its presentation of facts on contemporary social problems and possibilities for solving them. Goodwin's entry in the series follows in the footsteps of other books in the series "perfectly," Sherman concluded.

Also for young adults are two Goodwin works in Lucent's "Modern Nations of the World" series, *Mexico* and *India.* In the first title, Goodwin focuses on the contrasts of this vast nation, which the author contends are the result of mixing influences from indigenous and imported cultures across time and geography. Goodwin's language "assume[s] a sophisticated readership," noted *Booklist* reviewer Kathleen Squires, and this helps "keep the text from becoming too textbookish." Though not a textbook, *Mexico* does offer a wide spectrum of information on the country, presented in a manner that is both clear and interesting, according to this reviewer.

Works Cited

Sherman, Chris, review of *Teen Violence, Booklist,* May 15, 1998, p. 1614.

Squires, Kathleen, review of *Mexico, Booklist,* February 1, 1999, p. 968.*

* * *

GOTTESMAN, S. D.
See LOWNDES, Robert A(ugustine) W(ard)

GRAY, Elizabeth Janet
See VINING, Elizabeth Gray

* * *

GREY, Carol
See LOWNDES, Robert A(ugustine) W(ard)

* * *

GROENER, Carl
See LOWNDES, Robert A(ugustine) W(ard)

H

HAUGAARD, Kay

Personal

Name is pronounced "ho-guard"; daughter of Conrad (a garage and machine shop owner) and Catherine (a housewife; maiden name, Rink) Johnson; married Robert Duncan Haugaard (an architect); children: Brad, Erik, Kurt. *Education:* University of Oregon, B.A. (art history), 1952; Occidental College, M.A. (comparative litera-

Kay Haugaard

ture), 1966. *Hobbies and other interests:* Drawing, painting, studying other languages, gardening, cooking, reading classic literature.

Addresses

Home—390 North San Rafael Ave., Pasadena, CA 91105.

Career

Pasadena City College, Pasadena, CA, creative writing teacher, 1970—; writer.

Writings

Myeko's Gift, illustrated by Dora Ternei, Abelard-Schuman (New York City), 1966, translated into French as *La petite fille au kimono rouge,* Rouge et Or, 1971.

China Boy, Abelard-Schuman, 1971, translated into French as *Lee, chercheur d'or,* Castor Poche Flammarion, 1995.

(Self-illustrated) *A Perfect Fit,* Ivory Tower, 1986.

No Place, illustrated by Michelle Peterson-Albandoz, Milkweed Editions (Minneapolis, MN), 1999.

Regular contributor to the *Los Angeles Times* feature "The Kids Reading Room."

Work in Progress

Class Notes, "a book about my teaching experiences."

Sidelights

Children's author and illustrator Kay Haugaard began publishing books for children in the 1960s. Her first book, *Myeko's Gift,* which the author later translated into French, is an "appealing" account of a young Japanese girl learning to adjust to life in an American school, according to *Booklist* reviewer Jeanette Swickard. When Myeko and her parents move to the United States, the girl must decide what possessions and activities she will keep from her life in Japan and what she will adapt from her new environment. Though her American classmates initially rebuff her overtures at friendship, Myeko eventually learns that kindness is a universal language. One of the strengths of the narrative, observed a critic for *Kirkus Reviews,* is the way the author builds Myeko's realization, "slowly, gradually," so that the other schoolchildren "are intrigued by her playthings and past times just because they are different."

For her next book, *China Boy,* Haugaard produced a work of historical fiction for young adults. In the novel, a seventeen-year-old-protagonist sails to California in the 1850s to win his fortune during the Gold Rush. Fifteen years later, Haugaard published a self-illustrated picture book entitled *A Perfect Fit.* The 1990s saw another young adult novel, *No Place,* based in part on an actual event. Set in a poor Los Angeles neighborhood, a sixth-grade class raises money to purchase land and materials for a park. Together they overcome many obstacles, including parental disapproval, difficulty in dealing with government bureaucracies, and the willingness of adults to either take over the project or take credit for the children's hard work. "The courage required by these children as they learn how to get things done in an adult world comes through clearly," observed John Peters in *Booklist.*

"Words have fascinated me from infancy," Haugaard told *SATA.* "My parents tell me that I knew the alphabet from my blocks at eighteen months. My father, who read nursery rhymes and 'the funny papers' to me, says that my favorite book was the dictionary. It sounds good, but at that pre-literate age it was mainly the pictures that fascinated me. Art, in pencil, crayon, and watercolor, was my first love.

"School was easy for me. One of my grade school classmates yelled at me once during a recess wrangle what she intended to be an insult: 'You're a sophisticated brat!' I loved it. Modesty was not in me at the time. It took leaving my tiny town of Malin, Oregon (population 350), where I felt I was a very large intellectual frog in a tiny puddle, and attending the University of Oregon to give me a shockingly realistic view of my own capacities and limitations.

"What first motivated me to write was the urge to capture and keep my all too fleeting experiences and impressions. My best friend Gerri Lou gave me a diary at about age twelve, and I used it to conscientiously 'capture' Don Coleman's birthday party and getting crowded out of the tent my Girl Scout troop was sleeping in while camping at Diamond Lake. Every moment of my summer art school experience in Newport, Oregon, was so precious that I wrote page after page of verbal snapshots—by this time, on a portable typewriter. In junior high, I earned enough money to send off for an exotic dog, a Samoyede. He was not the round, fuzzy, white-haired, dark-eyed teddy bear I expected. He was long legged and scraggly, his fuzzy puppy coat gone. I loved him anyway, drew pictures of him and wrote a (still unpublished) book to tell the

world, which consisted of my parents, friends, and teachers, how he grew into a fine, handsome dog.

"The same impulse follows me. After I go on a long trip, I come home with my journal crammed with a tour through a cold, damp, black coal mine tunnel in West Virginia, what a Mississippi 'fried berry pie' is like, and a prim southern lady totally clad in pink, including her hair, stockings, and shoes, picking her way daintily around a service station. Research for my writing expands my knowledge and awareness of the world. That is the reason I enjoy writing about people very different from myself."

Works Cited

Review of *Myeko's Gift, Kirkus Reviews,* December 1, 1966, p. 1221.
Peters, John, review of *No Place, Booklist,* November 15, 1998, p. 590.
Swickard, Jeanette, review of *Myeko's Gift, Booklist,* February 15, 1973, p. 553.

*   *   *

HENRY, Marilyn 1939-

Personal

Born July 27, 1939, in Pittsburgh, PA; daughter of Wayne T. (an automotive mechanic) and Frances (a homemaker; maiden name, Cordell) Dickinson; married Guy H. Henry (a fine artist and financial adviser), August 18, 1961; children: Sharon, Tom. *Education:* Indiana University of Pennsylvania, B.S., 1961, and graduate study; also attended Maryland College of Art. *Politics:* Democrat. *Religion:* Presbyterian. *Hobbies and other interests:* Creating an "artist's garden," activities with granddaughters.

Addresses

Home and office—214 East Third St., Frederick, MD 21701. *E-mail*—ghenry5658@aol.com.

Career

St. John's School, Olney, MD, art teacher, 1970s; artist and illustrator, 1975—, with work represented at galleries in Pennsylvania, Maryland, Florida, and Delaware, and in Archives of the National Museum of Women in the Arts. Highland Studio, owner and teacher of adult drawing and painting; has done illustrations for Olney Theater, Sandy Spring Museum, Kennywood Park, Montgomery County Historical Society, and various corporations. Friends of East Third Street Park, president. *Exhibitions:* One-person retrospective at Hood College, 1999. *Member:* Society of Children's Book Writers and Illustrators, Baltimore Watercolor Society.

Marilyn Henry

Writings

ILLUSTRATOR

Gail S. Fleagle, *Play Ball!,* Richard C. Owen (Katonah, NY), 1998.
Marianne Mitchell, *Coo Coo Caroo,* Richard C. Owen, 1999.

Contributor to *Splash 3: Ideas and Inspirations,* by R. Wolf, North Light (Westport, CT), 1994. Contributor to *Artist's,* a fine art periodical.

Work in Progress

Writing and illustrating a book about SeeMore, a desert tortoise; creating a book about an armadillo, for Richard C. Owen.

Sidelights

Marilyn Henry told *SATA:* "I have always enjoyed creating drawings, paintings, and sculptures with children in mind. Many of my favorite artists, past and present, are children's book illustrators. Because I like working with children, I chose an art education major in college, and I have taught art to children of all ages throughout the years. Until recently, however, my professional art work has been primarily for galleries, shows, and adult publications.

"My desire to tell and illustrate the true story of my friend, Margie Nash, and her thirty-two-year friendship with a desert tortoise named SeeMore led me to learn the art of illustrating children's books. In the process of researching and drawing this book, which is still in progress, I discovered that I loved creating a story with pictures. To imagine the expressions, the gestures, the interactions, and the surroundings is fun, and as I sketch the characters interacting on the pages, their personalities emerge and develop.

"A few years ago, a representative of Richard Owen Publishers, Inc. saw the SeeMore illustrations and some others I'd done and hired me to illustrate *Play Ball!* Since then, I've illustrated *Coo Coo Caroo* and am working on a book about armadillos.

"When laying out the dummy for a picture book, I start with the image that interests me most, and then I develop the other illustrations around that one. In *Play Ball!,* I started with the 'It's an Armadillo' illustration first. I laid out the entire book, thinking of it as one piece of art, and continued making revisions until all pages coordinated and flowed.

"Even for a small book like *Play Ball!,* an enormous amount of research is necessary. Finding an ox wasn't easy. I eventually found two, Homer and Albert, right in my own community, where I could visit and study them as much as I needed. Getting to know their owner, Ernest Jackson, was an added bonus in the process. Learning about armadillos was also a challenge. For me to imagine an animal in different positions, I have to see it walk, run, sleep, et cetera. I visited the National Zoo, where they have one small armadillo from South America, and, better yet, I found an excellent videotape at the Pratt Library in Baltimore.

"The marriage of words and pictures in the SeeMore picture book is my current goal, no small task. To this end, I am in a writers and illustrators group, I am reading and studying all the children's books I admire most, attending book conferences, and enjoying all of it. Though much of my energy still goes toward my fine art career, painting for galleries and shows, I am finding that, at this time, the two activities don't conflict, but complement each other. I'm not sure where this new path will lead, but I am enjoying the process."

* * *

HODGES, Margaret Moore 1911-

Personal

Born Sarah Margaret Moore, July 26, 1911, in Indianapolis, IN; daughter of Arthur Carlisle (in business) and Anna Marie (Mason) Moore; married Fletcher Hodges, Jr. (a museum curator), September 10, 1932; children: Fletcher III, Arthur Carlisle, John Andrews. *Education:* Vassar College, A.B. (with honors), 1932; Carnegie Institute of Technology (now Carnegie-Mellon University), M.L.S., 1958. *Politics:* Republican. *Religion:* Episcopalian. *Hobbies and other interests:* Traveling, reading, folklore, and gardening.

Addresses

Home—48 Garden Court, Verona, PA 15147-3852. *Office*—University of Pittsburgh, Library and Information Science Building, Bellefield Ave., Pittsburgh, PA 15260.

Career

Carnegie Library of Pittsburgh, Pittsburgh, PA, special assistant and children's librarian, 1953-64; Pittsburgh Public Schools, story specialist in compensatory education department, 1964-68; University of Pittsburgh, Graduate School of Library and Information Science, lecturer, 1964-68, assistant professor, 1968-72, associate professor, 1972-75, professor 1975-77, professor emeritus, 1978—. Storyteller on program "Tell Me a Story," WQED-TV, 1965-76. *Member:* Zonta International, American Library Association (member of Newbery-Caldecott committee, 1960), Pennsylvania Library Association, Distinguished Daughters of Pennsylvania, Pittsburgh Bibliophiles, Pittsburgh Vassar Club.

Awards, Honors

Carnegie Library staff scholarship, 1956-58; American Library Association Notable Book citation, *New York Times* ten best picture books of the year award, both 1964, runner-up for Caldecott Award, and Silver Medal, Bienal (Brazil), both 1965, all for *The Wave; Lady Queen Anne: A Biography of Queen Anne of England* was selected as best book for young adults by an Indiana author, 1970; *The Making of Joshua Cobb* was selected as a *New York Times* outstanding juvenile book, 1971; American Library Association Notable Book citation, 1972, for *The Fire Bringer: A Paiute Indian Legend;* John G. Bowman Memorial grant, 1974; Distinguished Alumna, Carnegie Library School and Graduate School of Library and Information Science, 1976; Outstanding Pennsylvania Children's Author award, Pennsylvania School Librarians Association, 1977; Daughter of Mark Twain Award, 1980; *New York Times* Best Illustrated Children's Book Award, 1984, Carolyn W. Field Award for best children's book by a Pennsylvania author, *Horn Book* Honor Book Award, and Caldecott Award, all 1985, all for *Saint George and the Dragon: A Golden Legend;* "Margaret Hodges Day" citation from University of Pittsburgh School of Library and Information Science, 1985; Keystone State Reading Award, 1985; Margaret Hodges scholarship established, 1989; American Library Association Best Books for Young Adults citation, 1989, for *Making a Difference: The Story of an American Family;* Notable Children's Trade Book citation, National Council for Social Studies and Children's Book Council, 1989, for *The Arrow and the Lamp: The Story of Psyche;* Parents' Choice Honor for Story Books, and Children's Book Council award, both 1990, for *Buried Moon;* American Library Association Notable Books List, 1991, for *St. Jerome and the Lion;* Park Tudor (Tudor Hall) Distinguished Alumna Award,

Margaret Moore Hodges

1992; Parents' Choice Recommendation, 1999, for *Joan of Arc: The Lily Maid. Lady Queen Anne: A Biography of Queen Anne of England* was a Junior Literary Guild selection.

Writings

FICTION

One Little Drum, illustrated by Paul Galdone, Follett, 1958.
What's for Lunch, Charley?, illustrated by Aliki, Dial, 1961.
A Club against Keats, illustrated by Rick Schreiter, Dial, 1962.
The Secret in the Woods, illustrated by Judith Brown, Dial, 1963.
The Hatching of Joshua Cobb, illustrated by W. T. Mars, Farrar, Straus, 1968.
Sing Out, Charley!, illustrated by Velma Ilsley, Farrar, Straus, 1968.
The Making of Joshua Cobb, illustrated by W. T. Mars, Farrar, Straus, 1971.
The Freewheeling of Joshua Cobb, illustrated by Pamela Johnson, Farrar, Straus, 1974.
The High Riders, Scribner, 1980.
The Avenger, Scribner, 1982.

NONFICTION

Lady Queen Anne: A Biography of Queen Anne of England, illustrated with photographs, Farrar, Straus, 1968.
Hopkins of the Mayflower: Portrait of a Dissenter, Farrar, Straus, 1972.

Knight Prisoner: The Tale of Sir Thomas Malory and His King Arthur, decorations by Don Bolognese and Elaine Raphael, Farrar, Straus, 1976.

Making a Difference: The Story of an American Family, illustrated with photographs, Scribner, 1989.

Silent Night: The Song and Its Story, illustrated by Tim Ladwig, Eerdmans, 1997.

The True Tale of Johnny Appleseed, illustrated by K. B. Root, Holiday House, 1997.

Joan of Arc: The Lily Maid, illustrated by Robert Rayevsky, Holiday House, 1999.

RETELLINGS

The Wave (adapted from Lafcadio Hearn's *Gleanings in Buddha Fields*), illustrated by Blair Lent, Houghton, 1964.

The Gorgon's Head: A Myth from the Isles of Greece, illustrated by Charles Mikolaycak, Little, Brown, 1972.

The Fire Bringer: A Paiute Indian Legend, illustrated by Peter Parnall, Little, Brown, 1972.

Persephone and the Springtime: A Greek Myth, illustrated by Arvis Stewart, Little, Brown, 1973.

The Other World: Myths of the Celts, illustrated by Eros Keith, Farrar, Straus, 1973.

Baldur and the Mistletoe: A Myth of the Vikings, illustrated by Gerry Hoover, Little, Brown, 1974.

The Little Humpbacked Horse: A Russian Tale (adapted from a translation by Gina Kovarsky of a poem by Peter Pavlovich Yershov), illustrated by Chris Conover, Farrar, Straus, 1980.

Saint George and the Dragon: A Golden Legend (adapted from Edmund Spenser's *Faerie Queen*), illustrated by Trina Schart Hyman, Little, Brown, 1984.

If You Had a Horse: Steeds of Myth and Legend, illustrated by D. Benjamin Van Steenburgh, Scribner, 1984.

The Voice of the Great Bell (adapted from Lafcadio Hearn's *Some Chinese Ghosts*), illustrated by Ed Young, Little, Brown, 1989.

The Arrow and the Lamp: The Story of Psyche, illustrated by Donna Diamond, Little, Brown, 1989.

Buried Moon, illustrated by Jamichael Henterly, Little, Brown, 1990.

The Kitchen Knight: A Tale of King Arthur, illustrated by Trina Schart Hyman, Holiday House, 1990.

St. Jerome and the Lion, illustrated by Barry Moser, Orchard Books, 1991.

Hauntings: Ghosts and Ghouls from around the World, illustrated by David Wenzel, Little, Brown, 1991.

Brother Francis and the Friendly Beasts, illustrated by Ted Lewin, Scribner, 1991.

The Golden Deer, illustrated by Daniel San Souci, Scribner, 1992.

Don Quixote and Sancho Panza, illustrated by Stephen Marchesi, Scribner, 1992.

(With Margery Evernden) *Of Swords and Sorcerers: The Adventures of King Arthur and His Knights,* illustrated by David Frampton, Scribner, 1992.

Saint Patrick and the Peddler, illustrated by Paul Brett Johnson, Orchard, 1993.

The Hero of Bremen, illustrated by Charles Mikolaycak, Holiday House, 1993.

Hidden in Sand, illustrated by Paul Birling, Scribner, 1994.

Gulliver in Lilliput, illustrated by Kimberly Bulcken Root, Holiday House, 1995.

Comus (adapted from John Milton's *A Masque at Ludlow Castle*), illustrated by Trina Schart Hyman, Holiday House, 1996.

Molly Limbo, illustrated by Elizabeth J. Miles, Atheneum, 1996.

Up the Chimney, illustrated by Amanda Harvey, Holiday House, 1998.

EDITOR

Kathleen Monypenny, *The Young Traveler in Australia,* Dutton, 1954.

H. M. Harrop, *The Young Traveler in New Zealand,* Dutton, 1954.

Lucile Iremonger, *The Young Traveler in the West Indies,* Dutton, 1955.

Geoffrey Trease, *The Young Traveler in Greece,* Dutton, 1956.

(With others) *Stories to Tell to Children,* Carnegie Library of Pittsburgh, 1960.

Tell It Again: Great Tales from around the World, illustrated by Joan Berg, Dial, 1963.

Constellation: A Shakespeare Anthology, Farrar, Straus, 1968.

(With Susan Steinfirst) Elva S. Smith, *The History of Children's Literature: A Syllabus with Selected Bibliographies,* second edition, American Library Association, 1980.

OTHER

Also author of radio scripts; contributor to journals. Collections of Hodges's works are housed in the Kerlan Collection at the University of Minnesota, in the de Grummond Collection at the University of Southern Mississippi, and in the Elizabeth Nesbitt Room at the University of Pittsburgh.

Sidelights

Margaret Moore Hodges has led a distinguished career in children's books for half a century. Though she had already edited several works and worked as a children's librarian for many years, Hodges's first book, 1958's *One Little Drum,* was published when she was forty-seven. Since that time Hodges has gone on to publish over fifty books for young readers in three main areas: stand-alone fiction based on the antics of her own three boys, biographies, and retellings of myths and folktales in picture book format. It is with the last category that Hodges has made a name for herself in children's literature with such titles as the award-winning *Saint George and the Dragon: A Golden Legend, The Arrow and the Lamp: The Story of Psyche, St. Jerome and the Lion, Saint Patrick and the Peddler,* and *The Hero of Bremen.* Hodges sees herself not as a creator "but rather as a sort of midwife, simply bringing out life that already existed in itself," as she remarked in her essay in the *Something about the Author Autobiography Series* (*SAAS*).

Stories and books were an important part of Hodges's early years. When her mother died six months after the author's birth, Hodges's father brought an older cousin, Margaret Carlisle, into the household to take care of the family, which included Hodges, her brother, John, her father, and her paternal grandfather. Hodges heard "superb storytelling" at Sunday school, and both her cousin Margaret and her father gave her books and read to her. Robert Louis Stevenson's poems, Beatrix Potter's *Tale of Peter Rabbit,* and George Macdonald's *The Princess and the Goblin* and its sequel, *The Princess and Curdie,* were early loves. Lewis Carroll, Rudyard Kipling, and Charles Dickens followed. Long poems such as Kipling's "The Ballad of East and West" and Browning's "The Pied Piper of Hamelin," learned during this period, became useful for Hodges later in storytelling programs for children.

Hodges began writing at an early age, producing her first work at Public School Number 60 in Indianapolis—a paragraph titled "Miss Matty's Library" that was published in the school magazine. Around the same time, she sent a poem to *St. Nicholas,* a children's magazine that encouraged contributions from its readers and awarded silver and gold badges. Later, at Vassar College, she majored in English and took an active part in theater, studying the Stanislavsky method of acting developed at the Moscow Art Theatre. This method, which relies largely on the actor's establishing empathy with the character being portrayed, was also to help her in her storytelling.

Hodges tells the story behind the creation of "Silent Night," and how the song spread throughout the world. (Cover illustration by Tim Ladwig.)

Hodges graduated from Vassar and married Fletcher Hodges, Jr., in 1932. The couple moved to Pittsburgh in 1937, where they have lived ever since; they have three sons. Before their children went off to school, Hodges had, as a volunteer, written scripts for a radio program called "The Children's Bookshelf." In 1953, at the request of the Carnegie Library of Pittsburgh's Boys and Girls Department, she took a paid job as radio storyteller for the library's "Let's Tell a Story," which later became WQED-TV's "Tell Me a Story." Working in the Boys and Girls Room was part of the inspiration for her first book, *One Little Drum,* which is based on the real-life adventures of her children, as were several of the books that followed.

One of Hodges's early works, *The Hatching of Joshua Cobb,* tells of the adventures of a ten-year-old boy away from home for the first time at camp. Within a two-week period, his fears and worries fade away as he makes friends, learns to swim, and enjoys camp life. Jean C. Thomson, writing in the *Library Journal,* noted that Hodges "handles her small charge well, good-naturedly detailing the . . . metamorphosis." And a reviewer in the *Bulletin of the Center for Children's Books* called *The Hatching of Joshua Cobb* "pleasantly low-keyed and smoothly written." Joshua Cobb continues his adventures in *The Making of Joshua Cobb,* which follows him into the Fifth Form at boarding school. "A skillful handling of a school situation," declared a reviewer in *Horn Book.* Another critic in *Publishers Weekly* praised the "believable characters" and "relaxed and natural atmosphere" in Hodges's book. *Library Journal* contributor Sandra Scheraga concluded that *The Making of Joshua Cobb* is "an enjoyable, non-offensive pleasantry." The final book in the trilogy, *The Freewheeling of Joshua Cobb,* takes Josh on a summer vacation bike trip with his former camp counselor, Dusty, and a group of friends, including a girl named Cassandra who insists her name is "Crane" and eats health food. By the end of the trip, the group has accepted her as a friend. A reviewer in *Horn Book* noted the "fresh background" of the story, and praised Hodges's talent in knowingly portraying the "personality changes" of the characters. Another reviewer concluded in the *Bulletin of the Center for Children's Books,* "The writing style has vitality, the characters individuality."

Since her own children have grown, Hodges has turned her hand to other genres, including biography and retellings. *Lady Queen Anne: A Biography of Queen Anne of England* was the result of much burrowing through historical records. A *Publishers Weekly* reviewer found the book "worthwhile" and "interesting," while Nathan Berkowitz praised Hodges's work in the *Library Journal* as a "broad, thorough treatment" of the monarch's life, and a "good introduction to the lives and era of the later Stuarts."

In *Knight Prisoner: The Tale of Sir Thomas Malory and His King Arthur,* Hodges focuses on the widely known fifteenth-century English translator of Arthurian legend. While there is little information actually available about Thomas Malory, the author of *Morte d'Arthur,* Hodges

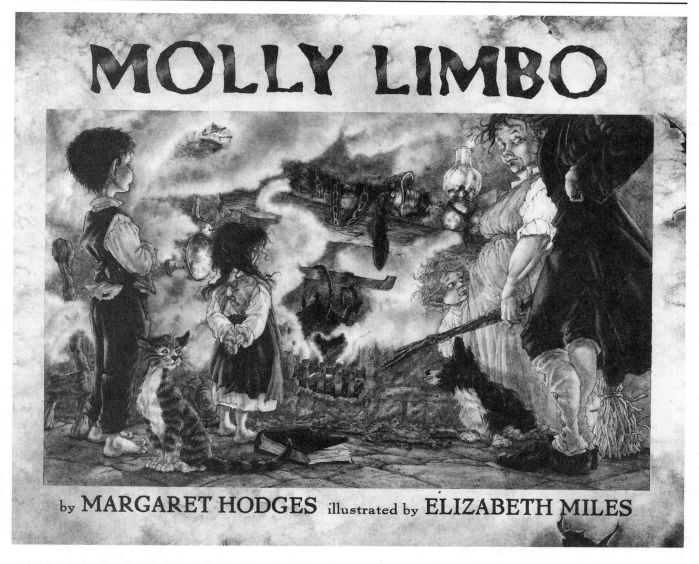

A miser living in a haunted house learns the value of human worth from the resident ghost. (Cover illustration by Elizabeth Miles.)

"makes the most of the ascertainable facts and speculations," noted a reviewer in *Horn Book.* Told in flashbacks, the book presents Malory recalling episodes of his life and his experiences with some of the most famous people of the time, including Joan of Arc, King Henry V, and King Edward IV. A reviewer in the *Bulletin of the Center for Children's Books* remarked that the multitude of historical and literary details may "prove too difficult" for some readers, but went on to note that *Knight Prisoner* "has both biographical and historical interest." Ruth M. McConnell concluded in *School Library Journal,* "The overall result is a most readable political and social history."

Less well-known characters are the subjects of *Making a Difference: The Story of an American Family,* a collective biography of the six members of the Sherwood family—mother and five children—during the first half of this century. The book traces the lives of these extraordinary people who faced adversity, overcame difficult circumstances, and excelled in their chosen fields. A *Publishers Weekly* reviewer noted the "tremendous amount of research" necessary to create the volume, while a *Horn Book* contributor praised *Making a Difference* as a "carefully crafted, . . . seamless" book. Jean Fritz, writing in the *New York Times Book Review,* called *Making a Difference* "well written," and concluded: "For all those readers who have been crying for good nonfiction about memorable women, here is your book."

With her 1999 biography, *Joan of Arc: The Lily Maid,* Hodges tells the story of a simple young girl who grew up in a French village listening to the stories of the saints' heroic deeds. The image of St. Michael the Archangel came to Joan at age thirteen, telling her she would save France. In a starred *Booklist* review, Ilene Cooper noted, "Hodges tells Joan's story with simplicity, distilling the myriad events of bravery and betrayal down to their essence." Cooper further commented that the artwork gives the whole a feel of a "medieval work," but one with "lots of child appeal."

Hodges is also a reteller of tales, and it is with these picture books that she has become most popular with young readers. *The Little Humpbacked Horse: A Russian Tale,* based on a translation of a poem by Peter Pavlovich Yershov, is the story of a younger son, Ivan, whose ownership of a magical, humpbacked horse changes his life. An "admirably clear and smooth English translation," commented a *Horn Book* reviewer. A *Publishers Weekly* critic declared *The Little Humpbacked Horse* to be "one of the most outstanding productions this year—handsome in all aspects."

The Caldecott Award-winning *Saint George and the Dragon: A Golden Legend* is another of Hodges's retellings, based on the first book of Edmund Spenser's *Faerie Queen.* Saint George, the hero, rescues a maiden and slays a dragon to save her family, and eventually the hero and his love marry and live happily ever after. The main portion of the story, though, is George's three-day battle with the dragon. "The dragon in full action virtually bursts off the page," proclaimed Rosalie Byard in the *New York Times Book Review,* praising Trina Schart Hyman's illustrations. Byard also noted that Hodges "offers a faithful translation of Spenser's detailed account" of the battle. A reviewer for the *Bulletin of the Center for Children's Books* called Hodges's adaptation "capable," highlighting her use of Spenserian language without becoming bogged down in it. *School Library Journal* contributor Janice M. Del Negro noted that the action is "fast-paced and immediate," further commenting that Hodges's *Saint George and the Dragon* "has made [Spenser's *Faerie Queen*] a coherent, palatable story suitable for a wide range of ages."

Hodges returned to folktales for her inspiration in producing *If You Had a Horse: Steeds of Myth and Legend.* A collection of nine tales drawn from different cultures and times, the volume features horses as the unifying theme. Celtic, Norse, Greek, and Arabian are among the folktales' cultures of origin. A reviewer for the *Bulletin of the Center for Children's Books* praised Hodges's "smooth narrative style," while a critic in *Publishers Weekly* felt that Hodges "intensifies the effects of the nine legends" with her convincing approximation of the "speaking manners of the original storytellers." Further, Gayle W. Berge commented in *School Library Journal* that "all these tales have broad appeal, action and drama."

In *The Arrow and the Lamp: The Story of Psyche,* Hodges further explores the field of myth and legend with her retelling of the ancient Greek myth of Psyche, a mortal whose love for a god changes her existence. A critic for the *Bulletin of the Center for Children's Books* called Hodges's work "a haunting myth well adapted by an experienced storyteller." *School Library Journal* contributor Connie C. Rockman judged *The Arrow and the Lamp* to be a "smooth, straightforward retelling."

Saints get the Hodges treatment in a trio of books. *St. Jerome and the Lion* tells the tale of the Christian Saint Jerome pulling a thorn from a lion's paw; the saint and lion form a strong bond as a result. Shirley Wilton, writing in *School Library Journal,* labeled *St. Jerome and the Lion* a "moral tale" and a "gentle story." Another critic for the *Bulletin of the Center for Children's Books* remarked on the "compassion" in Hodges's "simple and dignified adaptation." And a reviewer for *Publishers Weekly* called Hodges's book a "sensitive adaptation" with "language and rhythms sensitively attuned to contemporary readers." The story of Saint Francis of Assisi appears in *Brother Francis and the Friendly Beasts.* A reviewer for the *Bulletin of the Center for Children's Books* called Hodges's adaptation "graceful and smooth," while a *Horn Book* contributor described *Brother Francis and the Friendly Beasts* as "a graceful production." *Saint Patrick and the Peddler,* an adaptation from Irish sources, deals with yet another saint. Saint Patrick appears in the dreams of a peddler during the Irish potato famine, encouraging him to go to Dublin. There he meets another man who has had the same dream, and this leads to the discovery of buried gold. "Ever the storyteller," Judith Gloyer wrote in a *School Library Journal* review, "Hodges includes a two-page condensation of St. Patrick's life, as well as notes on how her version of the story came about."

In *Hauntings: Ghosts and Ghouls from around the World,* Hodges retells sixteen ghost stories drawn from cultures the world over, including Europe, the Orient, America, and India. The tales are "more mysterious than they are scary," noted Maeve Visser Knoth in *Horn Book,* calling *Hauntings* "one fresh, readable volume." "Hodges's polished retellings retain the flavor of the originals," declared Margaret A. Chang in *School Library Journal.* And Hodges's "meaty retellings" also won praise from Denia Hester in *Booklist.* Another "spooky" tale, according to Del Negro in *Bulletin of the Center for Children's Books,* is Hodges's *Molly Limbo,* an adaptation of a ghostly folktale. Molly, a pirate's wife, haunts Mr. Means's house and lends a helping hand to the housekeeper. "This is an entertaining tale," noted *Horn Book*'s Mary M. Burns, "told with flair and illustrated with fey delicacy." Burns further noted, "this adaptation reflects the touch of a true storyteller with its lilting phrases and narrative pace."

Hodges has also mined literary sources with retellings of the Don Quixote story and of the Arthurian legend, among others. Her *Don Quixote and Sancho Panza* "capture[s] famous incidents from Cervantes' novel," according to Betsy Hearne writing in *Bulletin of the Center for Children's Books.* Hearne went on to comment on the "pathetic-to-bitter range of humor" in the original which Hodges's "adaptation has captured so well." Reviewing her *Of Swords and Sorcerers: The Adventures of King Arthur and His Knights,* a writer for *Publishers Weekly* called the book a "carefully considered" retelling and that the nine tales gathered in the volume "sparkle with the rich language of professional storytellers."

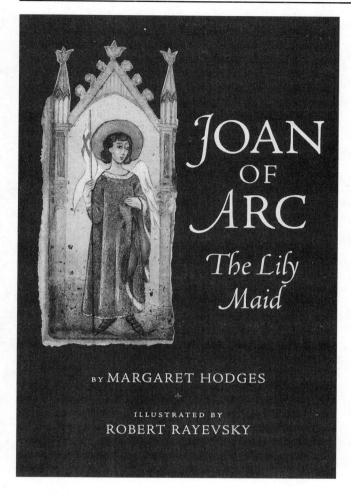

Hodges's tale takes place in the early 1400s, when young Joan led the French to battle against the English, helped crown Charles VII king of France, and was burned at the stake for witchcraft. (Cover illustration by Robert Rayevsky.)

Further literary retellings include *Gulliver in Lilliput,* an adaptation of Jonathan Swift's *Gulliver's Travels,* and *Comus,* from John Milton's *A Masque at Ludlow Castle.* Reviewing Hodges's adaptation of the Swift satire in *Gulliver's Travels, Horn Book*'s Ann A. Flowers called the book a "masterful retelling," and one which "emphasizes the adventures of Gulliver which are most appealing to children." *Booklist*'s Del Negro felt that Hodges retold Milton's tale of good and evil in "accessible, beautiful language."

More folktales and tall tales from around the world are served up in Hodges's *The Hero of Bremen, The True Tale of Johnny Appleseed,* and *Up the Chimney.* The medieval German city of Bremen is the scene for the first of these in which a shoemaker who is unable to walk helps out his hometown with the aid of the hero, Roland. "Hodges quickens her retelling with the assurance of a master storyteller," remarked Kate McClelland in a *School Library Journal* review of the book. In *The True Tale of Johnny Appleseed,* Hodges relates a "well-shaped, anecdotal account of the legendary Johnny

Chapman," according to Margaret A. Bush in *School Library Journal.* Chapman traveled west planting apple seeds along the way to make the country a better place to live. "A bit of tongue-in-cheek and a suggestion of tall tale spark the felicitous blend of biography and folklore," Bush further noted. With *Up the Chimney* Hodges retells an English folktale about two sisters who seek their fortune and receive very different fates. *Booklist*'s Cooper concluded that this was a "pleasant version of the Jacobs' 'The Old Witch.'"

Hodges has spent much of her life writing and telling stories for children. "The art of storytelling thrilled me because I saw it as the best way to lead children to good literature, to leap the boundaries between literacy and illiteracy, and to bring marvelous old tales to listeners of all ages," explained Hodges in her *SAAS* essay. With the timelessness of a good folktale, Hodges's retellings of classic legends and myths from around the world have insured her a place on the children's literature bookshelf.

Works Cited

Review of *The Arrow and the Lamp: The Story of Psyche, Bulletin of the Center for Children's Books,* February, 1990, pp. 138-39.

Berge, Gayle W., review of *If You Had a Horse: Steeds of Myth and Legend, School Library Journal,* January, 1985, p. 76.

Berkowitz, Nathan, review of *Lady Queen Anne: A Biography of Queen Anne of England, Library Journal,* September 15, 1969, p. 3218.

Review of *Brother Francis and the Friendly Beasts, Bulletin of the Center for Children's Books,* November, 1991, p. 64.

Review of *Brother Francis and the Friendly Beasts, Horn Book,* September-October, 1991, p. 611.

Burns, Mary M., review of *Molly Limbo, Horn Book,* November-December, 1996, p. 749.

Bush, Margaret A., review of *The True Tale of Johnny Appleseed, School Library Journal,* September, 1997, p. 203.

Byard, Rosalie, review of *Saint George and the Dragon: A Golden Legend, New York Times Book Review,* November 4, 1984, p. 22.

Chang, Margaret A., review of *Hauntings: Ghosts and Ghouls from around the World, School Library Journal,* November, 1991, p. 129.

Cooper, Ilene, review of *Joan of Arc, Booklist,* November 1, 1999, p. 524.

Cooper, Ilene, review of *Up the Chimney, Booklist,* November 15, 1998, p. 593.

Del Negro, Janice M., review of *Comus, Booklist,* March 1, 1996, p. 1182.

Del Negro, Janice M., review of *Molly Limbo, Bulletin of the Center for Children's Books,* October, 1996, p. 64.

Del Negro, Janice M., review of *Saint George and the Dragon: A Golden Legend, School Library Journal,* January, 1985, p. 76.

Flowers, Ann A., review of *Gulliver in Lilliput, Horn Book,* July-August, 1995, p. 450.

Review of *The Freewheeling of Joshua Cobb, Bulletin of the Center for Children's Books,* March, 1975.

Review of *The Freewheeling of Joshua Cobb, Horn Book,* October, 1974, p. 137.

Fritz, Jean, review of *Making a Difference: The Story of an American Family, New York Times Book Review,* July 23, 1989, p. 28.

Gloyer, Judith, review of *Saint Patrick and the Peddler, School Library Journal,* November, 1993, p. 99.

Review of *The Hatching of Joshua Cobb, Bulletin of the Center for Children's Books,* November, 1967, p. 43.

Hearne, Betsy, review of *Don Quixote and Sancho Panza, Bulletin of the Center for Children's Books,* February, 1993, p. 171.

Hester, Denia, review of *Hauntings: Ghosts and Ghouls from around the World, Booklist,* November 15, 1991, p. 624.

Hodges, Margaret Moore, *Something about the Author Autobiography Series,* Volume 9, Gale, 1990, pp. 183-201.

Review of *If You Had a Horse: Steeds of Myth and Legend, Bulletin of the Center for Children's Books,* January, 1985, p. 87.

Review of *If You Had a Horse: Steeds of Myth and Legend, Publishers Weekly,* November 30, 1984, p. 89.

Review of *Knight Prisoner: The Tale of Sir Thomas Malory and His King Arthur, Bulletin of the Center for Children's Books,* April, 1977, p. 126.

Review of *Knight Prisoner: The Tale of Sir Thomas Malory and His King Arthur, Horn Book,* December, 1976, pp. 632-33.

Knoth, Maeve Visser, review of *Hauntings: Ghosts and Ghouls from around the World, Horn Book,* November-December, 1991, pp. 747-48.

Review of *Lady Queen Anne: A Biography of Queen Anne of England, Publishers Weekly,* May 19, 1969, p. 71.

Review of *The Little Humpbacked Horse: A Russian Tale, Horn Book,* February, 1981, p. 61.

Review of *The Little Humpbacked Horse: A Russian Tale, Publishers Weekly,* November 14, 1980, p. 55.

Review of *Making a Difference: The Story of an American Family, Horn Book,* September, 1989, pp. 636-37.

Review of *Making a Difference: The Story of an American Family, Publishers Weekly,* April 28, 1989, p. 80.

Review of *The Making of Joshua Cobb, Horn Book,* June, 1971, p. 287.

Review of *The Making of Joshua Cobb, Publishers Weekly,* March 22, 1971, p. 53.

McClelland, Kate, review of *The Hero of Bremen, School Library Journal,* October, 1993, p. 118.

McConnell, Ruth M., review of *Knight Prisoner: The Tale of Sir Thomas Malory and His King Arthur, School Library Journal,* December, 1976, p. 60.

Review of *Of Swords and Sorcerers, Publishers Weekly,* May 3, 1993, p. 310.

Rockman, Connie C., review of *The Arrow and the Lamp: The Story of Psyche, School Library Journal,* December, 1989, p. 108.

Review of *Saint George and the Dragon: A Golden Legend, Bulletin of the Center for Children's Books,* October, 1984, p. 27.

Review of *St. Jerome and the Lion, Bulletin of the Center for Children's Books,* September, 1991, p. 12.

Review of *St. Jerome and the Lion, Publishers Weekly,* July 5, 1991, p. 64.

Scheraga, Sandra, review of *The Making of Joshua Cobb, Library Journal,* April 15, 1971, p. 1504.

Thomson, Jean C., review of *The Hatching of Joshua Cobb, Library Journal,* September 15, 1967, p. 118.

Wilton, Shirley, review of *St. Jerome and the Lion, School Library Journal,* September, 1991, p. 246.

For More Information See

BOOKS

Authors of Books for Young People, third edition, Scarecrow, 1990.

Children's Books and Their Creators, edited by Anita Silvey, Houghton, 1995.

Major Authors and Illustrators for Children and Young Adults, Volume 3, Gale, 1993.

PERIODICALS

Booklist, September 1, 1993, p. 64; September 15, 1996, p. 243.

Bulletin of the Center for Children's Books, October, 1993, p. 47; January, 1994, p. 156; January, 1995, pp. 12-13; April, 1996, pp. 266-67; December, 1997, p. 129; December, 1998, p. 133.

Horn Book, November-December, 1993, pp. 748-49.

Kliatt, January, 1993, p. 28.

New York Times Book Review, December 20, 1998, p. 24.

Publishers Weekly, November 23, 1984, p. 75; November 23, 1998, p. 66; February 1, 1999, p. 87.

School Library Journal, May, 1989, pp. 129-30; August, 1993, p. 174; September, 1996, p. 197; January, 1999, p. 116.

J

JAMES, Ann 1952-

Personal

Born October 6, 1952, in Melbourne, Australia; daughter of Bernard M. S. and Joan E. (Currie) James; companion of Ann Haddon. *Education:* Melbourne Teachers College, Higher Diploma in Teaching, 1973.

Addresses

Home—300 Beaconsfield Parade, Middle Park, 3206, Victoria, Australia. *Office*—Books Illustrated, 15 Graham St., Albert Park, 3206, Victoria, Australia.

Career

Teacher at Doveton High School and Ringwood High School, 1974-77; Ministry of Education's Publication Branch, art and design department, Victoria, Australia, designer and illustrator, 1978-88; freelance illustrator for various Australian publishing houses, 1981—; Books Illustrated Gallery, Victoria, co-director, 1988—. Director of Nutcote Trust. *Exhibitions:* James's work is represented in permanent collections of Australian children's book illustration, including the Lou Rees Archives at the University of Canberra, Dromkeen Collection, Fremantle Children's Literature Centre, Seasons Gallery, and Customs House Gallery. *Member:* Australian Society of Authors (Committee of Management illustrator representative, 1995—), Society of Book Illustrators (coordinator).

Awards, Honors

Children's Book Council of Australia, Junior Book of the Year, 1984, for *Bernice Knows Best;* Children's Book Council of Australia, Book of the Year Highly Commended, 1984, for *Penny Pollard's Diary;* Book Council of Australia Book of the Year Younger Honour, 1988, for *Looking Out for Sampson;* Best Books for Babies shortlist, United Kingdom, for *One Day: A Very First Dictionary;* Australian Children's Book Council Award shortlist for *A Pet for Mrs. Arbuckle, Penny Pollard's Letters, Wiggy and Boa, First at Last, Dog In, Cat Out, Hannah Plus One, The Midnight Gang,* and *Hannah and the Tomorrow Room; The Midnight Gang* has received several Children's Choice Awards.

Writings

FOR CHILDREN; SELF-ILLUSTRATED

The ABC of What You Can Be, Sugar and Snails Press, 1984.
One Day: A Very First Dictionary, Oxford University Press, 1989.
Finding Jack, Oxford University Press, 1992.
(With Ann Haddon) *Books Illustrated,* Ashton Scholastic, 1994.

FOR CHILDREN; ILLUSTRATOR

Gwenda Smyth, *A Pet for Mrs. Arbuckle,* Thomas Nelson, 1981, Crown, 1984.
Jenny Wagner, *Jo Jo and Mike,* Thomas Nelson, 1982.
Max Dann, *Bernice Knows Best,* Oxford University Press, 1983.
Robin Klein, *Penny Pollard's Diary,* Oxford University Press, 1983, reissued, Hodder Headline, 1999.
Robin Klein, *Snakes and Ladders,* Dent, 1984.
Where's My Shoe?, Longman Cheshire, 1984.
Robin Klein, *Penny Pollard's Letters,* Oxford University Press, 1984, reissued, Hodder Headline, 1999.
Robin Klein, *Penny Pollard in Print,* Oxford University Press, 1986, reissued, Hodder Headline, 1999.
Dangers and Disasters, Methuen, 1986.
Libby Hathorn, *Looking Out for Sampson,* Oxford University Press, 1987.
Hazel Edwards, *Sportsmad,* Bookshelf, 1987.
Robin Klein, *Penny Pollard's Passport,* Oxford University Press, 1988, reissued, Hodder Headline, 1999.
Anna Fienberg, *Wiggy and Boa,* Dent, 1988, Houghton, 1990.
Gwenda Smyth, *A Hobby for Mrs. Arbuckle,* Viking Kestrel, 1989.
Nette Hilton, *Prince Lachlan,* Omnibus, 1989, Orchard, 1990.

Robin Klein, *Penny Pollard's Guide to Modern Manners,* Oxford University Press, 1989, reissued, Hodder Headline, 1999.

Julia MacClelland, *First at Last,* Oxford University Press, 1990.

Pippa MacPherson, *Beryl and Bertha at the Beach,* Oxford University Press, 1990.

Judith Worthy, *Amy the Indefatigable Autograph Hunter,* Angus & Robertson, 1990.

Mike Dumbleton, *Dial-a-Croc,* Orchard, 1991.

Gillian Rubinstein, *Dog In, Cat Out,* Omnibus Books, 1991, Ticknor & Fields, 1993.

Kathleen Hill, *The Ding Dong Daily,* Heinemann, 1991.

Kathleen Hill, *The Ding Dong Daily Extra,* Heinemann, 1992.

Rod Quantock, *The Backsack Bulletin,* Mammoth Australia, 1992.

Margaret Clarke, *Ripper and Fang,* Omnibus Books, 1992.

Errol Broome, *Tangles,* Little Ark, 1993, Random House, 1994.

Roger Vaughn Carr, *The Butterfly,* Ashton Scholastic, 1994.

Errol Broome, *Rockhopper,* Little Ark, 1994.

Wendy Orr, *Jessica Joan,* Reed, 1994, reissued, Koala Books, 2000.

Wendy Orr, *Snap,* Reed, 1994.

Anna Fienberg, *Madeline the Mermaid and Other Fishy Tales,* Allen & Unwin, 1995.

Libby Gleeson, *Hannah Plus One,* Puffin, 1996.

Anna Fienberg, *Dead Sailors Don't Bite,* Allen & Unwin, 1997.

Anna Fienberg, *Pirate Trouble for Wiggy & Boa,* Allen & Unwin, 1997.

Margaret Wild, *The Midnight Gang,* Omnibus Books, 1997.

Krista Bell, *Pidge,* Unwin, 1997.

Janeen Brian, *Dog Star,* Omnibus Books, 1997.

Ted Greenwood, *After Dusk,* Penguin, 1997.

Jeri Kroll, *A Coat of Cats,* Lothian, 1998.

Kate Walker, *Elephant Lunch,* Omnibus Books, 1998.

Errol Broome, *Magnus Maybe,* Allen & Unwin, 1998.

Julia McClelland, *Lizzie and Smiley,* Penguin, 1999.

Margaret Wild, *The Midnight Feast,* ABC Books, 1999.

Robin Klein, *Penny Pollard's Scrapbook,* Hodder Headline, 1999.

Libby Gleeson, *Hannah and the Tomorrow Room,* Penguin, 1999.

Tania Cox, *Baby,* Working Title Press, 2000.

Errol Broome, *Missing Mem,* Allen & Unwin, 2000.

Libby Gleeson, *Shutting in the Chooks,* Scholastic, 2000.

Work in Progress

Illustrating *Big Red Hen* by Margaret Wild, for Penguin.

Sidelights

"I've always liked to draw from my memory—from my head as we said when we were kids," children's book author and illustrator Ann James told *SATA.* "It surprises me what comes out. But quite often, for illustration, I need to draw or paint things I don't know much about, like motorbikes or aardvarks, so I need to hunt these things out—pore over photos, devour books, scan the horizons. People and animals are the things I know best, and their expressions and moods interest me a lot.

"I like to do most things quickly, and my illustrations reflect this. I use materials that allow a spontaneous approach and have a life of their own. I like surprises, and happy accidents are welcome. Since I am a bit of a perfectionist, each piece of finished artwork has a long history—lots of preparatory drawings and self-rejected attempts. My photocopier is one of my handiest tools. It saves me from hours of tedious copying and redrawing.

"Other people's work is a great inspiration to me, and I have collected quite a library of illustrated books. Ann Haddon and I set up a gallery called Books Illustrated so that other people could have the opportunity to see the original artwork for children's books. We gather these from all over and have lots of exhibitions and visitors; many come to participate in our classes and workshops. We have a book shop, too, so I'm a bit of a jack-of-all-trades."

*   *   *

JENNINGS, Gary (Gayne) 1928-1999 (Gabriel Quyth)

OBITUARY NOTICE—See index for *SATA* sketch: Born September 20, 1928, in Buena Vista, Virginia; died of heart failure on February 13, 1999, in Pompton Lakes, New Jersey. Writer. Jennings specialized in writing broad historical novels backed with intensive research. The author was self-taught and received no college education. Jennings initially served as a war correspondent during his service in the Korean War. He later edited men's magazines and worked as a journalist and reporter. His self-illustrated nonfictional works for children covered a range of topics, including robots and movies. Jennings' extensive love of research was apparent in many of his novels—he lived in Mexico for twelve years to write *Aztec* (1980), his first success, which one reviewer in the *New York Times* called a "'dazzling and hypnotic historical novel,'" according to the publication. Other novels included *The Journeyer* (1984), the story of Marco Polo; and *Spangle* (1987), an account of circus life in the 1800s. Jennings authored the sequel *Aztec Autumn* in 1997. At the time of his death, Jennings was writing an opera based on Joe Hill, the labor activist.

OBITUARIES AND OTHER SOURCES:

PERIODICALS

Los Angeles Times, February 19, 1999, p. A22.
New York Times, February 18, 1999, p. C23.

K

KASTNER, Jill (Marie) 1964-

Personal

Born April 30, 1964, in Elizabeth, NJ; daughter of Arthur and Denna (Ragsdale) Kastner; married Timothy C. Rice (an accountant), September 20, 1991. *Education:* Rhode Island School of Design, B.F.A., 1986. *Politics:* "I would say fairly liberal." *Religion:* "Not practicing now; raised as a Presbyterian." *Hobbies and other interests:* "I'm a voracious reader and use books, magazines, newspapers, and any other reading material for procrastination purposes. I combat sitting at a drawing table for hours by engaging in any athletic activity that I can find."

Addresses

Home and office—511 Washington St., Hoboken, NJ 07030. *Agent*—Dilys Evans, Dilys Evans Fine Illustration, P.O. Box 400, Norfolk, CT 06058.

Career

Dilys Evans Fine Illustration, New York City, assistant to children's book packager Dilys Evans, 1986-88; Lucas/Evans Books Inc. (children's book packager), New York City, part-time projects director, 1988-91; illustrator of children's books, 1988—. *Exhibitions:* The Original Art Exhibition, Society of Illustrators, New York City, 1990. *Member:* Graphic Artists Guild.

Awards, Honors

Friends of American Writers Award, 1990, for *Night Owls;* Ohioana award, 1991, for *With a Name Like Lulu, Who Needs More Trouble?*

Writings

SELF-ILLUSTRATED

Snake Hunt, Four Winds, 1993.
Barnyard Big Top, Simon & Schuster, 1997.
Princess Dinosaur, Greenwillow, 1999.

ILLUSTRATOR

Tricia Springstubb, *With a Name Like Lulu, Who Needs More Trouble?*, Delacorte, 1989.
Ruth B. Gross, *True Stories about Abraham Lincoln,* Lothrop, 1989.
Scott Russell Sanders, *Aurora Means Dawn,* Bradbury, 1989.
Tricia Springstubb, *Lulu vs. Love,* Delacorte, 1990.
Sharon Phillips Denslow, *Night Owls,* Bradbury, 1990.
Sally Hobart Alexander, *Sarah's Surprise,* Macmillan, 1990.
Elvira Woodruff, *Mrs. McClosky's Monkeys,* Scholastic, 1991.
Alice McLerran, *I Want to Go Home,* Tambourine, 1992.
Phyllis Rose Eisenberg, *You're My Nikki,* Dial, 1992.
Virginia L. Kroll, *Naomi Knows It's Springtime,* Boyds Mill, 1993.
Nancy Luenn, *Song for the Ancient Forest,* Atheneum, 1993.
Sharon Chmielarz, *Down at Angel's,* Ticknor & Fields, 1994.
Kristine L. Franklin, *The Shepherd Boy,* Macmillan, 1994.
Nora Martin, *The Stone Dancers,* Atheneum, 1995.
Will Hobbs, *Beardream,* Atheneum, 1997.
Will Hobbs, *Howling Hill,* Morrow, 1998.
Jonathan London, *The Waterfall,* Viking, 1999.
Lucy A. Nolan, *The Lizard Man of Crabtree County,* Marshall Cavendish, 1999.
Cynthia Rylant, *In November,* Harcourt, 2000.

Sidelights

Jill Kastner once told *Something about the Author (SATA):* "I have always drawn and painted, and I've wanted to be 'an artist' since I was very young. During college I was most interested in painting as its own motivation, although I was majoring in illustration. I had trouble with the idea of creating art simply to fill editorial space and was unsure of what type of illustration I should pursue.

I decided to head home before
we attracted too much attention.

In Jill Kastner's self-illustrated **Barnyard Big Top**, **Ben and Clarence the pig keep an eye on Uncle Julius's circus while he's visiting.**

"I studied in Rome, Italy, my senior year at Rhode Island School of Design. I had absolutely no idea what I wanted to do when I graduated. A fellow student, who had spent some time in 'the real world,' gave me the names of several contacts in New York. Luckily, I stumbled into the office of Dilys Evans, an artist's representative. She looked at my portfolio and offered me a job as her assistant for a year. It was during this time that I realized I wanted to illustrate picture books. In college I could spend hours poring over the children's book section; yet I never equated my fascination and love of books with a potential career.

"While working for Evans, I had the wonderful opportunity to meet some of the mentors I look up to today. Illustrator David Wiesner was and still is a great inspiration; Troy Howell is another artist whose work I admire greatly. Evans represents both of these illustrators, so I had the opportunity to see firsthand how they, as well as others, dealt with picture books as fine art. My love of children's books was enhanced significantly by these three people. Evans gave me an intense education in both the history of children's book art and the authors and artists who helped create it.

"Although I illustrate jackets and books for older readers, the picture book will always be my favorite. It offers the artist thirty-two pages in which to both illustrate a story and add to and enrich the text with a visual story of one's own. I'm starting to write my own manuscripts now, but I want to continue illustrating other authors' works as well.

"I like to think of a book as a movie. The camera pans in and out and captures scenes from a wide variety of perspectives. The camera also allows the reader a look at intimate details, or juxtapositions, while obscuring the unnecessary and obvious. I have always had an obsession with figures in an environment and their relationship to specific things around them. I hope to focus more on these visual and emotional details in my next few books.

"As far as life experiences go, I grew up in a fairly rural area of New Jersey and spent my free time after school roaming woods and rivers. This may explain the rural setting of *Night Owls* and my attraction to the pioneer family in *Aurora Means Dawn*. I have two very active grandparents from Tennessee, who kept us (my two brothers and sister) busy on visits. We camped in the mountains, hiked, and even tubed down rapids in mountain rivers." Kastner based the story for her first self-illustrated children's book, *Snake Hunt,* on her own childhood "snake-hunting" expeditions with her grandfather. "I think that my interest in the environment also stems from these experiences," Kastner continued, citing the illustrations she contributed to the Native American tale *Song for the Ancient Forest.* This book represents the kind of illustrating projects Kastner hopes to do more of in the future, specifically ones "that are as exciting in design and visuals as they are in text and story."

Kastner is a popular children's book illustrator whose first self-illustrated book, *Snake Hunt,* was well received by critics. Based on similar incidents from her own childhood, the story of *Snake Hunt* focuses on a young narrator entranced by her grandfather's tall tales of

Kastner's illustrations cover a pioneer family's journey by covered wagon and their struggle to become the first settlers of **Aurora, Ohio.** *(From* Aurora Means Dawn *by Scott Russell Sanders.)*

adventures hunting snakes for dinner in years gone by. Grandmother shoos the two out of doors with the humorous command to hunt down a snake for that night's dinner, and with a storm gathering overhead the two head off into the woods. Kastner's illustrations "contrast Granddad's humorous fantasies of the hunt with his granddaughter's cautious anticipation and apprehensions," observed Ellen Mandel in *Booklist*. In addition to visually demonstrating the warm relationship between Jesse and her grandfather, Kastner's illustrations also carry the punch line for the humor of the story, according to a reviewer for *Kirkus Reviews*. At the height of Jesse's nervous anticipation, the wind from the impending storm makes a noise in the bushes like a rattlesnake and both jump back before collapsing on a nearby log in relief. But at the foot of the log, evident only to the reader, is coiled a large rattlesnake. "This is a satisfying adventure and good read-aloud choice," averred Carolyn Noah in *School Library Journal*.

Critics noted that Kastner drops the suspense and punches up the humor in her next solo effort, *Barnyard Big Top,* in which Ben's ordinary life on the farm with aunts Ginny and Gert is changed forever by the unexpected appearance of Uncle Julius and his Two-Ring Extravaganza circus. With his show-off pet pig Clarence taking the opportunity to ham it up, and Ben given all sorts of new responsibilities as the circus performers set up and rehearse in anticipation of performance, Kastner has provided herself with ample fodder for visual humor, according to reviewers. "The dauntless Clarence's preposterous acrobatic feats alone are worth the price of admission," attested a reviewer for *Publishers Weekly*. "Animals and people radiate charm and humor and vibrant joviality," remarked Virginia Opocensky in *School Library Journal*, who asserted that Kastner combines fantasy and realism in a perfectly humorous blend. Lauren Peterson likewise predicted in her *Booklist* review, "A good time will be had by all."

Works Cited

Review of *Barnyard Big Top, Publishers Weekly,* November 3, 1997, p. 84.
Mandel, Ellen, review of *Snake Hunt, Booklist,* December 15, 1993, p. 76.
Noah, Carolyn, review of *Snake Hunt, School Library Journal,* November 1993, pp. 84-85.
Opocensky, Virginia, review of *Barnyard Big Top, School Library Journal,* November, 1997, p. 85.
Peterson, Lauren, review of *Barnyard Big Top, Booklist,* November 1, 1997, p. 482.
Review of *Snake Hunt, Kirkus Reviews,* September 1, 1993, p. 1147.

For More Information See

PERIODICALS

Booklist, September 1, 1998, p. 126; April 1, 1999, p. 1421; November 15, 1999, p. 636.
Publishers Weekly, March 29, 1999, p. 103.
School Library Journal, October, 1999, p. 121.*

KEAMS, Geri 1951-

Personal

Born August 19, 1951, in Winslow, AZ; daughter of Lee and Helen Keams. *Education:* University of Arizona, B.F.A., 1978. *Politics:* Liberal. *Religion:* Native American, Holistic. *Hobbies and other interests:* Native American culture.

Addresses

Home—5152 La Vista Ct., Los Angeles, CA 90004. *E-mail*—Keams@pacbell.net.

Career

Actress and storyteller, c. 1980—. Also producer and director of films and videotapes. *Member:* Society of Children's Book Writers and Illustrators, Screen Actors Guild, American Federation of Television and Radio Artists.

Writings

Grandmother Spider Brings the Sun: A Cherokee Story, illustrated by James Bernardin, Northland Publishing (Flagstaff, AZ), 1995.
Snail Girl Brings Water: A Navajo Story, illustrated by Richard Ziehler-Martin, Northland Publishing, 1998.

Work in Progress

A children's novel; three folk tales.

Sidelights

Geri Keams told *SATA:* "I was born and raised in the Painted Desert region of the Navajo Indian Nation. As a child I grew up without television and had a community full of gifted storytellers. I grew up under their influence and developed a great fascination for my culture. I became an adventurous explorer by reading books about faraway places, and I listened to the stories of the Navajo.

"The seed was planted, and I grew into a curious person. I studied theater, film, psychology, philosophy, and other interesting subjects the world had to offer. I started writing down my experiences, which eventually led to poems being published. Today, I continue the journey as a writer. It has been a wonderful and marvelous journey, and I hope I continue on this path.

"Recently, I have published two books of Native American folk tales and am now writing a novel of my childhood experiences growing up on the reservation. The folk tales honor the many storytellers who influenced me, and the novel explores my relationship with my grandmothers when I was a child."

Geri Keams

For More Information See

PERIODICALS

Booklist, November 15, 1998, p. 583.
School Library Journal, May, 1999, pp. 108-09.

*   *   *

KENT, Mallory
See LOWNDES, Robert A(ugustine) W(ard)

*   *   *

KIRK, David 1955-

Personal

Born in 1955; married; wife's name, Kathy; children: Violet. *Education:* Graduated from Cleveland Institute of Art, 1977.

Addresses

Home—King Ferry, NY.

Career

Toy store owner and founder of Ovicular Toys and Hoobert Toys, 1979; cofounder of Callaway & Kirk Company.

Awards, Honors

In 1994, *Parents Magazine* named *Miss Spider's Wedding* to its list of top ten children's picture books.

Writings

Miss Spider's Tea Party, Scholastic, 1994.
Miss Spider's Wedding, Scholastic, 1995.
Miss Spider's New Car, Scholastic, 1997.
Miss Spider's Tea Party: The Counting Book, Scholastic, 1997.
Miss Spider's ABC, Scholastic, 1998.
Little Miss Spider, Scholastic, 1999.
Nova's Ark, Scholastic, 1999.
Miss Spider's New Car: The Board Book, Scholastic, 1999.
Little Miss Spider at Sunny Patch School, Scholastic, 2000.
Miss Spider's ABC: The Board Book, Scholastic, 2000.

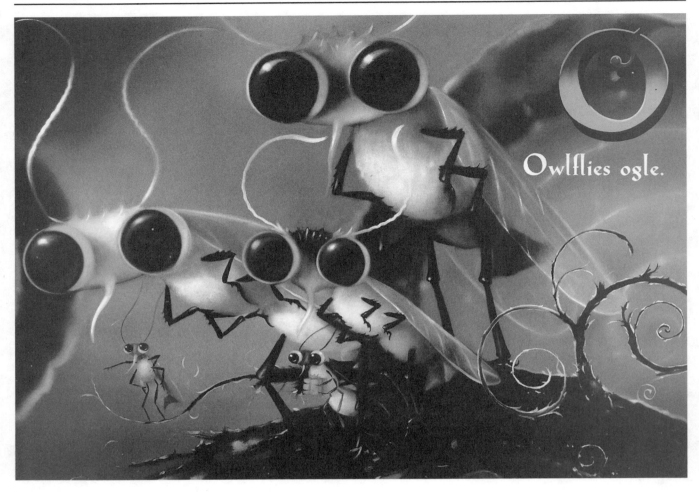

Owlflies ogle.

David Kirk's imaginative oil paintings illustrate his ant-to-zebra butterfly ABC book, Miss Spider's ABC.

Adaptations

Miss Spider's Tea Party was made into a CD-ROM game by Simon & Schuster Interactive. Several lines of toys, games, and other merchandise based on Kirk's characters have been released or are planned.

Sidelights

During the mid and late 1990s, author, artist, and toy maker David Kirk took the children's book world by storm with his high-color picture books featuring Miss Spider. Within six years, over four million copies of the Miss Spider titles were in the hands of readers worldwide. Kirk had not imagined such popular success; his accidental discovery by a children's book publisher is the dream of many would-be writers.

Kirk grew up in Columbus, Ohio, where he collected toy robots. After he earned a degree from the Cleveland Institute of Art in 1977, he lived in England until his art scholarship support ended. Upon the invitation of his brother Daniel, a children's book author and illustrator, Kirk settled in New York. There he opened a toy store to showcase his own creations, including toys, art, and furniture. Among his creations were animal figures,

which he sold in elaborately illustrated packages. After book publisher Nicholas Callaway bought a toy baby alligator for his daughter, he began to wonder about the toy maker. Kirk was working on a spider character when Callaway approached him about writing and illustrating picture books for children. "I generally didn't go out and drum things up," Kirk remembered to Michel Marriott in the *Detroit Free Press*. "If somebody came along and said 'Hey, you look like you'd be good at this,' I'd do it. That's how it happened." Kirk launched his literary career in 1994 with *Miss Spider's Tea Party*. In this story, told in rhyme and glossy oil paint illustrations, a lonely flower-eating spider wonders why her insect guests will not come to tea. Finally, at the end of this "sweet tale," to quote *School Library Journal* critic John Peters, Miss Spider convinces a moth that it is safe to visit.

A big attraction of the Miss Spider books is the artwork. According to Marriott, while Kirk's smooth, color-saturated illustrations resemble computer-generated art, they are really oil paintings. In her review of *Miss Spider's Wedding* for *School Librarian*, Jane Doonan described the illustrations as "luminous" and "surreally intense." Likewise, in *School Library Journal*, Karen James called Kirk's artwork "extraordinary."

Reviews of Kirk's next work, *Miss Spider's New Car,* in which Miss Spider and her husband Holley test drive vehicles made from insect parts, were generally positive. Writing for *School Library Journal,* Cynthia K. Richey praised Kirk's "energetic verse [which] conveys the movement of the vehicles" and "lavish, enthusiastic pictures." In *Miss Spider's ABC,* Kirk tells the story through such alliterations as "fireflies fandango" and "owlflies ogle," as well as through his signature illustrations. By the end of the book, readers realize that all of the insects and the few other garden creatures in the story are gathering for Miss Spider's birthday party. Even without Kirk's usual rhyming texts, "the juiced-up, color-saturated illustrations are thrilling" enthused a *Publishers Weekly* reviewer. In *School Library Journal,* Martha Link, remarking that the "text complements the paintings," predicted that this "child-friendly" book would appeal to younger readers more than the earlier Miss Spider books.

In 1999, Kirk departed from the Miss Spider series when he published *Nova's Ark,* the story of a square-headed robot named Nova who embarks on a mission to save his home planet, Roton. As with his Miss Spider books, Kirk's artwork captured critics' attention. Both *Booklist* reviewer John Peters and a *Publishers Weekly* critic noted the three-dimensional effect of Kirk's computer imaging. The plot, told in unrhymed prose this time, "may be rudimentary," remarked Peters, "but children will barely notice because of the dazzling visual effects and stylish machinery." *Nova's Ark* finishes with a happy outcome for the robots. "What sets Kirk's work apart from other visions of the future is a combination of adult sophistication and childlike innocence," remarked Marriott. "His robots are sweet and almost cuddly, rendered in a bright, warm palette and a style that appears both antique and futuristic."

Kirk mixed his art with 3-D computer imaging to produce the pictures for his self-illustrated Nova's Ark, *in which a young robot discovers the ultimate power source during a class field trip mishap.*

Works Cited

Doonan, Jane, review of *Miss Spider's Wedding, School Librarian,* spring, 1998, p. 34.

James, Karen, review of *Miss Spider's Wedding, School Library Journal,* October, 1995, p. 105.

Link, Martha, review of *Miss Spider's ABC, School Library Journal,* December, 1998, p. 86.

Marriott, Michel, "Children's Author Kirk Invents Toy Robot Line," *Detroit Free Press,* January 3, 2000, pp. E1-E2.

Review of *Miss Spider's ABC, Publishers Weekly,* October 5, 1998, p. 89.

Review of *Nova's Ark, Publishers Weekly,* November 23, 1998, p. 65.

Peters, John, review of *Miss Spider's Tea Party, School Library Journal,* June, 1994, p. 107.

Peters, John, review of *Nova's Ark, Booklist,* February 1, 1999, p. 980.

Richey, Cynthia K., review of *Miss Spider's New Car, School Library Journal,* January, 1998, p. 88.

For More Information See

PERIODICALS

Booklist, November 1, 1997, pp. 482-83; December 1, 1998, p. 671.

Kirkus Reviews, September 15, 1997, p. 1459.

New York Times Book Review, July 31, 1994, p. 20; September 10, 1995, p. 35.

Publishers Weekly, March 24, 1997, p. 85; March 8, 1999, p. 70.*

L

L., Barry
See LONGYEAR, Barry B(rookes)

*   *   *

LAING, Alexander (Kinnan) 1903-1976

Personal

Born August 7, 1903, in Great Neck, Long Island, NY; died April 23, 1976; son of Edgar Hall and Mary Adeline (Pray) Laing; married Isabel Lattimore Frost, June 10, 1930 (divorced); married Dilys Bennett, May 30, 1936 (died, 1960); married Veronica Ruzicka, March 22, 1961; children: (second marriage) David. *Education:* Dartmouth College, A.B., 1933, A.M., 1947.

Career

Radio News, technical editor, 1925-26; *Power Specialist,* editor, 1927-28; Erwin, Wasey Co., copywriter, 1929; Dartmouth College, Hanover, NH, tutorial adviser in English department, 1930, adviser to the arts, 1930-34, assistant librarian, 1937-50, director of public affairs laboratory, 1947-52, educational services adviser for library, 1952, professor of *belles lettres,* 1952-68, professor emeritus, 1968-76. Universities Committee for Postwar International Problems, chairperson of Dartmouth group, 1944-45; Americans United for World Organization, chairperson for Hanover. Also worked as a seaman.

Awards, Honors

Guggenheim fellowship for creative writing abroad, 1934-35.

Writings

FOR CHILDREN

Sailing In, Farrar, Rinehart, 1937.

NOVELS

End of Roaming, Farrar, Rinehart, 1930.
The Cadaver of Gideon Wyck, by a Medical Student, Farrar, Rinehart, 1934.
(With Thomas Painter) *The Motives of Nicholas Holtz; Being the Weird Tale of the Ironville Virus,* Farrar, Rinehart, 1936, published in England as *The Glass Centipede,* Butterworth, 1936.
Dr. Scarlett: A Narrative of His Mysterious Behavior in the East, Farrar, Rinehart, 1936.
The Methods of Dr. Scarlett, Farrar, Rinehart, 1937.
Jonathan Eagle, Duell, Sloan & Pearce (New York City), 1955.
Matthew Early, Duell, Sloan & Pearce, 1957.

POETRY

(With Richmond A. Lattimore) *Hanover Poems,* Harold Vinal, 1927.
Fool's Errand, Doubleday, 1928.
The Sea Witch, Farrar, Rinehart, 1933, reprinted, Ballantine, 1968.
The Flowering Thorn, 1933.
Brant Point: Poems, University Press of New England (Hanover, NH), 1975.

OTHER

Wine and Physic: A Poem and Six Essays on the Fate of Our Language, Farrar, Rinehart, 1934.
(Editor and author of foreword and afterword) *The Life and Adventures of John Nicol, Mariner,* Farrar, Rinehart, 1936.
(Editor and author of foreword and commentary) *The Haunted Omnibus,* Farrar, Rinehart, 1937, abridged edition published as *Great Ghost Stories of the World,* Blue Ribbon (Garden City, NY), 1939.
Way for America, Duell, Sloan & Pearce, 1943.
Clipper Ship Men, Duell, Sloan & Pearce, 1944, revised edition published as *Clipper Ships and Their Makers,* Putnam, 1966.
American Sail: A Pictorial History, Dutton, 1961.
The Pacific World, Delacorte, 1967.
(Editor) *The Collected Poems of Dilys Laing,* Press of Case Western Reserve University (Cleveland, OH), 1967.

American Ships, American Heritage Publishing (New York City), 1971.

The American Heritage History of Seafaring America, American Heritage Publishing, 1974.

Also author of *Scarce Ancient Ballads* and *The Thistle of Scotland.* Contributor to magazines, including *Esquire, Atlantic, Harper's, Nation, New Republic,* and *Saturday Review.*

Sidelights

The body of Alexander Laing's work includes a handful of poetry collections, a few mainstream novels, and several historical works related to ships and the sea. He is remembered chiefly, however, for four suspense novels penned in the 1930s, one of which was so gruesome that subsequent printings were abridged. The subject of the editor's pencil was *The Cadaver of Gideon Wyck, by a Medical Student.* This medical murder mystery was so heavily footnoted with scientific data and so adorned with meticulous detail that Mortimer Quick warned *Boston Transcript* readers: "the horrid events that transpire are ... imbued with reality and fascinate while they shock." According to Brian Stableford in the *St. James Guide to Horror, Ghost, and Gothic Writers,* the medical research focused on "the study of human monsters and mutations." Stableford continued, "The monstrousness of Gideon Wyck has, in the end, far less to do with conventional deformity than with the nature of his scientific speculations and endeavours." He found that "*The Cadaver of Gideon Wyck* is a conscientiously modern attempt to address some of the issues raised by Mary Shelley's classic *[Frankenstein]* regarding the nature of life, heredity and monstrousness." In the *New York Times Book Review,* Isaac Anderson predicted that the reader who "can stomach the grisly details which are absolutely essential" will enjoy "a really enthralling mystery yarn told with the skill of a master." Quick recommended the volume, stating, "here's a book to keep you going to the break of dawn."

Laing's other medical mystery was *The Motives of Nicholas Holtz; Being the Weird Tale of the Ironville Virus.* Stableford described it as "a moderately hard-boiled thriller ... solidly based in biological possibility ... in which an artificially created virus escapes from captivity with deadly consequences...." Writing in the *New York Times Book Review,* Anderson called it "a most uncomfortable book, one which proves that you do not need ghosts or vampires or werewolves to make a horror story. Science will do the trick if you give it enough rope." Quick commented in the *Chicago Daily* that "both thesis and material are interesting, only don't blame me it if changes your dreams to nightmares."

Laing also wrote two adventure novels, featuring an amusing ship's doctor best known for his execrable limericks and puns. *Dr. Scarlett* is set in the jungles beneath the Himalayas, and *The Methods of Dr. Scarlett* contains a set of the fictional doctor's case histories. *Books* reviewer Will Cuppy called *Dr. Scarlett* "a lively and often startling yarn." When Anderson announced in the *New York Times Book Review* that publishers intended to produce sequels to *Dr. Scarlett,* he added: "If they are to be stranger, or more exciting, or more mysterious than this one, Mr. Laing has undertaken a difficult task indeed. In the meantime, make sure that you do not miss this one." Stableford summarized the author's impact, saying, "Laing's thrillers are distinguished by considerable vigour and experimental enterprise, and he would doubtless have been able to produce interesting work had he not chosen to abandon the field of popular fiction."

Works Cited

Anderson, Isaac, review of *The Cadaver of Gideon Wick,* by a Medical Student, *New York Times Book Review,* January 21, 1934, p. 10.

Anderson, Isaac, review of *Dr. Scarlett, New York Times Book Review,* August 16, 1936, p. 20.

Anderson, Isaac, review of *The Motives of Nicholas Holtz; Being the Weird Tale of the Ironville Virus, New York Times Book Review,* January 26, 1936, p. 16.

Cuppy, Will, review of *Dr. Scarlett, Books,* August 23, 1936, p. 16.

Quick, Mortimer, review of *The Cadaver of Gideon Wick, by a Medical Student, Boston Transcript,* March 21, 1934, p. 2.

Quick, Mortimer, review of *The Motives of Nicholas Holtz; Being the Weird Tale of the Ironville Virus, Chicago Daily,* February 1, 1936, p. 14.

Stableford, Brian, "Alexander Laing," *St. James Guide to Horror, Ghost, and Gothic Writers,* St. James Press, 1998.

For More Information See

PERIODICALS

Booklist, December, 1936; March, 1937; October 1, 1937.

Books, January 21, 1934, p. 11; September 16, 1934, p. 22; January 26, 1936, p. 16; July 11, 1937, p. 9.

Boston Transcript, June 30, 1934, p. 1; January 25, 1936, p. 6; August 15, 1936, p. 4; February 6, 1937, p. 1; July 24, 1937, p. 3.

Chicago Daily Tribune, February 3, 1934, p. 14.

Christian Science Monitor, August 22, 1934, p. 12.

Nation, July 11, 1934.

New Republic, August 22, 1934.

New York Times Book Review, July 22, 1934, p. 3; July 11, 1937, p. 17; August 15, 1937, p. 21.

Saturday Review of Literature, January 20, 1934; July 14, 1934; August 22, 1936; January 30, 1937; July 24, 1937.

Spectator, June 18, 1937.

Time, February 3, 1936.

Times Literary Supplement, July 12, 1934, p. 493; June 19, 1937, p. 465.*

LASER, Michael 1954-

Personal

Born September 14, 1954, in Brooklyn, NY. *Education:* State University of New York at Binghamton, B.A., 1975; Johns Hopkins University, M.A., 1977.

Addresses

Home—51 Christopher St., Montclair, NJ 07042.

Career

Writer.

Writings

(Collector and editor, with Ken Goldner) *Children's Rules for Parents,* illustrated by Irene Trivas, Perennial Library (New York), 1987.

The Rain (picture book), illustrated by Jeffrey Greene, Simon & Schuster, 1997.

Old Buddy Old Pal (novel), Permanent Press (Sag Harbor, NY), 1999.

6-321 (middle-grade novel), Atheneum (New York), 2001.

Sidelights

Michael Laser told *SATA,* "*The Rain,* my first published children's book, was born as a concept for a series of books. I thought one day, 'Why not write about the simplest, most beautiful things around us, in the most simple and beautiful language I can manage?' The first step was to note everything that the word "rain" brought to mind. I soon found myself with an opening sentence, 'The rain fell on the city, the town and the forest,' and that sentence opened the door for three parallel rain-stories, which then of course had to come together, and their coming together turned into a nice surprise ending. It proved to be one of those rare writing experiences in which you set out with almost no idea where you'll end up . . . and luck (plus twenty years of diligent practice) carries you to the end of a story that feels whole and satisfying.

6-321 represents an opposite writing experience. This book is intensely autobiographical and jams every memorable experience I had in elementary school into one tale of a timid boy going through sixth grade. Because I cared so much about these memories, my sense of what worked and what didn't was cloudy. A very intelligent editor asked for changes, and I put the book through several major revisions, turning what began as a kaleidoscopic epic into a more streamlined plot. Where *The Rain* took less than a month to write, *6-321,* though less than one hundred pages long, has been a three-year project. There's very little left in the book that comes straight from life, but I think it works better now as a dramatic tale, thanks to the editor's suggestions.

Michael Laser's poetic tale follows an autumn rain from city to town and then to forest. (Cover illustration by Jeffrey Greene.)

"There are dozens of ideas for children's books in my files right now. I hope that many of them will find their way onto the page [and] into print."

Michael Laser's first picture book, *The Rain,* captured critical attention for its poetic text celebrating the rejuvenating, uplifting pleasures of an autumnal rain as experienced by five people. In a prose style "almost as peaceful and steadily rhythmic as the autumn shower he lauds," according to a reviewer in *Publishers Weekly,* Laser depicts the effects of a sudden autumn rain on a man boarding a commuter train, on a woman grading papers in a town, on two children playing in a forest, and on an elderly man who lets the rain run down his bare face as he stands in a city street. Each is changed or inspired by the ordinary miracle of the rainfall, and in this way the author captures the "universality and wonder" of a natural event, Shelley Townsend-Hudson wrote in *Booklist.* "Laser's low-key look at one of the gifts of nature is the perfect antidote to the weather-hysteria of local TV news," Jeanne Clancy Watkins similarly observed in *School Library Journal.* Although some critics noted that the relentlessly quiet, nostalgic tone of the book might disqualify its usefulness in certain settings, its unusual perspective and what Townsend-Hudson called its "joyful . . . appreciation of nature" make it a good book to pull out for quiet one-on-one readings, others observed.

Laser is also the author of a novel for adults, *Old Buddy Old Pal,* in which two long-time friends, Burt and Alan, re-evaluate their relationship after the break-up of Alan's marriage gives Burt the push he needs to finally express the feelings he has had for his friend's wife. A reviewer for *Publishers Weekly* described the strengths of *Old Buddy Old Pal* in the following way: "Deftly using flashbacks, this short novel proceeds at a smooth pace, with sharp observations and crisp dialogue."

Works Cited

Review of *Old Buddy Old Pal, Publishers Weekly,* May 10, 1999, p. 56.

Review of *The Rain, Publishers Weekly,* April 7, 1997, p. 91.

Townsend-Hudson, Shelley, review of *The Rain, Booklist,* April 1, 1997, p. 1338.

Watkins, Jeanne Clancy, review of *The Rain, School Library Journal,* May, 1997, pp. 102-3.

For More Information See

PERIODICALS

Bulletin of the Center for Children's Books, June, 1997, pp. 363-64.

Kirkus Reviews, April 1, 1999, p. 474.

Library Journal, June 1, 1999, p. 174.

*   *   *

LAVOND, Paul Dennis
See LOWNDES, Robert A(ugustine) W(ard)

*   *   *

LLOYD, Megan 1958-

Personal

Born November 5, 1958, in Harrisburg, PA; daughter of Warren (a history teacher) and Lois (a kindergarten teacher; maiden name, Hughes) Lloyd; married Thomas Thompson (an antiques dealer). *Education:* Attended Pennsylvania State University, 1976-78; Parsons School of Design, B.F.A., 1981. *Politics:* Independent. *Religion:* Presbyterian.

Career

Freelance illustrator of children's books, 1982—. Harper Junior Books, New York City, assistant to the art director, 1981-82; worked in restoration of American antique furniture, 1983—. Founding member and art director for the Children's Literature Council of Pennsylvania, 1985-96; former president and founding member of Citizens for Responsible Development (a local

A poor tailor who kills seven flies at one blow sets out on adventures outwitting savage giants and ogres, in Eric A. Kimmel's retelling of **Seven at One Blow,** *illustrated by Lloyd.*

community group working for sound city planning), 1986-87.

Awards, Honors

Colorado Children's Book Award runner-up and Keystone to Reading award, both 1988, for *The Little Old Lady Who Was Not Afraid of Anything;* Keystone to Reading award, 1989, for *More Surprises;* Parents' Choice, picture book category, 1991, for *Cactus Hotel.*

Writings

FOR CHILDREN; SELF-ILLUSTRATED

Chicken Tricks, Harper & Row, 1983.

FOR CHILDREN; ILLUSTRATOR

Surprises (poetry), selected by Lee Bennett Hopkins, Harper & Row, 1984.

Ida Luttrell, *Lonesome Lester,* Harper & Row, 1984.

Victoria Sherrow, *There Goes the Ghost,* Harper & Row, 1985.

Norma Farber, *All Those Mothers at the Manger,* Harper & Row, 1985.

Thom Roberts, *The Atlantic Free Balloon Race,* Avon, 1986.

Megan Lloyd illustrated the desert animals and the giant cactus they use for a hotel in Brenda Z. Guiberson's **Cactus Hotel.**

Tony Johnston, *Farmer Mack Measures His Pig,* Harper & Row, 1986.

Linda Williams, *The Little Old Lady Who Was Not Afraid of Anything,* Crowell, 1986.

More Surprises (poetry), selected by Lee Bennett Hopkins, Harper, 1987.

Nancy MacArthur, *Megan Gets a Dollhouse,* Scholastic, 1988.

Carolyn Otto, *That Sky, That Rain,* HarperCollins, 1990.

Patricia Lauber, *How We Learned the Earth Is Round,* HarperCollins, 1990.

Brenda Z. Guiberson, *Cactus Hotel,* Holt, 1991.

Jane O'Connor and Robert O'Connor, *Super Cluck,* HarperCollins, 1991.

Eric Kimmel, *Baba Yaga: A Russian Folktale,* Holiday House, 1991.

Paul Showers, *How You Talk,* HarperCollins, 1992.

Brenda Z. Guiberson, *Spoonbill Swamp,* Holt, 1992.

Melvin Berger, *Look Out for Turtles!,* HarperCollins, 1992.

Mary Neville, *The Christmas Tree Ride,* Holiday House, 1992.

Brenda Z. Guiberson, *Lobster Boat,* Holt, 1993.

Eric Kimmel, *The Gingerbread Man,* Holiday House, 1993.

Susan Tews, *The Gingerbread Doll,* Clarion, 1993.

Tom Birdseye, *A Regular Flood of Mishap,* Holiday House, 1994.

Ellen Kindt McKenzie, *The Perfectly Orderly House,* Holt, 1994.

Brenda Z. Guiberson, *Winter Wheat,* Holt, 1995.

Barbara Juster Esbensen, *Dance with Me* (poetry), Harper-Collins, 1995.

Carolyn Otto, *What Color Is Camouflage?,* HarperCollins, 1996.

Priscilla Belz Jenkins, *Falcons Nest on Skyscrapers,* HarperCollins, 1996.

Linda White, *Too Many Pumpkins,* Holiday House, 1996.

Melvin Berger, *Chirping Crickets,* HarperCollins, 1998.

Eric A. Kimmel, *Seven at One Blow: A Tale from the Brothers Grimm,* Holiday House, 1998.

Carolyn Otto, *Pioneer Church,* Holt, 1999.

Sidelights

"I was born and raised in south-central Pennsylvania," Megan Lloyd told *Something about the Author* (*SATA*), "growing up with my parents, one older sister, a cat, and a dog. Both my sister and I began taking ballet lessons when we were young, but my sister did not show any great love for that particular art form and stopped dancing shortly thereafter. I fell in love with ballet and pursued it with all that I had. For many years I was convinced that it would be my career—so convinced that I didn't really give a great deal of thought to anything else. Because ballet was 'my thing,' I wasn't allowed to take horse riding lessons when my sister and mother did, mainly because my sister fell off a horse and broke her arm while my mother fell off and broke her knee. Surely this was too risky a sport for an aspiring dancer!

"At fifteen the terrible blow fell. I discovered that there were practically NO five-foot-one-inch dancers with short legs, no matter how good they were at jumping and stretching and pirouetting. I was crushed. In my despair—and it truly felt like the world was crumbling—I decided that I would transfer my creative efforts to the visual arts, and I began to think of myself as an 'artist.' Fortunately, the high school I attended had an excellent art department with very talented and supportive teachers. Things seemed to run smoothly until it was time for the big college decision."

Lloyd "fell in love" with the idea of attending Harvard Law School and, with that goal in mind, started out her college career at Pennsylvania State University in the pre-law program. "That lasted for all of two semesters at which time I felt miserable, missed my art work, and was totally confused," Lloyd told *SATA*. "My mother, understanding my confusion, suggested that I might like to illustrate picture books. And to sweeten the suggestion, she showed me a copy of Brian Wildsmith's book *Circus.* That was all it took. I had never seen a book like that before. It was wonderful.

"I went to the Parsons School of Design and studied illustration. And I continue to work and work and work at learning, growing, and developing. The more I learn about illustrating books, the more I discover all that I don't know! That's great—it keeps illustrating a stimulating career. Each book presents a new puzzle to solve. Who could ask for more?

"Many of my early books are fiction. Recently, I have done a number of nonfiction books. I do a great deal of research for both types of story. With fictional pieces, I explore settings and characters, costumes and lighting, all of which make the illustration process interesting to me. With nonfiction books, I carry my research even further, usually traveling to the geographical location in which the book is set.

"In *Cactus Hotel,* for example, I did all of the research at the Saguaro National Monument in Tucson, Arizona. For *Lobster Boat* I traveled to Maine and found a lobsterman to take me out on his boat with him while he pulled his lobster traps. And for *Winter Wheat,* a story about a farmer growing winter wheat in the state of Washington, I drove clear across the country to photograph the wheat farm belonging to the author's father and mother! If I can't see what it is I am to draw, I simply can't make successful illustrations.

"When not working, I spend a great deal of time with my two Belgian Sheepdogs, Abel and Yonder. Both dogs are learning how to herd sheep and to be sled dogs, too. Most of the sheep-herding involves my trying not to be run over by a stampeding flock of sheep. Most of the sledding involves me running alongside the dogs, encouraging them onward! It's good fun."

For More Information See

PERIODICALS

Publishers Weekly, January 3, 2000, p. 78.

*   *   *

LONGBEARD, Frederick
See LONGYEAR, Barry B(rookes)

*   *   *

LONGYEAR, Barry B(rookes) 1942-
(Fan D. Ango, Barry L., Frederick Longbeard, Tol E. Rant, Mark Ringdalh, Shaw Vinest)

Personal

Born May 12, 1942, in Harrisburg, PA; married Regina Bedsun, May 4, 1967. *Education:* Attended Wayne State University, 1966-67. *Politics:* "No." *Religion:* "Independent."

Addresses

Home and office—P.O. Box 100, New Sharon, ME 04955-0100.

Barry B. Longyear

Career

Madison Corp., Detroit, MI, production manager, 1967-68; Sol III Publications, editor, publisher, and ghostwriter in Philadelphia, PA, 1968-72, owner in Farmington, ME, 1972-77; writer, 1977—. Conducts writer's workshops. *Member:* Authors Guild, Authors League of America, Science Fiction Writers of America.

Awards, Honors

Nebula Award, Science Fiction Writers of America, Hugo Award, World Science Fiction Convention, and Locus Award, all 1980, all for novella, "Enemy Mine"; John W. Campbell Award, World Science Fiction Association, 1980, for best new writer.

Writings

SCIENCE FICTION NOVELS

Elephant Song, Berkley, 1981.
The Tomorrow Testament, Berkley, 1982.
(With David Gerrold) *Enemy Mine* (novelization of screenplay based on Longyear's original novella), Charter (New York City), 1985.
Sea of Glass, St. Martin's, 1987.
Naked Came the Robot, Popular Library (New York City), 1988.
The God Box, Signet, 1989.

Infinity Hold, Popular Library, 1989.
The Homecoming (for young adults), Walker, 1989.
The Change ("Alien Nation" series), Pocket, 1994.
Slag Like Me ("Alien Nation" series), Pocket, 1994.
The Enemy Papers (contains newly edited and enlarged version of *Enemy Mine* and its two sequels, *The Last Enemy* and *The Tomorrow Testament*), White Wolf, 1998.

SCIENCE FICTION STORY COLLECTIONS

Manifest Destiny (contains short story "Enemy Mine"), Berkley, 1980.
Circus World, Berkley, 1980.
City of Baraboo, Berkley, 1980.
It Came from Schenectady, Bluejay (New York City), 1984.
Enemy Mine (novella; bound with *Another Orphan* by John Kessel), Tor, 1989.

OTHER

Science Fiction Writer's Workshop I: An Introduction to Fiction Mechanics, Owlswick (Philadelphia, PA), 1980.
St. Mary Blue (novel), Steel Dragon (Minneapolis, MN), 1988.
Yesterday's Tomorrow (meditations), Hazeldon (Minneapolis, MN), 1997.

Also author of *The Last Enemy,* 1997. Author of "Salty," a monthly column in *Empire Science Fiction*. Contributor (sometimes under pseudonyms Fan D. Ango, Barry L., Frederick Longbeard, Tol E. Rant, Mark Ringdalh, and Shaw Vinest) of stories, poems, and articles to science-fiction magazines and anthologies, including *Analog; Isaac Asimov's Science Fiction Magazine; Teaching Science Fiction: Education for Tomorrow,* edited by Jack Williamson, Owlswick, 1980; and *Carr's Best Science Fiction,* edited by Terry Carr, Del Rey, 1980.

Adaptations

The novella "Enemy Mine" was adapted for film by Edward Khamara and released by 20th Century-Fox, 1985.

Sidelights

When Barry B. Longyear's stories began appearing in the late 1970s, he was universally hailed by critics, readers, and other writers as a significant new talent in the science fiction field. Don D'Ammassa in the *St. James Guide to Science Fiction Writers* describes the "phenomenal impact" of Longyear's early work. Science fiction fans responded by voting Longyear both a Hugo Award and the John W. Campbell Award for best new writer; his fellow science fiction authors presented him with a Nebula Award.

What D'Ammassa considers the "four best" of Longyear's early stories were brought together in his first book, *Manifest Destiny*. This is a shared universe collection, all of the stories set in a future where an aggressively expanding Earth empire confronts and battles an alien empire known as Dracon. "Enemy Mine," the most acclaimed story in the book, served as the basis for a major motion picture with the same title and was later expanded to novel length by Longyear in a collaboration with David Gerrold. The story takes place on a primitive planet where a Dracon warrior and an Earth warrior, bitter enemies by race, are both marooned. They must learn to cooperate with one another or perish. As their cooperation leads to a common understanding and a kind of friendship, parallels are clearly drawn to the possibilities of understanding and peace between their two races. Longyear extended the Earth-Dracon saga in two novel-length sequels, *The Tomorrow Testament* and *The Last Enemy*. Published in 1981, *Elephant Song* features another popular shared world series by Longyear that also began with stories—collected in *Circus World* and *City of Baraboo*—and was eventually developed into a novel-length work. It deals with the adventures of an interstellar circus over several hundred years.

After Longyear's early successes his career was marked by a brief hiatus. In 1981, he was hospitalized for alcoholism and addiction to prescription drugs, an experience which he later chronicled in the semi-autobiographical novel *St. Mary Blue*. In 1987, Longyear returned to science fiction with *Sea of Glass,* a powerfully bleak dystopian tale of overpopulation that D'Ammassa sees as a "legitimate contender as [Longyear's] best novel" and "the last major work of [his] early career." The protagonist of the book, an illegal child, is taken from his parents at an early age and raised in a prison camp by the state, which is ruled by a monolithic super-computer that has scheduled a global war in order to reduce world population. D'Ammassa calls *Sea of Glass* a "searing indictment of selfishness and the human tendency to allow others to make their decisions for them." A *Publishers Weekly* reviewer found the book's premise tired, saying, "Violent and pumped up with the adrenalin of fear, the novel all too often seems a glib if flashy reworking of familiar dystopian themes." However, *Fantasy Review* critic Patricia Altner claims that "Longyear writes convincingly" and notes that the novel "is a book readers will find hard to put down."

Several more novels have followed *Sea of Glass,* including the young adult work *The Homecoming,* in which intelligent space-faring dinosaurs return to Earth, and two media tie-ins set in the world of the television series *Alien Nation.* Perhaps most noteworthy is *The God Box,* Longyear's first fantasy novel, which deals with a rug dealer who inherits a magical box of many drawers that can provide its owner with whatever he or she *needs*—not *wants*—at any given moment. Roland Green of *Booklist* observes: "Longyear tells this essentially episodic tale with imagination, deftness, a sound narrative technique, and a desirable light touch." A *Science Fiction Chronicle* reviewer ranks "Longyear's first fantasy . . . [as] every bit as good as his first rate SF."

While critics often suggest that although Longyear has continued to produce quality work, according to D'Ammassa, his fiction as a whole has not yet fulfilled the promise of his celebrated debut. D'Ammassa notes that few of his later short pieces—he singles out "Bloodsong" and "Portrait of Baron Negay" as exceptions—achieve "the enthusiasm and sheer gripping intensity" of his early stories.

Longyear once commented: "*Manifest Destiny* tells the story of Earth's early contacts and relations with alien cultures, and the movement to get the United States of Earth Planets to join the Ninth Quadrant Federation of Habitable Planets. *The Tomorrow Testament* is set against the tense backdrop of delicate treaty negotiations between the United States of Earth Planets and the Dracon Chamber, when a translation of the hermaphroditic Drac's *Talman,* the alien's nontheistic bible, is widely spread among human-populated planets. Reactions vary from the formation of fanatical cults to religious outrage. The negotiations are to be held in a station orbiting a planet half populated by humans and half by Dracs—the original point of issue that brought about the recent war.

Longyear's book is a compilation of his entire "Enemy" series, including the Hugo and Nebula award-winning **Enemy Mine.** *(Cover illustration by Matt Manley.)*

"*City of Baraboo* tells the story of John J. O'Hara and his efforts to preserve the institution of the canvas show. Toward this end he takes his moth-eaten circus show to an alien planet, then to other worlds on his circus starship, 'City of Baraboo,' against an enemy who grows more determined with each success O'Hara has. Momus is a planet inhabited by the descendants of O'Hara's Greater Shows some two hundred years before the story in *Circus World* takes place. In the intervening time, Momus has become strategically significant in a power struggle between two powerful forces in the galaxy. This forms the setting for Lord Ashly Allenby's efforts to inform the people of Momus, and then to protect and defend them against both forces. *Elephant Song* is an epic tracing the generations of bullhands (elephant handlers) who took to the star road with O'Hara's Greater Shows. The "Circus World" series begins on Earth, when O'Hara's show was little more than a carnival, and follows the success of the show until it is marooned on the planet Momus. *Elephant Song* continues the story, showing the development of Moman society, with *Circus World* reaching the tensions and eventual war with the Tenth Quadrant, concluding with the new mission of the Moman starshow: to get elephants."

Works Cited

Altner, Patricia, review of *Sea of Glass, Fantasy Review,* May, 1987, p. 45.

D'Ammassa, Don, "Barry B. Longyear," *St. James Guide to Science Fiction Writers,* 4th edition, St. James, 1996.

Review of *The God Box, Science Fiction Chronicle,* April, 1989, p. 38.

Green, Roland, review of *The God Box, Booklist,* April 15, 1989, p. 1435.

Review of *Sea of Glass, Publishers Weekly,* September 5, 1986, p. 92.

For More Information See

PERIODICALS

Booklist, December 15, 1984, p. 560; October 1, 1986, p. 192.

Detroit News, January 18, 1981.

Fantasy Review, February, 1986, p. 23; March, 1987, p. 45.

Publishers Weekly, October 12, 1984.

Science Fiction Chronicle, November, 1989, p. 41.

*   *   *

LORRIMER, Claire
See CLARK, Patricia Denise

LOWNDES, Robert A(ugustine) W(ard) 1916-1998
(Carol Grey, Carl Groener, Mallory Kent, Wilfred Owen Morley, Richard Morrison, Robert Morrison, Michael Sherman, Peter Michael Sherman; Arthur Cooke, S. D. Gottesman, Paul Dennis Lavond, John MacDougal, Lawrence Woods, joint pseudonyms)

Personal

Born September 4, 1916, in Bridgeport, CT; died July 14, 1998, in Newport, RI; son of Henry Irving (in electronics) and Fanny Raymond (Stevens) Lowndes; married Dorothy Barbara Sedor Rogalin, August 14, 1948 (divorced, 1974); children: Peter Michael Rogalin (stepson). *Education:* Attended Stamford Community College, 1936.

Career

Columbia Publications, New York City, editor, 1941-60; Health Knowledge, Inc., New York City, editor, 1960-70; *Sexology,* New York City, associate editor, 1971-77, managing editor, 1977-78; Radio-Electronics, Farmingdale, NY, in editorial production, 1978-89.

Awards, Honors

Guest of honor at Lunacon, 1969, and Boskone, 1973.

Writings

Mystery of the Third Mine (novel for children), Winston (Philadelphia, PA), 1953.

(With James Blish) *The Duplicated Man* (novel), Avalon (New York City), 1959.

(With Lloyd Biggle) *The Angry Espers,* Ace, 1961.

The Puzzle Planet (novel), Ace, 1961.

Believer's World (novel), Avalon, 1961.

Three Faces of Science Fiction (collected columns), NESFA Press (Boston, MA), 1973.

(Editor) *The Best of James Blish,* Ballantine, 1979.

(With Jeffrey M. Elliott) *Orchids for Doc: The Literary Adventures and Autobiography of Robert A. W. "Doc" Lowndes,* Borgo (San Bernardino, CA), 1993.

(With Mike Ashley) *The Gernsback Days: The Evolution of Modern Science Fiction from 1911 to 1936,* Borgo, 1995.

Columnist for *Famous Science Fiction.* Science fiction editor for Avalon Books, 1956-58, 1958-68. Contributor to magazines, including *Comet Stories, Outworlds,* and *Fantastic Novels,* often under pseudonyms Carol Grey, Carl Groener, Mallory Kent, Wilfred Owen Morley, Richard Morrison, Robert Morrison, Michael Sherman, and Peter Michael Sherman; joint pseudonyms include Arthur Cooke, S. D. Gottesman, Paul Dennis Lavond,

John MacDougal, and Lawrence Woods. Editor of *Future Science Fiction,* 1941-60, *Science Fiction Quarterly,* 1941-58, *Science Fiction,* 1943-60, *Dynamic Science Fiction,* 1952-54, *Exploring the Unknown, Science Fiction Stories, Original Science Stories, Magazine of Horror,* 1963-74, *Startling Mystery Stories,* 1966-71, *Famous Science Fiction,* 1967-79, *Weird Terror Tales,* 1969-70, and *Bizarre Fantasy Tales,* 1970-71; associate editor and producer of "Luz," 1971-78.

Sidelights

Although Robert A. W. Lowndes' contribution to genre fiction is generally viewed in terms of his considerable work as a science fiction editor and critic, Curtis C. Smith contended in the *St. James Guide to Science Fiction Writers* that Lowndes can also be viewed as a "fiction writer of considerable talent." Emphasizing that "economy, atmosphere," and "description" were "Lowndes' strongest points as a writer," Smith also made a significant distinction between the author's short stories and novels. Whereas Lowndes's stories fall into the horror genre, showing the direct influence of such writers as H. P. Lovecraft and Clark Ashton Smith, his novels are clearly science fiction, concerned with the "creation and description of alien worlds."

In the horrific premise of the short story "The Abyss," monsters from another dimension have invaded the Earth to mesmerize humans and consume the fluids from their bodies. Smith felt "The Abyss" "is as well done as anything in Lovecraft, and the economy of the story is beyond Lovecraft." In contrast, the novel *Believer's World* details the culture and lifestyle of a planet founded by exiles from Earth who have forgotten their origins and subsequently evolved a complex society where science and religion have become inextricably linked. According to Smith, the "Arabian Nights atmosphere" of the novel "creates a world that exemplifies Arthur C. Clarke's generalization that advanced technology is indistinguishable from magic." Lowndes's other novels also rely to a large extent on world-building and the convincing environments they create for the reader. The juvenile novel *Mystery of the Third Mine* depicts a future society set in the asteroid belt, a mining community in some ways reminiscent of California's 1848 gold rush. *The Puzzle Planet* posits a world where commonsense assumptions can no longer be taken for granted. "Once again," according to Smith, "Lowndes's descriptive powers are impressive."

Lowndes once commented, "I have been a science fiction fan since the 1930s. The appeal of science fiction to me in those days was what Sam Moskowitz and others have called the 'sense of wonder' relating to other worlds and possible technological progress and its effect upon the future, near or far.

"During most of my editorial career, science fiction meant science fiction magazines, though books had taken over in importance by 1971 when that part of my career ended. The changes I've seen are so many that it would take a book to deal with them adequately. I still enjoy a little contemporary science fiction—that little which bears some relationship to the kinds of stories I loved in the past. Nearly all of it, on the whole, is better written today but the distinction between science fiction and fantasy has blurred so thoroughly that I cannot tell from the label 'science fiction' on any book or magazine or story whether what I may read therein will bear any relationship at all to science fiction as I conceive it. (Speculative fiction is *not* science fiction to me.) I could depend on Robert A. Heinlein, for all the excursions into fantasy in some of his later books, and I can still depend on Isaac Asimov to satisfy me, and sometimes Frederik Pohl. I regard James Blish as one of the best science fiction authors of our time; among his other achievements, he was one of the pioneers in raising the literary level of science fiction above action-pulp standards.

"My novels arose from particular 'What if?' questions. There had been numerous 'duplicated man' stories before James Blish and I wrote *The Duplicated Man,* which, though published much later, was actually the first attempt at a novel-length story for each of us. My idea was: What if there were a duplication machine, operated by five different activators, or duplicators, that produced five duplicates of a person? But say that none of the five duplicates is exactly like the subject. Why? While all five duplicates are physically acceptable replicas, each one is based upon the individual duplicator's impressions of the subject. What the original sees when he emerges is five replicas of himself as the others—the duplicators—see him. All five have all of the original's memories, but only some of his attitudes, which are attributed to the replicas by the individual duplicators. I'd originally thought of the story as a short one, or a novelette; I needed someone more learned in science than I to handle the scientific aspects, and Jim Blish was fascinated by the underlying idea. The working title was *As Others See Us.* But when we got to the outline stage, we found that we had a novel on our hands—a highly complicated one.

"There have been many stories about Earth inhabitants who encounter distinctly superior alien civilizations; the Earth people must undergo tests to determine whether they are worthy of the aliens' acceptance. My novel *The Puzzle Planet* is both a 'test' story and a murder-mystery tale wherein the reader has a fair a chance to spot the solution as in a mainstream 'whodunit' that plays fair. The testing of the Earth people, however, is more carefully concealed, and the premise of the test is different from any I have ever read about: humor in the sense of being able to laugh at oneself.

"*Believer's World* is based upon a culture described at length in Oswald Spengler's *Decline of the West*—the Magian culture, a priestly caste or tribe of ancient Persia about which little is known. The Magi have been revered by classic authors as wise men, and they were reputed to have power over demons. Could such a culture arise on another world, hand in hand with high-class technology? While I consider it highly improbable, I do believe that such a society is not impossible. *Believer's World* is a light satire that takes off on, among other things, the time-worn story of the lone (or nearly) Earth man who completely masters an alien society and becomes its king."

Works Cited

Smith, Curtis C., "Robert A. W. Lowndes," *St. James Guide to Science Fiction Writers,* 4th edition, St. James Press, 1996.

For More Information See

BOOKS

Ashley, Mike, *The Work of Robert A. W. Lowndes: An Annotated Bibliography and Guide,* edited by Boden Clarke, Borgo, 1996.

Lowndes, Robert A. W., and Jeffrey M. Elliott, *Orchids for Doc: The Literary Adventures and Autobiography of Robert A. W. "Doc" Lowndes,* Borgo, 1993.

Lowndes, Robert A. W., and Mike Ashley, *The Gernsback Days: The Evolution of Modern Science Fiction from 1911 to 1936,* Borgo, 1995.

Obituaries

PERIODICALS

Locus, August, 1998; September, 1998.*

M

MacDOUGAL, John
   See LOWNDES, Robert A(ugustine) W(ard)

*   *   *

MAYER, Danuta 1958-

Personal

Born April 12, 1958, in London, England; daughter of Jerzy and Hanna (Szamota) Mayer; companion of Robert Cogswell (an actor). *Education:* Attended Central School of Art and Design, 1976-77, and Camberwell School of Arts and Crafts, 1977-80. *Hobbies and other interests:* Books, writing, working with animals.

Addresses

Home—51 Sunnyhill Rd., London SW16 2UG, England.

Career

Book illustrator. Also works in design and advertising. *Member:* Association of Illustrators.

Writings

ILLUSTRATOR; FOR CHILDREN

Rudyard Kipling, *Rikki Tikki Tavi,* Candlewick Press (Cambridge, MA), 1997.
Mary Joslin, *Do the Angels Watch Close By?,* Lion Publishing, 1997, Loyola Press (Chicago, IL), 1998.
Fiona Waters, *The Brave Sister,* Bloomsbury Children's Press (London, England), 1998.
Patrick Ardagh, *Ancient Egyptian Myths and Legends,* Dillon Press (New York City), 1999.

Work represented in anthologies published by Koala, Kingfisher, and Element. Creator of book covers.

Danuta Mayer

ILLUSTRATOR; FOR ADULTS

Caitlin Matthews, *The Celtic Book of the Dead,* Eddison Sadd, 1992.
Your Natural Dog, Eddison Sadd, 1992.
Your Natural Cat, Eddison Sadd, 1992.

Derek and Julia Parker, *The Sun and Moon Signs,* twelve volumes, Dorling Kindersley, 1992.

Kwok Man Ho, *Chinese Horoscope Library,* twelve volumes, Dorling Kindersley, 1994.

Also illustrator of *Dress Sense: Medieval,* 2000, and *Dress Sense: Modern,* 2000.

Work in Progress

A series of illustrated short stories for children.

Sidelights

Danuta Mayer told *SATA:* "I was born of Polish parents who moved to England after the war. From an early age, I usually had a crayon in hand, scribbling, and recollect that, even as an infant, I wanted to emulate the artists I admired and become an illustrator. I was encouraged by my family, and on leaving school, I went on to study art. I took a foundation course at what was then known as the Central School of Art and Design in London and a degree in illustration at Camberwell School of Arts and Crafts. My personal tutor there was fine artist Eileen Hogan, who was immensely influential and became a close personal friend. During this period and for some time afterward, I traveled widely around Europe with my sister, photographer Barbara Baran, drawing and painting at every available opportunity. I exhibited and sold the results of some of this work in a couple of joint exhibitions at Central London galleries.

"For a number of years following this, I abandoned painting to do voluntary work within the animal rights movement, campaigning to secure better rights for animals and rescuing homeless, ill-treated, or sick animals. This in its turn revived my interest in painting as a means of communicating, giving me motivation and a reason to illustrate—to raise money for my animal work and to use the medium eventually to speak of the uniqueness of animals. It was also at this time that I met my partner, Robert Cogswell, with whom I've now lived for thirteen years. We are both vegans, and we now run a refuge for disabled/unwanted animals; the household is chaotic and visitors must be prepared to be leaped on or squawked at by a variety of dogs, birds, and other creatures.

"I was encouraged in my return to the creative path by my family and also through my association with the illustrator Pauline Baynes, who has often been a voice of reason when one was lacking in my own mind. We struck up a postal friendship many years ago when my sister and I were looking for a copy of one of her books. The growing friendship with her, which continues to this day, gave me focus and direction, and I regarded it as one of the most influential to me at this time.

"Artists of the twentieth century inspired me when I was younger; nowadays I often look to and admire artists throughout a much broader spectrum, and my influences and taste could be said to be eclectic and diverse, and far too involved to give a comprehensive list. More

Mayer's rich illustrations depict angels singing, rejoicing, comforting, and helping humans in the Scripture-based **Do the Angels Watch Close By?,** *written by Mary Joslin.*

specifically since this is the field in which most of my work is now commissioned, I take an active interest in illustration and illustrators, studying and handling illustrated books, especially early editions, and I enjoy scouring auctions and secondhand bookshops for 'finds.' These finds make up part of a growing reference library which helps me to establish a visual integrity in a piece of work which requires historical accuracy. Apart from anything else, I just love books and am a voracious reader between jobs; I should say that witchcraft, magic, and the esoteric are strong personal interests and have been the subject of several commissioned works.

"Illustration is becoming an increasingly pressurized and competitive profession. There are so many gifted illustrators about, all of them trying to keep up with the ever-changing demands upon them to compete with technology and forcing them to look at new ways of exploring their creative potential, to diversify. It's difficult to know what place the illustrator will have in the new technological age; it is certain that our future has never been less certain, but uncertainty and struggle have always been obstacles for artists and we should take courage and inspiration from those who preceded us."

*   *   *

McALLISTER, Margaret 1956-

Personal

Born August 2, 1956, in Tynemouth, England; daughter of Douglas Hay (a research engineer) and Shiela Elizabeth (Turner) McAllister; married Tony Buglass (a

Margaret McAllister

Methodist minister), August 12, 1978; children: Elinor, Adam, Iain. *Education:* Newcastle Polytechnic, degree in education and English. *Politics:* "Center." *Religion:* Christian. *Hobbies and other interests:* Theater, dance, history.

Addresses

Home—Pickering, England.

Career

Buddle Arts Centre, Wallsend, England, teacher of dance and drama. Also works as teacher of creative writing.

Writings

A Friend for Rachel, Oxford University Press (Oxford, England), 1997.
Hold My Hand and Run, Oxford University Press, 1999, Dutton, 2000.
Never Wash Your Hair, illustrated by Tim Archbold, Oxford University Press, 1999.
Ghost at the Window, Oxford University Press, 2000.
The Worst of the Vikings, Oxford University Press, 2000.

The Mean Dream Wonder Machine, Oxford University Press, 2000.
The Doughnut Dilemma, Oxford University Press, 2000.

Work in Progress

Children's novels for Oxford University Press, including books for reluctant readers.

Sidelights

Margaret McAllister commented: "Why am I writer? You may as well ask why I'm not a brain surgeon. Writing is the only thing I'm any good at (apart from baking scones and having babies, which aren't really ways to make a living). I've always made up stories, since before I was old enough to write them down. Aspiring writers sometimes feel discouraged because they think you have to be brainy to succeed. I'm not! I just like words and stories.

"I suppose I write about the things that make an impression on me—ancient churches with their candlelit festivals, and the history of the north of England, for example. Writing is a way of immersing myself in these things and inviting the reader in, too.

"For me, the mark of a really good children's book is that you can enjoy it at any age. If you can fall in love with a book as a child, and come back to it as an adult without feeling patronized or uneasy, it has strength. I could go on reading C. S. Lewis and Lucy Boston forever."

For More Information See

PERIODICALS

Books for Keeps, May, 1997, p. 24; July, 1999.
School Librarian, August, 1997, p. 158.

*   *   *

McCOURT, Lisa 1964-
(Lisa M. Combs)

Personal

Born September 2, 1964, in Florida; daughter of Michael (a post office employee) and Bettye (an antiques shop owner; maiden name, Hogan) McCourt; married Gregory Combs (a C.O.O. for real estate developer), April 21, 1996; children: Tucker McCourt Combs. *Education:* Drew University, B.A., 1986.

Addresses

E-mail—lisa@lisamccourt.com.

Career

Children's book author; creative director/owner of Boingo Books, Inc. (book packaging company), 1995—.

Lisa McCourt

Awards, Honors

Finalist, Literary Marketplace Award, children's editorial category, 1996; Honor Title, IRA Storytelling World Award, 1998, for *The Never-Forgotten Doll;* National Parenting Publications Honors Award, 1998, for *I Love You, Stinky Face.*

Writings

PICTURE BOOKS

I Love You, Stinky Face, illustrated by Cyd Moore, Troll (Mahwah, NJ), 1997.

The Rain Forest Counts!, illustrated by Cheryl Nathan, Troll, 1997.

Raptors!, Troll, 1997.

(Adaptor) *Chicken Soup for Little Souls: The Best Night Out with Dad,* illustrated by Bert Dodson, Health Communications (Deerfield Beach, FL), 1997.

(Adaptor) *Chicken Soup for Little Souls: The Never-Forgotten Doll,* illustrated by Mary O'Keefe Young, Health Communications, 1997.

(Adaptor) *Chicken Soup for Little Souls: The Goodness Gorillas,* illustrated by Pat Porter, Health Communications, 1997.

Chicken Soup for the Soul Family Storybook Collection (includes *The Goodness Gorillas, The Best Night Out with Dad,* and *The Never-Forgotten Doll*), illustrated by Pat Porter, Bert Dodson, and Mary O'Keefe Young, Health Communications, 1997.

Chicken Soup for Little Souls: The Braids Girl, illustrated by Tim Ladwig, Health Communications, 1998.

Chicken Soup for Little Souls: A Dog of My Own, illustrated by Katya Krenina, Health Communications, 1998.

(Adaptor) *Chicken Soup for Little Souls: The New Kid and the Cookie Thief,* illustrated by Mary O'Keefe Young, Health Communications, 1998.

(With Cheryl Nathan) *The Long and Short of It,* illustrated by Cheryl Nathan, Troll, 1998.

Deadly Snakes, illustrated by Allan Eitzen, Troll, 1998.

I Miss You, Stinky Face, illustrated by Cyd Moore, Bridgewater Books, 1999.

Candy Counting: Delicious Ways to Add and Subtract, illustrated by Brad Tuckman, Troll, 1999.

(Adaptor) *Chicken Soup for Little Souls: Della Splatnuk, Birthday Girl,* illustrated by Pat Grant Porter, Health Communications, 1999.

Love You Until . . ., illustrated by William Haines, Paulist Press (New York), 1999.

(Under name Lisa M. Combs) *Rocket to the Moon: The Story of the First Lunar Landing,* illustrated by Robert F. Goetzl, Bridgewater Books, 1999.

(Under name Lisa M. Combs) *Construction Buddies #1: Dozer to the Rescue!,* Troll, 1999.

(With Aimee McCourt) *Attitude: Tips to Help You Deal, Feel, and Be Real,* Lowell House (Los Angeles, CA), 2000.

Time for School, Stinky Face, illustrated by Cyd Moore, Bridgewater/Troll, 2000.

(Under name Lisa M. Combs) *Construction Buddies #2: Dozer's Wild Adventure,* illustrated by Karl Gude, Troll, 2000.

Weird in the Wild: Wet 'n' Weird, illustrated by Cheryl Nathan, Lowell House/NTC Contemporary, 2000.

Weird in the Wild: Hairy 'n' Weird, illustrated by Cheryl Nathan, Lowell House/NTC Contemporary, 2000.

(With Lisa M. Bernstein) *Brain Builders: What's Inside My Body?,* illustrated by Pat Grant Porter, Lowell House / NTC Contemporary, 2000.

(With Lisa M. Bernstein) *Brain Builders: Mysterious Space,* illustrated by Cheryl Nathan, Lowell House/ NTC Contemporary, 2000.

OTHER

101 Ways to Raise a Happy Baby, Lowell House, 1999.

Work in Progress

Goodnight, Princess Pruney-Toes, for Troll; *101 Ways to Raise a Happy Toddler* for adults; young adult book *The Seven Secrets of Happy, Confident Girls.*

Sidelights

Lisa McCourt told *SATA,* "When I was in third grade, I heard about a contest for kids. You had to create a bumper sticker with a message about saving the planet. I was thrilled at the idea of writing something that people would stick on their cars! I drew a rabbit, a bird, and a squirrel, and wrote, 'We're not the only ones who live here. Don't ruin their world.' Believe it or not, the other entries must have been worse. It was the first time my writing ever won an award—and the last time my drawing ever won anything.

"I was the oldest kid in my family, so I spent a lot of time babysitting my brother, Michael, and my sister, Aimee. The first stories I ever wrote were for my brother. I made up a bunch of silly characters that lived inside the human body. (I've always thought that body stuff was so cool!) Eye One and Eye Two sat at control stations like pilots in tiny cockpits looking out through the windshield-like eyes. Miss Sneeze lived in the big toe. That's why it took her so long to run all the way up to the mouth once a person felt like he was going to sneeze.

"When I was in fifth grade, my teacher handed out the Arrow Book Club *Student News* and I found a book that changed my life. It was called the *Anything Book* and it was just a bunch of blank pages. The *Student News* said it was the perfect place to write down secret thoughts and ideas, and I had a lot of those! I ordered the *Anything Book,* but couldn't wait the two weeks for it to come. I was so excited to start writing that I wrote stuff down on scraps of paper, then copied it all into the book

Ben rescues an abused dog and uses love and patience to earn his confidence. (Cover illustration by Katya Krenina.)

when my order finally arrived. Ever since then I've been emptying my head on paper. (You should see my closet—it's full of old journals!)

"In seventh grade, I wrote a lot of stories about boys and girls falling in love. I was totally boy-crazy by then. One was called 'The Last Desk in the Fourth Row' and it was about a boy and girl who found out they liked each other by writing notes and leaving them in a desk that they both sat in during different classes. I tried leaving romantic notes in my own desks at school, but no boys ever answered them! Even when I was writing romantic stories, kids were still my favorite kind of people. Every job I've ever had has involved kids in some way. At twelve I became a camp counselor-in-training, and I loved it so much I kept working for camps until I finished college.

"In high school, English classes were always my favorite. I loved reading anything, and I even looked forward to writing reports. In my senior year I co-edited the yearbook and took three different English classes. In college, I knew from the first day that I would major in English and minor in writing. My favorite professor at Drew University was my writing teacher, Professor Berke. She made us edit one another's writing in class. It was kind of embarrassing, but it really let me see how important the editing process is. I would write every paper over and over again until I got it just right.

"My first job out of college was for a company I bet you know—Troll Communications. The original owners of Troll taught me all about what makes an awesome kids' book. I was so young when I started that they were kind of like on-the-job parents to me, and I'm forever grateful to them.

"I worked for children's book publishers for ten years before I started my own book packaging company, Boingo Books. Being a packager means publishing companies hire me to create each book as a whole package—including not just the story but the art, the design, the cover, the kind of type, and where the words go on each page."

To aspiring writers, McCourt had these words: "Go get your journal, a notebook, a napkin, or the back of last week's homework—and start writing!"

In a few short years, Lisa McCourt has published more than a dozen books for children, ranging from the moralistic "Chicken Soup for Little Souls" series to the exuberant antics of *I Love You, Stinky Face* and its sequels. McCourt has adapted a number of stories based on incidents related in the adult self-help book, *Chicken Soup for the Soul* for the picture-book audience. In *The Best Night Out with Dad* a little boy gives up his tickets to the circus when he realizes that a poor boy and his father can't afford to buy tickets for themselves. In *The Goodness Gorillas* a class dedicates itself to performing good deeds, even to the extent of reaching out to the class bully when his dog is killed. In *The Never-Forgotten Doll* Ellie buys her favorite babysitter an

A mother reassures her son that she would love him—no matter what—in McCourt's **I Love You, Stinky Face.** *(Illustrated by Cyd Moore.)*

antique doll to replace the one the elderly woman lost as a child.

In *The New Kid and the Cookie Thief* a shy little girl starts at a new school and mistakenly believes that the boy who sits next to her at the bus stop has stolen her cookies, and she makes her first new friend when she owns up to the mistake and apologizes. In *Della Splatnuk, Birthday Girl* Carrie's mother makes her go to the birthday party of weird classmate Della, but when no one else from their class shows up, the two girls and their mothers have a splendid time by themselves. In *The Braids Girl* Izzy and her grandfather befriend a poor girl at a homeless shelter where they volunteer, but when the girl reaches back in friendship, Izzy is unsure how to react until Grandpa Mike offers some gentle advice. In *A Dog of My Own* a little boy gives up his dream of adopting a new puppy in favor of rescuing a stray from a trip to the pound and coaxing the animal to tameness.

Critics were divided about the straightforward moral lessons embodied in each story, noting that some readers would likely find them unappealing for this reason, while parents and teachers might find them useful in talking to children about specific issues concerning the

treatment of others. In a review of three of the books in this series, for example, Nancy Menaldi-Scanlan wrote in *School Library Journal,* "Although they may prove to be a bit too sugarcoated for some, they are sure to provoke discussions about the need for kindness in our all-too-violent world."

Critics likened McCourt's *I Love You, Stinky Face* and its sequels to the popular book by Sam McBratney, *Guess How Much I Love You?* for its simple yet reassuring message of a common childhood fear. In *I Love You, Stinky Face* McCourt sets the scene in a child's bedroom as his mother tucks him in for the night and gently reassures him that even if he became a slimy green monster, a cyclops, or a stinky skunk, she would love him and care for him without question. "McCourt's sweet yet effective game sends a soothing message," observed a reviewer for *Publishers Weekly.* Reviewers noted that Cyd Moore's green and purple illustrations playfully exaggerate the child's fearful imaginings, while McCourt's text offers the "absolute" reassurance: "nothing could ever make me stop loving you," as Hazel Rochman put it in *Booklist.*

In McCourt's **I Miss You, Stinky Face,** *Mother is away but promises to return to her son even if by camel, hot-air balloon, or shark. (Illustrated by Cyd Moore.)*

In *I Miss You, Stinky Face* McCourt plays out a similar scenario based on a common childhood fear. In this story, the little boy and his mother are talking on the phone and for each time the little boy expresses a fear his mother won't be able to get home to him, she replies with an equally fantastic solution to the problem. *School Library Journal* reviewer Linda Ludke remarked on the similarity between *I Miss You, Stinky Face* and the question-and-answer format of the classic tale of the *Runaway Bunny,* both of which feature a mother going to extremes in a wide variety of locales in order to get to her child. "Although the formula is familiar, the message is reassuring," Ludke remarked. And Hazel Rochman, reviewing McCourt's sequel for *Booklist,* concluded, "Kids will welcome the reassurance as they laugh at the wild exaggeration and recognize their fears."

McCourt is also the author of *The Rainforest Counts!,* a counting book that uses the exotic plants and animals of the tropical rainforest to count from one to ten. The author's text rhymes, and the book concludes with factual information about the flora and fauna seen in the illustrations. This is "a book that can be enjoyed on several levels," contended Kathy Piehl in *School Library Journal.*

Works Cited

Review of *I Love You, Stinky Face, Publishers Weekly,* August 25, 1997, p. 70.

Ludke, Linda, review of *I Miss You, Stinky Face, School Library Journal,* May, 1999, pp. 92-93.

Menaldi-Scanlan, Nancy, review of *The Best Night Out with Dad, The Goodness Gorillas,* and *The Never-Forgotten Doll, School Library Journal,* January, 1998, p. 80.

Piehl, Kathy, review of *The Rain Forest Counts!, School Library Journal,* November, 1997, pp. 91-92.

Rochman, Hazel, review of *I Love You, Stinky Face, Booklist,* October 15, 1997, p. 403.

Rochman, Hazel, review of *I Miss You, Stinky Face, Booklist,* April 15, 1999, p. 1536.

For More Information See

PERIODICALS

Booklist, December 15, 1997, p. 704; February 1, 1999, p. 981; May 1, 1999, p. 1600.

School Library Journal, August, 1998, p. 143; December, 1998, p. 86.

McFARLANE, Todd 1961-

Personal

Born March 16, 1961, in Calgary, Alberta, Canada; son of a printer and a homemaker; married July 27, 1985; wife's name, Wanda (a business executive); children: two daughters and a son. *Education:* Eastern Washington State University, B.A. (general studies), 1984.

Addresses

Office—Todd McFarlane Productions, Inc., 40 W. Baseline Rd., Ste. E-105, Tempe, AZ 85283.

Career

Comic artist for Marvel and DC, 1984-92, drew titles such as *Scorpio Rose, The Incredible Hulk, Batman, Detective, Batman: Year Two, Invasion, Amazing Spider-Man,* and *Spider-Man;* co-founder of Image Comics, 1992; founder of McFarlane Toys, 1994; founder of Todd McFarlane Productions, Todd McFarlane Entertainment, and McFarlane Design Group; executive producer of *Todd McFarlane's Spawn,* HBO, 1998—; co-produced and directed animated video for Pearl Jam's "Do the Evolution," 1998, and co-directed video for Korn's "Freak on a Leash."

Awards, Honors

Globally, McFarlane has won more than 120 prestigious awards as either producer, director, writer, designer, toy manufacturer or comic book creator, including one of Ernst and Young's 1998 Entrepreneur of the Year Awards. Emmy Award for Outstanding Animated Program, Academy of Television Arts and Sciences, 1999, for *Todd McFarlane's Spawn,* HBO; Grammy Award nomination, Best Short Form music video, 1999, for Pearl Jam's "Do the Evolution"; Grammy Award, Best Short Form music video, 2000, for Korn's "Freak on a Leash."

Writings

(Illustrator) David Michelinie, *Stan Lee Presents Spider-Man Vs. Venom,* Marvel, 1990.
(With others) *Batman: Year Two,* Warner Books, 1990.
Stan Lee Presents Spider-Man: Torment, Marvel, 1992.
(With Rob Liefeld and Fabian Nicieza) *Stan Lee Presents X-Force and Spider-Man in Sabotage,* Marvel, 1992.

Todd McFarlane

(Illustrator with Sal Buscema) Gerry Conway and David Michelinie, *Spider-Man: The Cosmic Adventures,* Marvel, 1993.

(With Steve Ditko, John Romita, and Mark Bernardo) *Spider-Man Unmasked,* Marvel, 1997.

(And illustrator) *Spawn Book 1: Beginnings,* Image Comics, 1995.

(And illustrator) *Spawn Book 2: Dark Discoveries,* Image Comics, 1996.

(And illustrator) *Spawn Book 3,* Image Comics, 1996.

(And illustrator) *Spawn Book 4,* co-illustrated by Greg Capullo, Image Comics, 1997.

(And illustrator) *Spawn Book 5: Death and Rebirth,* co-illustrated by Marc Silvestri, Image Comics, 1998.

(And illustrator) *Spawn Book 6: Pathway to Judgement,* co-illustrated by Greg Capullo, Image Comics, 1998.

(And illustrator) *Spawn Book 7: Deadman's Touch,* co-illustrated by Greg Capullo, Image Comics, 1998.

(With Frank Miller) *Spawn-Batman,* Image Comics, 1998.

(Editor) Brian Holguin, *Todd McFarlane Presents: Kiss Psycho Circus,* illustrated by Angel Medina and Kevin Conrad, Image Comics, 1998.

(And illustrator) *Spawn Book 8: Betrayal of Blood,* co-illustrated by Alan Moore and Julia Simmons, Image Comics, 1999.

Spawn Book 9: Urban Jungle, illustrated by Greg Capullo and Tony Daniel, Image Comics, 1999.

Spawn Book 10: Vengeance of the Dead, illustrated by Greg Capullo and Tony Daniel, Image Comics, 2000.

(And illustrator) *Spawn Book 11: Crossroads,* co-illustrated by Greg Capullo and Tony Daniel, Image Comics, 2000.

Also contributor of cover art for the Korn album *Follow the Leader,* Sony/Columbia, 1998.

Sidelights

Comic fans feel fortunate that Todd McFarlane's dreams of playing professional sports never came to fruition. Instead, the Canadian-born baseball nut began drawing comics, first penciling for Marvel and DC, then injecting the long-running and popular *Amazing Spider-Man* series with some new blood by stylizing the artwork and adding a new villain to the tale. Thanks to some indignation at the way comic artists were treated in the business, he soon ventured out to form his own company and decided right away to showcase an original character he had devised as a college student. Thus, *Spawn* was born. McFarlane's creation was a runaway success, becoming the top-selling comic in the United States and in several European countries and leading to animated television episodes, a live-action film, and a line of hot-selling action figures. The comic's popularity entrenched McFarlane's fledgling firm, Image Comics, as one of the top three in the industry. And in early 1999, even those not fond of comics caught news of McFarlane with his eye-popping $3 million purchase of Mark McGwire's record-setting baseball that marked his seventieth home run during the 1998 season.

McFarlane was born on March 16, 1961, in Calgary, Alberta, Canada, but when he was a baby, his family

Spawn, a government assassin who makes a pact with the devil to return from the dead, is haunted by his memories in Spawn Book 5: Death and Rebirth.

moved to Southern California. His father was a printer, and his mother was a homemaker; they divorced when McFarlane was in college. Early on, he harbored a love of and talent for baseball and held dreams of turning professional. His family moved back to Calgary when he was fourteen, and McFarlane became an athlete at William Aberhart High School. However, he was also "the best doodler in the class," as he recalled in a *People* article. Although he never held an interest in comic books as a child, at age seventeen, McFarlane discovered the genre and eventually began collecting works and copying his favorites.

Remaining committed to his goal of playing baseball, McFarlane accepted an athletic scholarship in 1981 from Eastern Washington State University in Cheney, Washington, after attending community college. He studied art and printing in school and was sketching his own comic creations. Despite his talent, he did not pursue drawing as his livelihood until he broke his ankle sliding into home plate during a college game, dashing his hopes for a solid career on the baseball field. Subsequently, he began sending out drawings to almost all of the comic publishing companies in the United States and Canada, reaping more than 700 rejection letters.

In 1984, McFarlane graduated from college with a bachelor of arts in general studies with an emphasis in communications, fine arts, and graphic design. Shortly before graduation, after mailing his portfolio out for fourteen months, he finally received an offer from the comic giant Marvel to pencil a minor story called *Scorpio Rose,* which ran as an eleven-page back-up in the more well-known comic *Coyote.* McFarlane once remarked in a *People* article that his persistence apparently paid off. "Editors knew my package was coming in every month. After a while, they said, 'Just give him some work and shut him up.'"

Although the position at Marvel lasted only a short time, McFarlane went on to provide drawings for a number of issues of the popular series *The Incredible Hulk* in 1987. Soon he also began doing freelance penciling for DC's *Detective Comics* on titles like *Batman, Detective,* and *Batman: Year Two.* Later, when the two rival companies agreed to produce a book combining some of their top characters, called *Invasion,* they hired McFarlane to pencil such favorite characters as Superman, Wonder Woman, and the Green Lantern.

In 1989 McFarlane began drawing and providing covers for Marvel's longstanding *Amazing Spider-Man,* jazzing up the veteran title with a new look by replacing Spider-Man's web with a more rubbery-looking substance and enlarging his eyes to look more insect-like. The almost surreal appearance bowled over fans, boosting the book's sales ranking from number nine to number one and making McFarlane one of the hottest properties on the comic circuit. He then asked Marvel if he could also write the strip, and although they turned him down, they did offer the temperamental artist a companion title. The first issue of his creation, *Spider-Man,* was released in September 1990 and set a record for the best-selling comic book of all time, eventually surpassing 2.5 million copies.

Soon anything carrying McFarlane's name flew off the shelves, and he became the most recognized name in the comic artist field. Although he commanded nearly a $2 million annual salary, he did not own the rights to his work. McFarlane knew that artists had often been exploited by publishers, and in 1991 he conceived of a plan to start his own publishing firm where artists could retain the rights to their works. One day, in February 1992, McFarlane felt especially perturbed when he was ordered to re-do some panels that the Comics Code Authority had rejected, so he walked out. Leading six other prominent artists, McFarlane marched into the office of Marvel's president, Terry Stewart, and declared that they were all quitting. Unconcerned, Marvel executives wished them well and let them know they were welcome to return. "They thought we couldn't do the printing and that we were dumb," McFarlane noted in an article for *Success.* "I said, 'These guys are going to sit

back and do nothing because they think we'll be back in three months,' and that's what happened."

McFarlane and his new partners Erik Larsen, Jim Lee, Rob Liefeld, Whilce Portacio, Marc Silvestri, and Jim Valentino set up their own business, Image Comics, which allowed artists creative control over their characters and let them savor all the rewards of their success. McFarlane's first endeavor was *Spawn,* the concept for which had been occupying his imagination since high school. "Of all the characters I created," McFarlane told Joe Chidley in *Maclean's,* "Spawn was the guy. On some levels, his existence is pried from mine. He's got a bit of a bad attitude, and I'd say the same for me."

After the first issue of *Spawn* shipped in May 1992, it became the best-selling independent comic of all time, moving 1.7 million copies. *Spawn* would eventually be printed in twenty languages and sold in more than 120 nations. The macabre story centers on the character of Spawn. A grotesque and flawed protagonist, Spawn was formerly a top-notch government assassin named Al Simmons who is mysteriously killed and then makes a pact with the devil to regain life and return to see his beloved wife. She does not recognize the man she once knew as Al Simmons, however, and in fact has already remarried his best friend. Spawn also discovers that to fulfill his deal with Satan, he must again become a killer, ridding humankind of its criminal elements who then become part of Satan's army.

The artwork in *Spawn,* while appealing mainly to preteen and teenage males, is exceptionally grisly. Scenes depict still-beating hearts ripped from victims' chests, impalings with various blunt instruments, and a dismembered arm used as a writing utensil. However, the sophisticated themes and other intriguing elements added a fresh zest to the gory genre. For instance, the protagonist can definitely be recognized as an African American. "I got tired of Clark Kent and Superman and everyone all being good-looking white guys," noted McFarlane to David Wild in *Rolling Stone.*

Soon after the release of *Spawn,* McFarlane was swamped with offers from toy companies like Mattel, Hasbro, and Playmates seeking to license his characters. However, none were willing to give him creative control over the production, so he again forged his own business, McFarlane Toys, in 1994 to ensure that the quality of the goods met his standards. The large corporations scoffed at his plan, but he once again proved he was more than up to the task. The detailed, if somewhat disturbing, action figures sold millions of units, amassed several industry awards, and consistently ranked in the top ten in sales. McFarlane Toys soon became the fifth-largest action-figure maker in the United States.

Next came a short television run, with McFarlane serving as executive producer for six half-hour animated segments of *Todd McFarlane's Spawn* for the HBO network, which first aired the shows in May of 1997. Six more were shown in May of 1998, and another six in

May of 1999. The show won Emmy Awards in 1998 and 1999. All three seasons went to video/DVD. Seasons 1, 2, and 3 were HBO Home Video's top three selling products of all time. Other Spawn spin-offs include CD-ROM and video games, a board game, trading cards, and a number of other comic titles based on other *Spawn* characters. It was not long before Hollywood took note, fresh off the success of comics-turned-movies like *The Crow* and *The Mask.*

McFarlane agreed to work with New Line Cinema on a live-action version of *Spawn,* starring Michael Jai White as Spawn, Martin Sheen as Jason Wynn, and John Leguizamo as Clown (Satan). New Line allowed McFarlane to retain most of the merchandising rights, as well as have a hand in the creative side. The film debuted in 1997 with a respectable showing at the box office, reaping $50 million within a few weeks and eventually earning $100 million worldwide.

By mid-1997, McFarlane was worth an estimated $100 million. His long-term goal was to make his Spawn character as recognizable as Walt Disney's iconic Mickey Mouse. Branching out beyond *Spawn,* McFarlane was granted a license to produce action toys for the blockbuster 1998 summer movie *The X-Files* and later won the contract to produce figures for 1999's *Austin Powers: The Spy Who Shagged Me,* a sequel to the cult hit starring Mike Meyers. He also announced that he was creating a comic book and action figure based on veteran rocker Ozzy Osbourne, as well as a line of psychedelic Beatles figures to commemorate the twenty-fifth anniversary re-release of their film *Yellow Submarine.* In another realm, in 1998 he teamed with Pearl Jam lead singer Eddie Vedder to create an animated video for their song "Do the Evolution" from the *Yield* album. It collected more than forty international awards and was nominated for a 1999 Grammy. In 2000 McFarlane won a Grammy for his work on Korn's video "Freak on a Leash."

Although he was known as a superstar to the comic subculture—which is marked by its fervent fans—McFarlane was not as well known outside of his field. That changed when he announced that he was the purchaser of the baseball that Mark McGwire of the St. Louis Cardinals slammed for his record-setting seventieth home run in September 1998. He bought the ball for just over $3 million in an anonymous telephone bid in January 1999, and the following month went public with his identity. He added it to his growing collection of historic baseballs, which included other home run balls from McGwire and Sammy Sosa of the Chicago Cubs.

McFarlane married his college sweetheart, Wanda, on July 27, 1985, in Calgary. She has a degree from Eastern Washington State and taught high school biology before leaving that career to become an executive in her husband's business. They lived on Vancouver Island in British Columbia, and for a time in Portland, Oregon, then moved to an upper-middle class enclave of Phoenix, Arizona. McFarlane has two daughters and a son, all born in the 1990s. A self-described "sports geek," he

also is a part owner of the Edmonton Oilers hockey team and continues to play baseball in an amateur league in the Phoenix area.

Works Cited

Chidley, Joe, "Dawn of Spawn," *Maclean's,* August 11, 1997, p. 52.

Lipton, Michael A., "Spawn Meister: Todd McFarlane Draws a Superhero from beyond the Grave," *People,* August 18, 1997, p. 99.

"Renegades," *Success,* February, 1996, p. 32.

"Spidey's Man," *People,* May 6, 1991, p. 105.

Wild, David, "Satanic Majesty," *Rolling Stone,* June 12, 1997, p. 126.

For More Information See

PERIODICALS

Advertising Age, February 16, 1998, p. 41.
Arizona Republic, October 19, 1997, p. EV5.
Columbian, February 9, 1999.
Entertainment Weekly, February 21, 1997, p. 86; December 19, 1997, p. 81.
Newsweek, August 4, 1997, p. 68.
People, May 26, 1997, p. 16.
USA Today, February 9, 1999, p. 8C.
Washington Times, February 27, 1999, p. B4.

ON-LINE

Spawn Web site, located at http://www.spawn.com (April 1, 1999).

*　　*　　*

McKISSACK, Fredrick L(emuel) 1939-

Personal

Born August 12, 1939, in Nashville, TN; son of Lewis Winter (an architect) and Bessye (Fizer) McKissack; married Patricia Carwell (a writer), December 12, 1964; children: Fredrick Lemuel Jr., Robert and John (twins). *Education:* Tennessee Agricultural and Industrial State University (now Tennessee State University), B.S., 1964. *Politics:* Independent. *Religion:* African Methodist Episcopal. *Hobbies and other interests:* Collecting antique model ships, gardening, spending time with pet cat, Kit.

Addresses

Home—5900 Pershing Ave., St. Louis, MO 63112. *Office*—All-Writing Services, 225 South Meramec, #206, Clayton, MO 63115.

Career

Worked as a civil engineer for city and federal governments, 1964-74; owner of a general contracting company in St. Louis, MO, 1974-82; writer, 1982—; co-owner with wife, Patricia, of All-Writing Services. *Military service:* U.S. Marine Corps, 1957-60. *Member:* National

Writers Guild, Society of Children's Book Writers and Illustrators.

Awards, Honors

C. S. Lewis Silver Medal award, Christian Educators Association, 1985, for *Abram, Abram, Where Are We Going?;* Jane Addams Children's Book Award, Women's International League for Peace and Freedom, and Coretta Scott King Award, both 1990, both for *A Long Hard Journey: The Story of the Pullman Porter;* Woodson Outstanding Merit award, 1991, for *W. E. B. Dubois;* Coretta Scott King Award and *Boston Globe-Horn Book* Honor Book, both 1993, both for *Sojourner Truth: Ain't I a Woman?;* Hungry Mind Award, 1993, for *The World of 1492.*

Writings

FOR CHILDREN

Black Hoops: The History of African Americans in Basketball, Scholastic, 1999.

FOR CHILDREN; WITH WIFE, PATRICIA McKISSACK

Look What You've Done Now, Moses, illustrated by Joe Boddy, David Cook, 1984.

Abram, Abram, Where Are We Going?, illustrated by Joe Boddy, David Cook, 1984.

Cinderella, illustrated by Tom Dunnington, Children's Press, 1985.

Country Mouse and City Mouse, illustrated by Anne Sikorski, Children's Press, 1985.

The Little Red Hen, illustrated by Dennis Hockerman, Children's Press, 1985.

The Three Bears, illustrated by Virginia Bala, Children's Press, 1985.

The Ugly Little Duck, illustrated by Peggy Perry Anderson, Children's Press, 1986.

When Do You Talk to God? Prayers for Small Children, illustrated by Gary Gumble, Augsburg, 1986.

King Midas and His Gold, illustrated by Tom Dunnington, Children's Press, 1986.

Frederick Douglass: The Black Lion, Children's Press, 1987.

A Real Winner, illustrated by Quentin Thompson and Ken Jones, Milliken, 1987.

The King's New Clothes, illustrated by Gwen Connelly, Children's Press, 1987.

Tall Phil and Small Bill, illustrated by Kathy Mitter, Milliken, 1987.

Three Billy Goats Gruff, illustrated by Tom Dunnington, Children's Press, 1987.

My Bible ABC Book, illustrated by Reed Merrill, Augsburg, 1987.

The Civil Rights Movement in America from 1865 to the Present, Children's Press, 1987, second edition, 1991.

All Paths Lead to Bethlehem, illustrated by Kathryn E. Shoemaker, Augsburg, 1987.

Messy Bessey, illustrated by Richard Hackney, Children's Press, 1987.

The Big Bug Book of Counting, illustrated by Bartholomew, Milliken, 1987.

The Big Bug Book of Opposites, illustrated by Bartholomew, Milliken, 1987.

The Big Bug Book of Places to Go, illustrated by Bartholomew, Milliken, 1987.

The Big Bug Book of the Alphabet, illustrated by Bartholomew, Milliken, 1987.

The Big Bug Book of Things to Do, illustrated by Bartholomew, Milliken, 1987.

Bugs!, illustrated by Martin, Children's Press, 1988.

The Children's ABC Christmas, illustrated by Kathy Rogers, Augsburg, 1988.

Constance Stumbles, illustrated by Tom Dunnington, Children's Press, 1988.

Oh, Happy, Happy Day! A Child's Easter in Story, Song, and Prayer, illustrated by Elizabeth Swisher, Augsburg, 1989.

God Made Something Wonderful, illustrated by Ching, Augsburg, 1989.

Messy Bessey's Closet, illustrated by Richard Hackney, Children's Press, 1989.

James Weldon Johnson: "Lift Every Voice and Sing," Children's Press, 1990.

A Long Hard Journey: The Story of the Pullman Porter, Walker & Co., 1990.

Taking a Stand against Racism and Racial Discrimination, F. Watts, 1990.

W. E. B. DuBois, F. Watts, 1990.

The Story of Booker T. Washington, Children's Press, 1991.

Messy Bessey's Garden, illustrated by Martin, Children's Press, 1991.

From Heaven Above, Augsburg, 1992.

Sojourner Truth: Ain't I a Woman?, Scholastic, 1992.

God Makes All Things New, illustrated by Ching, Augsburg, 1993.

African-American Inventors, Millbrook Press, 1994.

African-American Scientists, Millbrook Press, 1994.

African Americans, illustrated by Michael McBride, Milliken, 1994.

Sports, Milliken, 1994.

Black Diamond: The Story of the Negro Baseball Leagues, Scholastic, 1994.

The Royal Kingdoms of Ghana, Mali, and Songhay: Life in Medieval Africa, Holt, 1994.

Christmas in the Big House, Christmas in the Quarters, illustrated by John Thompson, Scholastic, 1994.

Red-Tail Angels: The Story of the Tuskegee Airmen of World War II, Walker, 1995.

Rebels against Slavery: American Slave Revolts, Scholastic, 1996.

Let My People Go: Bible Stories of Faith, Hope, and Love, As Told by Price Jefferies, a Free Man of Color, to His Daughter, Charlotte, in Charleston, South Carolina, 1806-1816, illustrated by James Ransome, Atheneum, 1998.

Young, Black, and Determined: A Biography of Lorraine Hansberry, Holiday House, 1998.

Messy Bessey and the Birthday Overnight, illustrated by Dana Regan, Children's Press, 1998.

Messy Bessey's School Desk, illustrated by Dana Regan, Children's Press, 1998.

Black Hands, White Sails: The Story of African-American Whalers, Scholastic, 1999.

Fredrick L. McKissack with wife and writing partner, Patricia C. McKissack.

Messy Bessey's Holidays, illustrated by Dana Regan, Children's Press, 1999.

Messy Bessey's Family Reunion, illustrated by Dana Regan, Children's Press, 2000.

Miami Gets It Straight, illustrated by Michael Chesworth, Golden Books, 2000.

FOR CHILDREN; "GREAT AFRICAN AMERICANS" SERIES; WITH PATRICIA McKISSACK

Carter G. Woodson: The Father of Black History, illustrated by Ned Ostendorf, Enslow, 1991.

Frederick Douglass: Leader against Slavery, illustrated by Ned Ostendorf, Enslow, 1991.

George Washington Carver: The Peanut Scientist, illustrated by Ned Ostendorf, Enslow, 1991.

Ida B. Wells-Barnett: A Voice against Violence, illustrated by Ned Ostendorf, Enslow, 1991.

Louis Armstrong: Jazz Musician, illustrated by Ned Ostendorf, Enslow, 1991.

Marian Anderson: A Great Singer, illustrated by Ned Ostendorf, Enslow, 1991.

Martin Luther King, Jr.: Man of Peace, illustrated by Ned Ostendorf, Enslow, 1991.

Mary Church Terrell: Leader for Equality, illustrated by Ned Ostendorf, Enslow, 1991.

Mary McLeod Bethune: A Great Teacher, illustrated by Ned Ostendorf, Enslow, 1991.

Ralph J. Bunche: Peacemaker, illustrated by Ned Ostendorf, Enslow, 1991.

Jesse Owens: Olympic Star, illustrated by Michael David Biegel, Enslow, 1992.

Langston Hughes: Great American Poet, illustrated by Michael David Biegel, Enslow, 1992.

Zora Neale Hurston: Writer and Storyteller, illustrated by Michael Bryant, Enslow, 1992.

Satchel Paige: The Best Arm in Baseball, illustrated by Michael David Biegel, Enslow, 1992.

Sojourner Truth: Voice for Freedom, illustrated by Michael Bryant, Enslow, 1992.

Madam C. J. Walker: Self-Made Millionaire, illustrated by Michael Bryant, Enslow, 1992.

Paul Robeson: A Voice to Remember, illustrated by Michael David Biegel, Enslow, 1992.

Booker T. Washington: Leader and Educator, illustrated by Michael Bryant, Enslow, 1992.

OTHER

Also contributor, with Patricia McKissack, to *The World of 1492,* edited by Jean Fritz, Holt, 1992; author with P. McKissack of "Start Up" series for beginning readers, four volumes, Children's Press, 1985; editor with P.

McKissack of "Reading Well" series and "Big Bug Books" series, both for Milliken.

Sidelights

Fredrick L. McKissack is the author of over seventy books, primarily in collaboration with his wife, Patricia C. McKissack. The couple takes as their theme the history of African Americans and of race relations in the United States, often tracing the little-known byways of the past in labor relations, sports, politics, science, and the arts. In books such as the Enslow series "Great African Americans," and in stand-alone tiles such as *African-American Inventors* and *Rebels against Slavery,* McKissack and his wife paint a picture of men and women who have made a difference. In fiction titles such as *Christmas in the Big House, Christmas in the Quarters* and *Let My People Go,* the McKissacks deal in a more dramatic manner with the history of slavery. And in basic reading books, such as the "Messy Bessey" series, they provide relevant experiences with which young African American readers can identify.

McKissack was born on August 12, 1939, in Nashville, Tennessee, the son of an architect, Lewis Winter McKissack. After a stint in the Marines from 1957 to 1960, McKissack came back to Tennessee and graduated with a B.S. from Tennessee Agricultural and Industrial State University in 1964; he married his childhood friend and sweetheart, Patricia, that same year. These were turbulent times in the South, with the Civil Rights Movement transforming the segregationist culture. McKissack believed in the fight for changes and took part in sit-ins. "It was a time of violent change, it really was," McKissack once told *SATA.* "Life actually changed. In a sense we climbed from the Old South to the New South. We went from segregated schools to integrated situations."

McKissack worked as a civil engineer for city and federal governments from after his graduation until 1974, and from then until 1982 he had his own general contracting company in St. Louis, Missouri, where the family made its home. McKissack's wife began publishing books for children in 1978, and soon McKissack was collaborating with her on other titles. In 1982 he became a full-time writer and the operator of All-Writing Services in partnership with his wife. From the beginning, the McKissacks had a clear direction for their writing. The dearth of books on African American themes and topics was evident to Patricia McKissack, a junior high school English teacher who had to write her own book on the poet Paul Laurence Dunbar in order to share the man's work with her students. There were too few writers telling the stories of blacks in politics, the arts, the military—in all walks of life. "The reason we write for children," McKissack once said, "is to tell them about these things and to get them to internalize the information, to feel just a little of the hurt, the tremendous amount of hurt and sadness that racism and discrimination cause—for all people, regardless of race."

In the McKissacks' powerful collection, a former slave tells his daughter twelve Bible stories in answer to her questions about the injustices of her time. (Cover illustration by James E. Ransome.)

In a series of short books for the primary grades, McKissack and his wife detail the lives of "Great African Americans." Included in the series are biographies of strong women: *Madam C. J. Walker: Self-Made Millionaire* and *Zora Neale Hurston: Writer and Story-teller.* The feisty entrepreneur and trenchant author are profiled "in abbreviated form, which gives the basic facts of both women's lives," according to Ann Welton, writing in *School Library Journal.* Welton went on to note that "there are no other biographies of these notables for this age group." *Booklist*'s Hazel Rochman, reviewing three more titles in the series on Frederick Douglass, Louis Armstrong, and Mary McLeod Bethune, also commented on the lack of information on "these extraordinary people whose life stores will be of great interest to children." Each title in the series follows its subject from early childhood, through adversity, and on to adult achievements. Reviewing four more titles in the series on Langston Hughes, Jesse Owens, Satchel Paige, and Sojourner Truth, Susan Knorr noted in *School Library Journal* that these books "serve as accessible introductions to the highlights of the lives of the African-Americans."

McKissack and his wife have also produced such biographies for older readers. They employed material on Sojourner Truth to create a larger, more detailed picture of the freed slave who campaigned tirelessly for the cause of abolition and women's rights in *Sojourner Truth: Ain't I a Woman?* Born Isabella van Wagener, a slave, she was later freed and at age forty-six and felt the calling to "walk in the light of His truth"; thereafter she adopted the name of Sojourner Truth and fought for the rights of slaves and women. This tall woman (she was over six feet by some accounts) was able to popularize such ideas throughout the Midwest and New England despite the climate of the times. "With compassion and historical detail, the McKissacks offer a rich profile," remarked Gerry Larson in a *School Library Journal* review. "Middle grade readers and researchers will enjoy the readability, quotes, and documentary photos, all of which breathe life into the personality and times of Sojourner Truth." This biography won a Coretta Scott King Award, the second the husband-and-wife team garnered.

Other popular stand-alone titles include a history of medieval Africa, *The Royal Kingdoms of Ghana, Mali, and Songhay,* and American themes, *African-American Inventors* and *Rebels against Slavery: American Slave Revolts.* Reviewing the first title in *Bulletin of the Center for Children's Books,* Betsy Hearne called the book an "ambitious introductory survey" and "much needed to counter the persistent under-representation of African history in U.S. children's literature." Writing in *School Library Journal,* Susan Gifford commented that in *The Royal Kingdoms of Ghana, Mali, and Songhay* the

Bessey and her mother bake cookies for Christmas, Kwanzaa, and Hanukkah in this charming reader. (Cover illustration by Dana Regan.)

"authors have attempted something unique with their inclusions of indigenous and contemporaneous historical accounts . . . as well as in their substantial use of oral history."

With their *African-American Inventors,* the McKissacks created an "attractive, well-organized entry," according to *School Library Journal* critic Margaret M. Hagel. The book provides an overview of nineteenth- and twentieth-century inventors, some of whom were born slaves. Hagel concluded, "This title fills a real need; its readable text gives information not often found in books on inventions or on U.S. history." The husband-wife writing team turned their talents to slave revolts in *Rebels against Slavery,* in which they present "a fascinating cast," according to *Booklist*'s Ilene Cooper. Among those they profile are Toussaint-L'Ouverture, who led a slave revolt in Haiti, Gabriel Prosser in Virginia, and Nat Turner. Elizabeth Bush noted in *Bulletin of the Center for Children's Books* that "the tone is generally moderate; heroic legend and verifiable facts are carefully distinguished throughout the text."

McKissack has also turned his hand to a solo effort in nonfiction, 1999's *Black Hoops: The History of African Americans in Basketball.* This book was a follow-up to a joint effort with his wife on the Negro baseball leagues, 1994's *Black Diamond.* "Here he provides a concise but lively account of basketball from its earliest days to the present," according to *Booklist*'s Chris Sherman.

The McKissacks have also collaborated on fiction that explores race and black history. In *Christmas in the Big House, Christmas in the Quarters* they looked at one imaginary holiday in a Virginia Tidewater plantation in 1859. Two viewpoints were presented: that of the slaves in the quarters, and the slaveholders in the big house. Mary Harris Veeder wrote in the Chicago *Tribune Books,* "there is a careful attention to the way each group sees itself and its relationship to the other." *Horn Book* contributor Lois F. Anderson also commented on this attention to particulars: "Hardly a detail is missed in this vivid description of a traditional Christmas on a Virginia plantation." Anderson went on conclude, "Use of authentic language of the time helps the narrative flow, and carefully documented notes illuminate the interesting text."

Let My People Go: Bible Stories Told by a Freeman of Color to His Daughter is the fictional re-creation of Charlotte Jeffries Coleman, an abolitionist. Charlotte recalls the Bible stories her father told her when she was a child growing up in South Carolina in the early nineteenth century. Incidents from the death of one slave or the escape of another occasion a story from the father to illuminate the message of such events for the young girl. Janice M. Del Negro, writing in *Bulletin of the Center for Children's Books,* commented on the father's language which "rolls with a surprising, fierce splendor that embodies the solid faith he passes on to his daughter." Del Negro further noted, "This is an unusual combination of history, commentary, and Bible story that will lend itself to a wide variety of uses within

Kareem Abdul-Jabbar (formerly Lew Alcindor) showed that basketball players could achieve a good balance of academics and athletics. [AP/Wide World]

McKissack's thoroughly researched Black Hoops surveys the struggles, teams, and players involved in the history of African Americans in basketball.

curriculums and collections." Rochman concluded in another *Booklist* article, "With the rhythm and intimacy of the oral tradition, this is storytelling for family and group sharing and also for talking about history and our connections with the universals of the Old Testament." And a reviewer for *Publishers Weekly* called *Let My People Go* a "stunning achievement." This same reviewer further commented, "Readers will likely return to this extraordinary volume again and again, knowing that the answers to life's painful questions reside in the stories of faith that have comforted others for thousands of years."

Additionally, the McKissacks have developed several reading programs for beginning readers, including "Start Up," "Reading Well," "Big Bug Books," and the "Messy Bessey" books. In the last series, they follow the small adventures of a young African American girl who learns to tidy her room, garden, and her school desk, and who celebrates individual as well as national holidays, including Christmas, Hanukkah, and Kwanzaa. Reviewing *Messy Bessey's School Desk* in *School Library*

Journal, Sharon R. Pearce noted the reader "covers a familiar topic in a friendly way." In this story, Bessey decides to clean the useless things out of her school desk, and in doing so inspires the rest of the class to straighten up their desks. Finally, her leadership is not only recognized but also rewarded when she is elected class president. Pearce further commented that "readers see a strong African-American character who is recognized for her organizational and communication skills."

McKissack is a believer in the power of education and reaching students when they are young. That is why he and his wife concentrate their efforts toward younger readers. "You don't know who's going to be the puzzle part that you need," he once told *SATA*. "The solutions to all these problems are somewhere between kindergarten and Ph.D. I wonder who they are."

Works Cited

Anderson, Lois F., review of *Christmas in the Big House, Christmas in the Quarters, Horn Book,* January-February, 1995, p. 68.

Bush, Elizabeth, review of *Rebels against Slavery, Bulletin of the Center for Children's Books,* June, 1991, pp. 345-46.

Cooper, Ilene, review of *Rebels against Slavery, Booklist,* February 15, 1996.

Del Negro, Janice M., review of *Let My People Go, Bulletin of the Center for Children's Books,* December, 1998, p. 137.

Gifford, Susan, review of *The Royal Kingdoms of Ghana, Mali, and Songhay, School Library Journal,* June, 1994, pp. 140-41.

Hagel, Margaret M., review of *African-American Inventors, School Library Journal,* November, 1994, p. 115.

Hearne, Betsy, review of *The Royal Kingdoms of Ghana, Mali, and Songhay, Bulletin of the Center for Children's Books,* February, 1994, p. 194.

Knorr, Susan, review of *Langston Hughes: Great American Poet, School Library Journal,* January, 1993, pp. 116, 118.

Larson, Gerry, review of *Sojourner Truth: Ain't I a Woman?, School Library Journal,* February, 1993, p. 100.

Review of *Let My People Go, Publishers Weekly,* October 26, 1998, p. 62.

McKissack, Patricia C., and Fredrick McKissack, *Sojourner Truth: Ain't I a Woman?,* Scholastic, 1992.

Pearce, Sharon R., review of *Messy Bessey's School Desk, School Library Journal,* August, 1998, p. 144.

Rochman, Hazel, review of *Frederick Douglass: Leader against Slavery, Booklist,* January 1, 1992, p. 832.

Rochman, Hazel, review of *Let My People Go, Booklist,* October 1, 1998, p. 339.

Sherman, Chris, review of *Black Hoops, Booklist,* February 15, 1999, p. 1057.

Veeder, Mary Harris, review of "Up Pops Christmas," *Tribune Books* (Chicago), December 4, 1994, p. 9.

Welton, Ann, review of *Madam C. J. Walker: Self-Made Millionaire, School Library Journal,* December, 1992, p. 124.

For More Information See

PERIODICALS

Booklist, March 1, 1992, p. 1270; April 15, 1992, p. 1525; June 19, 1994; February 15, 1997, p. 1027; June 1, 1997, p. 1696; October 1, 1997, p. 329; February 15, 1998, p. 1696; February 15, 1999, p. 1068.

Bulletin of the Center for Children's Books, June, 1997, p. 367; February, 1998, p. 213.

Horn Book, May-June, 1997, p. 310.

Interracial Books for Children Bulletin, Number 8, 1985, p. 5.

Kirkus Reviews, December 15, 1991; February 15, 1998, p. 271.

Kliatt, May, 1999, p. 27.

New York Times Book Review, November 29, 1992, p. 34; June 21, 1998, p. 20.

Publishers Weekly, February 9, 1998, p. 98.

School Library Journal, September, 1994, pp. 251-52; September, 1997, p. 199.

Voice of Youth Advocates, August, 1998, p. 224.*

*   *   *

McKISSACK, Patricia C. 1944-
(L'Ann Carwell)

Personal

Born August 9, 1944, in Nashville, TN; daughter of Robert (a civil servant) and Erma (a civil servant) Carwell; married Fredrick L. McKissack (a writer), December 12, 1964; children: Fredrick Lemuel Jr., Robert and John (twins). *Education:* Tennessee Agricultural and Industrial State University (now Tennessee State University), B.A., 1964; Webster University, M.A., 1975. *Politics:* Independent. *Religion:* Methodist. *Hobbies and other interests:* Gardening.

Addresses

Home—5900 Pershing Ave., St. Louis, MO 63112. *Office*—All-Writing Services, 225 South Meramec, #206, Clayton, MO 63115.

Career

Junior high school English teacher in Kirkwood, MO, 1968-75; Forest Park College, St. Louis, MO, part-time instructor in English, 1975—. Children's book editor at Concordia Publishing House, 1976-81, and Institute of Children's Literature, 1984—; University of Missouri—St. Louis, instructor, 1978—; co-owner with Fredrick L. McKissack of All-Writing Services. Educational consultant on minority literature. *Member:* Society of Children's Book Writers and Illustrators.

Awards, Honors

Helen Keating Ott Award, National Church and Synagogue Librarians Association, 1980, for editorial work at Concordia Publishing House; C. S. Lewis Silver Medal awards, Christian Educators Association, 1984, for *It's the Truth, Christopher* and 1985, for *Abram, Abram, Where Are We Going?;* Caldecott Honor Award, 1989, for *Mirandy and Brother Wind;* Parents' Choice Award, 1989, for *Nettie Jo's Friends;* Jane Addams Children's Book Award, Women's International League for Peace and Freedom, and Coretta Scott King Award, both 1990, both for *A Long Hard Journey: The Story of the Pullman Porter;* Woodson Merit award, 1991, for *W. E. B. DuBois;* Hungry Mind Award, 1993, for *The World in 1492;* Newbery Honor Award and Coretta Scott King Author Award, both 1993, both for *The Dark-Thirty: Southern Tales of the Supernatural;* Coretta Scott King Honor Award and *Boston Globe-Horn Book* Award, both 1993, both for *Sojourner Truth: Ain't I a Woman?;* Image Award for Outstanding Literary Work for Children, National Association for the Advancement of Colored People, 1999, for *Let My People Go.*

Writings

FOR CHILDREN

(Under name L'Ann Carwell) *Good Shepherd Prayer,* Concordia, 1978.

(Under name L'Ann Carwell) *God Gives New Life,* Concordia, 1979.

Ask the Kids, Concordia, 1979.

Who Is Who?, Children's Press, 1983.

Martin Luther King, Jr.: A Man to Remember, Children's Press, 1984.

Paul Laurence Dunbar: A Poet to Remember, Children's Press, 1984.

Michael Jackson, Superstar, Children's Press, 1984.

Lights Out, Christopher, illustrated by Bartholomew, Augsburg, 1984.

It's the Truth, Christopher, illustrated by Bartholomew, Augsburg, 1984.

Patricia C. McKissack

The Apache, Children's Press, 1984.

Mary McLeod Bethune: A Great American Educator, Children's Press, 1985.

Aztec Indians, Children's Press, 1985.

The Inca, Children's Press, 1985.

The Maya, Children's Press, 1985.

Flossie and the Fox, illustrated by Rachel Isadora, Dial, 1986.

Our Martin Luther King Book, illustrated by Rachel Isadora, Child's World, 1986.

Who Is Coming?, illustrated by Clovis Martin, Children's Press, 1986.

Give It with Love, Christopher: Christopher Learns about Gifts and Giving, illustrated by Bartholomew, Augsburg, 1988.

Speak Up, Christopher: Christopher Learns the Difference between Right and Wrong, illustrated by Bartholomew, Augsburg, 1988.

A Troll in a Hole, Milliken, 1988.

Nettie Jo's Friends, illustrated by Scott Cook, Knopf, 1988.

Mirandy and Brother Wind, illustrated by Jerry Pinkney, Knopf, 1988.

Monkey-Monkey's Trick: Based on an African Folk-Tale, illustrated by Paul Meisel, Random House, 1989.

Jesse Jackson: A Biography, Scholastic, 1989.

(With Ruthilde Kronberg) *A Piece of the Wind and Other Stories to Tell,* Harper, 1990.

No Need for Alarm, Milliken, 1990.

A Million Fish—More or Less, illustrated by Dena Schutzer, Knopf, 1992.

The Dark-Thirty: Southern Tales of the Supernatural, illustrated by Brian Pinkney, Knopf, 1992.

History of Haiti, Holt, 1996.

(With Robert L. Duyff) *All Our Fruits and Vegetables,* Many Hands Media, 1996.

(With Robert L. Duyff) *It's a Sandwich!,* Many Hands Media, 1996.

A Picture of Freedom: The Diary of Clotee, a Slave Girl, Scholastic, 1997.

Ma Dear's Aprons, illustrated by Floyd Cooper, Atheneum, 1997.

Run Away Home, Scholastic, 1997.

Color Me Dark: The Diary of Nellie Lee Love, the Great Migration North, Scholastic, 2000.

Goin' Someplace Special, illustrated by Jerry Pinkney, Atheneum, 2000.

The Honest-to-God Truth, illustrated by Giselle Potter, Atheneum, 2000.

FOR CHILDREN; WITH HUSBAND, FREDRICK L. McKISSACK

Look What You've Done Now, Moses, illustrated by Joe Boddy, David Cook, 1984.

Abram, Abram, Where Are We Going?, illustrated by Joe Boddy, David Cook, 1984.

Cinderella, illustrated by Tom Dunnington, Children's Press, 1985.

Country Mouse and City Mouse, illustrated by Anne Sikorski, Children's Press, 1985.

The Little Red Hen, illustrated by Dennis Hockerman, Children's Press, 1985.

The Three Bears, illustrated by Virginia Bala, Children's Press, 1985.

The Ugly Little Duck, illustrated by Peggy Perry Anderson, Children's Press, 1986.

When Do You Talk to God? Prayers for Small Children, illustrated by Gary Gumble, Augsburg, 1986.

King Midas and His Gold, illustrated by Tom Dunnington, Children's Press, 1986.

Frederick Douglass: The Black Lion, Children's Press, 1987.

A Real Winner, illustrated by Quentin Thompson and Ken Jones, Milliken, 1987.

The King's New Clothes, illustrated by Gwen Connelly, Children's Press, 1987.

Tall Phil and Small Bill, illustrated by Kathy Mitter, Milliken, 1987.

Three Billy Goats Gruff, illustrated by Tom Dunnington, Children's Press, 1987.

My Bible ABC Book, illustrated by Reed Merrill, Augsburg, 1987.

The Civil Rights Movement in America from 1865 to the Present, Children's Press, 1987, second edition, 1991.

All Paths Lead to Bethlehem, illustrated by Kathryn E. Shoemaker, Augsburg, 1987.

Messy Bessey, illustrated by Richard Hackney, Children's Press, 1987.

The Big Bug Book of Counting, illustrated by Bartholomew, Milliken, 1987.

The Big Bug Book of Opposites, illustrated by Bartholomew, Milliken, 1987.

The Big Bug Book of Places to Go, illustrated by Bartholomew, Milliken, 1987.

The Big Bug Book of the Alphabet, illustrated by Bartholomew, Milliken, 1987.

The Big Bug Book of Things to Do, illustrated by Bartholomew, Milliken, 1987.

Bugs!, illustrated by Martin, Children's Press, 1988.

The Children's ABC Christmas, illustrated by Kathy Rogers, Augsburg, 1988.

Constance Stumbles, illustrated by Tom Dunnington, Children's Press, 1988.

Oh, Happy, Happy Day! A Child's Easter in Story, Song, and Prayer, illustrated by Elizabeth Swisher, Augsburg, 1989.

God Made Something Wonderful, illustrated by Ching, Augsburg, 1989.

Messy Bessey's Closet, illustrated by Richard Hackney, Children's Press, 1989.

James Weldon Johnson: "Lift Every Voice and Sing," Children's Press, 1990.

A Long Hard Journey: The Story of the Pullman Porter, Walker & Co., 1990.

Taking a Stand against Racism and Racial Discrimination, F. Watts, 1990.

W. E. B. DuBois, F. Watts, 1990.

The Story of Booker T. Washington, Children's Press, 1991.

Messy Bessey's Garden, illustrated by Martin, Children's Press, 1991.

From Heaven Above, Augsburg, 1992.

Sojourner Truth: Ain't I a Woman?, Scholastic, 1992.

God Makes All Things New, illustrated by Ching, Augsburg, 1993.

African-American Inventors, Millbrook Press, 1994.

African-American Scientists, Millbrook Press, 1994.

African Americans, illustrated by Michael McBride, Milliken, 1994.

Sports, Milliken, 1994.

Black Diamond: The Story of the Negro Baseball Leagues, Scholastic, 1994.

The Royal Kingdoms of Ghana, Mali, and Songhay: Life in Medieval Africa, Holt, 1994.

Christmas in the Big House, Christmas in the Quarters, illustrated by John Thompson, Scholastic, 1994.

Red-Tail Angels: The Story of the Tuskegee Airmen of World War II, Walker, 1995.

Rebels against Slavery: American Slave Revolts, Scholastic, 1996.

Let My People Go: Bible Stories of Faith, Hope, and Love, As Told by Price Jefferies, a Free Man of Color, to His Daughter, Charlotte, in Charleston, South Carolina, 1806-1816, illustrated by James Ransome, Atheneum, 1998.

Young, Black, and Determined: A Biography of Lorraine Hansberry, Holiday House, 1998.

Messy Bessey and the Birthday Overnight, illustrated by Dana Regan, Children's Press, 1998.

Messy Bessey's School Desk, illustrated by Dana Regan, Children's Press, 1998.

Black Hands, White Sails: The Story of African-American Whalers, Scholastic, 1999.

Messy Bessey's Holidays, illustrated by Dana Regan, Children's Press, 1999.

Messy Bessey's Family Reunion, illustrated by Dana Regan, Children's Press, 2000.

Miami Gets It Straight, illustrated by Michael Chesworth, Golden Books, 2000.

FOR CHILDREN; "GREAT AFRICAN AMERICANS" SERIES; WITH HUSBAND, FREDRICK L. McKISSACK

Carter G. Woodson: The Father of Black History, illustrated by Ned Ostendorf, Enslow, 1991.

Frederick Douglass: Leader against Slavery, illustrated by Ned Ostendorf, Enslow, 1991.

George Washington Carver: The Peanut Scientist, illustrated by Ned Ostendorf, Enslow, 1991.

Ida B. Wells-Barnett: A Voice against Violence, illustrated by Ned Ostendorf, Enslow, 1991.

Louis Armstrong: Jazz Musician, illustrated by Ned Ostendorf, Enslow, 1991.

Marian Anderson: A Great Singer, illustrated by Ned Ostendorf, Enslow, 1991.

Martin Luther King, Jr.: Man of Peace, illustrated by Ned Ostendorf, Enslow, 1991.

Mary Church Terrell: Leader for Equality, illustrated by Ned Ostendorf, Enslow, 1991.

Mary McLeod Bethune: A Great Teacher, illustrated by Ned Ostendorf, Enslow, 1991.

Ralph J. Bunche: Peacemaker, illustrated by Ned Ostendorf, Enslow, 1991.

Jesse Owens: Olympic Star, illustrated by Michael David Biegel, Enslow, 1992.

Langston Hughes: Great American Poet, illustrated by Michael David Biegel, Enslow, 1992.

Zora Neale Hurston: Writer and Storyteller, illustrated by Michael Bryant, Enslow, 1992.

Satchel Paige: The Best Arm in Baseball, illustrated by Michael David Biegel, Enslow, 1992.

Sojourner Truth: Voice for Freedom, illustrated by Michael Bryant, Enslow, 1992.

Madam C. J. Walker: Self-Made Millionaire, illustrated by Michael Bryant, Enslow, 1992.

Paul Robeson: A Voice to Remember, illustrated by Michael David Biegel, Enslow, 1992.

Booker T. Washington: Leader and Educator, illustrated by Michael Bryant, Enslow, 1992.

OTHER

Also contributor with Fredrick L. McKissack to *The World of 1492,* edited by Jean Fritz, Holt, 1992; author with F. L. McKissack of "Start Up" series for beginning readers, four volumes, Children's Press, 1985; editor with F. L. McKissack of "Reading Well" series and "Big Bug Books" series, both for Milliken. Writer for preschool series "L Is for Listening," broadcast by KWMU-Radio, 1975-77. Author of radio and television scripts. Contributor of articles and short stories to magazines, including *Friend, Happy Times,* and *Evangelizing Today's Child.* Co-author, with Mavis Jukes, of the short-subject film script, *Who Owns the Sun?,* Disney Educational Productions, 1991.

Sidelights

Patricia C. McKissack has written well over one hundred titles under her own name, as well as in collaboration with her husband, Fredrick L. McKissack. The author of historical fiction and biographies for children, McKissack focuses on religious as well as African American themes, and her love of writing is in part inspired by the fact that she has been for many years an English instructor at both the junior high and college levels. The recipient of a 1993 Newbery Honor Award for the short stories gathered in *The Dark-Thirty,* McKissack has also won several Coretta Scott King Awards, as well as a Caldecott Honor Award for her picture book *Mirandy and Brother Wind.* Teaming up with her husband, she has contributed numerous titles to Enslow's "Great African Americans" series, as well as many non-series books on little-known aspects of African American history, including *The Red-Tail Angels* and *Black Diamonds.*

The McKissacks' lives were shaped by one of the most optimistic eras in American history—the 1960s. "We're Kennedy products, and we were very idealistic," McKissack once told *SATA.* "That was the period in which African Americans were really looking up, coming out of darkness, segregation, and discrimination, and doors were beginning to open—ever so slightly, but still opening." The optimism of those days can be seen in such books as the *Civil Rights Movement in America from 1865 to the Present* and *Martin Luther King, Jr.: Man of Peace.*

Born in 1944 in Nashville, Tennessee, McKissack experienced firsthand many of the injustices about which she and her husband write. These were the days of segregation, in which a black person was not allowed to drink from the same public water fountain as a white, nor allowed into the same restaurants as whites. But at home, McKissack's life was rich and filled with the tales that her storytelling grandfather shared. She grew up with a love of narrative and a love of reading.

She also grew up with her future husband, Fred McKissack, "in the same town, where every family knew every other family," McKissack once told *SATA*, "but he was five years older and you just didn't date boys who were five years older than you. When I was fifteen and he was twenty that just would have been forbidden." But then Fred went away to the Marines for several years; later, they both attended college together, graduating in 1964 from Tennessee State University in Nashville, and suddenly the two seemed not so far removed in age. They were married after graduation. "All of our friends said it wouldn't last six months. They said it was ridiculous, and our families were a bit concerned," McKissack recalled for *SATA*. "But we just knew. We talked all the time and we still do. We have always had a very, very close relationship from the first date we had. We just had so much fun together that we knew."

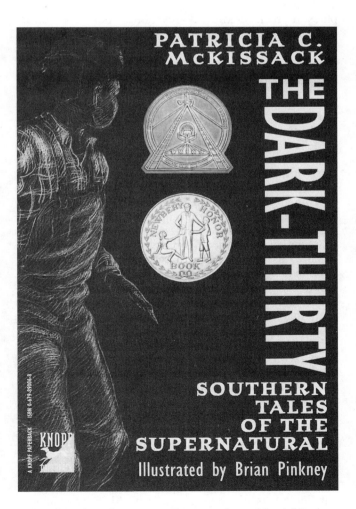

McKissack relates ten ghost stories with African-American themes in her award-winning book. (Cover illustration by Brian Pinkney.)

One thing the McKissacks discovered they had in common was a love of literature. Both recalled reading Ayn Rand's *Fountainhead, Atlas Shrugged,* and *Anthem,* as well as Aldous Huxley's *Brave New World* and other novels of similar futuristic themes. "We were talking about the future," McKissack noted. Other influences included Julius Lester, an author known for his historically accurate, heroic depictions of black characters. Lester had graduated in 1960 from Fisk University, also in Nashville.

While the era was filled with hope and opportunities, it was also a time of violent change. Sit-ins and demonstrations by Southern blacks were finally shaking the segregationist foundations of the region. Schools became desegregated; integration was in the works. "Our generation was the first to do it," McKissack recalled for *SATA*. "I remember when Fred took me to dinner at Morrison's. I was nervous as a flea because a sit-in had occurred only a few years earlier, and there had been people putting shotguns at young people's heads and saying, 'If you sit here we will blow you away.' And that happened to Fred" when he joined a sit-in at a Woolworth department store. The visit to Morrison's was among many firsts for the McKissacks; after years of seeing them only from the outside, the two finally entered a Kentucky Fried Chicken restaurant, a Shoney's, a McDonald's, and a Hardee's. When her younger brother got a job at Shoney's, McKissack realized that "things were opening up. And we were very proud that we were the first generation to come through that."

Then came the Vietnam War and the "white backlash" to the Civil Rights Movement. McKissack found the television footage at that time, the first ever shown of American soldiers in combat, profoundly disturbing. "That was horrible for us to watch—the body bags coming back in," she related. "I was a young mother—I had three little boys—and I said, 'My God, I hope we never have to go through anything this nonsensical again.'" The assassinations of John F. Kennedy and his brother Robert, Martin Luther King Jr., Medgar Evers, and Malcolm X, along with church bombings and innumerable other violent incidents, all served to temper the McKissacks' positive attitude. "Just as blacks experienced white resistance to equality during Reconstruction, there was another backlash to the Civil Rights Movement of the 1960s," McKissack commented. "By 1980 blacks were once again on the defense, trying to safeguard their and their children's rights."

These experiences have all combined to produce the variety and depth of writing McKissack has produced. One of her goals is to write in such a way that the past comes alive for her young readers. One of her first writing projects was a biography of Paul Laurence Dunbar, written for her class of eighth-grade English students in Kirkwood, Missouri. "The school was twenty-five percent black and I wanted to teach about an African American writer who I had come to know and appreciate when I was growing up," McKissack recalled. When she began researching Dunbar, "I couldn't find a biography, so I wrote his biography myself for my

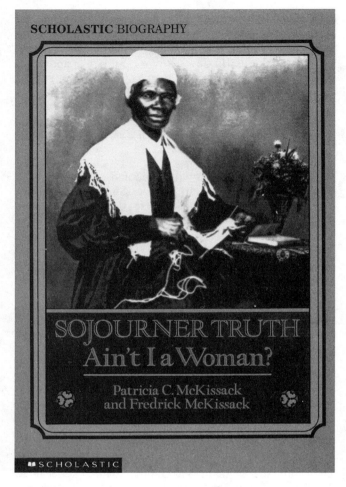

The McKissacks offer a historically detailed portrait of preacher, abolitionist, and activist Sojourner Truth.

students." She also sought information on Langston Hughes and James Weldon Johnson, both of whom she and her husband later wrote about. Many more biographies have followed.

James Weldon Johnson: "Lift Every Voice and Sing," co-authored with her husband, "makes Johnson come alive for young readers," Jeanette Lambert commented in *School Library Journal.* Readers learn that Johnson was the author of "Lift Every Voice and Sing," the song recognized as the African American national anthem, and also was the first African American to pass the bar in Florida, was principal of the first black high school in Jacksonville, Florida, and served as executive secretary of the NAACP.

Together, the McKissacks have penned nearly a score of biographies in Enslow's "Great African Americans" series, short nonfiction titles intended for the primary grades. These books describe the lives of important black leaders, both cultural and political, in brief chapters using a basic, concise style accompanied by photographs and other illustrations. In a review of the McKissacks' *Ida B. Wells-Barnett: A Voice against Violence, Marian Anderson: A Great Singer, Martin*

Luther King, Jr.: Man of Peace, and *Ralph J. Bunche: Peacemaker,* Phyllis Stephens noted that the authors present each of the subjects as people with convictions so strong that "not even a racially biased society could provide effective obstacles to deter them" from achieving their dreams. Writing about *Paul Robeson: A Voice to Remember* and *Booker T. Washington: Leader and Educator,* Laura Culberg noted in *School Library Journal* that these brief biographies "fill a need for materials on noted African-Americans for primary-grade readers." Culberg went on to conclude, "the books will find an eager audience among beginning readers." Reviewing a group of five more such biographies on notables, including black historian Carter G. Woodson, anti-slavery leader Frederick Douglass, scientist George Washington Carver, jazz musician Louis Armstrong, and equal rights proponent Mary Church Terrell, Anna DeWind noted in *School Library Journal* that all five books "have simplified vocabularies, large print, and plenty of black-and-white photographs and illustrations." DeWind further commented that in spite some "flaws . . . these [biographies] are a step in the right direction."

The McKissacks also have several non-series biographies to their credit. "A revealing book," *W. E. B. DuBois* "should entice readers to seek more information about this complex man," Lydia Champlin remarked in *School Library Journal. Voice of Youth Advocates* reviewer Bruce Lee Siebers recommended *W. E. B. DuBois* as "a good addition to African American history and biography collections." With *Sojourner Truth: Ain't I a Woman,* a Coretta Scott King Honor Book from 1993, they tell the story of this nineteenth-century preacher, abolitionist, and activist for the rights of both African Americans and women. They have also told the story of the brilliant black writer, Lorraine Hansberry in *Young, Black, and Determined.* The author of the acclaimed play, *A Raisin in the Sun,* Hansberry fought prejudice throughout her brief career. "The McKissacks' biography sparkles with the energy and passion that characterize her subject," observed *Booklist* contributor Anne O'Malley. Marilyn Heath, reviewing the same book in *School Library Journal,* called it a "well-written biography" that is "lively and engaging" and that "brings its subject to life by successfully capturing that unique spark that makes Hansberry noteworthy and interesting."

Other history books of note include *Black Diamond: The Story of the Negro Baseball Leagues, Red Tail Angels: The Story of the Tuskegee Airmen of World War II,* and *Black Hands, White Sails: The Story of African-American Whalers,* all collaborative efforts. Racism in sports is brought into focus in the first of these, "a lucid, comprehensive study of a vital chapter of baseball history," according to Randy M. Brough in a review of *Black Diamond* in *Kliatt.* In *Red-Tail Angels,* the authors tell the little-known story of black pilots who fought in World War II in a special squadron because the regular Air Force was still segregated. Mary M. Burns enthusiastically praised this history in a *Horn Book* review: "Impeccably documented, handsomely designed, thoughtfully executed, this book by two of our most committed and talented writers gives these pioneers' accomplishments meaning for a new generation." David A. Lindsey, reviewing the same title in *School Library Journal,* commented, "The prolific McKissacks have collaborated once again to produce yet another well-crafted, thoroughly researched account of a little-known facet of African American history." Of the McKissacks' 1999 book *Black Hands, White Sails,* a reviewer for *Booklist* felt it was a "fascinating look at the convergent histories of whaling and the abolitionist movement" that "weaves seemingly disparate threads into a detailed tapestry."

Patricia McKissack also has numerous solo books in history and fiction to her credit. Her books for very young readers, such as *Flossie and the Fox* and the Caldecott Honor Book *Mirandy and Brother Wind,* have won critical praise and a wide readership. A contributor for *Kirkus Reviews* called *Flossie and the Fox,* based on a tale McKissack's grandfather once told her, "a perfect picture book." *Mirandy and Brother Wind* was also inspired by McKissack's grandfather, more specifically from a photograph of both her grandfather and grandmother as teenagers after they had won a cakewalk contest in 1906. In the book, Mirandy enlists Brother Wind as her partner in a cakewalk contest in a "delightful book," according to Valerie Wilson Wesley, writing in the *New York Times Book Review.* Wesley concluded, "each page of *Mirandy and Brother Wind* sparkles with life." *Booklist*'s Ilene Cooper called the book "a graceful fantasy." Remembrances of her great-grandmother and her eternal apron inspired McKissack's 1997 work *Ma Dear's Aprons,* a book that a contributor to the *New York Times Book Review* called "[a]ffectionate, appealing and full of information about the routines of domestic life." In her 1999 title *The Honest-to-Goodness Truth,* McKissack tells the story of young Libby, who learns that truth-telling is not always as straightforward as it seems. "The story is very much a lesson," *Booklist*'s Hazel Rochman noted, "but it's a subtle one."

McKissack became the recipient of a Newbery Honor Award for the stories collected in *The Dark Thirty.* The title comes from that half-hour before dark in which kids were still allowed to play outside when McKissack herself was growing up. The ten original stories in the collection reflect African-American history or culture. "Some are straight ghost stories," commented Kay McPherson in a *School Library Journal* review, "many of which are wonderfully spooky and all of which have well-woven narratives." McPherson concluded, "This is a stellar collection." Other works for older readers include the fictionalized diaries of African American girls for Scholastic, including *A Picture of Freedom: The Diary of Clotee, a Slave Girl* and *Color Me Dark: The Diary of Nellie Lee Love, the Great Migration North.* The first title is set on a Virginia plantation in 1859, and the second title follows the fortunes of a young girl who migrates to Chicago after World War I. Reviewing *A Picture of Freedom* for *School Library Journal,* Melissa Hudek called the book "an inspiring look at a young girl coming of age in terrible circumstances who manages to

Libby learns it isn't necessary to tell the whole truth all the time in McKissack's amusing tale. (Cover illustration by Giselle Potter.)

live life to the fullest." *Booklist*'s Carolyn Phelan, reviewing *Color Me Dark,* felt "the strong narrative will keep children involved and give them a great deal of social history to absorb along the way." In *Run Away Home* McKissack tells the story of a young Apache who escapes federal custody and is aided by an African American family. Reviewing this historical novel in *Horn Book,* Burns noted, "McKissack knows how to pace a story, create suspense, and interweave period details of the late nineteenth century into a coherent narrative" to produce a book "sophisticated in content yet tuned to the understanding of a middle-school audience—no small accomplishment."

McKissack sees her work as something that can possibly unite disparate communities in this country. "It's a kind of freedom," she once told *SATA.* "Writing has allowed us to do something positive with our experiences, although some of our experiences have been very negative. We try to enlighten, to change attitudes, to form new attitudes—to build bridges with books." And for her, reaching the young with her books is vital. "It's quite interesting how your youth shapes how you think in the future," McKissack remarked to *SATA.* "The things that are happening to you now will affect how you parent, how you will function in your work, and how you will treat your neighbors." She stresses that intervention at this crucial time in a young person's development must help to provide a strong foundation for his or her future. "When I do a workshop with teachers, I always say, 'Someone in your class might be the person who has the cure for cancer. The cure for AIDS is sitting in someone's classroom right now. The solution for world hunger can be found by someone sitting in a classroom. You do not know whether you will be the person to touch that person. So, therefore, you have to respect and treat all of these students with an equal measure of concern.'"

Works Cited

Review of *Black Hands, White Sails, Booklist,* September 1, 1999.

Brough, Randy M., review of *Black Diamond, Kliatt,* November, 1998, p. 40.

Burns, Mary M., review of *Red-Tail Angels, Horn Book,* March-April, 1996, p. 226.

Burns, Mary M., review of *Run Away Home, Horn Book,* November-December, 1997, p. 681.

Champlin, Lydia, review of *W. E. B. DuBois, School Library Journal,* January, 1991, p. 103.

Cooper, Ilene, review of *Mirandy and Brother Wind, Booklist,* February 1, 1992, p. 1037.

Culberg, Laura, review of *Paul Robeson: A Voice to Remember, School Library Journal,* October, 1992, pp. 105-6.

DeWind, Anna, review of *Carter G. Woodson: The Father of Black History, School Library Journal,* February, 1992, p. 83.

Review of *Flossie and the Fox, Kirkus Reviews,* November 1, 1988, p. 1607.

Heath, Marilyn, review of *Young, Black, and Determined: A Biography of Lorraine Hansberry, School Library Journal,* April, 1998, pp. 148-49.

Hudek, Melissa, review of *A Picture of Freedom, School Library Journal,* September, 1997, p. 220.

Lambert, Jeanette, review of *James Weldon Johnson: "Lift Every Voice and Sing," School Library Journal,* February, 1991, p. 79.

Lindsey, David A., review of *Red-Tail Angels, School Library Journal,* February, 1996, p. 119.

Review of *Ma Dear's Aprons, New York Times Book Review,* August 3, 1997, p. 14.

McPherson, Kay, review of *The Dark Thirty, School Library Journal,* December, 1992, p. 113.

O'Malley, Anne, review of *Young, Black, and Determined: A Biography of Lorraine Hansberry, Booklist,* February 15, 1998, p. 995.

Phelan, Carolyn, review of *Color Me Dark, Booklist,* February 15, 2000, p. 1113.

Rochman, Hazel, review of *The Honest-to-Goodness Truth, Booklist,* December 15, 1999, p. 791.

Siebers, Bruce Lee, review of *W. E. B. DuBois, Voice of Youth Advocates,* October, 1990, p. 248.

Stephens, Phyllis, review of *Ida B. Wells-Barnett: A Voice against Violence, Marian Anderson: A Great Singer, Martin Luther King, Jr.: Man of Peace,* and *Ralph J. Bunche: Peacemaker, School Library Journal,* November, 1991, p. 111.

Wesley, Valerie Wilson, review of *Mirandy and Brother Wind, New York Times Book Review,* November 20, 1988, p. 48.

For More Information See

BOOKS

McKissack, Patricia, *Can You Imagine?,* Richard C. Owen, 1997.

PERIODICALS

Booklist, March 1, 1992, p. 1270; April 15, 1992, p. 1525; June 19, 1994; February 15, 1997, p. 1027; June 1, 1997, p. 1696; October 1, 1997, p. 329; February 15, 1998, p. 1696; February 15, 1999, p. 1068.

Bulletin of the Center for Children's Books, June, 1997, p. 367; February, 1998, p. 213; December, 1998, p. 137.

Horn Book, May-June, 1997, p. 310.

Interracial Books for Children Bulletin, Number 8, 1985, p. 5.

Kirkus Reviews, December 15, 1991; February 15, 1998, p. 271.

Kliatt, May, 1999, p. 27.

New York Times Book Review, November 29, 1992, p. 34; June 21, 1998, p. 20.

Publishers Weekly, February 9, 1998, p. 98; October 26, 1998, p. 62.

School Library Journal, September, 1994, pp. 251-52; September, 1997, p. 199; August, 1998, p. 144.

Voice of Youth Advocates, August, 1998, p. 224.*

* * *

MILLER, Judi

Personal

Education: Ohio University, B.F.A.; attended Juilliard School of Music and New York School of Visual Arts.

Addresses

Home—Apt. 2B, 75 Bank St., New York, NY 10014.

Career

New School of Social Research, instructor.

Awards, Honors

Virginia Readers Award; International Children's Choice Award.

Writings

FOR YOUNG READERS

Ghost in My Soup (novel), Bantam Doubleday Dell, 1987.

How I Kept the U.S. Out of War (novel), Dell, 1987.

Ghost a la Mode (novel; sequel to *Ghost in My Soup*), Dell, 1989.

Cry in the Night (novel), Avon, 1990.

The Middle of the Sandwich Is the Best Part (novel), Pocket Books, 1990.

How to Be Friends with a Boy/How to Be Friends with a Girl (nonfiction) Scholastic, 1990.

A Vampire Named Murray (novel), Bantam, 1991.

Confessions of an Eleven-Year-Old Ghost (novel), Bantam, 1991.

Purple Is My Game, Morgan Is My Name (novel), Pocket Books, 1998.

"COURTNEY" SERIES; FOR YOUNG READERS

My Crazy Cousin Courtney, Pocket Books, 1993.

My Crazy Cousin Courtney Comes Back, Demco Media, 1993.

Courtney Gets Crazier, Pocket Books, 1993, published as *My Crazy Cousin Courtney Gets Crazier,* Demco Media, 1993.

My Crazy Cousin Courtney Returns Again, Demco Media, 1994.

FOR ADULTS

Women Who Changed America (nonfiction), Kearny Publishing, 1977.

How to Ask a Man (nonfiction), Dell, 1978.

(With Eric Weber) *The Shy Person's Guide to Love & Loving* (nonfiction), Times Books, 1979.

Save the Last Dance for Me (fiction), Pocket Books, 1981.

Hush, Little Baby (fiction), Pocket Books, 1983.

I'll Be Wearing a White Carnation (fiction), Avon Books, 1985.

Also author, with Eric Weber, of *Shy Person's Guide to a Happier Love Life* (nonfiction), Symphony Press.

Judi Miller

Sidelights

After publishing a handful of psychological thrillers for adults during the early and mid-1980s, Judi Miller tried her hand at writing juvenile fiction. Seeing herself as a "humor writer," Miller told *SATA:* "For the most part, I like to entertain." Commentators have noted the humorous aspects of Miller's middle-grade novels, and some have found the humor to be the strong point of her work.

In *Ghost in My Soup* and its sequel, *Ghost a la Mode,* Miller follows eleven-year-old Scottie and Malcolm, a ghost Scottie meets when he moves to an old mansion, through a serious of adventures. Although Therese Bigelow, writing in *School Library Journal,* faulted Miller for using stock characters, a didactic tone, and occasionally "stilted" language, she predicted that because humorous tales about ghosts are "rare" for this readership, children "will enjoy" *Ghost in My Soup.* Ilene Cooper of *Booklist* judged the work to be a "pleasant enough diversion." Reviewing the sequel, *Ghost a la Mode,* for *School Library Journal,* Florence M. Brems found the novel's "subplots delightful" and the ghost's behavior "hilarious." However, she determined that as a whole *Ghost a la Mode* "never quite comes together."

With *How I Kept the U.S. Out of War, A Vampire Named Murray,* and *My Crazy Cousin Courtney,* Miller continues in a humorous vein. In the first novel, vacationing Robbie Belmont is mistaken for being the prince of a fictitious country and is kidnapped from the London airport. He recounts this tale in his school essay about what he did during his summer vacation. The novel caught critics' attention. In her *Booklist* review, Ilene Cooper praised *How I Kept the U.S. Out of War,* declaring it a "wild romp." Likewise, Blair Christolon, writing in *School Library Journal,* described the novel as "silly" but "not without good intent." Although he approved of the suspenseful chapter endings and fictional glossary of made-up words, he found the final ending to be marred by didacticism. "Silly" is also the word Alice Cronin used in her *School Library Journal* review to describe Miller's *A Vampire Named Murray.* She also found this novel, which revolves around the activities of Kelly and Kevin's Uncle Murray—a comedian who entertains children in hospitals—to be an "entertaining" book for challenged readers. Miller brings together two very different cousins in *My Crazy Cousin Courtney.* During the summer between sixth and seventh grade, Cathy and Courtney encounter adventure and misadventure in New York City as they find common ground. In a *Booklist* review, Susan DeRonne praised Miller for the novel's "humor and sensitivity to the concerns of young teens." *Publishers Weekly* reviewer Diane Roback also noted the work's humor and found the novel to be "generally promising," though at times flawed by cumbersome phrases.

Several of Miller's books deal with relationships, including her self-help book *How to Be Friends with a Boy/How to Be Friends with a Girl* and the novels *The Middle Part of the Sandwich Is the Best Part* and *Purple Is My Game, Morgan Is My Name.* In *How to Be*

Purple-obsessed Morgan takes action to get the things she wants—especially to reunite her divorced parents—with humorous results. (Cover illustration by Lina Levy.)

For two decades, Miller has published a steady stream of novels for both children and adults. Critics have commented on Miller's works for middle-grade students, particularly praising their humor. Miller encourages would-be writers to hold fast to their dreams of authorship. She told *SATA,* "My advice is never give up!"

Works Cited

Bigelow, Therese, review of *Ghost in My Soup, School Library Journal,* November, 1985, p. 88.

Brems, Florence M., review of *Ghost a la Mode, School Library Journal,* February, 1990, p. 92.

Christolon, Blair, review of *How I Kept the U.S. Out of War, School Library Journal,* January, 1988, p. 76.

Cooper, Ilene, review of *Ghost in My Soup, Booklist,* February 1, 1986, p. 811.

Cooper, Ilene, review of *How I Kept the U.S. Out of War, Booklist,* December 15, 1987, p. 714.

Cronin, Alice, review of *The Middle of the Sandwich Is the Best Part, School Library Journal,* April, 1991, pp. 121-22.

Cronin, Alice, review of *A Vampire Named Murray, School Library Journal,* July, 1991, p. 74.

Cufari, Cheryl, review of *Purple Is My Game, Morgan Is My Name, School Library Journal,* November, 1998, p. 126.

DeRonne, Susan, review of *My Crazy Cousin Courtney, Booklist,* March 1, 1993, p. 1230.

Dubois, Deborah L., review of *How to Be Friends with a Boy/How to Be Friends with a Girl, Voice of Youth Advocates,* June, 1991, p. 128.

Review of *Purple Is My Game, Morgan Is My Name, Publishers Weekly,* January 5, 1998, p. 68.

Roback, Diane, review of *My Crazy Cousin Courtney, Publishers Weekly,* February 8, 1993, p. 87.

*   *   *

MILLER, Ruth White
See WHITE, Ruth C.

*   *   *

MORLEY, Wilfred Owen
See LOWNDES, Robert A(ugustine) W(ard)

*   *   *

MORRISON, Richard
See LOWNDES, Robert A(ugustine) W(ard)

*   *   *

MORRISON, Robert
See LOWNDES, Robert A(ugustine) W(ard)

Friends, Miller advises readers on how to be friends with members of the opposite sex without having to become a "boyfriend" or "girlfriend." Such advice as being oneself, listening to others, and sharing common interests are "standard and would apply to almost any type of relationship," remarked Deborah L. Dubois in *Voice of Youth Advocates.* In *The Middle Part of the Sandwich Is the Best Part,* Miller explores the relationships between three siblings, concentrating on Betsi, the middle child. According to Cronin in another *School Library Journal* review, the novel is "well written" with "adequate plot development, characterizations, and development of theme." Yet, in her view, it lacks the depth of novels by Miller's contemporaries. The relationships in question in *Purple Is My Game, Morgan Is My Name* are between divorced parents living on different parts of the globe and their daughter Morgan, who wishes they would reunite. While a *Publishers Weekly* critic complained that some of plot events are implausible and the ending "unlikely," Cheryl Cufari, writing in the *School Library Journal,* declared the work "entertaining" and "fast-paced," predicting that it would appeal to reluctant readers.

N

NELSON, Julie L. 1970-

Personal

Born July 22, 1970, in Good Thunder, MN; daughter of John C. (a factory worker) and Donna (a secretary; maiden name, Smothers) Nelson. *Education:* Central College, Pella, IA, B.A., 1992; Mankato State University, M.F.A., 1996. *Politics:* Democrat. *Religion:* None.

Addresses

Home—R.R.3, Box 145, Good Thunder, MN 56037. *E-mail*—JulieNelson@hotmail.com.

Career

Mankato State University, Mankato, MN, adjunct instructor, 1992—. Also taught in Austin, MN, 1998; athletic coach for high school basketball and college softball.

Writings

NONFICTION

The History of the Los Angeles Sparks, Creative Education (Mankato, MN), 1999.
Indianapolis Colts, Creative Education, 2000.
Jacksonville Jaguars, Creative Education, 2000.
Kansas City Chiefs, Creative Education, 2000.
Miami Dolphins, Creative Education, 2000.
Minnesota Vikings, Creative Education, 2000.
New England Patriots, Creative Education, 2000.
New Orleans Saints, Creative Education, 2000.
New York Giants, Creative Education, 2000.
New York Jets, Creative Education, 2000.
Oakland Raiders, Creative Education, 2000.
Philadelphia Eagles, Creative Education, 2000.
Pittsburgh Steelers, Creative Education, 2000.
San Diego Chargers, Creative Education, 2000.
San Francisco 49ers, Creative Education, 2000.
Seattle Seahawks, Creative Education, 2000.
St. Louis Rams, Creative Education, 2000.

Julie L. Nelson gives the history and major player profiles of the Los Angeles Sparks professional women's basketball team.

Tampa Bay Buccaneers, Creative Education, 2000.
Tennessee Titans, Creative Education, 2000.
Washington Redskins, Creative Education, 2000.

Work in Progress

Young adult fiction with a sport theme.*

NILSSON, Eleanor 1939-

Personal

Born June 6, 1939, in Stirling, Scotland; daughter of Murdoch and Rose (Kane) Luke; married Neil Nilsson (a teacher), December 23, 1968; children: Martin, Catherine. *Education:* Adelaide University, B.A. (with honors), Dip.Ed.

Addresses

Home—416 Main Rd., Coromandel Valley, South Australia 5051, Australia.

Career

High school teacher, 1960-61; Adelaide Teachers' College, Adelaide, South Australia, lecturer in English, 1962-68; South Australia College of Advanced Education, lecturer in English, 1971-90; University of South Australia, Adelaide, lecturer in English, 1991-92; full-time writer, 1992—.

Awards, Honors

Australian Literature Board fellowships, 1988, 1993; Book of the Year shortlist, Children's Book Council of Australia, 1991, for *The Black Duck;* Book of the Year Award (older category), Children's Book Council of Australia, Victorian Premier's Literary Award, National Children's Literature Award, all 1992, all for *The House Guest.*

Writings

FOR CHILDREN

Parrot Fashion, illustrated by Craig Smith, Omnibus, 1983.
The Rainbow Stealer, illustrated by Leanne Argent, Omnibus, 1984.
Tatty, illustrated by Leanne Argent, Omnibus, 1985.
A Bush Birthday, illustrated by Kerry Argent, Omnibus, 1985.
Heffalump?, illustrated by Rae Dale, Puffin, 1986.
The 89th Kitten, Angus & Robertson, 1987, Scholastic, 1989.
Pomily's Wish, illustrated by Rae Dale, Puffin, 1987.
Mystery Meals, illustrated by Jane Disher, Omnibus, 1987.
There's a Crocodile There Now Too, Dent Australia, 1987.
Heffalump? and the Toy Hospital, illustrated by Rae Dale, Puffin, 1989.
A Lamb Like Alice, Angus & Robertson, 1990.
The Black Duck, illustrated by Rae Dale, Penguin Australia, 1990.
The House Guest, Viking, 1991.
Writing for Children, Penguin Australia, 1992.
Graffiti Dog, Omnibus, 1995.
Outside Permission, Viking, 1996.
Pearl's Pantry, illustrated by Betina Ogden, Puffin, 1996.
The Experiment, Omnibus, 1996.
Tiptoe round a Pony, illustrated by Betina Ogden, Puffin, 1998.
No One, illustrated by Ogden, Puffin, 1999.
The Bell of Germelshausen, Lothian, 1999.
The Way Home, Puffin, 2001.
The Good Dog, ABC Books, 2001.

Contributor to *Money!,* Angus & Robertson, 1989. Some of Nilsson's works have been published in the United Kingdom, Holland, Germany, Italy, France, and the United States.

Sidelights

In Australian author Eleanor Nilsson's books for children her young characters often have a greater affinity for animals than for people. An animal lover herself, Nilsson spoke with *Magpies* interviewer Moya Costello about her interest in children's relationships with animals as a method of revealing aspects in the children themselves. "Animals are the only thing children have power over," Nilsson observed. "Animals never criticise you, they love you whatever . . . you do, so they provide a lot of support." Fantasy literature has also had an influence on Nilsson's works, Costello noted, though she added that the author typically resolves her plots realistically rather than magically. Other critics have praised the author's intriguing characterizations, her poetic use of language, and her satisfying conclusions.

Nilsson's picture books for the youngest of children feature animal characters in gentle adventures. *Pomily's Wish* tells the story of young Pomily mouse, whose storytelling ability saves her from being eaten by a cat.

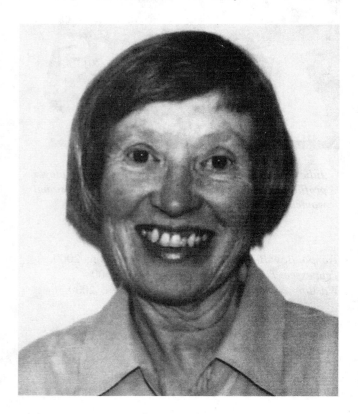

Eleanor Nilsson

In *Heffalump? and the Toy Hospital* a toy stuffed elephant complains about his boredom only to have his best friend, Bengal Tiger, disappear into the animal hospital without their owner Anne's knowledge. A *Books for Keeps* critic dubbed Heffalump's efforts to rescue his friend "a warm, reassuring story."

For slightly older children, Nilsson's *The Black Duck* tells the story of Tom, whose father loses his job, forcing the family to move and leave behind Tom's pet duck. Costello commended the book's multi-faceted theme of communication, which is centered on five-year-old Tom, who rarely speaks but is able to relate to his pet. A *Magpies* reviewer praised the lack of sentimentality in *The Black Duck,* adding that Nilsson keeps the reader's interest while supplying "a satisfying and reassuring ending." Another tale of animal rescue for this audience is *The 89th Kitten,* in which a lonely, elderly woman takes in more stray cats than her neighbors can tolerate. In this story of "loneliness, self-definition and self-determination," as Costello described it, young Sandy, with the help of the media and her distant father, finds good homes for the cats. An animal is also at the center of *A Lamb Like Alice,* in which two children decide to rescue a lamb being fattened by the local butcher for slaughter.

For older children, Nilsson has written an award-winning novel, *The House Guest,* which is about a small gang of children breaking into houses for money. One of the gang members, Gunno, becomes intrigued with Hugh, a boy who seems to be missing from the house. "The idea for *The House Guest,*" Nilsson related to *SATA,* "came from something that happened to our family. Our house was robbed, but in such a subtle, tidy way that we didn't even realise it had happened until several days after the event. Books were stolen as well as money. These two things, the tidiness and the books, gave me the idea for a rather unusual gang that operated by rules and also helped to give me the characters of Gunno and Jess. The fact that the children would have come into the house at all with our dog in it, who always barks furiously, even at friends, gave me the idea of Hugh, and of the very special relationship he has with Gunno. I knew the story would have to be told through Gunno's eyes, to preserve the sense of mystery and because he was the character who interested me most.

"I didn't really know what was going to happen," Nilsson continued; "I only knew that Gunno was going to be attracted back again and again to the house (my own!) and that in so doing, he would somehow unravel the mystery about Hugh (whatever that would turn out to be). Whenever I could imagine a scene, I wrote it down, even if it wasn't in sequence, almost as if I was filling in a jigsaw puzzle. The part that gave me the greatest trouble was the sequence where Gunno actually meets Hugh. The book was held up for almost a year because I couldn't get these few chapters right. When a friend suggested I visit the silver and lead mine at Glen Osmond, I knew I had found the setting where Hugh had his accident, and because I could visualise where it had happened, somehow the difficulty about writing this section disappeared. (The first version of *The House Guest* ended with a bushfire, the second with an open-hole mine like the copper mines in Coromandel Valley, the third with the cave-like mine of Glen Osmond.)"

In reviewing *The House Guest,* Costello noted that once again the author portrays her characters through their treatment of animals: in this case, through their differing reactions to the dog that greets them in the latest house they break into. "There's much that's playful in the book, but at the same time it is serious and sincere in intent. Its shape is impressive, providing pleasure through intrigue, and in so doing matching style to subject matter," Costello wrote.

Nilsson is also the author of *Graffiti Dog,* in which another teenager involved in illegal activities, this time a graffiti gang, is redirected from a life of crime by his growing attachment to a dog. *Magpies* reviewer Alan Horsfield praised Nilsson's "humane and perceptive" treatment of her two main characters, the boy and the dog, and found the juxtaposition of the sympathy shared by Derek and his canine friend with the "uncaring adults" who populate Derek's life "most thought provoking." In *Tiptoe round a Pony,* set in the English countryside, the arrival of an Australian veterinarian who is somewhat fearful of horses inspires timid Tess to stand up to her father, despite his impatience, and prove her abilities despite her own fears. The result is an "agreeably winsome story [with] a romantic conclusion," wrote Kevin Steinberger in *Magpies.*

"Ideas come from things that have happened to me or my family," the author told *SATA,* "from publishers, friends, from TV, from the newspaper, from anywhere, really." When writing, Nilsson told Costello, "I like language that has a certain rhythm and a lilting quality." The author also confessed an admiration for such writers as Philippa Pearce and William Mayne, "whose concern is with language," and who write for children "with the very best words." As the author concluded, "The way to do your best by children is to write in the best way you can from a child's point of view."

Works Cited

Review of *The Black Duck, Magpies,* May, 1991, p. 21.
Costello, Moya, "Know the Author: Eleanor Nilsson," *Magpies,* November, 1991, pp. 19-21.
Review of *Heffalump? and the Toy Hospital, Books for Keeps,* January, 1990, p. 6.
Horsfield, Alan, review of *Graffiti Dog, Magpies,* July, 1995, pp. 26-27.
Steinberger, Kevin, review of *Tiptoe round a Pony, Magpies,* March, 1998, p. 34.

For More Information See

PERIODICALS

Books for Keeps, July, 1988, p. 7.
Magpies, March, 1991, pp. 28-29; May, 1992, p. 31.
Papers: Explorations into Children's Literature, December, 1993.*

O–P

OCHILTREE, Dianne 1953-

Personal

Surname is pronounced *Ock*-el-tree; born July 10, 1953, in Warren, OH; daughter of Edward L. (a lawyer) and Lea (a homemaker; maiden name, Stoneman) Fairbanks; married Jamie Ochiltree III (an insurance executive), June 21, 1975; children: Jamie Andrew, Nathan Alexander. *Education:* Miami University, Oxford, OH, B.F.A., 1975; also attended University of Cincinnati and Montclair State University.

Addresses

Home—21 Lambert Dr., Sparta, NJ 07871. *E-mail*—ochiltre@ptdprolog.net.

Career

Freelance writer, including work in advertising and public relations. Cincinnati Arts Center, worked as docent; Sussex County Arts and Heritage Council, literary chairperson and presenter of adult writing workshops; presenter of writing workshops for young people; juror for school writing competitions; children's literature newsletter, book reviewer. *Member:* Society of Children's Book Writers and Illustrators, National Art Education Association, Authors Guild, Rutgers University Council on Children's Literature, Northwest Jersey Reading Council.

Awards, Honors

Awards for excellence from International Association of Business Communicators, for marketing newsletters.

Writings

Cats Add Up!, mathematics activities by Marilyn Burns, illustrated by Marcy Dunn-Ramsey, Scholastic Inc. (New York City), 1998.

Dianne Ochiltree

Bart's Amazing Charts, mathematics activities by Burns, illustrated by Martin Lemelman, Scholastic Inc., 1999.

Author of training materials. Contributor to periodicals. Editor of marketing newsletters.

Work in Progress

Ten Monkey Jamboree, a picture book, with illustrations by Anne-Sophie Lanquetin, for Margaret K. McElderry Books (New York City), completion expected in 2001; *Pillow Pup,* Margaret K. McElderry Books, 2002; research on American Indian customs and history, art history, and natural science.

Sidelights

Dianne Ochiltree told *SATA:* "I was born in a steel town in northeastern Ohio, near the Pennsylvania border. I grew up with lots of pets. My childhood home, at various times, was home to ducklings, chicks, cats, kittens, guinea pigs, rabbits, hamsters, white mice, and painted turtles. Caring for all these animals taught me the great importance of small kindnesses. I learned to respect my fellow creatures. My stories almost always include an animal character, because I can't imagine life without a pet. Today, however, my pets are limited to one small tiger-striped cat and one large yellow dog.

"My life goal was always to be a writer and an artist. I've been writing stories and drawing pictures to go with them for as long as I can remember. In fact, I started my writing life before I could actually read or write. I 'wrote' stories using only pencil or crayon drawings. These drawings were done on the back sides of scrap paper that my grandfather brought home from his bookkeeping office for me to use. I would punch holes in the drawings and bind them together into a book with strings of yarn tied in tight knots. Then I would show the book to all the friends, neighbors, or family members willing to listen to me, as I told them the story that went with the pictures. I still have some of these books, and I bring them with me on author visits to preschool and kindergarten classes. I want young students to know that they don't have to wait to be an author. A writer is, in essence, a storyteller, and stories can be told just as successfully when spoken aloud or communicated in pictures.

"I was lucky enough to grow up next door to my grandparents. Because of this, many of my stories involve a grandparent who shares a close relationship with a young person. Older relatives have much to teach us, if we take time to listen and do things together. I've also enjoyed a lot of support for my creative efforts from my extended family of aunts and uncles and cousins over the years. A lifelong interest in Native American history and culture is due to the influence of my great-grandmother, who was a full-blooded member of the Blackfoot tribe.

"Why did I switch from advertising and public relations writing to writing for children? Because it's the most challenging, enjoyable writing I've ever done. I hope to make learning fun for readers and to encourage a passion for reading. Good books open doors to other worlds which can enrich our lives. I know that growing up isn't always easy. My goal is to write stories that might help children understand their world, and themselves, a bit

Scooty pokes his nose inside the shopping bags.
He pushes boxes off the table.

A family adds more cats and then gives some away in Ochiltree's **Cats Add Up!,** *a reader with math activities. (Illustrated by Marcy Dunn-Ramsey.)*

better. With each book, I strive to write the best prose or poetry I can, because I believe a beginning reader deserves it. To build a lifelong love of reading, we've got to start children off with the very best literature we can offer.

"My college degree is in visual art. I continue to enjoy painting and drawing. However, my visual training has also helped me in my writing career. I tell students that the ability to observe life around us is the key to developing good writing skills. When we stop and take notice of the details, story settings and characters come to life. This observation process can't stop at what we *see.* All five senses have to be involved—sight, sound, taste, hearing, and touch. This gives readers a three-dimensional world to discover when reading a story.

"I work on my stories for a long time before I even think of sending them out to an editor at a publishing house. On author visits to schools, I stress to students the value and the necessity of writing several drafts of a story. Good writing means rewriting. I always show my stories to other writers and ask their advice before considering a manuscript finished. This is much like the process students go through when they show teachers their own stories or reports. Students and professional writers both need to learn how to listen to, and accept, criticism with a positive attitude, in order to learn how to make our stories the very best they can be.

"My office is in our family home in Sparta, New Jersey, where I live with my husband, two sons, cat, and dog. Besides writing stories for children, I review children's books, which is another job that I love. I think kids today have a lot more reading choice than earlier generations had. A tremendous amount of thought and energy is invested by publishers to ensure that today's children's books offer readers high quality in both writing and illustration."

For More Information See

PERIODICALS

Booklist, March 15, 1999.

*   *   *

PALLOTTA-CHIAROLLI, Maria 1960-

Personal

Born August 13, 1960, in Adelaide, Australia; daughter of Stefano (a factory worker and cleaner) and Dora (a cleaner and kitchen helper; maiden name, Fantasia) Pallotta; married Robert Chiarolli (a manager), December 17, 1983; children: Stephanie Cara. *Education:* University of Adelaide, B.A., 1980, diploma in education, 1981, M.A., 1991; University of Technology, Sydney, Australia, Ph.D., 2000.

Addresses

Home—15 Mountain Ash Ave., Ashwood, Victoria 3147, Australia. *Office*—Faculty of Health and Behavioural Science, Deakin University, Burwood Campus, 221 Burwood Highway, Burwood, Victoria 3125, Australia; fax 03-9244-6017. *E-mail*—mariapc@deakin.edu.au; chiar@ozemail.com.au; and http://www.ozemail.com.au/~chiar.

Career

Secondary schoolteacher in Adelaide, Australia, 1982-92; Maquarie University, Sydney, Australia, research officer, 1997-98; Deakin University, Burwood Campus, Burwood, Australia, lecturer, 1998—. Catholic Education Office, Adelaide, gender and equity officer, 1990-93. South Australian Indo-Chinese Women's Association, volunteer teacher of English, 1980-81; South Australian Migration Museum, volunteer consultant and adviser on Italian migration exhibitions, 1989-90; AIDS Council of South Australia, volunteer worker in Community Education Group, 1990-92; Doppio Teatro (bilingual theater group), board member, 1993-95; SchoolWatch, member, 1995—; conducts workshops

Maria Pallotta-Chiarolli

and seminars; guest on television and radio programs. Member of South Australian Writers' Centre, 1990-; New South Wales Writers' Centre, 1994-; Victorian Writers' Centre, 1994-; Australian Teaching Council, 1994—; Centre for Research on Women, Murdoch University, 1994—; Women's Studies Research Centre and Gay and Lesbian Research Centre, University of Sydney, 1994—; Sydney Bisexual Network and Australian Bisexual Network, 1995—; Australian Women's Studies Network, 1997—; and Emily's List, 1999—. *Member:* Australian Society of Authors, Association of Women Educators, National Organisation of Women in Further Education, Australian Federation of University Women, Society of Women Writers, Italian-Australian Writers Association, Association of NESB Women in Australia, Italo-Australian Women's Association, Multicultural, Assertive, Resourceful Women in Action in Education, Women in Multicultural Networks, Gay and Lesbian Teachers and Students Association, Victorian Association for the Teachers of English, Western Australian Association for the Teachers of English.

Awards, Honors

Community Advancement Award, from Australian Bisexual Network, 1996; first runner-up in short story competition, Sydney Women's Library and *Australian Women's Book Review,* 1997; Shortlisted for NSW Premier's Award and Children's Book Council Award, both 2000, both for *Tapestry.*

Writings

Someone You Know: A Friend's Farewell, Wakefield Press (Adelaide, Australia), 1991, new edition, 1999.
(Contributor) Wendy Parsons and Rob Goodwin, editors, *Landscape and Identity: Perspectives from Australia,* Auslib Press (Adelaide), 1994.
(Contributor) Rollo Browne and Richard Fletcher, editors, *Boys in Schools: Addressing the Issues,* Finch Publishing (Sydney, Australia), 1995.
(Contributor) Carmel Guerra and Rob White, editors, *Ethnic Minority Youth in Australia: Challenges and Myths,* National Clearinghouse on Youth Studies (Hobart, Australia), 1995.
(Contributor) Catherine Beavis and Louise Laskey, editors, *Schooling and Sexualities: Teaching for a Positive Sexuality,* Centre for Education and Change, Deakin University, 1996.
(Contributor) Judith Gill and Maureen Dyer, editors, *Schooldays Past, Present, and Future,* Centre for Gender Studies, University of South Australia 1997.
Girls Talk: Young Women Speak Their Hearts and Mind, Finch Publishing, 1998.
(Contributor) Gerard Sullivan and Peter Jackson, editors, *Multicultural Queer: Australian Narratives,* Haworth Press (New York City), 1999.
(Contributor) S. Calwell and D. Johnson, editors, *There's So Much More to Life than Sex and Money,* Penguin (New York City), 1999.
(Contributor) Debbie Epstein and James T. Sears, editors, *A Dangerous Knowing: Sexual Pedagogies and the Master Narrative,* Cassell (London, England), 1999.
Tapestry: Italian Lives over Five Generations, Random House (Milsons Point, Australia), 2000.
(With Wayne Martino) *Schooling Masculinities: Adolescent Boys, Health, and Education in Australia* (tentative title), Open University Press (London, England), in press.
(With Martino) *The Stuff That Boys Are Made Of,* Allen & Unwin (Sydney), in press.
(Contributor) Felicity Haynes and Tarquam McKenna, editors, *Transgenderism in Education* (tentative title), Falmer Press (London), in press.

Creator of audiovisual materials. Work represented in anthologies, including *Voicing the Difference,* edited by Peter Moss, Wakefield Press, 1994; *She's a Train and She's Dangerous: Women Alone in the 1990s,* edited by Lizz Murphy, Literary Mouse Press (Kalamanda, Australia), 1994; and *Motherlode: A Feminist Anthology on Mothering,* edited by Stephanie Holt and Maryanne Lynch, Sybylla Feminist Press (Melbourne, Australia), 1996. Contributor of articles, poems, stories, and reviews to periodicals, including *Meanjin, Catholic Ethos, Journal of Intercultural Studies, Gender and Education, English in Australia, Social Alternatives, Journal of Homosexuality,* and *Independent Education.* Member of editorial board, *Interpretations: Journal of the English Teachers' Association of Western Australia,* 1995—.

Work in Progress

A young adult novel, *Love You T(w)oo,* publication by Random House expected in 2001; research for *Border Sexualities, Border Families: Bisexual Students and Multi-Partnered Families in Schools* (tentative title).

Sidelights

Maria Pallotta-Chiarolli told *SATA:* "I believe in using stories, narratives, and other forms of writing to raise the awareness of children and young adults about the kinds of social justice issues that need to be addressed. Sometimes these issues are considered controversial. I like using storytelling devices, particularly in describing 'real-life' experiences and in biographies, so that young people can look beyond the myths, stereotypes, and prejudices and consider the so-called controversial issues from more informal and diverse perspectives. That's why my work deals with sexism, racism, homophobia and heterosexism, HIV/AIDS, and poverty.

"Coming from an Italian migrant background and living as a child in the racist Australian climate of the 1960s, and then choosing to live my life as a feminist woman, I have had first-hand experience of marginality, prejudice, and being stereotyped. I believe my own experiences drive my work. Indeed, much of my work is autobiographical.

"I believe young people are often more just, more open-minded than their elders, and I hope my writings act as catalysts to encourage them to pursue the goal of a society where all are treated with justice and diversity is celebrated rather than considered threatening."

For More Information See

PERIODICALS

Campaign, August, 1996.
GEN, March, 1994; May, 1996.

OTHER

Out in the Bush (film), Rantan Productions, 1997.

*   *   *

PATRICK, Susan
See CLARK, Patricia Denise

Autobiography Feature

Kit Pearson

1947-

When I'm in the middle of writing a book, I can't see what it is really about, what its theme is, until I've finished the first draft. The theme is like the root of the tree whose trunk, branches, and leaves are the plot, character, and surface details of my story.

I suppose one can never really see one's own life story clearly—see what the theme is. But now that I am fifty—half a century old!—I can look back and trace a pattern, a pattern that has certainly formed me as a writer. That pattern, that theme as clearly as I am able to perceive it, is one of stories. Stories told, read, imagined, and written down. Perhaps because I grew up in, and live in, a young country where so much seems to have happened somewhere else, I have spent my life first absorbing, then creating, other worlds that reflect my own.

I was born in the spring in a very wintry part of Canada, in Edmonton, Alberta, in 1947. My younger brother Ron was born not quite two years later, and I sometimes resent the fact that I can't remember existing before he did! We moved from a tiny house to a larger one soon after he was born, and my earliest memory is knocking at the door of our new house and waiting to be shown around. I remember my curiosity and excitement before the door opened, feelings I still experience when I open the cover of a new book.

I spent the first eight and a half years of my life in Edmonton, and all those years seemed to be centered on winter. Edmonton is in the middle of Alberta, which means it's at fifty-three degrees latitude. The short days of winter were often bitterly cold—as much as forty degrees below zero—with large amounts of snow that was so dry that it wasn't any good for making snowmen until the spring. My mother would bundle up my brother and me in cloth snowsuits with fur around the rims, double mitts, and scarves tied high around our faces so only our eyes showed. My eyelashes would freeze and thaw, dripping into my eyes. The scarf would slip down around my mouth, become moist, and then freeze, so I had a mouthful of stiff cold wool. We floundered in the deep drifts and made angels, clutched each other on toboggans, and learned to skate in the backyard that my father flooded every winter. Even though it was cold the sun always shone, turning the drifts into sparkling white hills. The blue prairie sky seemed to stretch on forever. I assumed that lines from two songs I heard in my childhood were about Alberta: "Where the skies are not cloudy all day" from "Home on the Range" and "Where the snow lay round about/Deep and crisp and even" from "Good King Wenceslas."

Spring was late (sometimes there was still snow on my birthday on the last day of April), short, and muddy, with water rushing along the curbs, fluffy white seed heads filling the air as if reminding us of winter's snowflakes, and pale green leaves finally appearing in May. I will never forget the sensation of stepping on a bare sidewalk for the first time each spring without boots, my feet feeling deliciously light. Summers were hot with many thunderstorms, and fall was crisp and yellow with blowing leaves. Then came the early morning when my mother would call up the stairs, "Look out the window!" and we would rush to pull open the curtains on the first snowfall—usually in October, sometimes even earlier. Once it even snowed in July, and we made snowballs and put them in the freezer.

Edmonton was a small city then, and I was always conscious that we were surrounded by gently rolling prairie. Somewhere at a very young age I must have heard that the earth was round, for I thought that we lived inside the earth, like being inside a snow dome, the high sky its round walls. I would lean out of my bedroom window at night and stare at the clear stars, which to me were on the outside of the dome shining in; it made me feel very secure. Once a jackrabbit hopped slowly by and paused, staring back at me, its white winter coat gleaming in the moonlight.

Three of my grandparents had roots on the prairies. I knew my father's parents the best—Granno and Grandad. They lived close to us, and we went to their house for Sunday lunch every week except in the summer. Grandad was born in Minnedosa, Manitoba. I was often told the story of his complicated family history, but it took many years for me to sort it out. His grandparents, John Pearson and Marianne Dyer, were a widow and widower living in Devon when three of their grown-up sons came to Manitoba and, liking what they saw, convinced their parents to join them. John and Marianne decided to get married, and then many of the combined family—there were seventeen children in all—moved to Minnedosa to farm and establish businesses. Three of the stepchildren married each other, including my great-grandparents, Frank Pearson and Edith Dyer. My grandfather therefore had several "double first cousins," many of whom ended up on

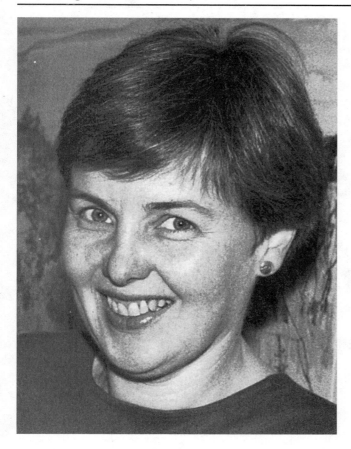

Kit Pearson

the West Coast; I still sometimes run into a Pearson or a Dyer who is related.

When Hugh, my grandfather, left Minnedosa in 1906 he became a Dominion land surveyor, mapping territory in northern Alberta and the Northwest Territories. He told stories of losing all his supplies and food as he hurtled down rivers in the far north. Later he started a very successful radio and automotive supply business in Edmonton, where my father also worked after he married.

My grandmother, Connie, had to me an even more interesting life, for her father was with the Northwest Mounted Police. His name was Colonel Sanders! Granno grew up in various Mountie barracks on the prairies. Her ancestors stretch the farthest back in Canada, some of them United Empire Loyalists who came to Ontario from New York State during the American Revolution. Granno's grandfather, Augustus Jukes, was a senior surgeon in the Mounties, one of the doctors who pronounced Louis Riel—a famous character in Canadian history—sane at his trial.

Granno would tell us stories about taming gophers or performing stunts riding bareback with her older sister Phoebe. She first met my grandfather in Athabasca Landing, Alberta, when she was nineteen. I guess she wasn't smitten with him then, for she became engaged to a man called Ernest Pinkham. When World War I began Granno quickly trained as a volunteer nurse and went over to England to be near Ernest—only to be greeted with the news he had been killed. His family gave her his gold watch, the watch that became the means for going back in

time in my book *A Handful of Time*. I never knew how Granno ran into Grandad again, but they were married in Scotland at the end of the war.

My other grandmother—her name was Auriol, but she was always known as Babs—I gave the unfortunate name of "Goggie" when I was two. She was born in Wetaskiwin, Alberta, but, being an incurable snob, always told people she was from Toronto, where she lived most of her life. She also took great pleasure in telling me about her illustrious "D'Auriol" relatives, who were originally Huguenots from France. Many years later I discovered that her great-grandfather, William Prinsep, a painter—I have several of his watercolours—was Virginia Woolf's great-uncle by marriage!

Goggie's husband, William Hastie, was a Scot from Glasgow who came to Canada in 1906 (the same year Grandad left home!). His father, John Hastie, an engineer, invented the steam steering gear. He married my grandmother in 1920, but I never knew him. He died of asthma when my mother, an only child, was eighteen. All I know of him is that he was quiet with a dry sense of humour. Perhaps he was quiet because Goggie talked so much! She was a vivacious and bossy woman who often visited us. Once my mother and Ronnie, as he was called then, and I went all the way to Toronto on the train and stayed with her. She liked girls better than boys and thus favoured me, providing me with lots of dolls and books and dresses properly hand-smocked all around the bodice. Knowing I was favoured I loved her back, although I later resented how much she dominated my mother. Goggie's strong personality was later useful to me, for she was a model for Aunt Florence in my World War II trilogy.

My Edmonton grandparents were easier to be with, and I adored them. They had two other children besides my father. The oldest, Mollie, lived in Toronto with her husband, Norris, and her children, eventually to number five; the youngest, Gerry, still lived at home then. Mollie's oldest daughter, Chris, has often told me how jealous she was of me for having Grandad all to myself. When I was a baby he would hold me up by the ankles despite everyone's warning that my legs would buckle. Sure enough, one day they did, and my hard forehead broke his nose, something he loved to tease me about in later years. Like my father, Grandad called me "Kitten," and I would sit on his knee while he fed me bits of blue cheese.

Granno was gentle, merry, and full of stories. She taught me how to knit one cold winter afternoon, and she always sat regally in her special chair with a burning cigarette hanging out of her mouth while she talked, catching the butt in an ashtray just in time.

All the time I knew them Granno and Grandad never criticized me, and they were always immensely interested in my life. I know my parents often chafed at having to spend every Sunday afternoon after church at their house, but those afternoons were some of the happiest of my childhood. My grandparents lived in a large, beautiful house on a wooded crescent by the river. There was a drawer in the hall full of small toys and tricks—glasses with eyeballs in them, a Jacob's ladder, a whoopee cushion. These were all the more special because you couldn't take them home. Ronnie and I were the only children for a while, and we basked in the attention the adults gave us. We would sprawl on the rug sipping ginger ale, making houses out of cards, and sucking humbugs, the striped candies Granno always had in a dish by her chair. Sunday dinner (at noon) was always a roast of some kind, with a huge crystal bowl of ice cream for dessert. As Granno brought it in we would all chant, "You scream, I scream, we all scream for ice cream!" After dessert Ronnie and I would race round and round the table while adult arms tried to catch us. Then we would have a rest upstairs while the adults played cards. "Supper" always made me laugh for it was like breakfast: cereal! Ronnie and I ate at the kitchen table while the adults crowded around us making sandwiches out of whatever they could find in the refrigerator.

My Uncle Gerry seemed like a big kid to us until he married my Aunt Margaret in Lethbridge. (I was a proud flower girl in a long organdy dress with a pink slip.) After my youngest brother, Ian, was born and, soon after, their son Geoff, there was a bigger crowd on Sundays. I once hit Ronnie (accidentally) and Ian once hit Geoff (on purpose?) with the same brass ashtray on the table.

In the spring and early fall we played in Granno and Grandad's huge backyard, where there was a rock garden like a small hill, masses of peonies, a birdbath, and an amazing lawn sprinkler that somehow "walked" across the lawn as it spewed out water. Granno and Grandad had a TV before anyone else in the family. (We all watched Queen

Parents, Kay and Sandy Pearson, with infant Kit, 1947.

Elizabeth's coronation in 1953.) And every year a few weeks before Christmas we would gather in their living room to make the "family record": a tape of each member of the family singing an original song set to a familiar tune, which my grandfather then had made into a record. I remember struggling to memorize my song before I could read; when I listen to the records now I am amazed at how well some of the songs were written and—by the more musical of the family—sung. The family in Toronto, including Goggie, also recorded songs, and the exchanged records were listened to after Christmas dinner. Each family always sang "We Wish You a Merry Christmas" at the end, bellowing out "We all want figgy pudding" and "Good tidings we bring/To you and your kin." Each family played charades—English charades, where you act out words instead of titles. Each family placed their children's stockings on the ends of their beds and drew out the delicious agony of waiting for the tree by having to get dressed and have breakfast first.

The clannish nature and rituals of my family I later reflected in Aunt Florence's family in my World War II books set in Toronto and Muskoka. Even now, when I walk into the house that is now lived in by my widowed Aunt Margaret in Edmonton, feelings of being cherished and protected come flooding back.

The east/west division in my extended family went as far back as my parents' marriage. My father, Sandy, grew up in Edmonton, my mother, Kay, in Toronto. Sandy and his older sister Mollie were both sent to boarding schools in Ontario for high school; Mollie attended the same school in Toronto where my mother was a day girl. Mollie suggested her friend Kay when my father needed a date for a dance. Sandy and Kay continued to see each other. When my father was fighting in World War II he proposed by letter and was accepted. They got married in Toronto immediately after the war, in early December 1945, and my father took his new bride back to Edmonton in time for Christmas.

Perhaps the reason landscape has always meant so much to me both in my life and in my writing is that I experienced so many contrasting ones in my childhood. The aspect of the prairies that gave me the greatest joy when I was young was "the lake." Many people in Alberta went to lakes for the summer, and everyone called their summer cottage simply "the lake." Our lake was Lake Wabamun, about forty miles west of Edmonton. When I was two my grandfather bought a cottage there for his three children to share, but our family used it the most. Eventually my father bought his siblings' shares of it and it became ours. I spent every summer there from age two to age seventeen, except for three summers on the West Coast.

Years later, when I read how my favourite author, Arthur Ransome, used to rush down to his lake and dip his hands in the water, I identified strongly with him. The lake was my childhood paradise. The drive seemed endless, and Ronnie and I competed to see who could see the glimpse of silvery water first. When we arrived I rushed out to the front of the green-and-white cottage to feast on the huge expanse of water that seemed to stretch on forever.

The part of the lake we went to consisted of a long line of cottages stretched along a cliff above the lake, connected by a thin dirt path. Every morning we would walk along

Young Kit, age two with maternal grandmother, Goggie; mother, Kay, holding baby Ronnie; paternal grandmother, Granno; and paternal great-grandfather, Colonel Sanders, 1949.

this path, loaded with pails and towels, to the main beach to join other families sprawled on the sand. A wide white pier stretched out to a raft. When we were young we paddled in the water close to shore; when we were older we took the Red Cross swimming lessons that two of the teenagers taught. Although the water was weedy and we often got hives from the snails in it, and although later the skyline was spoiled by two power plants, I adored the place. When I wasn't in the water I was building forts or playing cards or dolls with my friends, hanging around our small cottage reading the accumulation of books and comics that were a new surprise each summer, or walking to the store for groceries or to fill up water bottles from the pump. At first we had an outhouse and kerosene lamps, which I found an adventure. The sun always seemed to shine and the sky was always blue, except when we watched a thunderstorm approach across the water. I tried to capture the atmosphere of the lake in my second book, *A Handful of Time.*

Another childhood landscape was Jasper. The Rocky Mountains were only a five-hour drive from Edmonton, but

what a contrast with their stark grey peaks and rushing rivers. My grandparents spent part of each summer at Jasper Park Lodge, a resort on a large lake. When I was seven I was sent on the train—alone!—to spend a week with them. The train ride terrified me because I had been cautioned so much not to talk to strangers that I quaked whenever an adult kindly asked me questions. Once there, however, I reveled in the majestic beauty of the mountains and also in being the sole object of attention of my grandparents and their friends. The girls who worked as waitresses and chambermaids for summer jobs also indulged me, and I resolved that I, too, would work at the lodge one day. (I did, in the summer of 1968.) That fall my teacher praised me for my accurate drawings of mountains; previously I had drawn them as triangles, but now I knew how irregular their bumpy outlines were.

My early life wasn't all the security of my extended family and the bliss of running free at the lake every summer. I was a very timid child and had many fears. When we finally got a TV I missed the very first episode of

Davy Crockett because the neighbourhood bully, a girl a year older than I, told me that they had boxing on TV where the blood was in colour. I stayed in my room and refused to watch it. I was afraid of things under the bed, and I was sure some monster dwelt in the laundry chute in my room. I had mixed feelings about school; all the other kids made me even shyer, and it seemed so odd to have to sit in rows and put up your hand if you had to go to the bathroom.

I liked most of the work of school, however. I can still recall the intense pleasure of forming an "a" or an "s" on wide-lined paper with a fat pencil. Arithmetic was more complicated, for I made up personalities for each number and knew, for example, that "3," a spoilt little boy, didn't want to be on the same line as "6," a cross woman. This made addition tricky, which is perhaps why I'm still impossible with numbers.

We had Dick and Jane readers, and every day my reading group learned a few words by sight, then took turns reading sentences that contained that word. I will never forget the day I realized I could read the words myself before my teacher told us what they were. The first word on the column was "red." Forgetting my usual shyness I blurted out, "I can read!" and proceeded to sound out the whole list. My teacher looked very stern and said, "You are not to go ahead of the rest of the group." Luckily for me her indifference didn't turn me off reading but instead made me a secret reader. From then on I devoured the stories of Dick and Jane under the lid of my desk. Suddenly I could read all the books that had been read to me at home; I would sit beside my father and read a book while he read the paper.

The blandness of Dick and Jane didn't bother me but stimulated my imagination; at night I would lie in bed and make up more exciting adventures for the children in the stories. I was always pretending, especially with my family of dolls and especially just before I went to sleep. For a long time I was obsessed with fairies and often looked for them in the woods at the lake. After I was taken to my first Disney movie, *Peter Pan,* I became Peter Pan for several years, flying all over the world in adventures that involved fairies and Dick and Jane as well. I also had fantasies of living in a tree, like Piglet.

My imagination was, of course, stimulated by stories, and I was very lucky that my parents and grandparents read to me often. My earliest memories are of Mother Goose rhymes, which Goggie chanted often in her musical voice when she visited. She also knew most of the A. A. Milne verses by heart. I owned *The Real Mother Goose,* and the sharp-nosed figure on the cover still brings back early memories of sitting on someone's lap while the pages were turned. The small Beatrix Potter books also delighted me, although one summer I was afraid to put my feet in the water because of the picture in *Jeremy Fisher* where the huge fish is rising up to grab the frog. A moment of bliss I particularly remember is being read the end of *Winnie-the-Pooh* by my mother one afternoon. I stared at the picture of all the animals and toys having a party in the forest, and—as my mother described the scene—I was in that picture, feeling utterly satisfied: full of good food and good companionship, sitting outdoors in a beautiful place.

We all remember books we wish we could find as adults. Two of mine are a story of a horse who is lonely and is looking in a lighted window, which filled me with

At the lake, age three.

yearning; and a story of a dog in a circus who is first the smallest dog in the world and then the largest, but everyone loves him just the same.

When I began to read on my own one of the first books I read was *Ellen Tebbits* by Beverly Cleary. (It's amazing that she has been writing for so long!) I really identified with Ellen's feeling out of place, for at school there seemed to be a popular circle of girls with whom I never felt comfortable. And because I was always worried about how to behave—my parents put so much emphasis on manners that it was difficult to remember everything—I also identified with Jane in Eleanor Estes's books about the Moffats, especially in the hilarious chapter in *The Middle Moffat* where she doesn't know whether or not to ask for a second chop. I also liked two kinds of Betsy books, those by Carolyn Haywood and those by Maud Lovelace. This early love of books about families has stayed with me all my life. My own books emphasize families, especially *Awake and Dreaming,* where a child yearns to belong to a large family like those in books.

When I was seven a momentous event occurred: my youngest brother, Ian, was born. Ronnie and I were often at odds when we were young; I still have a scar on my wrist from when we pushed in the glass of the basement window from either side. I longed for a sister, but as soon as I saw Ian I melted. From then on he became my baby, a living doll I was allowed to feed and dress and take for walks.

There was always another sibling in our family—a dog. The first I remember was Jumbo, a black mutt who would walk beside Ronnie and support him when he was learning to walk. Then one morning we were told that Jumbo had gone to dog heaven. I was too awed to inquire further. Then came my favourite dog of my childhood, Peggy—a bushy black combination of husky, lab, and chow. We got her from the pound. She was perfectly behaved from the start and loved snow so much she'd dig herself a hollow in it. Peggy was an integral part of my life from ages eight to twenty. She belonged to us all, of course, but she and I knew she belonged to me the most.

A second major change in my life came at age eight and a half, when we moved to Vancouver. We went on the train, a great adventure: being rocked to sleep on narrow bunks with straps to hold you in, the long swaying walk to the baggage car to visit Peggy in her wooden crate, watching the Rockies from the dome car, and eating delicious meals with white tablecloths and heavy silver utensils. We arrived on a mild winter day in January and were greeted by Grandad's brother and sister-in-law, Uncle Ronnie and Aunt Margaret. Before we even saw our new house they whisked us off to Stanley Park where we watched the antics of the otters and rode on the miniature train.

That pleasant beginning was a sign of things to come; the four and a half years we lived in Vancouver were some of the happiest of my life. Perhaps it was because of my age, the upper years of childhood (the age I like writing about best), when I think girls, in particular, are especially strong, before the storms of adolescence set in. The West Coast's soft beauty appealed to me greatly. Vancouver, with its beaches, its wide harbour, its mountains rising straight out of the bay, and its huge trees and blossoms, was a gentle contrast to the stark prairies. I remember walking with my mother and brother to my new school on our first day. Ronnie and I wore our thick Edmonton parkas, which we had to unzip in the mild air; that was the last day we ever wore them. We walked under a canopy of huge chestnut trees and past bare lawns green even in winter, past gardens where snowdrops were already poking up green shoots.

School, too, was much more enjoyable than in Edmonton. That first recess I was surrounded by a group of grade-three girls, all eagerly offering me friendship; what a contrast to the clique that—I thought—spurned me in Edmonton!

I also relished our new house and neighbourhood. The house was much larger and older and more interesting than the one in Edmonton. All the bedrooms were upstairs surrounding a huge hall where Ian, who was always pretending, would construct a sleigh of chairs every Christmas and dress up as Santa Claus. At first I had to share a room with Ronnie. But that, too, was a novelty; we would talk for hours and for the first time became tentative friends.

Ron was always springing things on his gullible sister. When he told me that every night he became Superboy and flew out the window, a large part of me believed him. He also stated that only Cubs—he was one—were allowed to read Rudyard Kipling's *Jungle Books,* so I didn't dare touch his copies. At age seven he firmly told me, his nine-year-old sister, that there was no Santa Claus, a belief I was somewhat desperately clinging to. And shortly after he said he was now going to call Mummy and Daddy "Mum and

Dad"; I could do what I wanted. As usual I never wanted change, but since I was the oldest, what choice did I have?

Back to the delights of Vancouver. Down the street there was an abandoned golf course where all the neighbourhood kids ran wild. We made forts in the trees and told each other horror stories about a pond called the Polio Pool: if you even put a finger in it you would get polio and die.

The crowning glory of Vancouver for me was that I finally had some real friends. First came Lizzie, whom I met at the beginning of grade four. Immediately we were soulmates. A year later Gretchen moved across the street and the three of us became inseparable. As is usual in threesomes, there were sometimes power struggles, but as these seemed to happen more with the other two than with me most of my memories of this friendship are of an incredible security.

Together, and often including Lizzie and Gretchen's younger sisters and sometimes other kids as well, we created a fantasy world that was probably the strongest influence of my childhood. We all read, but Lizzie read far more widely than the rest of us did and introduced us to the legends of King Arthur and to Greek mythology. Every free moment we were involved in some elaborate game. We were cowboys or Indians riding stick horses made out of bamboo that we stole from a neighbour's garden. We were the children in the Narnia books, or we gave flying lessons to younger kids on the golf course. We were the characters from *Johnny Tremain,* which we had seen on Walt Disney. We were gods and goddesses (I was always Pan), or—most of all—we were knights. The knight game even extended to school; secretly we pretended that art or arithmetic was really harping or archery, and we would smile secretly at each other during those periods. I was Sir Lancelot; Lizzie

Kit and Ronnie, ages six and four.

Ronnie, Kit, and younger brother, Ian, with Jumbo, 1954.

was Sir Gawain, and Gretchen was Sir Galahad. (She infuriated us one day when she showed us a picture in the encyclopedia that said the latter was the "perfect knight.") Another game we extended to school was centered on the tiny stuffed Steiff animals we each had. Mine was a rabbit—Susie; Lizzie's was a bear, and Gretchen's a raccoon. We dressed them in capes and hid them under our desk lids; for a short period even the most sophisticated girls began bringing small stuffed animals to school. Later Susie was lost, an event I magnified out of all proportion. That this was the most tragic event of those years is an example of how extremely protected and innocent I was.

It is hard to convey the intensity and magic of those games, which lasted right to the end of grade six. Our mothers began to worry about us still riding around on stick horses. When Lizzie asked for a set of holsters for her twelfth birthday they worried even more. Once the three of us even made a pact that we would never grow up, for surely adults could never know the joy we took in our games.

But of course everyone has to grow up, and I think the games became an unhealthy escape that I, in particular, had a very difficult time weaning myself from later on. Yet I value them for what they contributed to my creative life. Turning oneself into Sir Lancelot or Pan was wonderful practice for turning into my characters when I later wrote books. Writing is pretending, making things up; by the time I came to write books I was very good at that.

No time period is entirely happy, yet I seem unable to remember many unhappy times from those Vancouver years. My family became great friends with Gretchen's, and we all went on many excursions around Vancouver and

shared Easter and Thanksgiving meals. On warm summer evenings after we had been sent to bed Gretchen and I, our rooms (I now had my own) opposite each other, would lean out our windows and talk to each other across the street. Aunt Margaret and Uncle Ronnie lived just up the street—a few houses down from Lizzie's—and even Ian would walk up there on his own and stay for hours. Aunt Margaret's sister Molly also lived with them, and the three old people doted on us. So I continued to enjoy the clannish security we had in Edmonton. And some Christmases Granno and Grandad and even Goggie would visit, although one year Goggie stayed so long and bossed us all so much that four-year-old Ian said to her, "Old woman, go home."

We rode our bikes (which of course were horses) around the neighbourhood, played on the golf course, and walked to and from school in a large chattering group. I enjoyed the simple pleasures of a fifties Vancouver childhood: *Lassie* and *Name That Tune* on TV, eating in the car at the White Spot drive-in restaurant on Sunday evenings, the hula-hoop craze, skiing (the only sport I was ever good at) at Grouse Mountain, piano lessons (where I also shone), being taken to musicals like *Kiss Me Kate* and *South Pacific* at Theatre Under the Stars in Stanley Park— my first theatre experiences—and my first mixed party where we danced to Elvis Presley records. I reveled in Vancouver's trees (I had a favourite I spent hours in) and flowers and even liked the constant rain. Although we spent one summer traveling back to the lake, for the other three we went to a resort on Vancouver Island called Oyster River, where we made houses out of driftwood, fished for salmon (I was so proud when I caught one), and whizzed down the river in homemade kayaks.

And of course I continued to read. I discovered *Little Women* and C. S. Lewis and *The Princess and the Goblin* and Frances Hodgson Burnett, and—lest anyone think I only read "good books"—I also devoured a series called the Happy Hollisters and many dog and horse stories. I never took to Nancy Drew, but I loved the Bobbsey Twins and Enid Blyton. My great-aunt in Scotland sent me lots of British *Girls' Annuals,* which often had stories about boarding schools in them and which made me want to go to one. She also sent me an excellent series called Joy Street. I read a remarkable story in one of them, "A Bad Day for Martha" by Eleanor Farjeon. Despite my happy life in Vancouver there was still part of me that felt like an outsider, someone who was always observing. Perhaps all writers feel like this in their childhoods. The character of Martha riveted me, for most of the books I read were about the outer, not the inner, lives of children. I identified strongly with Martha's fears, her ideas that backfired, and especially her imagination. This book was later lost, and for years I wished I could find it. When I was an adult I read Eleanor Farjeon's autobiography, *A Nursery in the Nineties,* and to my delight one of the chapters was an adapted version of her story. Several years later I actually found the right volume of Joy Street in a secondhand bookstore, so I now own both versions.

Besides the rich fantasy life I led with my friends, I still made up stories every night before I went to bed. And one Saturday morning, prancing around as a horse on a glorious spring day, a surprising thought came into my head: "Someday I will write about this." That was my first inkling of my future career.

The disadvantage of having an overly protected and secure childhood is that it is hard to leave. Eventually Lizzie and Gretchen and I would have to cast aside our imaginary worlds; but I had an especially difficult time because my growing up coincided with our move back to Edmonton.

I was devastated. Apparently my parents knew all along that they were only staying in Vancouver temporarily, but I had no idea that it wasn't forever. Lizzie came to me one day, accusing and frantic, after she heard my mother tell hers on the telephone that we were moving. I dashed home and demanded if it was true; it was. Once again we put Peggy in her crate and traveled by train to our new house in Edmonton; but for me, at twelve, every mile was too far from the friends and city I loved.

We moved into a larger house on the same street we had lived on before. I dreaded going into grade seven at the enormous junior high school a few blocks away, and all my fears came true. There were eight classes for each grade, and I knew only one person in mine. Outside of class I hung around the same group of girls I'd known since grade one. We all walked to school together, picking up each other along the way. We formed a club, the Mysterious Eleven, which met at a different girl's house every Saturday night; sometimes there were sleep-overs where we practised dancing.

Proudly showing her first salmon, 1956.

On the surface, it appeared that I was a normal preteen with many friends. Underneath it was much different. I was still scared of these girls, who seemed so much more confident than I. Looking back I can see that none of us was confident and that if I'd made more of an effort to like them they would have liked me better back. Gradually I made friends with two of the girls—one, Barbara, I knew from the lake, and the other, Louise, was a tomboy like me who preferred to climb trees and explore the ravine by the river rather than giggle about boys. But even with Louise and Barbara I felt removed; although I knew I was now too old for games, I missed them, and Lizzie and Gretchen, so desperately that my new friendships seemed dull by comparison.

Some of the gang began to bully me with the cruelty that girls that age are so good at. Because my mother had forgotten how cold Edmonton winters were, she'd bought me a jacket that was too light and had to buy me a warmer one. "Kit has two winter coats," the girls would chant outside my window. They also made subtle allusions to the fact that I was the only one of the group not to wear a bra.

I've never been as miserable as I was that year, a misery that lessened somewhat in grades eight and nine but always hung over me. My body was changing much too fast for my liking. I couldn't seem to do my hair in the current style; the after-school "sock hops" terrified me; I couldn't seem to learn how to jive (I still can't); and I didn't want a bra, high heels, a straight skirt, or any of the other symbols of being a teenager that were important then. Some of these early teen miseries I later gave to the character of Norah when she is thirteen in *Looking at the Moon.*

Like Peter Pan, I had an unhealthy wish never to grow up. I still played with my dolls, and I had a constant, secret fantasy that I was a child aged ten called Robin; I even wrote a letter to a children's magazine under her name. I became so shy in school that I barely talked to anyone, and every night I wept for my former life in Vancouver.

That summer I at least had the opportunity to visit one of my friends. Gretchen's family had just moved to Toronto, and I went there for a few weeks to stay with Goggie, to visit my eastern relatives, and to stay with Gretchen at her family's cottage in Muskoka—a cottage that became the inspiration for Gairloch in *Looking at the Moon.* It was wonderful to see Gretchen again, but it wasn't the same. She had grown up faster than I had, and there was no mention of games. Her cousins also ganged up on me, calling me "Split Personality." (I gave this agonizing experience of being taunted by a group to Patricia in *A Handful of Time.*) I did enjoy seeing Niagara Falls and my first Shakespeare play, *A Midsummer Night's Dream,* in Stratford. When I got home, however, I found out my brothers had been taken to Vancouver! I felt betrayed and even more homesick for my former life.

What saved me during those miserable three years was reading. Every week, sometimes with Louise, I would take my bike or the bus to the library. I never asked for help but scanned the shelves for what I wanted. It must have been a particularly good library because I found real treasures. Every day after school I would go up to my room with a handful of cookies, lie on my bed, and read, so absorbed in the story that I ate the pages as well as the cookies, tearing off a corner and munching on it without realizing—and ruining a lot of library books in the process! Many of the books I owned as a child have the corners of their pages missing.

This is the time in my life when I did the most reading, sometimes devouring (literally!) a book a day. I remember especially the Borrowers series, *Tom's Midnight Garden*, Arthur Ransome's Swallows and Amazons series (still my favourite children's books), fairy tales by Andersen and Grimm, all the Edward Eager books, and those by E. Nesbit. I also continued to read dog stories. Louise and I shared a passion for dogs; she had a fox terrier called Pixie, and my family now had a second dog, Buff, a comical Hungarian vizsla who would sit in front of the mirror admiring himself and who loved to be dressed up.

One afternoon I found a trunk of old books in my grandparents' basement. Most had belonged to my aunt, and I was allowed to take them home. One was a wonderful family story set in Australia called *The Family at Misrule*. Another was the book that has had the greatest influence on my life: *Emily of New Moon* by L. M. Montgomery. I had already read the Anne books, but I was lukewarm about them; I thought Anne talked too much. Emily, however, bowled me over. Like me, she was lonely and felt an almost mystical kinship with nature. And she wanted to be a writer! After I finished the book I rushed to the drugstore, bought a blank notebook, and started a diary as Emily did. From then on my ambition, vaguely felt in Vancouver, was confirmed: I would be a writer.

I don't remember doing much creative writing in school then. I did have an excellent grammar teacher in grade eight, who once praised a story we had to make up out of our spelling words. Mine went on for pages more than necessary, and she said, "I see we have a future writer in the class"—words I hugged to myself. Although I have written in a journal ever since that first one—and later, regrettably, burned all the ones I'd kept before age twenty—why didn't I try writing fiction? I think I thought writing was something you did when you grew up. Being a writer also seemed a strange thing to want to be. I'd never met one and never did in all my school years; there certainly weren't very many in Canada at the time. So I kept my ambition secret; when asked what I wanted to be when I grew up I said I was going to be a teacher.

There were two comforts in Edmonton I was glad to return to in those unhappy years: my grandparents and the lake. We still spent many afternoons at Granno and Grandad's house. Uncle Gerry and Aunt Margaret now had three young children, and I enjoyed taking care of them and telling them, and Ian, stories. And I loved the lake more than ever. There I swam, made rafts, and played cards on rainy days with the same friends from before.

One Easter holiday when I had just turned fifteen our family went to Harrison Hot Springs near Vancouver. Aunt Margaret and Uncle Ronnie came to visit and offered to take me back with them for a few days. I was ecstatic about finally seeing my old neighbourhood again. With great trepidation I ventured to Lizzie's door and knocked. She welcomed me with warmth and asked me to a party that evening. Many of my friends from elementary school were there, and they were all friendly, but all I could think of was how we had all changed; I missed my childhood more than ever.

The author with her parents on her thirty-third birthday, 1980.

Soon after that I was sent back to Vancouver when I went to a girls' boarding school for high school. Since I had boarding school romanticized from all the stories I'd read about it, I was eager to go. Of course it was nothing like the books, but I fell into it with relief.

When I look back I don't know how I could bear the lack of privacy, the regulated life, and the awful food. But I was back in my favourite city. Still painfully shy, the lack of boys meant no more worrying about how I never went on dates like other girls; still a tomboy, I loved wearing a uniform and not worrying about what to put on every day. Many of the teachers were stimulating, and because we were forced to study every night I began to really like academic work for the first time. The other girls in my class were bright and interesting and ambitious; girls were allowed to be brainy, not pretending not to be to attract boys, as they had in junior high. I was still very quiet, but I made some good friends. One of them, Ann Blades, grew up to become a children's book illustrator; in 1990 she and I did a book together, a retold folk tale, *The Singing Basket*.

The consistent world behind the ivy-covered walls soothed me. I became much happier and more confident, and by grade twelve I even had a sort-of boyfriend, whom I would secretly meet when the school took us skiing. He gave me my first awkward kiss on the school verandah. He missed my mouth and got my ear, but I didn't care; this was what being a teenager was supposed to be like! Those three years at boarding school were so rich that I turned them into my first book, *The Daring Game.*

I had never stopped reading children's books, but now I made the leap into adult literature. The first adult novel I read was *Gone with the Wind;* I was proud of how thick it was. Then I discovered the Brontes and Jane Austen and Shakespeare and Robert Frost and Emily Dickinson. English was my best subject (math was my poorest), so I decided to major in it at university.

But what of writing? Again, I don't remember doing much creative writing, even in high school. Deep inside I still wanted to write, but in those days—the mid-sixties—young women were expected to be teachers, nurses, or librarians. And that was just a stopgap until you got married and stayed home with your children. Like most of my friends, I decided to get a B.A. and put off the decision of what to do until later.

I went to the University of British Columbia (UBC) for my first year of university. After boarding school the freedom was heady. I lived in residence and was free from classes every day at two. My best friend Jane lived with friends of her family who let her have the use of one of their cars, a light blue Mustang that matched Jane's blue coat. She and I and another friend, Jennifer, would take off every day, sometimes driving around the city, or even on trips to Seattle or to the Okanagan to ski. I loved my courses, especially my English course that introduced me to Beat poets and modern art and during which my teacher had us do some creative writing as well.

I would happily have stayed at UBC, but my parents wanted me to return to Edmonton for the rest of university. They said I didn't know anyone there anymore, which was true. Edmonton was just as clannish as my family; I think my parents hoped I would meet my future husband there and stay. I protested a little, but not much, and went home to finish my degree at the University of Alberta.

Just as when I returned to Edmonton at age twelve, I was plunged into misery. Now I wonder, why did I agree to go? I'm sure that if I had made a stronger case I would have been allowed to stay at UBC. But then I was still timid and did what was expected of me.

I continued to like my courses, especially English, but for the first two years there was nothing else about U. of A. I liked. To make friends I joined a sorority. There I was with basically the same group of girls I'd been on the fringe of since age six—still on the fringe. Desperate to be liked, I threw myself into sorority activities with a frenzy and was even elected vice president in my third year. I tried to ignore that part of me that found the activities trivial and phoney. I was doing what was expected of me, and I even had boyfriends, various fraternity boys I met at dances. But none of them were serious, and I felt as shallow as I increasingly found the sorority world.

If you suppress your real self it is bound to burst forth somehow, and in my third year it finally did. Everything began to change at once. I found myself in an experimental English class where the professor led us in encounter groups where we bared our souls to each other. The people in that class became my closest friends. I fell in love for the first time, resigned from the sorority, attended meetings of Students for a Democratic University, grew my hair long, wore flowered tops and a bell on a leather cord, listened to

At Saltspring Island, 1991: Patricia Runcie; Kit Pearson, holding her cairn terrier, Flora; Sarah Ellis; and Nancy Bond.

Bob Dylan and the Rolling Stones, and read many books about Zen Buddhism. My parents were, understandably, concerned at my sudden change, and we began to argue. I moved out, sharing a house near the university with three others. After I got my degree I worked in the library for the summer and that fall went on an extended trip to Europe with four friends; eventually we hoped to travel to India in a van, but after a series of disasters we all split up. I ended up working as a chambermaid and filing clerk in London for several lonely months. Then followed several messy, confusing years during which I wondered what to do with my life and during which I still wasn't writing, except in my journal. I was bewildered but not unhappy; it was the late sixties and early seventies, a tumultuous time when society was changing drastically. Looking back, it seems that I was just the right age for those times. I would alternate working in menial jobs and traveling in Europe, sometimes living in Edmonton and sometimes on the West Coast. I attempted a year at the University of Victoria, getting my teaching degree but flunking the practicum; they said I was too nice to the children! That year was valuable only because it made me realize how little I wanted to be a teacher.

This prolonged adolescence—I was now twenty-five—was brought to an abrupt end when Aunt Mollie—to whom I was very close—and Uncle Norris were killed in a plane crash on a holiday in Greece. The whole family united in comforting my Toronto cousins, my grandparents, and each other, and I appreciated their warmth. My brother Ron decided to get married, and I finally had a "sister," Betty Anne. My haphazard life was beginning to seem like a waste of time, and I decided I needed a career.

So did I begin to write? Not yet. I did the next best thing: I decided to become a children's librarian.

It was a good decision. I already had experience working in libraries; I already knew a lot about children's books from all my reading, and I had always liked children. I took a two-year course at UBC where I studied children's literature with the renowned Sheila Egoff, a wonderful teacher with high standards. Sheila believed that children's books are just as much a part of literature as adult books. Her ideas have always made my reach in writing exceed my grasp.

I assumed that library school, except for the children's librarian courses, would be dull; I never expected it to be so much fun! I met three of my closest friends there, Sarah Ellis (now also a children's book writer), Judi Saltman (who replaced Sheila Egoff when she retired), and Linda Shineton (the mother of three of my youngest friends).

I wanted to stay in Vancouver and work, but there were no jobs there. So I took my first job in Saint Catharines, Ontario. I longed to be in Toronto, however, and eventually moved there and got a job at North York Public Library, where I worked for four years.

Those were busy, satisfying years. I sunk deeper and deeper into the world of children's literature, and I enjoyed the city my mother had grown up in and where my brother Ian now lived. At this time Canadian children's literature was just beginning to blossom. I asked many authors to do readings at the library and got sent to many conferences; the ones I enjoyed the most were the Loughborough conferences in Britain and New England. I was enjoying

single life in my own apartment with a good salary and a cat, Harriet.

One fall I took an evening storytelling course from Alice Kane, a respected Toronto storyteller. She told us how she used to tell stories to the "war guests," children who had been sent to Canada during World War II. I had never heard of these children, so that was when the seeds for my trilogy about them became planted.

The urge to write became stronger and stronger. Now I knew what I wanted to write: children's novels. My job was extremely busy, however, and although I tried to write on Sundays or after work, I simply couldn't give it the time it needed. I did write a picture book text about the antics of our dog Buff, which was turned down; it just whetted my appetite to do more. I was also beginning to experience children's librarian burnout and wanted a change.

I decided to take a year off work and get my M.A. at the Simmons College Center for the Study of Children's Literature in Boston. Judi Saltman did the same thing, and we shared an apartment in Brookline. From 1981 to 1982 I took ten courses in children's literature—what bliss! My teachers—including Betty Levin, Ethel and Paul Heins, Jill Paton Walsh, and John Rowe Townsend—were inspiring. I became good friends with one of my classmates, Joan Tieman, who lived in Boston; she and I and Judi had great trips together exploring New England.

One of my courses was "Writing for Children," taught by Nancy Bond. Remarkably, I almost didn't take this; I thought that if I was a "real" writer I shouldn't need a course. That is partly true; you don't have to take a course to be a writer, but if you find the right one, as I did, it can be a powerful motivation. As soon as I wrote my first assignment—a childhood memoir of how Ron told me there was no Santa Claus—I felt an immense relief. At last I was writing! I adored every moment of that class. Nancy was very encouraging, and she has since become a friend; we've done a lot of traveling together. She was also my advisor for my thesis, which I wrote on Arthur Ransome. In the spring I took a special week-long seminar in writing from Jane Langton, who was equally inspiring and encouraging.

At this time Granno died, and my father sent me a diary that she had kept when she was nineteen. It seemed like a sign to finally do what I was meant to do: my grandmother had written this wonderful document (which I will turn into a book one day), and she had left me a bit of money. I decided to use it to finance myself while I worked part of the week, leaving the other days free to write. I also decided to move back to Vancouver after I finished Simmons; somehow it seemed easier to write in a city where I felt more at home—and where it was easier to stay in and write because it rained all the time.

In the fall of 1982 I drove across Canada with all my possessions in my little yellow Honda. When I reached Vancouver I got a part-time children's librarian job with Burnaby Public Library. On November 12 I sat down to finally begin what I'd decided to create twenty-three years earlier—a book.

The Daring Game was the easiest of all my books to write. Perhaps it was because I thought about it all during that long drive, or perhaps I just did it because I didn't know how hard it was to write. I wrote it the same way I've written all my novels. I don't have much of a plan but

Reading to her goddaughters, Marit and Charlotte Mitchell, 1993.

simply sit down and write by hand with a pen and lined paper, letting whatever comes out come out. Then I make a plan and type the second draft—then on a typewriter, now on a computer. In the second draft I concentrate on the characters and plot; in the third, which consists of scribbling all over the second, I work on the words. Then I keep printing out drafts and revising them until I can't change any more.

I'll never forget the ecstasy I felt when, a year after beginning it, I reached this stage with my first book. I'd finally done it!

But now the hard part began: finding a publisher. That took me another year. After it was rejected twice, Penguin Books Canada in Toronto finally accepted it. I have been with them ever since and have been lucky enough to have had the same insightful editor, David Kilgour, for all six of my novels.

I found it very difficult to begin a second novel, especially when the first one hadn't yet found a publisher. A big mistake was attempting another book only a week after I'd finished the first one. I now know that I have to wait months before I am ready to start a new book; I have to wait for the tide of inspiration to come back in. Because I began writing so late I have dozens of ideas for books; another problem has always been which one to try next.

I seem to write the way I cook; I like to try new recipes. I have tried writing realistic fiction (*The Daring Game*); time travel (*A Handful of Time*); historical fiction

(*The Sky Is Falling, Looking at the Moon,* and *The Lights Go on Again*); and a ghost fantasy (*Awake and Dreaming*). Now I'm trying adult fiction, which is almost like beginning again; it's interesting how different it feels. But I have far more ideas for children's books than adult books. I can still remember those magic ages from nine to twelve vividly, much more clearly than I can remember adolescence.

Right from the beginning I was lucky in the reception of my books. I've never written to please anyone but the child within me, so I was pleasantly surprised when *The Daring Game* became popular. I've won nine awards for my books, and among them they are published in French, Japanese, Dutch, and German and in the United States, Britain, Australia, and New Zealand as well as in Canada. I am constantly asked to schools and conferences, and I get lots of mails from fans. All of this seems like a dream, and I am grateful for my success; the only problem is that it doesn't leave me enough time to write! I stopped being a librarian in 1990, but I still do many other things to do with writing, such as teaching writing to adults and book reviewing.

I still live in Vancouver, with two naughty terriers, Flora and Poppy. I love to travel and have been to Britain many times, as well as to Iceland, New Zealand, and Bali. My greatest pleasure is still reading. I also like playing the piano—alas, much more poorly than when I stopped taking lessons at age seventeen—gardening, going to films, walking, birdwatching, and visiting with old friends in Vancouver, Victoria, Montreal, Toronto, Boston, and Concord, as well as with all the new Canadian writer friends I have made over the last decade. The biggest regret in my life is that I never had children, but I have many children and young adults in my life: my niece and nephews—Anne, Joe, and Will Pearson—and the children of close friends—Marit, Charlotte, and Joey Mitchell and Anne Barringer.

And that is the story so far. In some ways the plot of my life seems predictable: I will carry on creating as many books as I can fit in. Yet every day is like opening up a new book, beginning a new story. Anything can happen, and whatever does it will never fail to be interesting.

Writings

The Dating Game, Penguin Books Canada, 1986.
A Handful of Time, Penguin Books Canada, 1987.
The Sky Is Falling, Penguin Books Canada, 1989.
The Singing Basket, illustrated by Ann Blades, Douglas & McIntyre, 1990.
Looking at the Moon, Penguin Books Canada, 1991.
The Lights Go on Again, Penguin Books Canada, 1993.
Awake and Dreaming, Penguin Books Canada, 1996.

POMASKA, Anna 1946-

Personal

Born July 27, 1946, in Edinburgh, Scotland; daughter of Maksimilian (a storekeeper) and Maria (a storekeeper; maiden name, Koltko) Pomaski; married Wyatt Portz (a printer), December 31, 1989. *Education:* Pratt Institute, B.F.A., 1968; Visual Studies Workshop, Rochester, NY, M.F.A., 1979. *Politics:* "Green."

Addresses

Home—871 Alice St., No. 12, Monterey, CA 93940. *E-mail*—wyatt@concentric.net.

Career

Art teacher at public schools in Brooklyn, NY, 1968-69; Pratt Institute, Brooklyn, photographer in public relations department, 1969-71; freelance illustrator of children's books, 1978—. Destiny Design, studio owner, photographer and artist, 1979-84; work represented in numerous solo exhibitions and group shows, primarily in New York and California; performance artist in California, 1989—. Genesee Community College, art teacher, 1973-75 and 1984; Visual Studies Workshop, art teacher, 1976-77; Communiversity, art teacher, 1977; visiting artist and lecturer at various institutions, including Rochester Institute of Technology and State University of New York at Buffalo. Arroyo Arts Collective, member, 1991—, member of board of directors, 1992-93; Site, member, 1993-94; Perimeter Arts Collective, member, 1994-96. Central American Refugee Center, member, 1985-97; Florence Crittenton Center, volunteer, 1996-97. *Member:* Society of Children's Book Writers and Illustrators.

Writings

AUTHOR AND ILLUSTRATOR

Write Your Own Story Coloring Book, Dover (Mineola, NY), 1979.
Hidden Picture Puzzle Coloring Book, Dover, 1980.
Make Your Own Calendar Coloring Book, Dover, 1981.
Follow the Dots Coloring Book, Dover, 1983.
What's Wrong with This Picture Coloring Book, Dover, 1983.
Create Your Own Pictures Coloring Book, Dover, 1984.
Fun with Numbers Coloring Book, Dover, 1984.
Fun with Crossword Puzzles Coloring Book, Dover, 1985.
Fun with Letters Coloring Book, Dover, 1986.
The Little ABC Coloring Book, Dover, 1986.
The Little Mother Goose Coloring Book, Dover, 1986.
The Little Old MacDonald's Farm Coloring Book, Dover, 1986.
The Little Follow-the-Dots Book, Dover, 1986.
The Little Numbers Coloring Book, Dover, 1987.
The Little Dinosaur Activity Book, Dover, 1987.
Easy Mazes Activity Book, Dover, 1987.
The Little Seashore Activity Book, Dover, 1988.
The Little Alphabet Follow-the-Dots Book, Dover, 1988.
The Little Christmas Activity Book, Dover, 1988.
(With Suzanne Ross) *Fun with Opposites Coloring Book,* Dover, 1989.
(With Ross) *Easy Animal Mazes,* Dover, 1990.
(With Ross) *Easy Search-a-Word Puzzles,* Dover, 1991.
Alphabet Hidden Picture Coloring Book, Dover, 1992.
Easter Activity Book, Dover, 1994.
ABC, Dover, 1997.
Dot-to-Dot, Dover, 1997.
Numbers, Dover, 1997.
Same and Different, Dover, 1997.
What's Wrong?, Dover, 1997.
Dinosaurs, Dover, 1998.
Let's Go!, Dover, 1998.
Opposites, Dover, 1998.

Hidden Pictures, Dover, 1998.
Birds, Dover, 1999.
Flowers, Dover, 1999.
Rhyming Words, Dover, 1999.
The Night before Christmas, Dover, 1999.
My First Crossword Puzzle Book, Dover, 2000.

AUTHOR AND ILLUSTRATOR; "FULL-COLOR STICKER STORY BOOKS"

Make Your Own "The Night before Christmas" Sticker Storybook, Dover, 1996.
Make Your Own "Puss in Boots" Sticker Storybook, Dover, 1997.

AUTHOR AND ILLUSTRATOR; "INVISIBLE MAGIC PICTURE BOOKS"

Invisible ABC Magic Picture Book, Dover, 1994.
Invisible Circus Magic Picture Book, Dover, 1994.
Invisible Mother Goose Magic Picture Book, Dover, 1995.
Invisible Numbers Magic Picture Book, Dover, 1995.
Invisible Animals Magic Picture Book, Dover, 1995.
Invisible Scary Creatures Magic Picture Book, Dover, 1995.
Invisible Sea Life Magic Picture Book, Dover, 1996.
Invisible Christmas Magic Picture Book, Dover, 1996.
Invisible Dinosaur Magic Picture Book, Dover, 1997.
Invisible Birds Magic Picture Book, Dover, 1997.
Invisible Flowers, Dover, 1997.
Invisible Fairies and Elves, Dover, 1997.
Invisible Valentines, Dover, 1997.
Invisible Cars and Trucks, Dover, 1998.

Anna Pomaska

ILLUSTRATOR

Fairy Tale Hidden Picture Coloring Book, Dover, 1982.
A Fairy Tale Toy Theater, Dover, 1984.
Mother Goose: A Very First Coloring Book, Random House (New York City), 1988.
The Little Spanish ABC Coloring Book, Dover, 1988.
My Diary, Dover, 1989.
Hey Diddle, Diddle: Rhymes to Color, Random House, 1989.
The Little French ABC Coloring Book, Dover, 1991.
My Camp Book Diary, Dover, 1991.

ILLUSTRATOR; "COLOR YOUR OWN POSTCARD BOOKS"

Color Your Own Ready-to-Mail Postcards, Dover, 1984.
Color Your Own Happy Birthday Postcards, Dover, 1993.
Color Your Own Thank You Postcards, Dover, 1993.
Color Your Own Valentine Postcards, Dover, 1993.
Color Your Own Easter Postcards, Dover, 1993.

ILLUSTRATOR; "FULL-COLOR POSTCARD BOOKS"

Birthday Party Invitation Postcards, Dover, 1990.
Six Happy Birthday Postcards, Dover, 1990.
Six Thank You Postcards, Dover, 1990.
Six Valentine Postcards, Dover, 1990.
Six Halloween Postcards, Dover, 1990.
Six Thanksgiving Postcards, Dover, 1990.
Six Christmas Postcards, Dover, 1990.
Six Get Well Postcards, Dover, 1991.
Six Summer Camp Postcards, Dover, 1991.
Six Hidden Picture Postcards, Dover, 1994.

ILLUSTRATOR; "FULL-COLOR STICKER BOOKS"

Fun with Alphabet Stickers, Dover, 1985.
Little Rainbow Stickers, Dover, 1989.
Little Dinosaur Stickers, Dover, 1989.
Little Animal Stickers, Dover, 1989.
Little ABC Stickers, Dover, 1989.
Little Thanksgiving Stickers, Dover, 1989.
Little Christmas Stickers, Dover, 1989.
Awards Stickers, Dover, 1999.
Sea Life ABC Stickers, Dover, 1999.
Sun, Moon, and Stars Stickers, Dover, 1999.
ABC Picture Book, Dover, 1999.
Decorative Sun, Moon, and Stars, Dover, 1999.

ILLUSTRATOR; "FULL-COLOR TATTOO BOOKS"

Scary Tattoos, Dover, 1995.
Sun, Moon, and Stars Tattoos, Dover, 1996.
Christmas Tattoos, Dover, 1996.

ILLUSTRATOR; BASED ON WORKS BY BEATRIX POTTER

Peter Rabbit Stickers and Seals, Dover, 1984.
Cut and Assemble Peter Rabbit Toy Theater, Dover, 1984.
The Tale of Jeremy Fisher Coloring Book, Dover, 1985.
The Little Tale of Peter Rabbit Coloring Book, Dover, 1986.
Peter Rabbit Bookmarks, Dover, 1987.
Peter Rabbit Notepaper to Color, Dover, 1988.
Favorite Beatrix Potter Character Prints, Dover, 1992.
Little Bunny Rabbit Stickers, Dover, 1993.
Little Tom Kitten Stickers, Dover, 1993.
Little Jeremy Fisher Stickers, Dover, 1993.
Little Jemima Puddle-Duck Stickers, Dover, 1993.

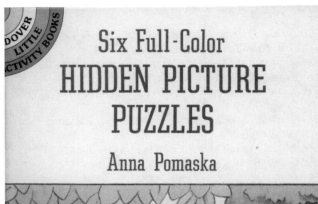

Young children can search for hidden objects in the six different scenes of Pomaska's self-illustrated puzzle book.

The Tale of Peter Rabbit, text by Potter, Dover, 1995.
The Tale of Benjamin Bunny, text by Potter, Dover, 1995.
The Tale of Jemima Puddle-Duck, text by Potter, Dover, 1995.
The Tale of Tom Kitten, text by Potter, Dover, 1995.
Make Your Own Peter Rabbit Sticker Story Book, Dover, 1996.
The Tale of Squirrel Nutkin, text by Potter, Dover, 1996.
The Tale of Mr. Jeremy Fisher, text by Potter, Dover, 1996.

Several of these works have been translated into Spanish, French, and German.

Work in Progress

Digitally imaged illustrations for compact disks; a series of children's activity books, for Grosset & Dunlap; a series of paper-doll career cutouts.

Sidelights

Anna Pomaska told *SATA:* "I am one of those fortunate persons who knew from childhood what she wanted to become—an artist. Born to Polish refugees in Scotland just after World War II, I became a voracious reader and especially responded to the illustrations in the books I read. My Scottish birth guaranteed a familiarity with Britain's longest-lived children's comic character, Rupert Bear, who began his existence in the pages of the *Daily Express* in 1920. My brother gave me a Rupert annual, and I fell in love with the illustrations and adventures created by Alfred Bestall. Looking back, Rupert was one of the first influences that determined my future career as a children's book illustrator. Later influences include Winsor McCay (*Little Nemo in Slumberland*), the *Playmate* magazine of the forties and fifties, and other children's annuals and activity books of Britain and America of the thirties and forties.

"I immigrated with my family to the United States in the fifties, just in time to find myself in a nation beginning a profound self-reflection in its legacy of racism. *Brown vs. Board of Education,* troops mobilized to enforce integration in Mississippi, the civil rights movement, and finally the Vietnam war all had a profound influence on me, as on all Americans. These events, combined with my history of being a refugee, all combined to create a deep social consciousness that has affected my art. It shows itself in my choice of children's projects, and also in the fine photographic/drawing art I have made.

"For the last twenty years, I have created more than a hundred different books and projects for children. Most are activity books—hidden pictures, dot-to-dot, what's wrong?, create your own stories, create your own calendars—but I have also created toy theaters and specialty books. I feel activity books are far more important than most people give them credit for; they develop creativity, problem-solving ability, and perseverance in completing a task, and they provide children with a feeling of accomplishment when finished. These are important building blocks for creating self-esteem.

Cheerful animals and bold, bright colors highlight Pomaska's **Hidden Alphabet Adventure.**

"In my photographic work, I combine my photographs with drawn imagery to create a magical world based upon the real, on the one hand, and on the other to call attention to the challenges—social and environmental—that face the human family as we move into the twenty-first century."

Q–R

QUYTH, Gabriel
See JENNINGS, Gary (Gayne)

*   *   *

RANT, Tol E.
See LONGYEAR, Barry B(rookes)

*   *   *

RASCHKA, Chris
See RASCHKA, Christopher

*   *   *

RASCHKA, Christopher 1959-
(Chris Raschka)

Personal

Born March 6, 1959, in Huntingdon, PA; son of Don (a historian) and Hedda (a translator; maiden name, Raschka) Durnbaugh; married Lydie Olson (a teacher), August 4, 1984. *Education:* St. Olaf College, B.A., 1981. *Hobbies and other interests:* Yoga, walking, playing solitaire, going to movies.

Addresses

Office—310 Riverside, #418, New York, NY 10025.

Career

Writer, artist, and musician. Art teacher in St. Croix, Virgin Islands, 1985-86; freelance artist, cartoonist, and editorial illustrator, Ann Arbor, MI, 1987-89; freelance artist and children's book writer and illustrator, New York City, 1989—. Member, New York City School Volunteers Program; member, Ann Arbor Symphony Orchestra, Ann Arbor, 1982-84 and 1986-89; member, Flint Symphony Orchestra, Flint, MI, 1983-84. Also worked as an intern in an orthopedic clinic in Germany, 1981-82, and as a respite care worker in Ypsilanti, MI, 1982-84. *Exhibitions:* Artwork has been shown in many exhibitions, including *From Sea to Shining Sea—An American Sampler: Children's Books from the Library of Congress,* Library of Congress, Washington, DC, 1998; *America Illustrated,* Bolzano, Padua, Rome, and Venice, Italy, 1998-2000; and *The Art of the Book,* Grand Valley State University, Michigan, 1999. *Member:* Authors Guild, Authors League of America, Society of Children's Book Writers and Illustrators, New York-New Jersey Trail Conference, Municipal Art Society.

Awards, Honors

Best Books of the Year citation, *Publishers Weekly,* 1992, Notable Children's Book citation, American Library Association (ALA), 1992, and Pick of the Lists citation, American Booksellers Association, 1992, all for *Charlie Parker Played Be Bop;* Caldecott Honor Book award, ALA, 1994, and U.S. winner of UNICEF-Ezra Jack Keats Award, 1994, both for *Yo! Yes?*

Writings

FOR CHILDREN; SELF-ILLUSTRATED

UNDER NAME CHRIS RASCHKA, EXCEPT AS NOTED

(Under name Christopher Raschka) *R and R: A Story about Two Alphabets,* Brethren Press, 1990.
Charlie Parker Played Be Bop, Orchard, 1992.
Yo! Yes?, Orchard, 1993.
Elizabeth Imagined an Iceberg, Orchard, 1994.
Can't Sleep, Orchard, 1995.
The Blushful Hippopotamus, Orchard, 1995.
Mysterious Thelonious, Orchard, 1997.
Arlene Sardine, Orchard, 1998.
Like Likes Like, DK Publishing, 1999.
Moosey Moose, Hyperion, 2000.
Doggy Dog, Hyperion, 2000.
Goosey Goose, Hyperion, 2000.
Lamby Lamb, Hyperion, 2000.
Ring! Yo?, DK Ink, 2000.

A hippopotamus prone to blushing gains self-confidence from his friend Lombard in Chris Raschka's self-illustrated **The Blushful Hippopotamus.**

Sluggy Slug, Hyperion, 2000.
Snaily Snail, Hyperion, 2000.
Whaley Whale, Hyperion, 2000.
Wormy Worm, Hyperion, 2000.

ILLUSTRATOR

James H. Lehman, *The Saga of Shakespeare Pintlewood and the Great Silver Fountain Pen,* Brotherstone, 1990.
James H. Lehman, *Owl and the Tuba,* Brotherstone, 1991.
Phyllis Vos Wezeman and Colleen Aalsburg Wiessner, *Benjamin Brody's Backyard Bag,* Brethren Press, 1991.
George Dolnikowski, *This I Remember,* Brethren, 1994.
Nikki Giovanni, *The Genie in the Jar,* Holt, 1996.
Simple Gifts: A Shaker Hymn, Holt, 1998.
Margaret Wise Brown, *Another Important Book,* Harper-Collins, 1999.
bell hooks, *Happy to Be Nappy,* Hyperion, 1999.
Sharon Creech, *Fishing in the Air,* HarperCollins, 2000.

Sidelights

Caldecott Honor-winning author and illustrator Chris Raschka likes to take chances. Employing only thirty-four well-chosen words in his book *Yo! Yes?,* and artwork that is, according to *Publishers Weekly* contributor Diane Roback, "brash, witty, and offbeat," Raschka manages to convey volumes about not only the process of making friends, but also race relations and the subtle nuances of emotion. His *Charlie Parker Played Be Bop,* constructed like a jazz piece itself with text forming the rhythm and cadence of be bop, "stretched the definition of picture book," according to Roback in another *Publishers Weekly* review. Raschka is a chance-taker in

his private life as well: accepted to medical school in the early 1980s, he made an eleventh-hour decision to forego the material security of a doctor's life for the risk and reward of being a freelance artist. It is a decision he has never regretted.

Born in Pennsylvania, Raschka is the only one of his siblings not born abroad. Raschka's parents met while both were doing refugee work after World War II: his father is an American from Detroit, and his mother is originally from Vienna, Austria. "So I grew up with a little bit of both in me," Raschka told *SATA* in an interview. "My earliest stories were Viennese fairy tales and sagas of Vienna that my mother would tell me." Growing up speaking both German and English, Raschka attended first grade in Marburg, Germany, where his father, a college history professor, was on sabbatical. "At that time of my life, I actually forgot English," he said. "When I got back to the United States, I remember my first grade teacher, Mrs. Ericson, saying 'Do you understand, Christopher?' I thought this was strange." But his childhood was not spent solely in distant locales. Living in suburban Chicago, "I played in the storm sewers and ditches," he said. "They were the one interesting place in the whole bleak environment."

Though he remembers some of the American cultural artifacts from his youth, such as the "Dick and Jane" readers, it is primarily the picture books from his mother's part of the world that informed his earliest imaginings and that still influence his own work. "I loved books such as *Die kleine Hexe* (*The Little Witch*) by [Otfried] Preussler," Raschka told *SATA.* "Another all-time favorite is the illustrator Winnie Gebhardt Gayler and Wilhelm Busch with his 'Max and Moritz' stories. I even liked *Struwelpeter* when I was growing up. I know they are all pretty frightening, with horrific things happening to children who disobey their parents, but I think that kids are so used to seeing dangers all around them that they can deal with it. I was disturbed by some of the cruelty of the old German stories, but I loved the drawings and still do." Only now as an adult is Raschka "catching up on" the great illustrators known to British and American audiences.

Raschka was involved in art and music from an early age. As a child, he loved to draw, and also started studying the piano at age six. From the piano he went on to the recorder and then violin. "But I was such a bad violinist," Raschka said, "that the director of the junior high orchestra made me take up viola." He went on to play in both high school and college orchestras. "But all the while I planned to be a biologist. I just loved animals of all types, especially crocodiles and turtles. I also loved drawing and music, but never thought I could make a living at those." Raschka was a biology major at college, and after graduation he planned to work on a crocodile farm in India on a project to restore the crocodile population in the country's rivers, thereby reviving a limited harvesting of the animal. But when these plans were put on hold, he took a position as an intern in a children's orthopedic clinic in Germany instead. "I learned so much from those kids," Raschka

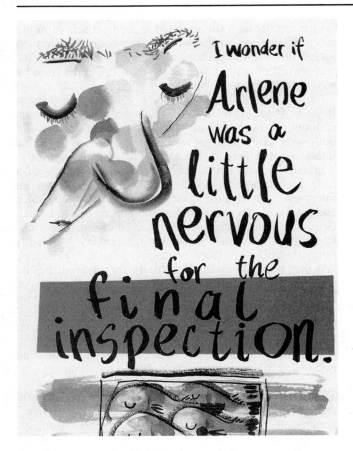

Raschka follows the life of Arlene from a fjord to a sardine can in his self-illustrated **Arlene Sardine.**

said, "and I loved the work. It was after that experience that I decided to go to medical school." After studying for and passing the entrance tests, Raschka was ultimately admitted to medical school, but again he put his plans on hold while he and his new wife went to St. Croix, Virgin Islands.

"I had a lot of luck in St. Croix," Raschka recalled. "My wife and I both decided to try our art—we had met in an art class—and we had shows there. My work was in galleries and I began to get freelance work as an illustrator. It was there that I first realized I might be able to make it as an artist." But the time came to enter medical school, and Raschka and his wife returned to the United States and the University of Michigan in Ann Arbor. The very night of his orientation, Raschka decided not to go to school. Instead, he opted to work as an illustrator for various regional newspapers and magazines, doing everything from political cartoons to illustrations for legal text. Meanwhile, Raschka's wife trained as a Montessori teacher. "After a couple of years illustrating, I thought I would try a children's book," Raschka said. "That's how *R and R* came about."

Raschka's first picture book explored a theme he continues to develop: finding commonality in difference and allowing tolerance to bridge the gaps between people and peoples. "Actually the second 'R' in the title

should be backwards, like in the Russian alphabet," Raschka told *SATA*. "The book is a story that contrasts the English and Russian alphabets and the two letters are the main characters. It's a Russian-American friendship book and the text is both in English and Russian." With this first book, Raschka was already demonstrating the care and attention to detail that would be seen in his later picture books. "My goal is to create a book where the entire book—text, pictures, shape of book—work together to create the theme. The placement of images and text on the page is crucial for me."

Raschka began painstaking work toward this goal with *R and R,* which he finished in only three weeks. Encouraged by a professor of children's literature at the University of Michigan, Raschka prepared a complete package with lettering, design, and layout all camera-ready, and submitted it to a small regional publisher. "The idea was to get into print," Raschka told *SATA*. "The publishing house I worked with in Illinois liked my work and this led to other illustration jobs." He worked on three picture books with text by other authors at this time. "It was all sort of my apprenticeship period," Raschka recalled. "It taught me the amount of work involved in creating a picture book and how to put books together. And most of all this work taught me to see the book as a whole work and not just one illustration after another."

Meanwhile, Raschka was still pursuing his second love, music. As a member of two professional symphony orchestras, he still held hope of a career as a viola player. New York City also began to beckon. "My wife and I spent a couple of summers in New York and it was a wonderful experience. For me, New York City is the best blend of two worlds. It has the feeling of a big European city." In 1989, with no job prospects, Raschka and his wife decided to make the leap. For Raschka, this would be a time where he would make the decision between art or music. All that summer he practiced on a new viola, hoping to audition for the big orchestras in the fall. He even experimented with a new hand position on the instrument, and then nature took over. "I developed this incredibly painful case of tendinitis," he related in his interview. "I simply couldn't play anymore. My decision was made for me." Years later, Raschka still suffers from tendinitis and can no longer play viola, though his love of music has not diminished.

It was this musical inclination that won Raschka his first big break. After struggling to find freelance illustration work for a couple of years, and creating a small body of work in children's books, Raschka felt he knew the children's book trade and was ready to take some chances with something really innovative. "I start work early every morning," Raschka said. "And I like to listen to the radio when I work. In New York there is this one show on morning radio that plays all the music of [jazz saxophone player] Charlie Parker. This is every morning, and the man who does the show, Phil Schaap, plays every last scrap of the music. I was caught up by his enthusiasm for Parker. That and my own love for the music convinced me I should do a book on him.

Ultimately I dedicated my book to Schaap." Convinced that jazz will be the classical music of the next century, Raschka decided it was time that kids learned something more about the jazz greats like Parker other than that their lives were messed up by drugs. "I wanted to write about Parker for the birth of be bop, and not for the downside of his life."

Initially planning to write a straightforward biography of the musician, Raschka's intention was derailed after the very first sentence of the book: "Charlie Parker played be bop," which also became the book's title. "I realized these words could fit one of the great be bop tunes of the time, 'Night in Tunisia,' by Dizzy Gillespie," Raschka recounted for *SATA*. "After these first words I put away the notion of a regular biography and decided to convey just two facts: that Parker played the saxophone and played be bop. The rest was like a be bop tune itself, based on a repeating stanza or motif, with pure nonsense stanzas in between—a simple line that gets modified over and over again." Raschka blended this text with art done in charcoal and watercolors, angular and skewed and quite humorous. The finished book was turned down by one publisher, and then an illustrator friend of Raschka's suggested he submit it to Richard Jackson at Orchard Books, who took immediate interest in the project.

Doubts as to whether the public would understand what Raschka was trying to do with the book were quickly dispelled by reviews. "Rather than attempting to teach his young audience about Parker's music," *Booklist* contributor Bill Ott noted, "Raschka allows them to hear it—not with sounds but with words and pictures." Raschka's text sticks in the head like a persistent ditty: "Charlie Parker played *be bop*./ Charlie Parker played *saxophone*./ The music sounded like *be bop*./ Never leave your cat alone./ Be bop./ Fisk, fisk./ Lollipop./

Boomba, boomba./ Bus stop./ Zznnzznn./ Boppity, bibbitty, bop. BANG!" In addition, Raschka's artwork gives his figures "extraordinary energy; creating jaunty, fantastical creatures to move with the beat," explained a *Kirkus Reviews* critic. Roback, writing in *Publishers Weekly,* added that "even the typeface joins in the fun as italics and boldface strut and swing across the pages." Roback also noted the inside jokes Raschka plays, such as the birds which are used as decorative motifs on some pages—Parker's nickname was "Bird." Raschka "has created a memorable tribute" to Parker, wrote Elizabeth S. Watson in *Horn Book,* calling the book "one of the most innovative picture books of recent times." And jazz great Dizzy Gillespie himself praised the book in *Entertainment Weekly.* Comparing the text to scat singing, Gillespie liked the "drawings of Bird, too; they're funny. So was he. I think this book would make him laugh a lot. It will surely make kids laugh."

The positive reception to this book encouraged Raschka to push ahead with another project that had started germinating about the same time as the Charlie Parker book. "I was walking to the post office one day," Raschka recalled for *SATA,* "and was suddenly struck with how rich the street scene was. I've got a real interest in language and how words such as 'Yo' come into use. And so I began thinking about how language and culture and race all seem so big, but are actually small. They shouldn't really stand between people and keep us apart." With this germ of an idea—the interplay of language and race—Raschka started playing with story ideas. He wanted to talk about friendship, about the process of making friends. And he wanted to keep it simple and direct. "When I was a kid, my dad would play this little one-word game with us. We used to carry on whole dialogues with just one word back and forth." From these elements, *Yo! Yes?* was born.

the moon will watch
you in your room.

Little dog takes a poetic journey to dreamland in Raschka's **Can't Sleep.**

on the Black loom   on the Black loom

Raschka's illustrations portray a dancing young African-American girl between her mother and members of her community in Nikki Giovanni's The Genie in the Jar.

With just thirty-four words, Raschka manages to portray a potential racial stand-off that turns into friendship. On the left-hand page, an African-American boy, coolly outfitted in baggy shorts and unlaced sneakers, calls "Yo!" across the book to a shy white boy who seems to be inching off the right-hand page. From this beginning, the picture book progresses through one-word exchanges that show the white kid to be lonely for lack of friends, and culminates in the more outgoing black kid offering friendship, an offer accepted in an ecstatic high-five as the two join together on the final page and shout "Yow!" with joy. "Raschka exhibits an appreciation of the rhythms of both language and human exchange in his deceptively simple story," Maeve Visser Knoth wrote in *Horn Book.* "The succinct, rhythmic text and the strong cartoon-like watercolor-and-charcoal illustrations are perfect complements," Judy Constantinides similarly commented in *School Library Journal.* Raschka's artwork and layout are "bold, spare and expressive," summarized a *Bulletin of the Center for Children's Books* reviewer, who concluded that "the language has the strength of a playground chant; the story is a ritual played out worldwide."

Named a Caldecott Honor Book, *Yo! Yes?* was a further step in Raschka's attempt at a complete work of art, where placement of illustrations on the very bottom edge of the page was as important as the hand-lettered text. The structure of the book itself also adds to the story, as the two boys seem to be looking across, and eventually

bridge, the gap between left and right pages. The book is also a distillation of some of the kids Raschka plays basketball with in New York and of himself as the shy new white kid on the block. "Beneath it all," Raschka told *SATA,* "the black kid is shy too. It's a risk for him to offer friendship. I hope it's always a risk worth taking."

Raschka's next book was inspired by a poem by Elizabeth Bishop, "The Imaginary Iceberg," which explores the theme of inner strength as one's own "inner iceberg." *Elizabeth Imagined an Iceberg* is a story about a kid "who uses this inner strength to protect herself from another character who could swallow her up," Raschka explained. "It's about child abuse, but a wide range of such abuse, psychological and not just physical." It is a story that had been germinating ever since Raschka lived in St. Croix and worked for a short time with abused children. In the book, Elizabeth manages to "freeze out" the domineering Madam Uff Da by picturing what her imaginary iceberg friend would do in the same situation. Employing charcoal and oil glazes, Raschka managed to convey a darker and denser atmosphere with more background and a stronger line in *Elizabeth Imagined an Iceberg.* "Raschka's breezy illustration style is as wittily offbeat as ever," Roback noted in *Publishers Weekly,* although she expressed reservations about determining just what the message of the book was. *School Library Journal* contributor Kate McClelland, however, found Raschka's "provocative but chilling book" successful in portraying how a child can deal with a frightening stranger.

Raschka generally has several projects going at once. "I may be finishing up one book while another one is in the early stages of artwork and still another one is just a few words scribbled onto a bit of scrap paper and left to ripen for a time," he said. "With my illustrations, I am working very close to the surface. Most of the information is right up front without great detail in the background. That's why I like to position them on the bottom of the page. To make them almost come out of the frame, to jump off the page. I work for young kids who want things close up and are immediate and tactile." As for content and theme, Raschka writes out of personal experience and necessity: "My books are my own thoughts about things that are important to me," he explained to *SATA.* "I work through how I feel about such things as language, art, music, and friendship with these loose, colorful and slightly wild drawings."

"I hope that my books create an openness to the world," Raschka told *SATA.* "An openness to cultural and racial differences. So far, I've looked at language and music and diversity. I want kids to be able to be positive toward these things. To enjoy difference and not be frightened by it."

In *The Blushful Hippopotamus* Raschka offers up his signature combination of expressionistic depictions of characters and unusual, rhythmic text. Like the earlier *Yo! Yes?*, Raschka tells much of the story in *The Blushful Hippopotamus* visually, using the simple technique of rendering confident characters large and timid characters small. Roosevelt Hippopotamus is so overpowered by his sister's teasing that he practically slinks off the right-hand page while his sister looms so large that only part of her face and body can fit on the left-hand page. But, as Roosevelt's bird friend Lombard boosts his confidence, Roosevelt grows in stature (and his sister shrinks correspondingly). The book ends with a grateful embrace by the two friends. "Ah, the sweet balm of friendship," beamed a reviewer for *Publishers Weekly,* continuing: "its magic works as admirably on these pages as it does in real life." Raschka's *Like Likes Like* is another celebration of friendship with a story played out mainly in the author/illustrator's expressive drawings. This book "features Raschka at his most amenable," contended Julie Corsaro in *Booklist.*

Of *The Blushful Hippopotamus,* School Library Journal reviewer Barbara Kiefer predicted: "This simple story will comfort any child who's ever been teased unmercifully." Reviewers likewise praised Raschka's evident sympathy for the uncomfortable feelings of children demonstrated in *Can't Sleep.* Horn Book reviewer Mary M. Burns described Raschka's illustrations as "a minimum of detail but supercharged with emotion," depicting a small dog as he goes to bed and lies awake listening to the sounds of the rest of his family preparing for sleep. Burns singled out for praise the author's "brilliantly imaginative and completely childlike conclusion," in which the moon watches over the fearful child/dog at night so that, during the day, when the moon is asleep and the dog awake, the child can watch over the moon "and keep her safe."

Critics likened another of Raschka's books of the late 1990s, *Mysterious Thelonious,* to the earlier *Charlie Parker Played Be Bop.* Like the earlier book, *Mysterious Thelonious* is a tribute to a famous figure in jazz history; this time it is composer Thelonious Monk. And like *Charlie Parker,* the text of *Mysterious Thelonious* mimics the music of its subject. Critics compared the text of the earlier book to the improvisational be-bop music it celebrates; in the latter book, the author/illustrator associates the placement and color of each page's illustration with placement of a note on the musical scale. Thus the book may be "played" as music to the tune of the composer's famous "Mysterioso." Watson, in another *Horn Book* review, remarked that while not all readers would be able to access this aspect of Raschka's tribute, those who could would find "Raschka's fresh, inventive use of color, rhythm, and melody will sing."

Though these books, along with his earlier works, have been considered innovative, pushing at the boundaries and expectations attached to children's literature, none got the kind of reaction from critics evoked by *Arlene Sardine.* In this book, Raschka chronicles the two-year life of Arlene from birth in a fjord among thousands of her kind, to death on the deck of a fishing boat, and beyond, to processing in a sardine factory. Ilene Cooper observed that the sardine's short life and subsequent death "seems a dubious topic upon which to write a book for preschoolers," in a *Booklist* review. *School Library Journal* reviewer Carol Ann Wilson was similarly ambivalent about *Arlene Sardine,* observing that "the graphic design [of the book] is masterful," and praising the touches of whimsy injected into the fact-based account of Arlene's life via the poetic rhythms and use of repetition in the text. Still, "Arlene's saga, like sardines, is an acquired taste," Wilson concluded. While Betsy Hearne, in her commentary in *Bulletin of the Center for Children's Books,* acknowledged the issues raised by other critics concerning the propriety of the book for its intended audience, she also cast *Arlene Sardine* as the culmination of Raschka's daring approach to children's books. "In the wake of the conventional cliches that too often plague literature of all kinds, including children's, it's refreshing to have a visual storyteller trying innovative things," Hearne declared, noting: "One thing for sure, Raschka's work always surprises, challenges, and intrigues us one way or another."

Works Cited

Review of *The Blushful Hippopotamus, Publishers Weekly,* August 5, 1996, p. 441.

Burns, Mary M., review of *Can't Sleep, Horn Book,* March-April, 1996, p. 191.

Review of *Charlie Parker Played Be Bop, Kirkus Reviews,* July 1, 1992, p. 853.

Constantinides, Judy, review of *Yo! Yes?*, *School Library Journal,* May, 1993, p. 90.

Cooper, Ilene, review of *Arlene Sardine, Booklist,* September 1, 1988, p. 126.

Corsaro, Julie, review of *Like Likes Like, Booklist,* April 1, 1999, p. 1409.

Gillespie, Dizzy, "What about Bop?," *Entertainment Weekly,* October 9, 1992, p. 70.

Hearne, Betsy, review of *Arlene Sardine, Bulletin of the Center for Children's Books,* September, 1998, pp. 3-4.

Kiefer, Barbara, review of *The Blushful Hippopotamus, School Library Journal,* September, 1996, pp. 117-18.

Knoth, Maeve Visser, review of *Yo! Yes?*, *Horn Book,* May-June, 1993, p. 323.

McClelland, Kate, review of *Elizabeth Imagined an Iceberg, School Library Journal,* April, 1994, p. 112.

Ott, Bill, review of *Charlie Parker Played Be Bop, Booklist,* June 15, 1992, p. 1843.

Raschka, Chris, *Can't Sleep,* Orchard, 1996.

Raschka, Chris, *Charlie Parker Played Be Bop,* Orchard Books, 1992.

Raschka, Chris, telephone interview conducted by J. Sydney Jones for *Something about the Author,* June 14, 1994.

Raschka, Chris, *Yo! Yes?*, Orchard Books, 1993.

Roback, Diane, review of *Charlie Parker Played Be Bop, Publishers Weekly,* July 6, 1992, p. 54.

Roback, Diane, review of *Elizabeth Imagined an Iceberg, Publishers Weekly,* December 13, 1993, p. 69.

Roback, Diane, review of *Yo! Yes?*, *Publishers Weekly,* February 15, 1993, p. 236.

Watson, Elizabeth S., review of *Charlie Parker Played Be Bop, Horn Book,* November-December, 1992, pp. 718-19.

Watson, Elizabeth S., review of *Mysterious Thelonious, Horn Book,* January-February, 1998, p. 68.

Wilson, Carol Ann, review of *Arlene Sardine, School Library Journal,* September, 1998, p. 179.

Review of *Yo! Yes?*, *Bulletin of the Center for Children's Books,* April, 1993, pp. 262-63.

For More Information See

PERIODICALS

Los Angeles Times Book Review, June 20, 1993, p. 3.
School Library Journal, October, 1992, p. 108.

*   *   *

REEVE, Kirk 1934-

Personal

Born April 25, 1934, in Oregon City, OR; son of Walter and Celia (Blomquist) Reeve; married Nancy Overstreet, February 25, 1961; children: Karen Reeve Roberts, David. *Education:* Whittier College, B.A., 1956, M.Ed., 1965. *Politics:* Republican. *Religion:* Protestant. *Hobbies and other interests:* Writing, reading, playing handball and racquetball, listening to jazz, "keeping up with current events."

Kirk Reeve and young friends.

Addresses

Home—61 Candlewood Way, Buena Park, CA 90621. *Office*—South Hills Academy, 1600 East Francisquito Ave., West Covina, CA 91791.

Career

Elementary and junior high school teacher and principal in Whittier, CA, 1962-96; South Hills Academy, West Covina, CA, teacher of mathematics, 1996—. *Military service:* U.S. Naval Reserve, 1952-72, active duty, 1956-60; became commander. *Member:* National Education Association, Naval Reserve Association, Reserve Officers Association.

Awards, Honors

Commendation, Americas Award for Children's and Young Adult Literature, 1998, Notable Children's Trade Book in the Field of Social Studies citation, National Council for the Social Studies and Children's Book Council, 1999, and Best Children's Books of the Year selection, Bank Street College of Education, 1999, all for *Lolo and Red-Legs.*

Writings

Lolo and Red-Legs, Northland Publishing (Flagstaff, AZ), 1998.

Work in Progress

Research on Indian cultures of the American southwest.

Sidelights

Kirk Reeve told *SATA:* "Writing fiction for children has been an ambition of mine for well over thirty years—since my early years as an elementary schoolteacher. Finding the time was the challenge. My writing efforts had to take third place to earning a living and raising a family. It wasn't until my own kids were grown and on their own that writing crept into second place. Several short stories later, I was into my first novel. That was a learning experience in itself! The blessings of a talented mentor and lots of persistence paid off. *Lolo and Red-Legs* was published in 1998 by Northland Publishing. What a thrill it was to receive that first copy sent to me! The feeling of creative accomplishment was—and still is—euphoric. I want to do it again . . . and again . . . and again!"

*   *   *

RINALDI, Ann 1934-

Personal

Born August 27, 1934, in New York, NY; daughter of Michael (a newspaper manager) and Marcella (Dumarest) Feis; married Ronald P. Rinaldi (a chief lineman for Public Service Gas & Electric), July, 1960; children: Ronald P. Jr., Marcella.

Addresses

Home and office—302 Miller Ave., Somerville, NJ 08876.

Career

Writer. *Somerset Messenger Gazette,* Somerset, NJ, columnist, 1969-70; *Trentonian,* Trenton, NJ, columnist, feature writer, and editorial writer, 1970-91. Lecturer, making visits to schools and educational conferences around the United States. Former member, Brigade of the American Revolution.

Awards, Honors

First place awards for newspaper columns, New Jersey Press Association, 1978, 1989; New Jersey Institute of Technology award, 1987, for *Time Enough for Drums,* and 1988, for *The Good Side of My Heart;* National History Award for contributions in "bringing history to life," Daughters of the American Revolution, 1991, for her historical novels; Best Book Award, Senior Division, Pacific Northwest Library Association, 1994, and M.

Ann Rinaldi

Jerry Weiss Book Award, 1998, both for *Wolf by the Ears;* several second place awards for newspaper columns; *Time Enough for Drums, The Last Silk Dress, A Break with Charity* and *Wolf by the Ears* were named American Library Association Best Books for Young Adults.

Writings

YOUNG ADULT NOVELS

Term Paper, Walker, 1980.
Promises Are for Keeping, Walker, 1982.
But in the Fall I'm Leaving, Holiday House, 1985.
Time Enough for Drums, Holiday House, 1986.
The Good Side of My Heart, Holiday House, 1987.
The Last Silk Dress, Holiday House, 1988.
Wolf by the Ears, Scholastic, 1991.
A Ride into Morning: The Story of Tempe Wick, Harcourt, 1991.
A Break with Charity: A Story about the Salem Witch Trials, Harcourt, 1992.
In My Father's House, Scholastic, 1993.
The Fifth of March: The Story of the Boston Massacre, Harcourt, 1993.
A Stitch in Time (first book in the "Quilt Trilogy"), Scholastic, 1994.
Finishing Becca: The Story of Peggy Shippen and Benedict Arnold, Harcourt, 1994.
The Secret of Sarah Revere, Harcourt, 1995.

Broken Days (second book in the "Quilt Trilogy"), Scholastic, 1995.

Hang a Thousand Trees with Ribbons: The Story of Phillis Wheatley, Harcourt, 1996.

Keep Smiling Through, Harcourt, 1996.

The Blue Door (third book in the "Quilt Trilogy"), Scholastic, 1996.

The Second Bend in the River, Scholastic, 1997.

Mine Eyes Have Seen, Scholastic, 1997.

Nightflower, Harcourt, 1997.

An Acquaintance with Darkness, Harcourt, 1997.

Cast Two Shadows: The American Revolution in South Carolina, Harcourt, 1998.

My Heart Is on the Ground: The Diary of Nannie Little Rose, a Sioux Girl, Scholastic, 1999.

The Coffin Quilt: The Feud between the Hatfields and the McCoys, Harcourt, 1999.

Amelia's War, Scholastic, 1999.

The Journal of Jasper Jonathan Pierce: A Pilgrim Boy, Plimoth Plantation, 1620, Scholastic, 2000.

The Education of Mary: A Little Miss of Color, 1832, Hyperion, 2000.

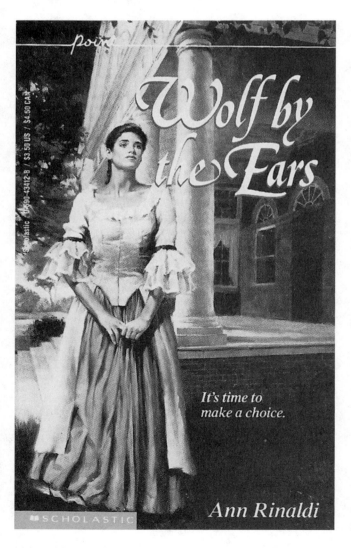

Rinaldi's novel portrays the life of Harriet Hemings, the illegitimate daughter of Thomas Jefferson.

Contributor of columns, editorials, and stories to the *Trentonian;* author of self-syndicated column to eighteen daily papers in New York, New Jersey, and Pennsylvania, 1969-70. Rinaldi's works have been translated into four languages.

Sidelights

The author of nearly thirty novels for young adults, Ann Rinaldi specializes in historical fiction, viewing the events of pivotal periods in American history through the eyes of young female protagonists. Rinaldi's heroines come of age and make consequential personal decisions regarding public events during the Revolutionary War era, as in *Time Enough for Drums, A Ride into Morning, Finishing Becca, Cast Two Shadows,* and *The Secret of Sarah Reeve,* or in the Civil War era, as in *The Last Silk Dress, In My Father's House, An Acquaintance with Darkness, Mine Eyes Have Seen,* and *Amelia's War.* She has also explored the consequences of slavery in *The Education of Mary, Wolf by the Ears,* and *Hang a Thousand Trees with Ribbons.* Additionally, she has written a dramatic re-creation of the Salem witch trials in her *A Break with Charity,* and a family saga in her "Quilt Trilogy." Known for meticulous research and compelling plots, Rinaldi's historical fiction has helped create the resurgence in the genre experienced in young adult literature in the late 1980s and throughout the 1990s. As Susan Dove Lempke noted in *Booklist,* "Rinaldi's books are always impeccably researched, vividly detailed, and filled with very human characters; they are also about something that matters."

Rinaldi worked for many years as a journalist before publishing her first young adult title in 1980, *Term Paper.* "I was my mother's fifth child, and she died right after I was born," Rinaldi once told *SATA.* "For two years I lived in Brooklyn with an aunt and uncle who wanted to adopt me. In the household were a lot of older teenage cousins who pampered and spoiled me, but my father came one day and took me home abruptly. The only happy part of my childhood ended."

Although Rinaldi's father worked for a newspaper as a manager, the author continued, "he did everything he could to prevent me from becoming a writer. At school they attempted to take out of me what spirit had eluded my stepmother. My father did not believe in college for his daughters, so I was sent into the business world to become a secretary." Rinaldi worked in typing pools for several years until her marriage. After having two children, she began to write fiction. She wished to become a novelist, but her work was "terrible," she recalled.

Rinaldi's introduction to professional writing came through the newspaper business, which she has been in since 1969. Then, over a decade later, she published *Term Paper,* and by 1991 was able to devote her energies to writing novels full time. The term paper of the title of that debut novel is written by Nicki as an attempt to articulate her feelings about her father's death. The assignment is given to her by a substitute

ANN RINALDI

An Acquaintance with Darkness

Emily suspects her doctor uncle of stealing bodies for research in Rinaldi's shocking account of the growth of the medical profession during the Civil War. (Cover illustration by Michael Hussar.)

English teacher who just happens to be Nicki's much-older brother. Through her efforts to finish the paper, Nicki matures and learns to understand how events have affected other members of the family. The result, according to *School Library Journal* contributor A. B. Hart, is a work that "declares strongly for family obligations of love and forgiveness." Nicki also appears in a sequel, *Promises Are for Keeps,* which details the hospital volunteer service she performs as a way to make up for some childish pranks. The book stands well on its own, M. K. Chelton wrote in *Voice of Youth Advocates,* and "Nicki sounds like a real kid, not an imitation." Two other early Rinaldi novels are set in contemporary times, *But in the Fall I'm Leaving* and *The Good Side of My Heart,* both featuring rebellious, teenage Brie and her coming-of-age angst.

At this same time, Rinaldi was already beginning to turn her hand to historical matters, inspired in part by her son's and then her daughter's involvement in historical reenactments. Her initial focus was on the events of the Revolutionary War; her first novel on the subject, *Time Enough for Drums,* was published in 1986. This novel tells the story of Jemima Emerson, a fifteen-year-old resident of Trenton, New Jersey, who watches in fascination as the American struggle for independence from Great Britain divides her town and her family. The novel is based roughly on the historical background of Washington's retreat before the battle of Trenton, though Rinaldi makes the story accessible by adding intrigue, romance, and a variety of interesting characters to the historical facts. "A stirring book which brings history to life accurately," a contributor for *Kirkus Reviews* wrote. "Rinaldi's enthusiasm for her subject is catching."

Since that first historical fiction, Rinaldi has returned many times to the American Revolution era for inspiration. Her 1991 *A Ride into Morning* follows the tale of Tempe Wick, who, along with her cousin, Mary Cooper, both ardent Patriots, must run her farm despite the ravages of the war going on all around them. The book is based on the legend of a young New Jersey woman who supposedly hid her horse in her house to keep it from being commandeered by Revolutionary soldiers. *Booklist* critic Candace Smith felt "the book is a suspenseful read with enough everyday detail to make it realistic and enough adventure to make it exciting." In *The Fifth of March* Rinaldi tells the story of the Boston Massacre through the eyes of a young servant indentured to John and Abigail Adams. A *Publishers Weekly* contributor called the book a "painstakingly researched tale," while *Booklist* reviewer Chris Sherman noted it "will be a wonderful selection to use in language-arts and social-studies classes."

More spirited heroines from Revolutionary times, both fictional and real, followed. Young Becca Syng becomes the maid to Peggy Shippen, soon to be married to General Benedict Arnold, in *Finishing Becca.* Set in Philadelphia during the Revolution, the ensuing action is seen through the eyes of Becca. "Rinaldi's intriguing approach depicting the life of Peggy Shippen through the eyes of Becca Syng will appeal to young adults with an interest in history," according to Laura L. Lent, writing in *Voice of Youth Advocates.* The daughter of Paul Revere makes an appearance in *The Secret of Sarah Revere,* in which young Sarah tells of her father's rides and of the intelligence network of the patriot community just before the Revolutionary War. "Once again Rinaldi has given readers a young woman's perceptions of what has too often been the all-male story of American history and politics," wrote Kay E. Vandergrift in a *School Library Journal* review. *Booklist* critic Susan Dove Lempke found that Rinaldi's "technique of framing the story within Sarah's recollections creates some initial confusion," but went on to conclude that "the swift pace and credible characters combined with impeccable research make the novel an involving and informative venture into history." And in *Cast Two Shadows* young Caroline learns about the realities of the Revolutionary War in South Carolina. Brenda Moses-Allen, reviewing the book in *Voice of Youth Advocates,* noted "the author's painstaking research is evident" and called the novel "thought-provoking."

Rinaldi has also produced a family saga with her "Quilt Trilogy," set in Salem, Massachusetts, and relating the adventures of the Chelmsfords, a shipping merchant family between the years 1788 and 1841. The first book in the series, *A Stitch in Time,* is narrated by sixteen-year-old Hannah, who sees her family pulled apart shortly after the War of Independence. One sister marries a sea captain and others prepare to move to the Northwestern Territory. Reviewing the initial novel in the trilogy, a writer for *Publishers Weekly* concluded, "With her infectious fascination for American history and her sensitive characterizations, Rinaldi again creates an adventurous, heart-catching story that will leave readers in eager anticipation of its successors." The second novel, *Broken Days,* moves forward in time to just before the War of 1812. Hannah is now Aunt Hannah, and this new tale is related through the eyes of her niece, fourteen-year-old Ebie, whose life is complicated by the arrival of a half-Indian girl who claims to be her cousin. Marylee Tiernan, writing in *Voice of Youth Advocates,* found "the setting is richly woven with the history of the period, and the plot enriched by the family's involvement with events of the time."

The final book in the trilogy, *The Blue Door,* is set in 1841 in South Carolina and in Lowell, Massachusetts. Amanda, granddaughter of a character from *A Stitch in Time,* travels north from her beloved plantation and witnesses firsthand the exploitation of women in the textile mills. A contributor for *Kirkus Reviews* concluded that it was unnecessary for readers to have read the previous books in order to "enjoy this rip-roaring tale of adventures and suspense; Amanda and all the other characters inhabit a revealing and credible historical milieu." And speaking of the trilogy in total, *Booklist*'s Carolyn Phelan called it an "ambitious" undertaking, and despite some shortfalls in the books, Phelan felt the "trilogy tells involving stories of several strong female characters, shows people at different stages in their lives, and ties together three periods in America's past."

Rinaldi moved on to the Civil War as a topic in several other historical novels. *The Last Silk Dress,* another coming-of-age novel, is based on an actual incident involving the capture of a Confederate balloon. The teenage female protagonist must again overcome the tumultuous and chaotic conditions caused both by the war and the corrupt society in which her family lives. As the novel progresses, Susan Chilmark gradually comes to understand the world around her and even to challenge it. Zena Sutherland, writing in the *New York Times Book Review,* praised Rinaldi for her "convincing" portrayal of Susan's awakening to the realities of racial inequality. *The Last Silk Dress,* Sutherland concluded, is "interesting not only for its theme and story, but also for the evidence it gives of Ms. Rinaldi's respect for her adolescent audience."

Mine Eyes Have Seen uses the backdrop of the incidents at Harper's Ferry and John Brown's raid to "weave fact and fiction into an involving story," according to Phelan in a *Booklist* article. The book is narrated by Brown's daughter, Annie. Pat Matthews, reviewing the title in

Bulletin of the Center for Children's Books, commented, "Mounting suspense charges the story with dramatic intensity." The moral ambiguities of body-snatching for medical research at the close of the Civil War are explored in *An Acquaintance with Darkness,* a work that blends "impressive" research with "a fast-paced and dramatic" plot, according to a reviewer for *Publishers Weekly.* Rinaldi blends the assassination of Lincoln with the fictional story of a young orphaned girl to create "some deliciously macabre elements of gothic potboilers," as Elizabeth Bush noted in the *Bulletin of the Center for Children's Books.* And the Confederate ransom of Hagerstown, Maryland, forms the backdrop for *Amelia's War,* set in 1861 and featuring an eleven-year-old female protagonist from that town. A contributor for *Publishers Weekly* remarked, "Among the book's strengths are some riveting characters both real . . . and imagined." *Booklist* writer Debbie Carton dubbed the novel "gripping" and "fast-paced."

Rinaldi has also dealt with the issue of slavery. In *Wolf by the Ears* the author returns to the Colonial era to follow the partially fictionalized tale of Harriet Hemings, the illegitimate daughter (by a slave mother) of

Twelve-year-old Amelia and her friend Josh save their Maryland town in Rinaldi's story of danger, loyalty, and love during the Civil War. (Cover photo by Marc Tauss.)

Thomas Jefferson. In her "Author's Note" section of the work, Rinaldi explains that it was, in part, the alienation which Jefferson's assumed illegitimate children must have felt that appealed to her. "The theme of alienation has always appealed to me," she notes. "My own mother had died when I was born. I never knew her family or even saw a picture of her until I was married. So there was always a part of me I could not acknowledge, a part of me I yearned to understand." As a result, she continues, "when looking for a real figure in American history to write about in connection with alienation, I recalled Harriet Hemings and her brothers."

While Rinaldi did a great deal of research about Hemings and Thomas Jefferson, she ultimately had to fill in the historical gaps by creating many of the details of her character's life. "Using every fact I could find about Monticello, Thomas Jefferson and the Hemings family, I put my story together," she writes. "My research, however, only told me bits and pieces about Harriet Hemings. And, so, within a framework of fact, I invented my own Harriet." A slave who looks almost white, Harriet is perplexed by her role on Jefferson's plantation and struggles to find a place for herself in society. "Harriet's plight is poignant, and she is a finely drawn, believable character," Bruce Anne Shook observed in *School Library Journal*. Sister Mary Veronica also praised the novel, writing in *Voice of Youth Advocates* that "it is history brought to life by a skillful and imaginative author."

With *Hang a Thousand Trees with Ribbons* Rinaldi presents a fictionalized biography of America's first black poet, Phillis Wheatley, who was purchased as a slave when a child in 1761 and later gained renown throughout the colonies for her verses. *Booklist* contributor Laura Tillotson concluded, "Strong characterization and perceptive realism mark this thoughtful portrait." With *The Education of Mary,* Rinaldi tells the story of the scandal caused by the admission of black girls to an exclusive Connecticut school in 1832.

Rinaldi's abiding interest in history has also led her to write books as disparate as *A Break with Charity: A Story of the Salem Witch Trials* to ones dealing with Native Americans in *The Second Bend in the River* and *My Heart Is on the Ground.* With the first of these, Rinaldi deals with the witch trials of 1692. As usual, Rinaldi uses historical fact for the basis of her story and fills in the gaps with her own imagination, again using a teenage girl as the protagonist: Susanna English. An acquaintance of the girls accused of instigating the witch trials, Susanna narrates the story from the perspective of fourteen years after the event. Carolyn Noah, writing in *School Library Journal,* praised Rinaldi's historical accuracy, as well as her well-constructed plot. "The plot is rich with details and names that will be familiar to those who have read about the trials," Noah writes. While she faulted the characters as "rigid," she concluded that *A Break with Charity* "portrays an excruciating era in American history from a unique perspective." Similar praise for the work was echoed by other critics. *Voice of Youth Advocates* contributor Sally Kotarsky

declared that Rinaldi has "once again chosen a historical character who quickly draws the reader into the story." And a critic for *Kirkus Reviews* asserted that Rinaldi has created "an enthralling, authentic story that makes the results of compounding malicious lies with false confessions of terrified victims tragically believable."

With *The Second Bend in the River* Rinaldi "crafts an elegant and moving account of the budding romance between Shawnee chief Tecumseh and a young frontier girl," according to a reviewer for *Publishers Weekly.* Kay Weisman, writing in *Booklist,* also lauded Rinaldi's "attention to period details . . . and careful separation of fact from fiction" in this "powerfully romantic tale." And in *My Heart Is on the Ground* Rinaldi presents the fictional diary of a twelve-year-old Sioux girl living in a Pennsylvania boarding school for Indian children. Part of Scholastic's "Dear America" series, Rinaldi's book is written in diary entries that "burst with details about culture and custom, adding wonderful texture to this thought-provoking book," according to *Booklist*'s Stephanie Zvirin.

The Journal of Jonathan Pierce: A Pilgrim Boy is another Rinaldi title in journal form, telling the story of an orphaned boy, this time, who is indentured as a servant and travels on the Mayflower to the Colonies. *Keep Smiling Through* is also something of a departure for Rinaldi, as it is set on the home front during World War II and portrays a young girl who must come face to face with prejudice and overcome propaganda. And in *The Coffin Quilt* the author tells the story of the feud between the McCoys and Hatfields, a "colorful" and "tautly plotted historical novel," according to a reviewer for *Publishers Weekly.*

"I write young adult novels because I like it," Rinaldi once commented. "But, as with my first book, I don't write for young people. I just write; I have an aim to write good stuff for them, to treat them as people, not write down to them with stories about romance and acne and the spring dance. Real life, as I know it, as I've learned it to be from my newspaper experience and own past, goes into my books. . . . I draw all my characters fully, give my adults as many problems and as much dimension as the young protagonist. I give them good, literary writing."

Works Cited

Review of *An Acquaintance with Darkness, Publishers Weekly,* April 19, 1999, p. 75.

Review of *Amelia's War, Publishers Weekly,* December 20, 1999, p. 81.

Review of *The Blue Door, Kirkus Reviews,* August 15, 1996, p. 1241.

Review of *A Break with Charity, Kirkus Reviews,* July 15, 1992, p. 924.

Bush, Elizabeth, review of *An Acquaintance with Darkness, Bulletin of the Center for Children's Books,* October, 1997, pp. 66-67.

Carton, Debbie, review of *Amelia's War, Booklist,* November 15, 1999, p. 627.

Chelton, M. K., review of *Promises Are for Keeping, Voice of Youth Advocates,* August, 1982, p. 36.

Review of *The Coffin Quilt, Publishers Weekly,* November 29, 1999, p. 72.

Review of *The Fifth of March, Publishers Weekly,* November 8, 1993, p. 78.

Hart, A. B., review of *Term Paper, School Library Journal,* January, 1981, p. 72.

Kotarsky, Sally, review of *A Break with Charity, Voice of Youth Advocates,* December, 1992, p. 285.

Lempke, Susan Dove, review of *The Secret of Sarah Revere, Booklist,* November 15, 1995, pp. 548-49.

Lempke, Susan Dove, review of *Cast Two Shadows, Booklist,* September 15, 1998, p. 229.

Lent, Laura L., review of *Finishing Becca, Voice of Youth Advocates,* February 15, 1995, pp. 340-41.

Matthews, Pat, review of *Mine Eyes Have Seen, Bulletin of the Center for Children's Books,* April, 1998, pp. 293-94.

Moses-Allen, Brenda, review of *Cast Two Shadows, Voice of Youth Advocates,* October, 1998, p. 278.

Noah, Carolyn, review of *A Break with Charity, School Library Journal,* September, 1992, p. 279.

Phelan, Carolyn, review of *The Blue Door, Booklist,* November 1, 1996, p. 491.

Phelan, Carolyn, review of *Mine Eyes Have Seen, Booklist,* February 15, 1998, p. 1000.

Rinaldi, Ann, *Wolf by the Ears,* Scholastic, 1991.

Review of *The Second Bend in the River, Publishers Weekly,* January 13, 1997, p. 76.

Sherman, Chris, review of *The Fifth of March, Booklist,* January 15, 1994, p. 925.

Shook, Bruce Anne, review of *Wolf by the Ears, School Library Journal,* April, 1991, pp. 142-43.

Sister Mary Veronica, review of *Wolf by the Ears, Voice of Youth Advocates,* June, 1991, p. 101.

Smith, Candace, review of *A Ride into Morning, Booklist,* August, 1991, p. 141.

Review of *A Stitch in Time, Publishers Weekly,* January 24, 1994, p. 56.

Sutherland, Zena, review of *The Last Silk Dress, New York Times Book Review,* April 10, 1988, p. 38.

Tiernan, Marylee, review of *Broken Days, Voice of Youth Advocates,* April, 1996, p. 28.

Tillotson, Laura, review of *Hang a Thousand Trees with Ribbons, Booklist,* September 1, 1996, p. 119.

Review of *Time Enough for Drums, Kirkus Reviews,* April 1, 1986, p. 552.

Vandergrift, Kay E., review of *The Secret of Sarah Revere, School Library Journal,* November, 1995, p. 122.

Weisman, Kay, review of *The Second Bend in the River, Booklist,* February 15, 1997, p. 1016.

Zvirin, Stephanie, review of *My Heart Is on the Ground, Booklist,* April 1, 1999, p. 1428.

For More Information See

BOOKS

Authors and Artists for Young Adults, Volume 15, Gale, 1995.
Children's Literature Review, Volume 46, Gale, 1998.

St. James Guide to Young Adult Writers, second edition, St. James, 1999.

PERIODICALS

Booklist, September 1, 1999, p. 124; February 15, 2000, p. 1114.
Bulletin of the Center for Children's Books, October, 1980, p. 39; September, 1992, p. 22; December, 1993, p. 132; April, 1994, p. 269; April, 1996, p. 277; March, 1997, p. 256; February, 1999, p. 215.
Kirkus Reviews, August 15, 1998, p. 1194; February 1, 1999, p. 228.
Publishers Weekly, August 3, 1992, p. 72; November 8, 1993, p. 78; January 24, 1994, p. 56; May 10, 1999, p. 70.
School Library Journal, April, 1982, p. 84; May, 1986, pp. 108-09; August, 1987, p. 98; May, 1988, pp. 112-13; May, 1991, p. 113; January, 1994, pp. 132-34; May, 1994, p. 132; June, 1996, p. 124; November, 1996, pp. 124, 126; June, 1997, p. 126; September, 1998, p. 208; April, 1999, p. 141; June, 1999, p. 16.*

*   *   *

RINGDALH, Mark
See LONGYEAR, Barry B(rookes)

*   *   *

ROBINS, Deri 1958-

Personal

Born June 16, 1958, in Cardiff, Wales; daughter of Roy and Jean (a teacher; maiden name, Rhydderch) Cumberlidge; married James Robins (an illustrator), 1987; children: Ben, Tom, Nell. *Education:* University of London, B.A. (with honors), 1979; attended London College of Printing, 1985. *Politics:* "Leftish." *Religion:* None.

Addresses

Home—Bath, England. *Agent*—Clare Pearson, 22 Upper Grosvenor St., London W1Y 9PB, England.

Career

Charles Letts and Co., began as proofreader, became editor, 1980-82; Grisewood & Dempsey, began as assistant editor, 1983, became senior editor of children's nonfiction, 1985-88; freelance writer and editor, 1989—.

Writings

An A-Z Activity Book of Animal Fun, illustrated by Charlotte Stowell, Kingfisher (New York City), 1989.
(With Meg Sanders) *An A-Z Activity Book of Outdoor Fun,* illustrated by Stowell, Kingfisher, 1989.
(Editor) *The Spies and Detectives Cut and Colour Book,* Kingfisher, 1989.
(Editor) *Flags and Uniforms,* Kingfisher, 1991.

(With Sanders) *By Myself Book,* illustrated by Stowell, Kingfisher, 1991.

Holiday Book, illustrated by Stowell, Kingfisher, 1991.

Gardening Book, illustrated by Stowell, Kingfisher, 1992.

(With Sanders and Kate Crocker) *The Kids Can Do It Book,* illustrated by Stowell, Kingfisher, 1993.

Making Prints, illustrated by husband, Jim Robins, Kingfisher, 1993.

Papier Mache, illustrated by J. Robins, Kingfisher, 1993.

Santa's Sackful of Best Christmas Ideas, illustrated by George Buchanan, Kingfisher, 1993.

The Kids' around the World Cookbook, illustrated by Stowell, Kingfisher, 1994.

In Roman Times, illustrated by David Salariya and others, Kingfisher, 1994.

The Great Pirate Activity Book, illustrated by Buchanan, Kingfisher, 1994.

Making Books, illustrated by Stowell, Kingfisher, 1994.

Christmas Fun, illustrated by Maggie Downer, Kingfisher, 1995.

Easter Fun, illustrated by Downer, Kingfisher, 1996.

Birthday Fun, illustrated by Annabel Spenceley, Kingfisher, 1996.

Top Tips for Girls, Hippo (London, England), 1997.

Mystery of the Monster Party, illustrated by Anni Axworthy, Candlewick Press (Cambridge, MA), 1998.

The Stone in the Sword: The Quest for a Stolen Emerald, illustrated by J. Robins, Candlewick Press, 1998.

Spooky Time!, illustrated by Martin Chatterton, Scholastic (London), 1999.

Other books include *Brat Packs: Making Jewellery* and *Secret File for Girls,* Scholastic; *The Ultimate Activity Book, My Secret Personality Profile,* and *My Secret Astrology Profile,* all Robinson; *Learning with Ozmo,* activity books for BBC Publications; *Action Packs: Friendship Bracelets,* Hat Trick; *Let's Start: Fabric Art,* Design Eye; *Arts and Crafts for all Seasons,* Two-Can; and *Animals All Around: Farm Animals,* Reader's Digest. Contributor to *The Millennium Encyclopedia.* Contributor to magazines, including *Art Magic* and *Smart.*

Work in Progress

Research on young people in history, especially in medieval times, with publications expected to result.

Sidelights

Deri Robins told *SATA:* "I became an author because, after fifteen years of editing other people's work, I decided I preferred the idea and writing side of

Deri Robins

publishing to the job of dotting all the 'i's' and crossing all the 't's.' (I was also very bad at administration and at chasing tardy authors and illustrators.) I still drift in and out of editorial work to pay the mortgage and the nursery fees, but I live by writing as and when I can. I have several ideas in progress, but I also have several small children and a dog who, together, take up a lot of my waking hours. More by luck than design, I think I've become pigeonholed as a writer of craft, puzzle, and story books—this is something I never intended!"

For More Information See

PERIODICALS

Booklist, April, 1998, p. 1322.
School Library Journal, July, 1998, p. 81.*

ROBINS, Patricia
See CLARK, Patricia Denise

*   *   *

RONSON, Mark
See ALEXANDER, Marc

S

SAN SOUCI, Robert D. 1946-

Personal

Surname is pronounced "San-*Soo*-see"; born October 10, 1946, in San Francisco, CA; son of Robert Abraham (a business consultant) and Mary Ellen (Kelleher) San Souci. *Education:* St. Mary's College, B.A., 1968; California State University at Hayward, graduate study,

Robert D. San Souci

1968-70. *Hobbies and other interests:* Travel, collecting old children's books.

Addresses

Office—2261 Market St., Suite 503, San Francisco, CA 94114. *Agent*—Barbara S. Kouts, Literary Agent, P.O. Box 558, Bellport, NY 11713.

Career

Freelance writer, 1974—. Books, Inc., Walnut Creek, CA, book buyer, 1966-72; California State University, Hayward, CA, lecturer in English, 1969-70; Campus Textbook Exchange, Berkeley, CA, assistant store manager and book department manager, 1972-73; Graduate Theological Union Bookstore, Berkeley, general manager, 1973-79; Harper & Row Publishers, Inc., San Francisco, CA, promotion coordinator, copy writer, and editorial coordinator, 1979-86; Walt Disney Feature Animation, Burbank, CA, story consultant, 1993—. Lecturer at elementary and middle schools, colleges, and universities, and to professional organizations. *Member:* Society of Children's Book Writers and Illustrators.

Awards, Honors

Ten Best Illustrated Children's Books of the Year citation, *New York Times,* and Notable Children's Trade Book in the Social Studies, National Council for Social Studies and the Children's Book Council, both 1978, and *Horn Book* Honor List citation, 1979, all for *The Legend of Scarface: A Blackfeet Indian Tale;* Notable Children's Trade Book in the Social Studies, 1981, and Children's Choice citation, International Reading Association-Children's Book Council (IRA-CBC), 1982, for *Song of Sedna: Sea-Goddess of the North;* Notable Children's Trade Book in the Social Studies, 1986, for *The Legend of Sleepy Hollow: Retold from Washington Irving,* 1987, for *The Enchanted Tapestry: A Chinese Folktale,* and 1992, for *The Samurai's Daughter;* Children's Choice citation, IRA-CBC, 1987, for *Short & Shivery: Thirty Chilling Tales;* Irma Simonton Black

Book Award, Bank Street College of Education, 1989, American Library Association (ALA) Notable Book citation, 1989, and state readers' awards from Tennessee, Colorado, Nebraska, Virginia, and Georgia, all for *The Talking Eggs;* ALA Notable Book citation, 1992, for *Sukey and the Mermaid;* Aesop Award, Children's Folklore Section, American Folklore Society, 1993, for *Cut from the Same Cloth;* Caldecott Honor Book, 1996, for *The Faithful Friend;* Texas Bluebonnet Award, 1999-2000, for *A Weave of Words.*

Writings

FOR CHILDREN

Casey's Color Surprise (picture book/cassette), Playskool/Hasbro, 1985.

The Loch Ness Monster: Opposing Viewpoints (nonfiction), Greenhaven Press, 1989.

N. C. Wyeth's Pilgrims (nonfiction), illustrations by N. C. Wyeth, Chronicle, 1991.

The Christmas Ark, illustrated by Daniel San Souci, Doubleday, 1991.

Kate Shelley: Bound for Legend (biography), illustrated by Max Ginsberg, Dial, 1994.

Red Heels, illustrated by Tom Pohrt, Dial, 1995.

Also author of *Cinderella Skeleton,* illustrated by David Catrow, *Six Foolish Fishermen,* illustrated by Doug Kennedy, and *The Silver Charm,* illustrated by Yoriko Ito, 1999.

FOLKLORE ADAPTATIONS; FOR CHILDREN

The Legend of Scarface: A Blackfeet Indian Tale, illustrated by brother, Daniel San Souci, Doubleday, 1978.

Song of Sedna: Sea-Goddess of the North, illustrated by Daniel San Souci, Doubleday, 1981.

Jacob and Wilhelm Grimm, *The Brave Little Tailor,* illustrated by Daniel San Souci, Doubleday, 1982.

Washington Irving, *The Legend of Sleepy Hollow: Retold from Washington Irving,* illustrated by Daniel San Souci, Doubleday, 1986.

Short & Shivery: Thirty Chilling Tales, illustrated by Katherine Coville, Doubleday, 1987.

The Enchanted Tapestry: A Chinese Folktale, illustrated by Laszlo Gal, Dial, 1987.

The Six Swans, illustrated by Daniel San Souci, Simon & Schuster, 1988.

The Boy and the Ghost, illustrated by Brian Pinkney, Simon & Schuster, 1989.

The Talking Eggs: A Folktale from the American South, illustrated by Jerry Pinkney, Dial, 1989.

Madame d'Aulnoy, *The White Cat: An Old French Fairy Tale,* illustrated by Gennady Spirin, Orchard Books, 1990.

Young Merlin, illustrated by Daniel Horne, Doubleday, 1990.

The Firebird, illustrated by Kris Waldherr, Dial Books, 1991.

Larger Than Life: The Adventures of American Legendary Heroes, illustrated by Andrew Glass, Doubleday, 1991.

Feathertop: Based on the Tale by Nathaniel Hawthorne, illustrated by Daniel San Souci, Doubleday, 1992.

The Samurai's Daughter: A Japanese Legend, illustrated by Stephen T. Johnson, Dial, 1992.

The Tsar's Promise: A Russian Tale, illustrated by Lauren Mills, Philomel, 1992.

Sukey and the Mermaid, illustrated by B. Pinkney, Four Winds Press, 1992.

The Snow Wife, illustrated by Stephen T. Johnson, Dial, 1993.

Cut from the Same Cloth: American Women of Myth, Legend, and Tall Tale, illustrated by Brian Pinkney, introduction by Jane Yolen, Philomel, 1993.

Young Guinevere, illustrated by Jamichael Henterly, Doubleday, 1993.

Donkey Ears, illustrated by Fabricio Vanden Broeck, Philomel, 1994.

Sootface: An Ojibwa Cinderella Story, illustrated by Daniel San Souci, Doubleday, 1994.

The House in the Sky: A Bahamian Folktale, illustrated by Wil Clay, Dial, 1994.

The Hobyahs, illustrated by Alexi Natchev, Doubleday, 1994.

More Short and Shivery: Thirty Terrifying Tales, illustrated by Katherine Coville, Doubleday, 1994.

The Faithful Friend, illustrated by Brian Pinkney, Four Winds, 1995.

The Hired Hand, illustrated by Jerry Pinkney, Dial, 1995.

Two White Pebbles, Dial, 1995.

The Little Seven-Colored Horse: A Spanish American Folktale, illustrated by Jan Thompson Dicks, Chronicle Books, 1995.

Young Lancelot, illustrated by Jamichael Henterly, Doubleday, 1996.

Pedro and the Monkey, illustrated by Michael Hays, Morrow, 1996.

John and Mr. Bear: An African-American Folktale, Dial, 1996.

Nicholas Pipe, illustrated by David Shannon, Dial, 1997.

Even More Short and Shivery: Thirty Spine-Tingling Stories, Bantam, 1997.

Young Arthur, illustrated by Jamichael Henterly, Bantam, 1997.

A Weave of Words: An Armenian Tale, illustrated by Raul Colon, Orchard Books, 1998.

Cendrillon: A Caribbean Cinderella, illustrated by Brian Pinkney, Simon & Schuster, 1998.

A Terrifying Taste of Short and Shivery: Thirty Creepy Tales, illustrated by Lenny Wooden, Delacorte, 1998.

Fa Mullan: The Story of a Woman Warrior, illustrated by Jean and Mou-Sien Tseng, Hyperion, 1998.

Brave Margaret, illustrated by Sally Wern Comport, Simon & Schuster, 1999.

Tarzan, illustrated by Michael McCurdy, Hyperion, 1999.

The Secret of Stones, illustrated by James Ransome, Penguin Putnam, 1999.

FOR ADULTS

Emergence, Avon, 1981.

Blood Offerings, Dorchester Press, 1985.

(With Kate Strelley) *The Ultimate Game: The Rise and Fall of Bhagwan Shree Rajneesh* (biography), Harper, 1987.

The Dreaming, Berkley, 1989.

Contributor of short stories and book and theater reviews to numerous publications.

Work in Progress

Several juvenile, young adult, and adult works of fiction and nonfiction.

Sidelights

Author of both adult and children's books, Robert D. San Souci is highly regarded for his adaptations of folktales from around the world, including Europe, Asia, and the Americas. These include such popular titles as _The Samurai's Daughter, The Enchanted Tapestry, The Talking Eggs, Sukey and the Mermaid, Cut from the Same Cloth, The Hired Hand, Nicholas Pipe, A Weave of Words,_ and the Caldecott Honor book _The Faithful Friend._ He has also produced several collections of spooky stories, the "Short and Shivery" series, an Arthurian sequence, and retellings of Native American myths, most of which are directed to middle graders. San Souci's adaptations are, according to Mary M. Burns in _Horn Book,_ typified by "impeccable scholarship and a fluid storytelling style." In addition to making more obscure or almost-forgotten stories accessible to young children, San Souci's work features female and male heros from many different places and ethnicities, with a particular emphasis on strong female protagonists.

San Souci was born in San Francisco and still makes his home in the Bay area. At an early age he knew he would become a writer: one of his favorite preoccupations was retelling stories he had heard to his siblings, one of whom, Daniel, has become a well-respected illustrator of children's books. San Souci wrote for his school newspapers and yearbook throughout school, and in college he majored in creative writing and world literature, doing graduate work in folklore, myth, and world religions. Once out of college, he worked variously as a bookstore manager and as a copy editor before breaking into publishing as a full-time children's writer.

San Souci's career writing children's books began with a book based on a Blackfeet Native American tale: _The Legend of Scarface,_ which is about a young warrior cut off from the others of his tribe in part because of a birthmark on his face. This debut title was illustrated by San Souci's brother, Daniel; this sibling collaboration has continued through many more titles written by Robert San Souci. Reviewing _The Legend of Scarface, School Library Journal_ critic Gale Eaton praised the "strong" and "accessible story." Other books retelling Native American myth and legends followed. _Song of Sedna,_ a story from the Eskimo people, presents one of San Souci's strong female protagonists, a young Inuit girl who searches for her own Prince Charming. "If Sedna loses out on Prince Charming, the reader only gains from this book," commented Carole Paikin in the _New York Times Book Review._ With _Sootface_ San Souci adapts another Native American tale, this time a Cinderella story from the Ojibwa. In the 1998 title _Two Bear Cubs,_ San Souci retells a Miwok Indian legend

Two young men struggle against a wizard to win the hand of his niece in **The Faithful Friend,** _San Souci's retelling of a Martinique folktale. (Illustrated by Brian Pinkney.)_

about two cubs who are rescued by the lowly measuring worm when they fall asleep on a rock formation at Yosemite. Once again collaborating with his illustrator brother on this title, San Souci creates a "story dramatically told to hold young listeners," according to Betsy Hearne in _Bulletin of the Center for Children's Books._ Hearne further noted, "San Souci is careful to document his sources, describe the context, and suggest related background readings."

San Souci has also tapped other cultures in the United States in folktale retellings, most notably African American. Among these are _The Boy and the Ghost, The Talking Eggs, Sukey and the Mermaid,_ and _The Hired Hand,_ which feature African American characters and stories from the oral tradition. In a review of the first two books, Malcolm Jones Jr. described San Souci in the _New York Times Book Review_ as "a wise adapter" and added that he left these tales "more or less as he found them, their plots unsullied, their lingo and custom still that of the 19th century rural South." In _The Boy and the Ghost_ the main character, Thomas, wins a treasure by being brave enough to spend a night in a haunted house. According to a _Publishers Weekly_ critic, "This story will delight long after the last embers have died down." And in the opinion of _Booklist's_ Ilene Cooper, _The Talking Eggs,_ a Cinderella tale, is a "vibrant adaptation of a Creole folktale." The story concerns a widow who lets her older, favorite daughter, Rose, live lazily while she makes her younger daughter, Blanche, do all the work.

Sukey and the Mermaid is based on a story from South Carolina and the earliest version is probably African. In this tale a beautiful, brown-skinned, black-eyed mermaid saves the young girl, Sukey, whose stepfather's rough treatment makes her want to escape to the sea. Describing San Souci as "a seasoned teller of folktales," a reviewer for *Publishers Weekly* wrote that the adapter "outdoes himself here with pungent, lyrical prose." *Booklist*'s Hazel Rochman noted that the mermaid is "a powerful woman, and she helps make Sukey strong." With *The Hired Hand,* San Souci weaves "themes of magic, rebirth and retribution into another splendid retelling of an African American folktale," according to a contributor for *Publishers Weekly*. A stranger turns up at a sawmill looking for work, and it turns out he has magical powers. But when the manager's sly son attempts to reproduce some of the hired hand's magic, tragedy ensues.

San Souci's adaptations of tales penned by well-known American authors include *The Legend of Sleepy Hollow: Retold from Washington Irving.* This revision of the classic is described as "little more than a simple, rather conventional ghost story" by Eleanor K. MacDonald in the *School Library Journal,* although a *Publishers Weekly* writer found it "a fine alternative" for reading aloud. In another revision of a story by an early American writer, San Souci's *Feathertop* is based on a Nathaniel Hawthorne tale, but it has been "greatly altered," according to a reviewer for *Publishers Weekly*. Nevertheless, the critic wrote that the story "preserves a surprising amount of drama," while *School Library Journal* critic Shirley Wilton admired the "smoothly flowing oral quality" of San Souci's adaptation.

Ghosts and things that go bump in the night are the subject of several collections of stories that began with *Short and Shivery: Thirty Chilling Tales,* and continued with *More Short and Shivery, Even More Short and Shivery,* and *A Terrifying Taste of Short and Shivery.* Each volume contains thirty samplings of spooky tales based on urban legends, folktales, and myths from around the world. Reviewing the third title in the series, Jennifer A. Fakolt wrote in *School Library Journal,* "San Souci continues to blend quality and high-entertainment value in this chilling feast for the imagination."

Readers who have enjoyed San Souci's individual adaptations of American folktales might be interested in his American folktale collections. *Larger Than Life: The Adventures of American Legendary Heroes* consists of five stories: "John Henry," "Old Stormalong," "Slue-Foot Sue and Pecos Bill," "Strap Buckner," and "Paul Bunyan and Babe the Blue Ox." In the opinion of *School Library Journal* contributor Eve Larkin the text and illustrations are "exuberant" and the work is an "excellent choice for all collections." *Cut from the Same Cloth: American Women of Myth, Legend, and Tall Tale* features Native American, African American, Mexican American, Eskimo, Hawaiian, and Anglo American stories, and includes notes and a bibliography. The focus in this collection is on the strength of each story's female protagonist. A reviewer for *Kirkus Reviews* criticized the "substantial revisions" of the stories, while Janice Del Negro voiced complaints in *Booklist* about the "use of pseudodialect" in some tales and noted that

"San Souci's retellings are uneven, lacking both definitive voice and focus." A *Publishers Weekly* reviewer, however, praised the author for adding "the flavor and vigor of its individual subculture" to each tale, while a *Bulletin of the Center for Children's Books* critic called the work "a first-class resource."

The *Enchanted Tapestry, The Samurai's Daughter, The Snow Wife,* and *Pedro and the Monkey* all feature tales from Asia and the Pacific Rim. The text of *The Enchanted Tapestry,* woven with the threads of several Chinese folktales, relates the story of a weaver woman and her fantastic tapestry. A reviewer for *Publishers Weekly* concluded that the text of this "beautiful book" is "skillful and immediate," while a *Kirkus Reviews* critic remarks that "children should be enchanted" by it. *The Samurai's Daughter* is San Souci's version of a medieval Japanese legend. As John Philbrook asserted in *School Library Journal,* the "strong, independent" heroine of this work "will inspire many admirers." Tokoyo, the daughter of a Samurai, does not stay home and grieve when her father is exiled by an insane ruler. Instead, she leaves home in search of him. A *Kirkus Reviews* writer commented that the "action-filled story is admirably retold," and praised its "unusual glimpse" of a legendary, heroic female. *The Snow Wife,* which, as with

San Souci retells an Armenian folktale in which a prince must learn to read, write, and weave before his love will marry him; these new skills later save him from a three-headed monster. (Cover illustration by Raul Colon.)

The Samurai's Daughter, is illustrated by Stephen T. Johnson, is based on an ancient Japanese legend. In this tale, two woodcutters seek shelter from a mountain storm and one is saved by the intervention of the lovely ice woman, but at a cost. "San Souci spins a compelling, atmospheric tale," Linda Boyles remarked in *School Library Journal,* making the tale "a fine addition to any collection." *Pedro and the Monkey* is a Filipino variant of the classic "Puss in Boots," in which a poor farmer is rewarded for the kindness he shows to a monkey. *Booklist* reviewer Michael Cart called this "a carefully researched" version in a "sober and straightforward retelling."

San Souci has also adapted tales and legends from the Caribbean, including the Martinique story *The Faithful Friend, The House in the Sky: A Bahamian Folktale,* and *Cendrillon: A Caribbean Cinderella.* Two young men raised as brothers set off to win the hand of lovely Paula for one of the duo, overcoming the machinations of her wizard uncle, in *The Faithful Friend.* This is an "excellent title," according to Marlene Lee in *School Library Journal,* which "contains all the elements of a well-researched folktale, and convincingly conveys the richness of the West Indian culture." Hearne noted in *Bulletin of the Center for Children's Books* that the story "celebrates a friendship threatened by forces of evil" and that older picture book readers "will relish the story's suspense." San Souci was awarded a Caldecott Honor for this book.

In *The House in the Sky* the Bahamas is the setting for a story of a "younger brother's greed and an old brother's cunning," according to Elizabeth Bush in *Bulletin of the Center for Children's Books.* Bush further remarked, "The text is a read-aloud delight, with its magical chant, wordplay, and comic conversations." And in *Cendrillon* readers get a Caribbean Cinderella story told from the godmother's point of view. Judith Constantinides, writing in *School Library Journal,* called the book "an outstanding Cinderella variant."

San Souci's adaptations and retellings of European tales include *The Brave Little Tailor,* a retelling of a Grimm Brothers story, which was hailed as a "fresh, dynamic version" by a *Publishers Weekly* critic. San Souci's retelling of *The Six Swans,* another Grimm tale, along with the book's illustrations, was described as "graceful and elegant" by a reviewer for *Publishers Weekly.* According to another *Publishers Weekly* reviewer, San Souci's retelling of Madame d'Aulnoy's old French tale, *The White Cat,* is "suitably magical" and "his words flow like music," while Boyles noted in *School Library Journal* that San Souci's "tighter, more direct" retelling will "appeal to young readers." And of *The Hobyahs,* San Souci's adaptation of an English folktale, a *Publishers Weekly* critic wrote that the work is "a strange hybrid of lyrical narrative and amusing illustrations"; Dot Minzer concluded in *School Library Journal* that it is "a fun scary book that will be a hit as a read-aloud."

Europe has proven to be a rich and fertile ground for San Souci in yet other adaptations from that continent.

Nicholas Pipe is a retelling of a folktale about a merman who falls in love with a woman of the land, a tale that can be traced back to twelfth-century legends. "San Souci has woven his magic once again," declared Beth Tegart in a *School Library Journal* review. A writer for *Kirkus Reviews* called the results "very bold and heroic," and concluded that "San Souci may be invoking an old story, but he also frames a few timeless ideas about responsibility, tolerance, and that simple thing called love." *A Weave of Words* comes from Armenian folklore and features another spunky heroine. It tells of Anait, a young weaver who refuses to have the spoiled Prince Vachagon, who has become smitten with her, until he learns to apply himself to the art of weaving—a skill that saves him years later when he is king. *Booklist's* Carolyn Phelan felt "the story weaves strong characters, an adventurous plot, and underlying wisdom into a fabric as beautiful as the carpet King Vachagon weaves to save his life."

Ireland is the setting for *Brave Margaret,* the story of a young woman who overcomes a deadly sea serpent to win her love, in a "smoothly written, and rhythmic" turn-around of the classic dragon-slaying tale, according to *Booklist's* Phelan. A reviewer for *Publishers Weekly* noted, "San Souci's adaptation of a traditional West Irish tale races along at fever pitch, bringing Margaret to the brink of disaster again and again." San Souci has also turned his hand to a retelling of the Arthurian legend in a series of books, including *Young Merlin, Young Guinevere, Young Lancelot,* and *Young Arthur.*

Unlike most of San Souci's work, *The Christmas Ark* is not based on a folktale. Nevertheless, as a critic for *School Library Journal* wrote, San Souci's understanding of "themes from a variety of literary traditions gives an added depth and richness to his story." In this tale, two sisters traveling to San Francisco with their mother by boat worry that they will not reach their destination, and their father, by Christmas, until St. Nicholas intervenes. Other original tales from San Souci include *Kate Shelley: Bound for Legend* and *The Red Heels.* In the former, San Souci tells the heroic story of a young girl who saves a train and its passengers when a railroad bridge goes out, while *The Red Heels* blends fantasy and folklore in the story of a cobbler lost in the woods and his encounter with a gentle witch. *Booklist's* Stephanie Zvirin thought the latter story was as "wistful and romantic a tale as any to come out in recent years." A tale from Arkansas, by way of Zaire, is 1999's *The Secret of the Stones,* involving two orphans turned into pebbles, a conjurer, and a childless couple. Reviewing this book, *Booklist* critic John Peters commented, "Children will be riveted and delighted by the tale's suspense, its see-saw climax, and the scary conjureman's squishy demise."

Fans of San Souci will be happy to learn that, as he once told *SATA,* he plans "to continue writing as long as I have stories to tell—and an audience that is willing to listen. . . . Retelling a Grimm Brothers' fairytale or a Pueblo Indian myth allows me scope to tell a story that has a solid structure derived from the inner truths that

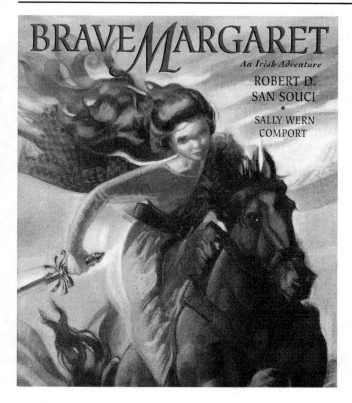

Brave Margaret battles sea creatures and other dangers to save her true love in San Souci's retelling of a traditional Irish folktale. (Cover illustration by Sally Wern Comport.)

are the kernels of all legends, myths, and fairytales. In all my writing I'm first of all concerned with the story; but (and I see this more and more as I write) I'm also using the narrative to explore ideas and suggest answers to questions about why and how the world works. I hope my books are entertaining, and I also get pleasure from thinking they may be sharing a little more substance with readers."

Works Cited

Review of *The Boy and the Ghost, Publishers Weekly,* September 8, 1989, p. 68.

Boyles, Linda, review of *The White Cat, School Library Journal,* October, 1990, p. 112.

Boyles, Linda, review of *The Snow Wife, School Library Journal,* March, 1994, p. 218.

Review of *The Brave Little Tailor, Publishers Weekly,* December 3, 1982, p. 60.

Review of *Brave Margaret, Publishers Weekly,* February 8, 1999, p. 214.

Burns, Mary M., review of *The Samurai's Daughter, Horn Book,* November/December, 1992, pp. 733-34.

Bush, Elizabeth, review of *The House in the Sky, Bulletin of the Center for Children's Books,* February, 1996, pp. 201-2.

Cart, Michael, review of *Pedro and the Monkey, Booklist,* September 1, 1996, p. 140.

Review of *The Christmas Ark, School Library Journal,* October, 1991, pp. 32-33.

Constantinides, Judith, review of *Cendrillon, School Library Journal,* September, 1998, p. 198.

Cooper, Ilene, review of *The Talking Eggs, Booklist,* August, 1989, p. 1982.

Review of *Cut from the Same Cloth, Bulletin of the Center for Children's Books,* June, 1993, pp. 328-29.

Review of *Cut from the Same Cloth, Kirkus Reviews,* April 1, 1993, p. 464.

Review of *Cut from the Same Cloth, Publishers Weekly,* April 26, 1993, p. 81.

Del Negro, Janice, review of *Cut from the Same Cloth, Booklist,* April 15, 1993, pp. 1508, 1510.

Eaton, Gale, review of *The Legend of Scarface, School Library Journal,* March, 1979, p. 144.

Review of *The Enchanted Tapestry, Kirkus Reviews,* March 15, 1987, p. 475.

Review of *The Enchanted Tapestry, Publishers Weekly,* March 13, 1987, p. 82.

Fakolt, Jennifer A., review of *A Terrifying Taste of Short and Shivery, School Library Journal,* November, 1998, p. 142.

Review of *Feathertop, Publishers Weekly,* November 2, 1992, pp. 70-71.

Hearne, Betsy, review of *The Faithful Friend, Bulletin of the Center for Children's Books,* September, 1995, pp. 28-29.

Hearne, Betsy, review of *Two Bear Cubs, Bulletin of the Center for Children's Books,* March, 1998, p. 259.

Review of *The Hired Hand, Publishers Weekly,* April 14, 1997, p. 75.

Review of *The Hobyahs, Publishers Weekly,* February 21, 1994, p. 251.

Jones, Malcolm Jr., review of *The Talking Eggs* and *The Boy and the Ghost, New York Times Book Review,* January 28, 1990, p. 29.

Larkin, Eve, review of *Larger than Life, School Library Journal,* November, 1991, p. 113.

Lee, Marlene, review of *The Faithful Friend, School Library Journal,* June, 1995, pp. 104-5.

Review of *The Legend of Sleepy Hollow, Publishers Weekly,* November 28, 1986, p. 74.

MacDonald, Eleanor K., review of *The Legend of Sleepy Hollow, School Library Journal,* December, 1986, p. 108.

Minzer, Dot, review of *The Hobyahs, School Library Journal,* April, 1994, p. 122.

Review of *Nicholas Pipe, Kirkus Reviews,* May 15, 1997, p. 807.

Paikin, Carole, review of *Song of Sedna, New York Times Book Review,* October 4, 1981, p. 38.

Peters, John, review of *The Secret of the Stones, Booklist,* January 1, 2000, p. 934.

Phelan, Carolyn, review of *Brave Margaret, Booklist,* March 1, 1999, p. 1217.

Phelan, Carolyn, review of *A Weave of Words, Booklist,* March 15, 1998, p. 1241.

Philbrook, John, review of *The Samurai's Daughter, School Library Journal,* November, 1992, p. 86.

Rochman, Hazel, review of *Sukey and the Mermaid, Booklist,* February 1, 1992, p. 1034.

Review of *The Samurai's Daughter, Kirkus Reviews,* October 15, 1992, p. 1316.

Review of *The Six Swans, Publishers Weekly,* June 9, 1989, p. 65.

Review of *Sukey and the Mermaid, Publishers Weekly,* January 13, 1992, p. 56.

Tegart, Beth, review of *Nicholas Pipe, School Library Journal,* May, 1997, p. 124.

Review of *The White Cat, Publishers Weekly,* August 31, 1990, p. 65.

Wilton, Shirley, review of *Feathertop, School Library Journal,* December, 1992, p. 90.

Zvirin, Stephanie, review of *The Red Heels, Booklist,* September 1, 1996, p. 131.

For More Information See

BOOKS

Children's Literature Review, Volume 43, Gale, 1997.

PERIODICALS

Booklist, November 15, 1991, p. 625; January 1, 1998, p. 819; October 15, 1998, p. 417; March 15, 1999, p.1302.

Bulletin of the Center for Children's Books, January, 1983, p. 89; October, 1989, p. 42; January, 1992, p. 138; March, 1992, p. 192; July-August, 1994, pp. 372-73; July-August, 1997, p. 411; April, 1998, p. 295; January, 1999, pp. 181-82; May, 1999, p. 327.

Horn Book, September-October, 1992, p. 593; January-February, 1996, p. 94; November-December, 1998, p. 747.

Kirkus Reviews, April 15, 1997, p. 649; January 15, 1999, p. 151.

New York Times Book Review, November 9, 1997, p. 24.

Publishers Weekly, November 28, 1986, p. 74; March 1, 1993, p. 57; July 19, 1993, pp. 252-53; November 25, 1996, pp. 77, 78; December 22, 1997, p. 61; January 25, 1999, p. 98; March 29, 1999, p. 106.

School Library Journal, September, 1989, p. 244; September, 1990, p. 220; May, 1992, p. 108; September, 1994, p. 235; November, 1994, p. 101; January, 1996, pp. 105, 117; October, 1996, pp. 105-6; March, 1998, p. 206; April, 1998, P. 125; September, 1999, p. 203; February, 2000, p. 115.*

*   *   *

SAUL, Carol P. 1947-

Personal

Born September 3, 1947, in New York, NY; married Mark E. Saul (a teacher), 1968; children: Susanna, Michael, Peter. *Education:* Barnard College, B.A., 1969; Bank Street College of Education, M.S., 1977.

Addresses

Office—c/o Publicity Director, Simon and Schuster Children's Books, 15 Columbus Cir., New York, NY 10023.

Career

Author of books for children. Day care teacher and elementary school teacher in New York City; has also worked as an accompanist. Resources for Children with Special Needs advocate, New York City; volunteer in schools. *Member:* Society of Children's Book Writers and Illustrators.

Awards, Honors

Peter's Song was named one of the Best Books of 1992 by the Oppenheim List, 1992.

Writings

Peter's Song, illustrated by Diane de Groat, Simon & Schuster, 1992.

Someplace Else, illustrated by Barry Root, Simon & Schuster, 1995.

The Song of the Last Miguel, illustrated by Minh Uong, Whispering Coyote Press, 1995.

Barn Cat: A Counting Book, illustrated by Mary Azarian, Little, Brown, 1998.

Contributor of articles to periodicals, including *Sesame Street.*

Sidelights

Carol P. Saul told *SATA:* "I have always made up stories, either on paper or in my head. At camp, I loved making up song parodies with my friends. My parents encouraged drawing, painting, and writing, and they provided my brother and me with music lessons. So there was always some messy creativity happening. I am thrilled when a person tells me that my story has touched them. I love to hear other people talk—and not only about my book. I love hearing other people's stories. I think if more people were allowed to speak the words in their heart and were able to listen to other people's stories, we'd have a lot more peace and understanding. And it wouldn't hurt for schools and governments to provide more opportunities for creativity: more arts education, more writing time, more showcases for young talent."

Saul's first book, *Peter's Song,* is the tale of a singing piglet who is proud of his musical abilities yet is ignored by the animals in his barnyard. Determined to share his music with someone, Peter goes to the pond and meets Frank the frog. Frank is eager to hear Peter's song and share his own music. After appreciating each other's creations, the new friends compose music together. Peter sings the piggy highs and Frank takes the froggy lows, beginning a partnership in music and a wonderful friendship.

For her next picture book, *Someplace Else,* Saul presents an older woman, Mrs. Trilby, who suddenly announces that she longs to live somewhere other than in the white house by the orchard where she has always lived. So she drives off in a pick-up truck to visit her son in the city,

She winds around my legs and purrs
And drinks the bowl of milk that's hers.

Waiting for something better, a finicky feline ignores a procession of animals in Carol P. Saul's counting book, **Barn Cat.**
(Illustrated by Mary Azarian.)

but soon leaves there to visit her daughter by the sea, and then her other son who lives in the mountains. The story is "filled with opportunities for youngsters to practice identifying patterns and making predictions," observed Lauren Peterson in *Booklist.* Though Mrs. Trilby never finds the place that feels just like home, she does realize that with a spiffy new trailer she can spend part of the year with each of her grown-up, far-flung children around the country. "The text is quiet and thoughtful," remarked Susan Dove Lempke in *Bulletin of the Center for Children's Books,* adding that "it's refreshing to see a picture book about an older person who's more than a grandparent."

Saul is also the author of *Barn Cat,* a counting book of exceptional quality, according to some reviewers. With a simple, rhyming text emphasizing the activities of the farm animals that are depicted, *Barn Cat* tells the story of a lazy feline who can not be bothered to chase after one grasshopper, or two crickets, or three butterflies, or even ten sparrows, but finally jumps to attention when it sees a girl appear with a bowl of milk. "Saul's rhyming text is simplicity itself . . . and her measured cadences are attuned to a read-aloud audience," remarked a contributor for *Publishers Weekly. School Library Journal* reviewer Barbara Elleman noted that the author's inclusion of colors and animal behavior in her text offers adults further teaching opportunities with young listeners, and like other reviewers, Elleman lauded illustrator Mary Azarian's woodcuts. The critic concluded, "Many counting books are available, but the potential here makes this collaboration one that should not be overlooked."

Works Cited

Review of *Barn Cat, Publishers Weekly,* August 24, 1998, p. 55.

Elleman, Barbara, review of *Barn Cat, School Library Journal,* November, 1998, p. 95.

Lempke, Susan Dove, review of *Someplace Else, Bulletin of the Center for Children's Books,* October, 1995, p. 68.

Peterson, Lauren, review of *Someplace Else, Booklist,* November 15, 1995, p. 565.

For More Information See

PERIODICALS

Bulletin of the Center for Children's Books, November, 1998, p. 111.

Publishers Weekly, August 14, 1995, p. 82.*

*　　*　　*

SCHWARTZ, Ellen 1949-

Personal

Born June 7, 1949, in Washington, DC; daughter of Bernard (a physician) and Ruth (a homemaker; maiden name, Shur) Rosenberg; married William Schwartz (a communications consultant), 1973; children: Elora Merri, Amy Jill. *Education:* Attended University of Chicago, 1967-69; University of Wisconsin, B.Sc. (special education), 1971; University of British Columbia, M.F.A. (creative writing), 1988. *Religion:* Jewish.

Addresses

Home and office—6637 Emerson St., Burnaby, British Columbia, V5E 1W5 Canada. *E-mail*—polestar@axionet.com.

Career

Polestar Communications Inc., Burnaby, British Columbia, writer and editor, 1989—; Simon Fraser University, Vancouver, British Columbia, writing instructor, 1990-94, 1997—. *Member:* Writers' Union of Canada, Children's Writers and Illustrators of British Columbia (recording secretary), Federation of British Columbia Writers, Hadassah.

Awards, Honors

Silver Birch Award nomination, 1997, for *Starshine on Televison; Starshine!, Starshine on Television,* and *Mr. Belinsky's Bagels* were all named Our Choice books by the Canadian Children's Book Centre.

Ellen Schwartz

Writings

FOR CHILDREN

Dusty, illustrated by Ann Swanson Gross, Solstice Books, 1983.

Starshine!, Polestar (Custer, WA), 1987.

Starshine at Camp Crescent Moon, Polestar, 1994.

Starshine on Television, Polestar, 1996.

Mr. Belinsky's Bagels, illustrated by Stefan Czernecki, Tradewind, 1997, Charlesbridge (Watertown, MA), 1998.

Jesse's Star, Orca, 2000.

Starshine and the Fanged Vampire Spider, Polestar, 2000.

OTHER

Born a Woman, Polestar, 1988.

Sidelights

"Ever since I began writing, I have always known that I wanted to write for children," Ellen Schwartz told *SATA.* "I've always loved children's books, especially the magic and humor in them, and the way children identify so strongly with the books they read. For me, writing is about characters. A story always starts with a character in a situation. I wonder: who is this character? Why is he or she in this situation? What's the problem? What happens next?

"For example, with *Mr. Belinsky's Bagels* I had an image of a little old man who made bagels, only bagels. I wanted to know: why does he make only bagels? What if his customers aren't happy about that? What if he switches in order to please his customers? How will he feel? What will he do? The story becomes a process of finding the answers to those questions.

"I spend a long time getting to know my characters— many months, in the case of novels. I walk with them, imagine them, dream them. They start talking in my ear. I see them doing things in clearer and clearer situations. I feel their feelings. Then I'm ready to start writing. Figuring out the plot is the hardest part of writing for me. Usually I have to go back and spend more time with the characters. Sometimes it's frustrating. But when the scene is unfolding in my mind like a movie, and I can hear the characters talking and feel what they're feeling, and the words are pouring out of my pen as fast as I can get them down, that's the best feeling in the world."

In Schwartz's first book, *Dusty,* a young girl becomes strongly attached to the blue bicycle that helps relieve her homesickness during the year she and her parents live in Copenhagen, Denmark. Though the bicycle cannot return to Vancouver with her, the note Pam leaves under the seat is found by the little girl to whom the bicycle is sold, and Pam soon has a new pen pal. Joan McGrath, who reviewed *Dusty* for *Quill & Quire,* remarked that while it seems a little farfetched that Pam's loving parents would not be willing to ship her

Mr. Belinsky's Bagels

Ellen Schwartz • Illustrated by Stefan Czernecki

Mr. Belinsky's fancy cakes and cookies can't satisfy his loyal customers, so he returns to his specialty. (Cover illustration by Stefan Czernecki.)

beloved bicycle back home with them, "never mind, it all turns out for the best." McGrath also called Schwartz's first book "a pleasant story."

In her next book, Schwartz created a character successful enough to resurrect in sequels. In *Starshine!,* the author introduces the ten-year-old daughter of parents who believe in an alternative lifestyle, which causes their daughter some inconvenience as well as some embarrassing moments. For example, when Starshine's fourth-grade class decides to raise money for a camping trip, her parents will not allow her to sell the sugary cookies because they believe that sugar makes people feel bad. So Starshine and her friend Julie devise another way to earn the money for the trip. After setting up her scenario, "the action moves along very quickly with lively dialogue and entertaining adventures," remarked Norma Charles in *Canadian Matters.*

Schwartz's first sequel, *Starshine at Camp Crescent Moon,* allows the author to expand upon the idea that it is not just Starshine's parents that make her different, but she herself is different, especially since her hobby is collecting spiders. In this book, Starshine's nervousness about going away to camp is offset by her excitement over the prospect of hunting a rare fanged vampire spider, which is said to be native to the area around the campgrounds. "This cheerful and lighthearted story about finding new friends is full of fun and mischief, and should quickly find an audience, particularly among young female readers," predicted Fred Boer in *Quill & Quire.* Reviewer Lian Goodall, writing in *Canadian Children's Literature,* places *Starshine at Camp Crescent Moon* among other series offerings for eight-to-ten-year-olds, featuring likable characters and providing "reasonable and sturdy reading fodder." However, Starshine's interest in spiders and Schwartz's ability to find the possibilities for humor in the simplest scenarios of childhood make this book a standout among others like it, Goodall concluded.

In a third book in this series, *Starshine on Television,* Schwartz's young heroine is torn between her excitement over participating in the school science fair and her desire to star in a television commercial. The result is "enjoyable and entertaining reading," according to Fred Boer in *Quill & Quire,* who concluded that Schwartz's readership is unlikely to be bothered by the plot's few flaws because they "will be too busy laughing. . . . This lively and funny novel is a winner."

Schwartz left Starshine aside for a time to write a picture book, *Mr. Belinsky's Bagels,* a story a reviewer for *Publishers Weekly* described as having an "old-fashioned tone." In this book, Mr. Belinsky is a beloved baker who refuses to expand his repertoire beyond bagels until a fancy pastry shop opens across the street and he is convinced that he must compete with them in order to stay in business. But Mr. Belinsky's loyal old customers are disappointed by this turn of events and the old baker himself finds something missing in his new career. So he goes back to making bagels and everyone is happy. "If the story is a bit weak, the message is solid," contended Stephanie Zvirin in *Booklist.*

Schwartz is also the author of *Born a Woman,* an examination of seven contemporary Canadian women folk singer/songwriters, including Sylvia Tyson, Lucie Blue Tremblay, Connie Kaldor, Heather Bishop, Ferron, Marie-Lynn Hammond, and Rita MacNeil. As Kieran Kealy writes in *Canadian Literature,* Schwartz's subjects "are not simply singers; they are also poets who provide a remarkably full portrait of the varied roles women play in Canadian life." Schwartz provides biographical information, excerpts from songs, extensive quotes from the women themselves, and concludes with a discography. "Above all else," Kealy concluded, "Schwartz convinces her reader that these voices deserve to be heard."

Works Cited

Boer, Fred, review of *Starshine at Camp Crescent Moon, Quill & Quire,* February, 1995, p. 39.

Boer, Fred, review of *Starshine on Television, Quill & Quire,* April, 1996, p. 42.

Charles, Norma, review of *Starshine!, Canadian Matters,* July, 1988, p. 131.

Goodall, Lian, review of *Starshine at Camp Crescent Moon, Canadian Children's Literature,* spring, 1998, p. 55.

Kealy, Kieran, "Be We Spirit," *Canadian Literature,* autumn, 1990, pp. 160-61.

McGrath, Joan, review of *Dusty, Quill & Quire,* August, 1983, pp. 34-35.

Review of *Mr. Belinsky's Bagels, Publishers Weekly,* June 29, 1998, p. 57.

Zvirin, Stephanie, review of *Mr. Belinsky's Bagels, Booklist,* July, 1998, p. 1988.

*   *   *

SELZNICK, Brian 1966-

Personal

Born July 14, 1966, in New Jersey; son of Roger (an accountant) and Lynn (a homemaker) Selznick. *Education:* Rhode Island School of Design, B.F.A., 1988. *Politics:* Democrat. *Religion:* Jewish. *Hobbies and other interests:* Cycling, swimming, movies, designing theater sets.

Addresses

Office—c/o Random House/Alfred A. Knopf Books for Young Readers, 201 East 50th St., New York, NY 10022.

Career

Eeyore's Books for Children, New York City, bookseller and painter of window displays, 1988-91; freelance painter of window displays, New York City, 1991-93; writer and illustrator of children's books, 1991—.

Member: Society of Children's Book Writers and Illustrators.

Awards, Honors

Texas Bluebonnet Award and Rhode Island Children's Book Award, both 1993, for *The Houdini Box.*

Writings

FOR CHILDREN; SELF-ILLUSTRATED

The Houdini Box, Knopf, 1991.
The Robot King, Laura Geringer Book, 1995.
The Boy of a Thousand Faces, Laura Geringer Book, 2000.

FOR CHILDREN; ILLUSTRATOR

Pam Conrad, *Dollface Has a Party!* HarperCollins, 1994.
Andrew Clements, *Frindle,* Simon & Schuster, 1996.
Norma Farber, *The Boy Who Longed for a Lift,* Laura Geringer Book, 1997.
Pam Munoz Ryan, *Riding Freedom,* Scholastic, 1998.
Pam Munoz Ryan, *Amelia and Eleanor Go for a Ride,* Scholastic, 1999.
Laura Godwin, *Barnyard Prayers,* Hyperion, 2000.
Ann Martin and Laura Godwin, *The Doll People,* Hyperion, 2000.

Freelance illustrator for *Cricket* and *Spider* magazines.

Sidelights

Brian Selznick's first book, *The Houdini Box,* published in 1991, brought a burst of recognition and popularity rare in children's book publishing, where reputations are generally built slowly, one book at a time. The book is about magic, the kind created by performers like Harry Houdini, as well as the everyday magic that grows from the human heart—the magic of growing up, creating a family, making dreams come true. Reviewers responded enthusiastically to this debut work, applauding the evocative pencil illustrations, the smooth prose blending fact and fiction, and the sense of mystery and fantasy the book brings to its readers.

Although he published his first book at the age of twenty-three, Selznick did not originally plan on a career in juvenile literature, as he explained in an interview for *SATA.* He related that when he graduated from the Rhode Island School of Design (RISD) in 1988, he wanted to design theater sets. But when he did not get into the graduate theater program he wanted, he decided to take some time off and think things over, during which time he realized that "what I love to do most of all is draw." Selznick told *SATA,* "I always loved children's books, so I thought, why am I fighting this? This is the most natural, obvious thing for me to do." The revelation prompted the artist to direct his efforts toward illustrating children's books.

His new plan was temporarily stalled, however, when he realized he had nothing in his portfolio he could send to children's book publishers. While trying to come up with ideas for illustrations that he could send to editors, he remembered a story he had written as part of a school project at RISD. "One week we got an assignment to do something about Houdini," Selznick recalled, "and I was really excited about that because when I was a kid Houdini was a hero of mine." The Houdini project, which Selznick sometimes brings with him to readings at schools and libraries, is a series of seven Plexiglas panels the artist described as "taped together back and forth like a Chinese folding screen," creating a three-dimensional display roughly the shape of a box. Each of the panels is painted with parts of a scene; when viewers look through the work they are presented with a complete picture of "Houdini on stage performing the Chinese water torture test," one of the most famous escapes of the renowned magician and escape artist. Selznick had been so charmed by the project that he went one step further and wrote a story and put it on the back of the painted parts of each panel. "It's the exact same story that's in *The Houdini Box*," said Selznick, "except in a much shorter version."

The artist made some black-and-white drawings of scenes from the rediscovered story and sent them to a number of editors, including Anne Schwartz at Knopf. "She liked the pictures," he remembered, "but she loved the story and she wanted to publish the whole thing." Selznick worked on the book for a year and a half, refining the text and making sketches, and the finished book appeared in 1991. *The Houdini Box* features ten-year-old Victor, who receives a box from Harry Houdini's widow that is supposed to contain all the great magician's secrets. Victor cannot find out if this is true or not because the box is locked. When Victor notices that the initials on the box are E. W., he decides he has been the victim of a trick. "This wasn't Houdini's box at all!" continues the story. "The owner was some E. W. There could be no secrets in here." In his sadness and disappointment, Victor takes the box and buries it "forever at the bottom of his closet." It is not until many years later, after Victor is grown and married and has a young son of his own, that he learns Houdini's real name

Amelia was Amelia Earhart, the celebrated aviator who had been the first female pilot to fly solo across the Atlantic Ocean. And when two of the most famous and adventurous women in the world got together, something exciting was bound to happen.

Brian Selznick illustrated the true story of Amelia Earhart and Eleanor Roosevelt's flight over Washington, D.C., in **Amelia and Eleanor Go for a Ride.** *(Written by Pam Munoz Ryan.)*

was Ehrich Weiss, whose initials match those on the long-forgotten box. That night, after his wife and child are asleep, Victor creeps up to the attic to find the box. The lock has rusted through, and it opens easily, revealing to Victor the secrets hidden for so long. *The Houdini Box,* according to a *Publishers Weekly* reviewer, expresses "the importance of faith and the ability to believe in the impossible."

The humorous and sensitive story soon sold out its first printing of ten thousand copies. The *Publishers Weekly* critic praised the story and stated that the illustrations "bring added vitality to a captivating plot." "The strong, rhythmic prose is great for reading aloud," wrote Hazel Rochman in her review in *Booklist.* Rochman also lauded the way the full-page drawings "with close cross-hatching show a dreamy, determined Victor." Roger Sutton, writing in the *Bulletin of the Center for Children's Books,* felt the story would appeal "to adult nostalgia," calling the book's ending "a big-boy's delight."

When *The Houdini Box* was published, Selznick was working at Eeyore's Bookstore in New York City, where he sold books and painted window displays. One customer, Laura Geringer, was a writer and editor of children's books with her own imprint at HarperCollins. She soon suggested Selznick illustrate a book by Pam Conrad called *Dollface Has a Party.* When Conrad wrote the book, she had in mind some little Asian dolls she used to play with as a girl. But Selznick thought Dollface sounded "like a gangster's moll from those old black-and-white gangster movies," he remarked in his interview. He based the character of Dollface on a doll from the 1920s that he found in a flea market. She was wearing a 1970s-era pink pants suit, and since she was bald, Selznick gave her a pink bouffant hairdo made of yarn to match. "She is always looking at the world through this one arched eyebrow," Selznick commented. Conrad had envisioned a very quiet little book, but when she saw Selznick's bright and wry drawings, he reported that her response was, "You made it really *Broadway!*"

Selznick's next solo effort was *The Robot King.* The idea for the story came from an announcer talking about a piece of music that had just finished playing on the radio. "I was only paying half-attention," Selznick recalled, "and it seemed like he said, 'That was "Waltz of the Robots."'" To this day, Selznick does not know if such a piece of music exists, but the idea stayed with him, and he made a note in his journal, "Why would a robot dance?" The answer he came up with is "because his heart is a music box." Selznick worked on the story for three years. It concerns a brother and sister who build a robot from the odds and ends they find in their house. For his heart, they use an old music box which belonged to their mother, who died many years before. When the music plays, the robot comes to life. The story takes place in the early part of this century, around the same period as *The Houdini Box.*

Critics noted that Selznick takes a step beyond fantasy into the realm of the surreal in *The Robot King.* The newly animated robot soon animates other small objects in the house and takes the children to the magical fairgrounds from one of Lucy's stories. "This has the flavor of a Victorian fairy tale," remarked Deborah Stevenson in *Bulletin of the Center for Children's Books,* "with electricity and technology forces of silent and incalculable magic and the sensibility more significant than the plotting." When the children see their father, they return home. Jane Gardner Connor praised the illustrations over Selznick's original story, writing in her review of *The Robot King* in *School Library Journal* that the pictures "do a good job of reflecting the somber, detached mood of the story."

Works Cited

Connor, Jane Gardner, review of *The Robot King, School Library Journal,* October, 1995, pp. 139-40.
Review of *The Houdini Box, Publishers Weekly,* May 3, 1991, p. 72.
Rochman, Hazel, review of *The Houdini Box, Booklist,* June 1, 1991, p. 1875.
Selznick, Brian, *The Houdini Box,* Knopf, 1991.
Stevenson, Deborah, review of *The Robot King, Bulletin of the Center for Children's Books,* October, 1995, p. 69.
Sutton, Roger, review of *The Houdini Box, Bulletin of the Center for Children's Books,* June, 1991, p. 250.

For More Information See

PERIODICALS

American Bookseller, March, 1991, p. 47; January, 1992, p. 8.
Children's Book Review Service, May, 1991, p. 117.
Kirkus Reviews, April 15, 1991, p. 538.
New York, February 19, 1990, p. 26.
Passaic Herald-News (New Jersey), April 21, 1991.
San Diego Union, May 5, 1991.
School Library Journal, September, 1991, p. 241.*

*   *   *

SHERMAN, Michael
See LOWNDES, Robert A(ugustine) W(ard)

*   *   *

SHERMAN, Peter Michael
See LOWNDES, Robert A(ugustine) W(ard)

SIMMS, Laura 1947-

Personal

Born April 7, 1947, in Brooklyn, NY; daughter of Louis (a dentist) and Claire (a concert pianist) Simms; children: Ishmael Beah (adopted from Sierra Leone).

Addresses

Home—814 Broadway, No. 3, New York, NY, 10003. *E-mail*—storydevi@earthlink.net.

Career

Author, storyteller, and educator, 1968—. Conducts writers' workshops and storytelling retreats. Lectures and consults in storytelling. Artist in residence, Lincoln Center's Institute for Arts in Education, 1997-99.

Awards, Honors

Young Readers Book Award, *Scientific American,* 1995, for *Moon and Otter and Frog;* 1996 Circle of Excellence in Storytelling Award; Sunny Days Award, *Sesame Street Parents,* 1999, for "contributions to children in the world"; Storytelling World Honor Award, for *Rotten Teeth.*

Writings

The Squeaky Door, illustrated by Sylvie Wickstrom, Crown, 1991.
Moon and Otter and Frog, illustrated by Clifford Brycelea, Hyperion, 1995.
The Bone Man: A Native American Modock Tale, illustrated by Michael McCurdy, Hyperion, 1997.
Rotten Teeth, illustrated by David Catrow, Houghton, 1998.

Also author of essays and articles on storytelling.

RECORDINGS

Women and Wild Animals Howl the Morning Welcome, Audio Press, 1992.
Nightwalkers (collection of ghost stories), Audio Press, 1994.
Dance without End: A Collection of Creation Myths, NorthWord Audio, 1995.
Making Peace, Earwig Records, 1996.
Four-Legged Tales: Stories from Here and Away, Lyrichord, 1999.
Fish Tales: Fish Stories from Here and Away, Lyrichord, 1999.
The Gift of Dreams, Sounds True Recordings, 2000.

RECORDINGS; FOR CHILDREN

Old As the World, Yellow Moon, 1999.
Just Right for Kids, Yellow Moon, 1999.
Horse in My Pocket, Yellow Moon, 1999.

OTHER

Also contributing editor and writer for *Parabola* magazine, and a contributing writer for *Sesame Street Parents, Humanity* magazine, and *Shambhala Sun.*

Work in Progress

A collection of essays for Yellow Moon Press; stories for *Globekids.net* website.

Sidelights

Laura Simms told *SATA:* "In quest of the power of oral narrative in the modern world, I became a storyteller, bringing together my love of literature, theater, anthropology, and psychology. It was my intention to create a new oral literature with the meaning and potency of traditional ritual in myth-based cultures. I have done that over these past thirty years.

"My work is distinguished by my study and respect for cultures and the process of spontaneous oral storytelling. I began as a writer and have returned again to the written word side by side with my performance work. I adapt traditional stories, write original tales, plays, and essays.... I have worked for the past ten years on a monumental retelling of the pre-Hellenic myth of the Mother and Daughter: *Demeter and Persephone.* I tell the tale combined with true life narrative to uncover, without didactic explanation, the way in which myth illumines our every day lives."

An experienced storyteller who has performed for children in schools and theaters, Simms has also written several children's books. Her passion for storytelling has its roots in the way an audience relates to a well-told tale. "A story is a journey into the unknown," Simms told Fran A. Snyder in an interview for *Natural History,* "and yet when we get there we respond to something entirely familiar." In her pursuit of stories that will appeal to children, Simms, a skilled storyteller who has performed at such places as the American Museum of Natural History in New York City, has mined the myths and folktales of many cultures from around the globe, many of which are obscure. Most of these stories, which come from cultures as diverse as the Native Americans, the Maori of New Zealand, and the Siberian Chukchi, are oral tales that have been handed down through the generations from ancient times.

Simms has stated that when she is searching for stories that appeal to her, she looks for certain features. "I mainly tell stories that I hear orally; ones that defy logic, grapple with the nature of spirituality, the attainment of wisdom, and how one can expand one's heart to contain a greater compassion," Simms stated in an interview for *Storypower* online. She has also shown a great deal of interest in Eastern European folktales, especially those with the Hasidic background she shares. "I began telling Hasidic stories in 1968, when I began my career," Simms recalled to *Storypower.* "It was natural since I grew up in an Eastern European family rooted in the tradition, in a Hasidic neighborhood—Borough Park.

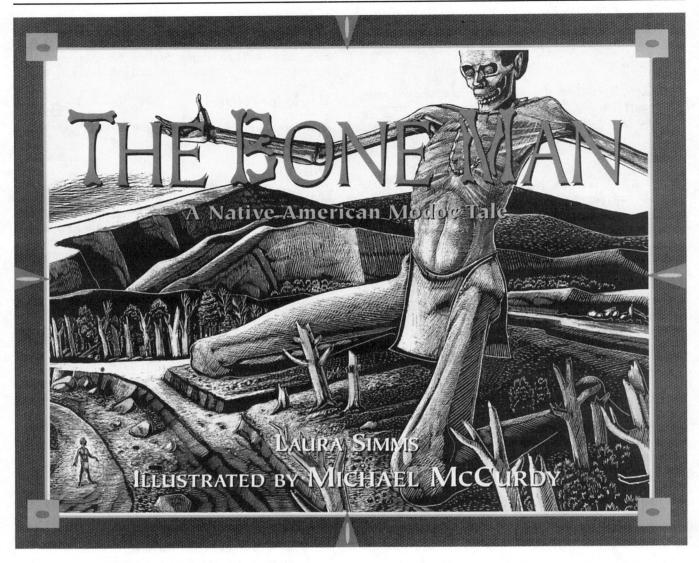

Nulwee must face the Bone Man and bring back the waters and people to his land in Laura Simms's retelling of this story of courage, wisdom, and compassion. *(Cover illustration by Michael McCurdy.)*

My great-grandfather on my mother's side from Dorohoi in Romania was the grand rabbi of Moldavia. My grandmother on my father's side, who was quite modest and magical, and knew ten languages, came from a very famous Rabbinical family."

Not only does Simms perform these stories live, she has retold many of them in print as well, such as in her as in her 1991 book *The Squeaky Door,* which is based on a folktale that originated in Puerto Rico. Two of her other publications, *Moon and Otter and Frog* (1995) and *The Bone Man: A Native American Modoc Tale,* are traditional folktales taken from a Native American tribe called the Modoc. Simms has also compiled and narrated cultural tales in audio form, as is the case with *Dance without End: A Collection of Creation Myths* (1995) in which she imparts a variety of origin stories from mostly tribal societies, as well as *Women and Wild Animals Howl the Morning Welcome* (1992). In addition to retelling the stories of other cultures, Simms has also

written an original story, titled *Rotten Teeth,* which she published in 1998. On top of her own writing and storytelling activities, Simms also leads writer's workshops, in which she tries to pass on to others her love of storytelling.

Moon and Otter and Frog, which earned the 1995 *Scientific American* Young Readers Book Award, is typical of the kind of story that appeals to Simms. As she writes in the book's introduction, it is her hope that the tale will foster "faith in children to trust their inner beauty." The book, which is illustrated by Clifford Brycelea, relates the Modoc tale about how the moon, after looking down upon Earth, sees his own reflection on some water. Hoping the reflection is a possible mate, Moon comes to Earth wearing the traditional dress of the Modoc, white buckskin and silver beads. Upon his arrival, he meets Otter, who had thought Moon to be a white-faced otter looking down from the sky. In the end, Moon ends up marrying Frog, an ugly, but loving mate.

By marrying Frog, rather than one of her ten prettier companions, Moon shows that character is more important than physical beauty. Reviewers Philip and Phylis Morrison of *Scientific American* described the narration as "songlike" and the illustrations "luminous and strange."

Simms again looked to the Modoc for her 1997 picture book *The Bone Man.* Only a young boy and his grandmother survive the wrath of the evil Bone Man, a gigantic creature who, in a fit of rage, ate all of the people in the region and washed them down with all of the water in the river. Raising her grandson alone, the grandmother prophesies to the young boy that he will one day defeat the Bone Man and people will return to the land. Indeed, when young Nulwee finally tires of the Bone Man's demands, a fierce battle erupts and the young boy calls on his deceased warrior father and medicine woman mother for strength in defeating the monster. Praising the "powerful language," *Bulletin of the Center for Children's Books* reviewer Janice M. Del Negro wrote that "Simms' text has the ring of the spoken works and the immediacy of a told tale as she succinctly delivers this tale of love, faithfulness, and heroism." Writing in *School Library Journal,* Barbara Elleman suggested that "The monster element will spark children's imaginations, making this a good tale to use beyond Native American studies."

Rotten Teeth, Simms's 1998 effort, is one of her most critically lauded works. The story is about Melissa Herman, a shy first grader who comes up with something unique to display at school on show and tell day. Upon the urging of her brother Norman, Melissa goes into her father's dentist office where she finds a bunch of pulled teeth in a bottle. Putting the bottle in a paper bag, Melissa heads to school ready to make her presentation. When it is her turn, a nervous Melissa stands at the head of the classroom. "Finally she opened up the bag, held up the bottle, and blurted out, "'ROTTEN TEETH! FROM REAL MOUTHS!,'" Simms describes the scene in the book. Although she had not talked much before this, Melissa is thrilled when her entranced classmates begin to ask her questions about the teeth. The discussion continues during the recess break, as Melissa realizes that she is suddenly a popular person. She also realizes the power of storytelling, which is the purpose of the tale. Jackie Hechtkopf, reviewing *Rotten Teeth* for *Library Journal,* called the book "a winner." Also appreciating the book's illustrations, Hechtkopf felt the "visual humor" to be "sensational." A contributor to *Publishers Weekly* was also impressed with the work, saying "This not-for-the-squeamish volume should impress future fans of Southern gothic." Reviewing the work in *Bulletin of the Center for Children's Books,* Del Negro admitted, "On a scale of one to ten, the grossout level is in the double digits, high enough to make this a readaloud favorite."

Despite her literary success, Simms's talents may best be utilized in a live performance, or on audio, where her expressive storytelling can take full effect. Such is the case with *Women and Wild Animals Howl the Morning Welcome,* which was released on audiocassette. On the tapes, which include the musical compositions of Steve Gorn, Simms verbally relates several cultural tales from places such as Africa, Siberia, and Romania. The team of Simms and Gorn works well together, largely because the two of them have a long history of performing live together, mostly in front of public school audiences. Using several traditional instruments, Gorn performs music that is evocative of tribal origins, matching the tone of the tales. In addition, Simms showcases her talents by lending a different voice for each of the book's different characters. The book opens with the Inuit legend about the energy of celebration as told by the Eagle Mother. "That's the trouble with you human beings. If you knew the nature of celebration, you'd never be lonely," Simms says in the voice of Eagle Mother. Critical response to the work was very emphatic. Preston Hoffman of *Wilson Library Bulletin* called the project "special" and Simms "one of the most expressive and versatile stylists I've heard."

Simms continued to *SATA:* "I am deeply struck by the misunderstanding of authentic storytelling today, and love the challenge of writing about the process of spoken reciprocal story. The ramifications of storytelling have to do with healing, conflict resolution, awakening imagination, and creating an embodied literature. Storytelling has become a buzzword for any narrative that holds attention. However, actual storytelling is a living language that more than holds attention. It engages

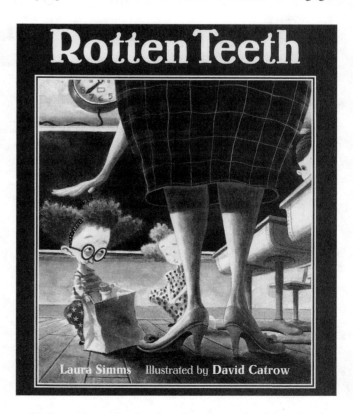

Melissa takes a bottle of real teeth to school for show-and-tell in Simms's hilarious story. (Cover illustration by David Catrow.)

listeners at a profoundly dynamic level. Drawn into the unfolding story, the listener becomes the story directly.

"I recently won the Sunny Days Award for contributions to children in the world for the healing power of my words. The award is given by *Sesame Street Parents* magazine. It is like the Emmy of children's theater. I think I received it for my work with children all over the world, bringing storytelling into the forefront of education, and for work with refugee children."

Works Cited

Del Negro, Janice M., review of *The Bone Man: A Native American Medoc Tale, Bulletin of the Center for Children's Books,* December, 1997, p. 140.

Del Negro, Janice M., review of *Rotten Teeth, Bulletin of the Center for Children's Books,* December, 1998, p. 145-46.

Elleman, Barbara, review of *The Bone Man: A Native American Medoc Tale, School Library Journal,* November, 1997, p. 112.

Hechtkopf, Jackie, review of *Rotten Teeth, Library Journal,* May 1, 1995, p. 149.

Hoffman, Preston, review of *Women and Wild Animals Howl the Morning Welcome, Wilson Library Bulletin,* May, 1992, p. 74.

Morrison, Philip, and Phylis Morrison, review of *Moon and Otter and Frog, Scientific American,* December, 1995, p. 108.

Review of *Rotten Teeth, Publishers Weekly,* August 24, 1998, p. 56.

Simms, Laura, interview with *Storypower* web site, www.storypower.com/hasidic/tellers/simms.

Simms, Laura, introduction to *Moon and Otter and Frog,* Hyperion, 1995.

Simms, Laura, *Rotten Teeth,* Houghton, 1998.

Simms, Laura, *Women and Wild Animals Howl the Morning Welcome,* Audio Press, 1992.

Snyder, Fran A., interview with Laura Simms, *Natural History,* October, 1983, pp. 88-92, 94-95.

For More Information See

PERIODICALS

Geo, August, 1983, p. 57.

Kliatt, September, 1992, pp. 65-66.

School Library Journal, May, 1991, p. 84; November, 1991, pp. 70-71; January, 1996, p. 106; September, 1998, p. 182.

*   *   *

SMITH, Craig 1955-

Personal

Born in 1955, in Woodside, South Australia; married Lisa Young (an artist); children: Hannah, Huw. *Education:* South Australian School of Art, received degree. *Hobbies and other interests:* Gardening.

Addresses

Office—15 Hardy St., Goodwood, South Australia 5034.

Career

Freelance illustrator. Has worked variously as a rust scraper and a nurse's aide.

Awards, Honors

Children's Book Council of Australia's Picture Book of the Year Award commendation, 1982, for *Whistle up the Chimney;* Children's Book Council of Australia's Book of the Year Award honor book, younger readers category, 1987, KOALA, secondary category, 1988, and Young Australian Best Book award, Fiction Younger Reader category, 1987, all for *Sister Madge's Book of Nuns;* Young Australian Best Book award, Fiction Younger Reader category, 1988, for *The Cabbage Patch Fib; Where's Mum?* was shortlisted in the Children's Book Council of Australia Picture Book of the Year Award, 1993; *Black Dog* was commended in the ABPA Book Design Awards; Young Artists Award.

Illustrator

PICTURE BOOKS

Christobel Mattingley, *Black Dog,* Collins (Sydney, Australia), 1979.

Nan Hunt, *Whistle up the Chimney,* Collins, 1981.

Geoffrey Dutton, *The Prowler,* Collins, 1982.

Nan Hunt, *An Eye Full of Soot and an Ear Full of Steam,* Collins, 1983.

Eleanor Nilsson, *Parrot Fashion,* Omnibus Books (Adelaide, Australia), 1983.

Nan Hunt, *Rain, Hail, or Shine,* Collins, 1984.

Sally Odgers, *Dreadful David,* Omnibus Books, 1984.

Doug MacLeod, *Sister Madge's Book of Nuns,* Omnibus Books, 1986.

Mary O'Toole, *A Strange Visitor,* Macmillan (Melbourne, Australia), 1987.

Duncan Ball, *My Dog's a Scaredy Cat,* Walter McVitty (Sydney), 1987.

Marcia Vaughan, *Still Room for More,* Australian Publishing (Sydney), 1989.

Phil Cummings, *Goodness Gracious!,* Omnibus Books, 1989, Orchard Books, 1992.

Mem Fox, *Sophie,* Ian Drakeford (Melbourne), 1989.

Nan Hunt, *The Whistle Stop Party,* Collins Ingram (Sydney), 1990.

Colin Pearce, *The Monkey and the Crocodile,* Tyndale House (Wheaton, IL), 1990.

Rachel Flynn, *I Hate Fridays,* Penguin (Melbourne), 1990.

Richard Tulloch, *The Brown Felt Hat,* Omnibus, 1990.

Nigel Gray, *Anna's Ghost,* Ashton Scholastic (Gosford), 1991.

Pamela Rushby, *All the Flavours in the World,* Ginn (Aylesbury), 1992.

Libby Gleeson, *Where's Mum?,* Omnibus, 1992.

June Loves, *I Know That,* SRA School Group (Santa Rosa, CA), 1992.

Diana Noonan, *Fat Cat Tompkin,* SRA School Group, 1992.

Robyn McIlhenny, *Our Baby,* SRA School Group, 1992.

Gillian Rubinstein, *The Giant's Tooth,* Viking, 1993.

Margaret Watts, *Trouble with Hairgrow,* SRA School Group, 1994.

Michael Dugan, *The Emu Who Wanted to Be a Horse,* SRA School Group, 1994.

Marcia K. Vaughan, *The Stick-Around Cloud,* SRA School Group, 1994.

Anthony Holcroft, *Bootlace Soup,* SRA School Group, 1994.

Cecily Matthews, *Captain Orinoco's Onion,* SRA School Group, 1994.

Anne Houghton, *There Stood Our Dog,* SRA School Group, 1994.

Nigel Gray, *Fly,* Cygnet Books/University of Western Australia Press, 1994.

June Loves, *I Know That,* SRA School Group, 1994.

Jessica Carroll, *Billy the Punk,* Red Fox (Sydney, Australia), 1995.

Garry Disher, *Ermyntrude Takes Charge,* Angus & Robertson (Sydney, Australia), 1995.

Emily Rodda, *Yay!,* Greenwillow, 1997.

Lesley Jane, *The Rain,* Folens (Dunstable), 1997.

Philippa Jean, *Insects That Bother Us,* Folens, 1997.

Meg Stein, *A Day Shopping,* Folens, 1997.

Julia Wall, *The Best Guess,* Folens, 1997.

OTHER

Contributor of illustrations to poetry collections, including *Petrifying Poems,* Scholastic, 1988, and *Vile Verse.*

Sidelights

Craig Smith told *SATA:* "I was born in Woodside, outside of Adelaide, Australia. I have an older sister, Maire, who has always been passionate about drawing. My parents were involved in a family business selling footwear in two neighbouring towns. Woodside has an Army barracks and was the biggest influence on my playtime. With a few friends we spent day after day involved in pretend combat, often kitted out from the local dump, which the Army used. My earliest remembered ambition was to be a cartoonist. I spent a lot of time copying Walt Disney characters. Nonetheless,

going into the early teens I seriously wanted to make a career in either Army or Navy. My sister went to the South Australian School of Art. It was through her that the interesting world of graphic design was opened to me. I followed in her footsteps.

"The illustrations lecturer George Tetlow was an enthusiast for children's book illustrations and set a major project in that area. It was on the strength of this project that I sent slides of the drawings to a number of publishers, from which came an invitation to provide roughs for a book. This was Christobel Mattingley's text for *Black Dog.* After graduation I began work as a freelance illustrator and have remained so since. However, for the first eight years I needed to work elsewhere part time. The principal employment was as a nurse's aid for a hospital for geriatrics.

"In 1981 Lisa and I had our first child, Hannah, and the following year had another, Huw. These were hectic times. It was in response to this that a friend, John Nowland, offered me space in his graphic design studio to work from. The few years spent there were very instructive as a first-class example of professional practice, also the need to give attention to the *whole* design concept and particularly the typography. Then a few of us came together and formed our own studio of illustrators and graphic designers. This went along quite nicely for about six years. Then someone burnt the studio down."

Smith now works in a garden studio. He states in his Angus & Robertson profile that he hopes the quiet atmosphere will inspire him to explore other illustration techniques, such as 3D. Smith notes that he enjoys illustrating children's books "because of the freedom to develop the character *of* the book, as well as the characters *in* the book. Children's books offer a good scope for humour and satire, both of which I love to use." Reading to his own children made him realize that "good books are far more than good pictures, it's the synthesis of text and image that's important."

Works Cited

"Craig Smith" (profile), Angus & Robertson, c. 1993.*

V

VANDERWERFF, Corrine 1939-

Personal

Born October 15, 1939, in Cathlamet, WA; daughter of Ernest (a fisherman and logger) and Margery (a homemaker) Kandoll; married Date Vanderwerff (a missionary, educator, and community development specialist), August 28, 1960; children: Joann Vanderwerff Chabaylo, Jon.

Corrine Vanderwerff

Addresses

Office—Box 57214, EPO Eastgate, 2010A Sherwood Dr., Sherwood Park, Alberta, Canada T8A 5L7. *E-mail*—104474.1654@compuserve.com.

Career

Elementary schoolteacher in British Columbia, 1966-68; high school journalism teacher in British Columbia, 1971-78; newspaper reporter and columnist in British Columbia, 1978-80; high school journalism teacher in British Columbia, 1979-81; missionary in Rwanda, Zaire (now Congo), 1981-99. Freelance writer and motivational speaker, 1988—. Reach Italy Child Sponsorship Programs in Zaire, manager, 1986-98; adviser and facilitator for African women's groups, 1993-98.

Writings

Ten Days, Pacific Press Publishing (Boise, ID), 1986.
An Arrow Returned, Review & Herald (Hagerstown, MD), 1986.
Way to Go! Jesus Answered, I Am the Way (devotional text for children), Review & Herald, 1993.
They Called Me Bwana Munaga, Amundsen Publishing, 1994.
Kill Thy Neighbor: One Man's Incredible Story of Loss and Deliverance in Rwanda, Pacific Press Publishing, 1996.
The Mists of Mbinda: Kate's Busy Life Concealed the Soul of a Woman Lonely for Love, Pacific Press Publishing, 1998.
Angry like Jonah: Finding Healing for Angry Feelings, Review & Herald, 1998.
Lucy, the Curiously Comical Cow (juvenile), Pacific Press Publishing, 1998.

Work in Progress

Breakfast with God, seven volumes of inspirational material on various facets of trust; research on the concept of trust from spiritual and psychological angles.

Sidelights

Corrine Vanderwerff told *SATA:* "Writing is a way of life for me. When I'm home, I'm usually in my office and at my computer by five o'clock a.m. I work for three to four hours before breakfast. Then I fit in another three or four hours of writing around the other tasks of the day.

"Living on the long-wintered Canadian prairies as we now do, I find that I write like I shovel snow. To keep the job interesting, I start at a favorite point, push ahead full speed until the load gets too heavy, then go back, scape and clean, then push off again. I keep pushing ahead, going back, cleaning and scraping sections to perfection until, *voila,* the job's done.

"I also write in spurts, frequently shifting pace to keep my focus and interest at an optimum. *Lucy the Curiously Comical Cow* happened like that. My publishers wanted a story about a kid and an exotic pet. 'My niece has a cow named Lucy,' I said. 'A Cow!' they responded, 'exotic?' 'You'll see!' I answered. Like when I shovel snow, I started at the most fun place and sent them chapter six. 'We see!' they said. 'Send us the rest as soon as you can.' And I did.

"We were still based in Africa (as missionaries) at the time, but I was home on furlough. My aunt let me use an upstairs bedroom of her farmhouse for a writing room. Before going back overseas, I had a concentrated session of dental work to finish, and lots of the final rewriting was done in a dental chair. Jen and her aunt and uncle read the manuscript and gave suggestions which helped to make the story true to detail, and real.

"Much of my writing, though, is set in the central part of Africa where we lived and worked as missionaries for eighteen years. My husband is still working part-time in Africa, but I'm living in North America most of the time, writing and speaking. With so many of my earlier professional years spent in the classroom, I find that I am still a teacher at heart. Thus, the focus of my work is sharing the good things I've learned because I'd like everyone to know how to have a happier, more peaceful life.

"I like living where we are now because of our grandsons, Matthew and Aaron: we can do things together. We explore the city, riding bus and underground, visiting museums and other places, and talking about important things. We can also go sledding. Sometimes we even shovel snow together."

*   *   *

VINEST, Shaw
See LONGYEAR, Barry B(rookes)

*   *   *

VINING, Elizabeth Gray 1902-1999
(Elizabeth Janet Gray)

OBITUARY NOTICE—See index for *SATA* sketch: Born October 6, 1902, in Philadelphia, PA; died November 27, 1999, in Kennett Square, PA. Author. Elizabeth Gray Vining was a Quaker woman summoned to be the tutor for Akihito, the Crown Prince of Japan, from 1946 to 1950. Her 1952 best-seller *Windows for the Crown Prince* tells of her experiences teaching Akihito and his peers while working and forging lifelong friendships with the royal family. Vining's thirty books include novels, story collections, and children's fiction. Her first book, *Meredith's Ann,* was published in 1929, and her *Adam of the Road,* the story of a boy's adventures in medieval England, won the Newbery Award in 1943.

OBITUARIES AND OTHER SOURCES:

PERIODICALS

Los Angeles Times, December 7, 1999, p. A28.
New York Times, December 1, 1999, p. C31.

W

WALLACE, Rich 1957-

Personal

Born January 29, 1957, in Hackensack, NJ; divorced in 1996; remarried in 2000; children: two sons. *Education:* Montclair State College (now University), B.A., 1980.

Rich Wallace

Addresses

Home—P.O. Box 698, Honesdale, PA 18431. *Office*—Highlights for Children, 803 Church St., Honesdale, PA 18431.

Career

Herald News, Passaic, NJ, editorial assistant, 1978-79; sports reporter, 1979-82; *Daily Advance,* Dover, NJ, sports editor, 1982-84, news editor, 1984-85; *Trenton Times,* Trenton, NJ, copy editor, 1985-86, assistant city editor, 1986-87; *Highlights for Children* magazine, copy editor, 1988-90, assistant editor, 1990-92, coordinating editor, 1992-98, senior editor, 1998—.

Awards, Honors

American Library Association Best Books for Young Adults selection, and American Library Association Recommended Book for Reluctant Young Adult Readers, both 1996, both for *Wrestling Sturbridge.*

Writings

Wrestling Sturbridge, Knopf, 1996.
Shots on Goal, Knopf, 1997.
Playing without the Ball, Knopf, 2000.

Adaptations

Wrestling Sturbridge was recorded on audio cassette, Recorded Books, 1996; *Shots on Goal* was recorded on audio cassette, Recorded Books, 1998.

Sidelights

In his novels *Wrestling Sturbridge* and *Shots on Goal,* young adult author Rich Wallace has used "the metaphors of sports to explore universal themes of emerging adulthood and self-definition," according to *Horn Book* reviewer Maeve Visser Knoth. "Like other good writers," stated Ken Donelson in the *St. James Guide to Young Adult Writers,* "Wallace recognizes the importance of telling a story that involves readers—mostly boys, but also girls and women—who recognize that the book is about sports and much, much more."

Wallace was born January 29, 1957, in Hackensack, New Jersey. Raised by his college-educated parents along with six brothers and sisters, Wallace, as he told *Authors and Artists for Young Adults,* started writing "little stories" in the first grade. But academics were not Wallace's strong suit. As he remembered, "I found school generally a bit boring, and I stopped reading much of anything I didn't have to from about sixth grade until well after college." What did capture Wallace's interest? "My ambitions as a teenager," he told *Artists and Authors for Young Adults,* "were focused on being the best runner I could possibly be. I was heavily into sports and devoted myself to track and cross country running."

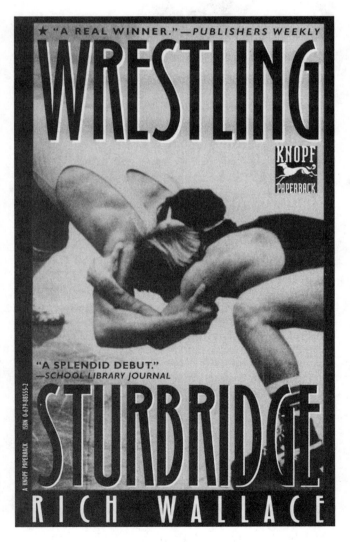

High-school senior Ben challenges his friend for his spot on the wrestling squad in Wallace's portrait of adolescence in small-town America. *(Cover photo by Mike Valeri.)*

In high school, however, Wallace "began to write extensively . . . just diaries in which I sorted out my life and purged a lot of emotion." He also gained valuable experience by working on his school's newspaper. Wallace's evolution as a writer continued at New Jersey's Montclair State College. He took creative writing classes, including one that required him to pen a novel, one chapter per week. He also interned at the Passaic *Herald-News,* where he was later offered a paid writing and reporting position. Sports once again captured the majority of Wallace's attention, though. "I spent most of my energy on the track and cross country teams," he admitted. In fact, Wallace left college just two credits short of a degree. A couple of years later, he returned and completed "two one-credit, half-semester physical education courses (bowling and soccer) so I could get my degree and stop lying on my resume."

Wallace revealed that after graduating from Montclair State in 1980 with a bachelor of arts degree, he "played around with that novel [from creative writing class] for quite a few years." He finished the work and sent it to publishers, but "none took it because it's a disjointed, poorly planned book." Wallace did receive a "nice rejection letter" from Patricia Gauch, an editor at Philomel. Gauch also shared some positive comments from the in-house staff, including several from Tracy Gates. Gates would later play a pivotal role in the publication of *Wrestling Sturbridge.*

Over the next eight years, Wallace continued his newspaper career, working variously as a sports reporter, news editor, and assistant city editor at a variety of New Jersey newspapers. He also married and became a father to two boys. In 1988, Wallace began working for *Highlights for Children* as a copy editor. Today, he is a senior editor at the magazine, and publishing well-written stories has become Wallace's passion. "I love the field," he told *Author's and Artists for Young Adults.* "I've met virtually no one who works editorially in this field—children's publishing—whose first and overwhelming priority isn't to bring out great books and magazines."

Wallace had continued his own writing efforts during this period. In 1996, after working on a number of novels that "showed promise but didn't go anywhere," as he told *Publishers Weekly* contributor Heather Vogel Frederick, Wallace finally had a story that was different. "This one gelled right from the beginning," Wallace continued, "I knew where it was going." Wallace sent the manuscript to Gates, who years earlier had complimented his first, failed effort. Gates, now an editor at Knopf, suggested changes to the new work, including a few additional scenes and chapters that fleshed out the story. "*Wrestling Sturbridge* wouldn't be what it is without Tracy, not by a long shot," Wallace remarked to Frederick.

Wrestling Sturbridge is the story of Ben, a high school senior and varsity wrestler who tires of being practice fodder for Al, his teammate and close friend. Faced with a bleak future in a dead-end town, Ben decides to challenge for Al's spot on the squad, despite the fact that Al is a top contender for the state title. Ben also begins a romance with the intelligent, tough-minded Kim, who believes in Ben more than he believes in himself. But "Wallace isn't writing a sports fairy story," a *Publishers Weekly* contributor declared. Instead, *Wrestling Sturbridge* offers a "strong portrait of a smothering small town," *Horn Book* reviewer Maeve Visser Knoth remarked, "and the hopelessness that it engenders in an adolescent." "Anyone even remotely curious about small-town America need look no further than this exemplary first novel," stated the *Publishers Weekly* critic.

Reviewers also praised the author's narrative voice. Wallace, "like Ben, whose voice is so strong and clear here," wrote Debbie Carton in *Booklist,* "weighs his words carefully, making every one count." "He [Ben] tells the story in a spare way appropriate to his undemonstrative, nonverbal nature," a *Kirkus Reviews* critic stated, "recording fast and furious wrestling action, the steady burn of his own anger and frustration, and brief but telling glimpses of the people around him." *Wrestling Sturbridge,* Donelson concluded, "is about young people who care about life and about keeping promises they've made to themselves and others. It is a rare sports story because there is no super-hero and no villain."

The setting for *Shots on Goal,* Wallace's next book, remains in Sturbridge but moves to the soccer field. A critic in *Kirkus Reviews* declared, "Wallace flattens the sophomore jinx in this taut, present-tense tale of an underdog high-school soccer team battling internal dissension." The instigators of this internal dissension are Barry "Bones" Austin and his best friend, Joey. Bones realizes that he is stuck in "second place," not only on the soccer field, where he is the team's second-best player (after Joey), but also at home, where his older brother, Tommy, is the favored son of their parents.

Tension arises when Bones' object of desire, Shannon, begins dating Joey. Bones also grows resentful of Joey's increasingly selfish play on the field. As the soccer season rolls on, "a face-off [begins] between the two teens," *Booklist* critic Frances Bradburn stated, "each striving to find his own identity without the other, in spite of the other." The face-off finally comes to an end after "the two friends square off in a fight which makes both aware how important their soccer team and their friendship are," according to Donelson.

Like *Wrestling Sturbridge, Shots on Goal* earned praise for its fully-developed characters and exciting action. Dina Sherman, writing in *School Library Journal,* felt that the "situations and emotions that Bones experiences are all very real, and young people will relate to them." A critic in the *Bulletin of the Center for Children's Books* added that "the soccer matches are fast, the interaction with girls unromantically realistic, and the voice is engaging, as Bones tells his story as a rueful eyewitness account."

Fifteen-year-old Bones deals with a crush on his best friend's girlfriend while helping his soccer team toward the league championship.

In his book, *Playing without the Ball* Wallace again invites readers to enter the world of high school sports in Sturbridge. The main character is Jay, a high school basketball player who supports himself by working part-time in a bar, while also living by himself above the bar. Jay meets Spit, a singer in a band that often performs at the bar. Wallace admitted that "you could say the book is about sex, drugs and rock and roll, but it's as much about basketball as anything."

The writing process is a lengthy one for Wallace, and patience is the key element. The author "starts with a character and a situation. Plotting comes after I've gotten well under way, if at all." These characters or situations have often originated from Wallace's old journals, his children, or "from experiences I have as an adult that I can twist a little bit and think I can picture happening to me when I was a teenager." The next step is research, "but not in any traditional way," Wallace declares. His books are set in "contemporary small-town Pennsylvania, which is where I live. So I pay attention to the world I live in." Details are important, Wallace added, "like the arrangement of soda bottles in the Turkey Hill convenience store or the way the streets look at dusk on an October evening from the cliff overlooking the town." Finally, Wallace will "write intensely for a few months" until the book is finished. The author also stated that he doesn't "fight writer's block. I expect long dry periods in which something may be incubating in my head, but I'm not really working on it."

Why does Wallace write about sports? As the author told *Authors and Artists for Young Adults,* he simply doesn't "know any other way to approach what I do. Sports has been my mindset since a very young age, and I'd have trouble getting inside a head that didn't function that way." Furthermore, the author sees "sports as a metaphor for life." But Wallace adds that he "didn't set out directly to draw a parallel between the growth and stresses of a friendship and the internal strife of a soccer team [in *Shots on Goal*]." Nor did Wallace see "wrestling as a metaphor for self-awareness [in *Wrestling Sturbridge*] or basketball playing as potentially akin to addiction [in *Playing without the Ball.* They just came out that way.]"

Wallace has but one goal for his writing: "I really just want to be honest," honest in the representation of how teenage boys struggle to find themselves while "striving to be the best that they can be, making continual mistakes, and eventually seeing the light." Wallace also hopes that, after reading his books, "some kids will realize their potential. I have kids tell me all the time, for example, that *Wrestling Sturbridge* changed their lives. They can't articulate why, but they don't have to." Critics agree that Wallace's novels have touched young adults; as Donelson stated, "It's safe to say that many readers . . . await whatever Wallace has to offer."

Works Cited

Bradburn, Frances, review of *Shots on Goal, Booklist,* September 15, 1997, p. 224.

Carton, Debbie, review of *Wrestling Sturbridge, Booklist,* September 1, 1996, p. 128.

Donelson, Ken, *St. James Guide to Young Adult Writers,* St. James Press, 1999, pp. 860-61.

Frederick, Heather Vogel, "Flying Starts: Six Children's Book Newcomers Share Thoughts on Their Debut Projects," *Publishers Weekly,* July 1, 1996, pp. 34-37.

Knoth, Maeve Visser, review of *Wrestling Sturbridge, Horn Book,* November-December, 1996, p. 747.

Sherman, Dina, review of *Shots on Goal, School Library Journal,* November, 1997, pp. 124-25.

Review of *Shots on Goal, Bulletin of the Center for Children's Books,* December, 1997, pp. 143-44.

Review of *Shots on Goal, Kirkus Reviews,* July 15, 1997, p. 1118.

Wallace, Richard, e-mail interview with *Authors and Artists for Young Adults,* November, 1999.

Review of *Wrestling Sturbridge, Kirkus Reviews,* May 15, 1996, p. 752.

Review of *Wrestling Sturbridge, Publishers Weekly,* June 3, 1996, p. 84.

For More Information See

PERIODICALS

Horn Book, November, 1997, p. 687.

Kliatt, August, 1997, p. 53; September, 1997, p. 15.

Los Angeles Times Book Review, September 15, 1996, p. 11.

Tribune Books (Chicago), April 14, 1996, p. 7.

Voice of Youth Advocates, June, 1997, p. 114.

—*Sketch by Ann Schwalboski*

*   *   *

WATLING, James 1933-

Personal

Born February 7, 1933, in Newcastle-upon-Tyne, England; immigrated to Canada; married; children: five. *Education:* Attended Barrow-in-Furness School of Art, 1945-53; Leeds School of Art, A.T.C., 1954; postgraduate study. *Hobbies and other interests:* Birds, the outdoors, cabinet making, home construction.

Addresses

Home—4151 Lakeshore Drive, Rawdon, Quebec, Canada J0K 1S0. *Agent*—Portfolio Solutions, Suite 8, Billings Plaza, 2419 Route 82, P.O. Box 74, Billings, NY 12510-0074.

Career

Illustrator and educator. McGill University, Montreal, Quebec, associate professor and art program director, faculty of education, 1963-1995.

Awards, Honors

Notable Children's Trade Book in the Field of Social Studies, 1990, for *Samuel's Choice;* Child Study Association Children's Book of the Year, 1994, for *Bound for Oregon;* Georgia Author of the Year Award for Juvenile Literature, 1996, and Storytelling World Award, 1997, for *The Tree That Owns Itself and Other Adventure Tales from Out of the Past;* Georgia Author of the Year Award, 1999, for *The Devil's Highway;* Children's Pick of the Lists, American Booksellers Association, 1999, for *Seaman: The Dog Who Explored the West with Lewis & Clark.*

Illustrator

Hans Christian Andersen, *The Emperor and the Nightingale,* Troll Associates (Mahwah, NJ), 1979.

Corinne Denan, reteller, *Tales of Magic and Spells,* Troll Associates, 1980.

Keith Brandt, *Wonders of the Seasons,* Troll Associates, 1982.

Susan Gold Purdy, *Eskimos,* Watts (New York), 1982.

Laurence Santrey, *Discovering the Stars,* Troll Associates, 1982.

Raymond Harris, editor, *Best Short Stories,* Jamestown Publishers, 1983.

Peter Zachary Cohen, *The Great Red River Raft,* Whitman (New York), 1984.

K. Brandt, *Deserts,* Troll Associates, 1985.

Louis Sabin, *Grasslands,* Troll Associates, 1985.

Eileen Curran, *Life in the Meadow,* Troll Associates, 1985.

E. Curran, *Mountains and Volcanoes,* Troll Associates, 1985.

Kim Jackson, *The Planets,* Troll Associates, 1985.

Linda Walvoord Girard, *Earth, Sea, and Sky: The Work of Edmond Halley,* Whitman (Niles, IL), 1985.

Drollene P. Brown, *Belva Lockwood Wins Her Case,* Whitman, 1987.

David Cutts, reteller, *King of the Golden Mountain,* Troll Associates, 1988.

Judy Donnelly, *Tut's Mummy Lost—and Found,* Random House (New York), 1988.

Stephen Krensky, *Witch Hunt: It Happened in Salem Village,* Random House, 1989.

Janet Palazzo-Craig, *Discovering Prehistoric Animals,* Troll Associates, 1990.

Stephen Caitlin, *Wonders of Swamps and Marshes,* Troll Associates, 1990.

Linda Hayward, *The First Thanksgiving,* Random House, 1990.

Richard Berleth, *Samuel's Choice,* Whitman, 1990.

Robert McConnell, *Nip and Tuck,* Napoleon (Toronto), 1990.

Stephen Krensky, *Children of the Earth and Sky,* Scholastic Inc., 1991.

Anita Larsen, *The Roanoke Missing Persons Case,* Maxwell Macmillan International (New York)/Crestwood House (Toronto), 1992.

Gail Stewart, *Why Buy Quantrill's Bones?* Maxwell Macmillan International/Crestwood House, 1992.

Barbara Diamond Goldin, *Fire! The Beginnings of the Labor Movement,* Viking (New York), 1992.

Anita Larsen, *Raoul Wallenberg: Missing Diplomat,* Maxwell Macmillan International/Crestwood House, 1992.

Nancy Antle, *Hard Times: A Story of the Great Depression,* Viking, 1993.

Kathleen V. Kudlinski, *Night Bird: A Story of the Seminole Indians,* Viking, 1993.

Marion Russell, *Along the Sante Fe Trail: Marion Russell's Own Story,* adapted by Ginger Wadsworth, Whitman (Norton Grove, IL), 1993.

Jean Van Leeuwen, *Bound for Oregon,* Dial (New York), 1994.

Stephen Krensky, *Children of the Wind and Water: First Stories about Native American Children,* Scholastic (New York), 1994.

Kathleen V. Kudlinski, *Facing West: A Story of the Oregon Trail,* Viking, 1994.

Lisa Sita, *The Rattle and the Drum: Native American Rituals and Celebrations,* Millbrook Press, 1994.

Laurie Stedling, *Birthstones: Make Your Own Birthstones, Rings, and Other Projects!* (book and ring kit), Watermill Press, 1995.

Mary Packard, *Rocks and Minerals,* Troll Associates, 1995.

Mary Packard, *Stars and Planets,* Troll Associates, 1995.

Stephen Krensky, *The Iron Dragon Never Sleeps,* Dell (New York), 1995.

Lisa Banim, *The Hessian's Secret Diary,* Silver Moon Press (New York), 1996.

Candace Fleming, *Women of the Lights,* Whitman, 1996.

Loretta Johnson Hammer and Gail Karwoski, *The Tree that Owns Itself and Other Adventure Tales from Out of the Past,* Peachtree (Atlanta), 1996.

Eric Carpenter, *Young Thurgood Marshall: Fighter for Equality,* Troll Associates, 1996.

Avi, *Finding Providence: The Story of Roger Williams,* HarperCollins (New York), 1997.

Lynne Reid Banks, *Key to the Indian,* Avon (New York), 1998.

Joseph Bruchac, *The Arrow over the Door,* Dial, 1998.

Stanley Applegate, *The Devil's Highway,* Peachtree, 1998.

Deborah Heligman, *The Story of the Titanic,* Random House, 1998.

Stanley Applegate, *Natchez Under-the-Hill,* Peachtree, 1998.

John J. Loeper, *Meet the Drakes on the Kentucky Frontier,* Marshall Cavendish, 1998.

John J. Loeper, *Meet the Dudleys in Colonial Times,* Marshall Cavendish, 1999.

Gail Karwoski, *Seaman: The Dog Who Explored the West with Lewis & Clark,* Peachtree, 1999.

Ann McGovern, *Christopher Columbus,* Econo-Clad Books, 1999.

Watling is also the illustrator of *Buddy: The Picture Storybook,* written by Alison Inches and published by Landolf's, Inc.

Adaptations

The Emperor and the Nightingale was released as a sound recording by Troll Associates in 1998. Teacher's Guides for *The Devil's Highway* and *Natchez Under-the-Hill* were issued by Peachtree Publications.

Sidelights

An English-born Canadian illustrator of picture books, fiction, nonfiction, and retellings, James Watling is regarded as a prolific artist whose distinctive works have graced a variety of books. Focusing mainly on works directed to primary and middle graders, Watling has also illustrated books for preschoolers and young adults. The artist's pictures appear most often in works with historical themes, although he has also illustrated science books, concept books, fantasy, and retellings of folk and fairy tales. Watling has provided the pictures for books by Hans Christian Andersen and the Brothers Grimm, as well as for more current writers such as Avi, Lynne Reid Banks, Joseph Bruchac, Jean Van Leeuwen, Stephen Krensky, Robert McConnell, Anita Larsen, Barbara Diamond Goldin, Keith Brandt, Eileen Curran, and Stanley Applegate.

Watling's pictures often introduce children to historical events, generally from American history. For example, he has illustrated volumes that describe such landmarks as the first Thanksgiving at New Plymouth Colony; the

James Watling's colored ink and pencil drawings illustrate seven-year-old Marion Russell's story of her wagon-train journey along the Santa Fe Trail. (From Along the Santa Fe Trail, *adapted by Ginger Wadsworth.)*

disappearance of the English colonists on Roanoke Island; the founding of Providence, Rhode Island; the Salem witch trials; the building of the transcontinental railroad; the sinking of the *Titanic;* the Great Depression; the beginning of the Labor Movement in New York City; and the discovery of the tomb of King Tut. He has also illustrated several biographies of well-known historical figures, such as the explorers Christopher Columbus and Lewis and Clark, as well as biographies of figures who are less well known but still had a powerful impact on history, such as Belva Lockwood, the nineteenth-century presidential candidate who was the first woman to practice law before the Supreme Court; Thurgood Marshall, the first African American to become a Supreme Court justice; Raoul Wallenberg, the Swedish diplomat who helped thousands of Jews to escape during World War II and then mysteriously disappeared; and a group of women—Ida Lewis, Kate Walker, Harriet Colfax, and Emily Fish—who lived and worked in lighthouses across America.

In addition to his books about notable contributors to history, Watling has provided the pictures for biographies of unusual or notorious figures such as William Clarke Quantrill, the leader of a Confederate army during the Civil War who massacred nearly two hundred civilians in Lawrence, Kansas, and the naturalist Gertrude Lintz, a socialite in the 1920s who adopted a huge menagerie of wild animals and kept them on her Long Island estate. The subject of *Buddy: The Picture Storybook* by Alison Inches, Lintz raised a baby gorilla named Buddy from birth, treating him as if he was a human child. Their story was dramatized in a 1997 film on which the book, which contains Watling's colorful illustrations, is based. In Gail Stewart's *Why Buy Quantrill's Bones?,* Watling depicts incidents from the life of Quantrill, the leader of a guerrilla band who fought in a border war between Missouri and Kansas and whose bones currently rest in three states; the book presents brief biographies of Quantrill and other related figures in the form of mysteries with possible solutions.

Watling has also illustrated many books about science and nature. His books introduce children to such subjects as prehistoric animals; the seasons; the sun, moon, and planets; deserts, grasslands, swamps, meadows, and marshes; mountains and volcanoes; and rocks and minerals. In addition, Watling has illustrated fiction and nonfiction about Native Americans, historical fiction that often is set during the American Revolution or describes the lives of the pioneers in the American West, and craft books about making jewelry and Eskimo artifacts.

Watling once told *SATA* that he is "particularly interested in historical illustration and illustration of nature/wildlife." Born in Newcastle-upon-Tyne, England, Watling studied art in England before moving to Canada. He and his wife, who live on a lake in the Laurentians, have five grown children, as well as a stable of animals, both wild and domestic. In 1963 Watling began teaching art at McGill University in Montreal, Quebec. Before his retirement he had become an associate professor, as well as the director of the university's art program. Watling illustrated his first book, a picture book version of Hans Christian Andersen's tale *The Emperor and the Nightin-*

...a suddon squall of wind struck us...near overseting the perogue....
—JOURNAL OF CAPTAIN MERIWETHER LEWIS, April 13, 1805

Watling's illustrations bring to life one of the greatest American expeditions in Seaman, *written by Gail Langer Karwoski.*

A fourteen-year-old Quaker and a young Indian scout meet in Joseph Bruchac's The Arrow over the Door, *illustrated by Watling.*

gale, in 1979. He then began to balance his teaching career with his new occupation. As an illustrator, Watling characteristically works in both color (watercolor and colored pencil) and black and white (pencil or ink). His works, which often appear on full pages and are sometimes accompanied by maps and photographs, range from simple line drawings and soft watercolor washes to dramatic, gleaming paintings. Credited with enhancing and adding atmosphere to their texts, Watling's pictures are generally considered attractive, accurate, detailed, and well-designed. Watling's art is generally considered both educational and entertaining, and he is a well-respected figure in the field of children's literature.

Among Watling's most acclaimed illustrations are those for *Nip and Tuck,* a picture book by Canadian author Robert McConnell that is written in verse. In this work, which features a family of beavers, the parents of the title characters feel that their children are too young to help build the family's new dam. Nip and Tuck insist that they are big enough to assist their parents, but their protests are ignored. After disaster strikes the dam when their parents are away, Nip and Tuck fix the dam, save the pond, and become heroes. Writing in the *Midwest Book Review,* a critic noted that the "lovely story is wonderfully illustrated and brought visually to life by the artistry of James Watling." Another well-received work is *Along the Santa Fe Trail: Marion Russell's Own Story,* an adaptation by Ginger Wadsworth of *Land of Enchantment: Memoirs of Marion Russell.* Written for a middle-grade audience, the volume describes young Marion's exciting adventures as she travels from Kansas to California with her mother and brother along the Santa Fe Trail. Writing in *Booklist,* Julie Corsaro stated that the illustrations in colored ink and pencil "capture the setting through the haze of memory" and that the book conveys "a sense of the danger, boredom, and natural beauty that accompanied these trailblazers." A critic in *Kirkus Reviews,* calling Watling's pictures "[l]ively with authentic detail," noted that he provided "dramatic, well-designed watercolors with panoramic sweeps that are rich in detail." Writing in *Publishers Weekly,* a reviewer stated that "his polished colored ink and colored pencil drawings are historically accurate and filled with energy."

With their picture book *Finding Providence: The Story of Roger Williams,* Watling and author Avi introduce children to the Puritan preacher who was driven from the Massachusetts Bay Colony in 1635 because he stood up for the separation of church and state. Told by Williams's young daughter, Mary, the story describes the founding of a new settlement in Rhode Island that was based on religious freedom; the settlement was later named Providence by Mary Williams. Hazel Rochman commented in *Booklist,* "Watling's glowing illustrations on every page create a strong sense of the period, though at times they almost overpower the spare text." Although a critic in *Kirkus Reviews* called the pictures "soft and pale, lacking drama," *Horn Book* reviewer Maeve Visser Knoth concluded that Watling's watercolors "contribute to the portrait of Williams as a serious man driven by strong beliefs."

Joseph Bruchac's novel *The Arrow over the Door* is based on an actual incident: a meeting between the Quakers and the Abenaki Indians that took place in 1777 near Saratoga, New York. In this story, fourteen-year-old Samuel Russell, a Quaker who hates being called a coward, learns to become friends with Stands Straight, a Native boy of the same age whose parents were murdered by white men. The Quakers and the Indians meet together in the Quaker Meetinghouse and shake the handshake of peace. At the end of the novel, an arrow is placed over the cabin door in order to show other Native Americans that the Quakers are people of peace. Praising the book as a tale of "pacifism triumphant," *School Library Journal* critic Elaine Fort Weischedel concluded that Watling's full-page illustrations in shades of gray "fit the mood of the story without breaking the narrative flow." Karen Hutt noted in *Booklist,* "Simple black-and-white drawings reflect the dignified tone of the story," while a critic in *Publishers Weekly* stated that

Watling's "rugged, textured pen-and-ink drawings provide an atmospheric backdrop."

Watling also illustrated a well-received biography of Lewis and Clark, *Seaman: The Dog Who Explored the West with Lewis & Clark,* that revolves around Lewis's Newfoundland dog and is drawn from journals of the period. The book, which is directed at middle graders, describes how Seaman becomes the first canine to cross the continent in 1804. He proves his worth as a hunter, navigator, and watchdog while serving with the Corps of Discovery. Writing in *Booklist,* Carolyn Phelan concluded that Watling's "many handsome pencil-shaded drawings will help readers visualize the setting, hardships, and dramatic moments of the story, and two maps will enable them to follow the explorers' routes."

Works Cited

Review of *Along the Santa Fe Trail: Marion Russell's Own Story, Kirkus Reviews,* August 15, 1993.

Review of *Along the Santa Fe Trail: Marion Russell's Own Story, Publishers Weekly,* August 9, 1993, p. 479.

Review of *The Arrow over the Door, Publishers Weekly,* March 9, 1998, p. 68.

Corsaro, Julie, review of *Along the Santa Fe Trail: Marion Russell's Own Story, Booklist,* January 15, 1994, p. 928.

Review of *Finding Providence: The Story of Roger Williams, Kirkus Reviews,* January 1, 1997.

Hutt, Karen, review of *The Arrow over the Door, Booklist,* February 15, 1998.

Knoth, Maeve Visser, review of *Finding Providence: The Story of Roger Williams, Horn Book,* May-June, 1997, pp. 313-14.

Review of *Nip and Tuck, Midwest Book Review,* http://transmedia95.com/Napoleon/html/nip.htm.

Phelan, Carolyn, review of *Seaman: The Dog Who Explored the West with Lewis & Clark, Booklist,* August 19, 1999.

Rochman, Hazel, review of *Finding Providence: The Story of Roger Williams, Booklist,* February 1, 1997, p. 949.

Weischedel, Elaine Fort, review of *The Arrow over the Door, School Library Journal,* April, 1998, p. 128.

For More Information See

PERIODICALS

School Library Journal, July, 1996, p. 85.

*   *   *

WATSON, Mary 1953-

Personal

Born September 5, 1953, in Redbank, NJ; married John Conn (divorced); married Pete Watson (a museum director), October 26, 1986; children: Winston Conn, Ryan Conn, Kevin Watson, Harry Watson. *Education:* School of Visual Arts, B.F.A., 1976.

Addresses

Home and office—129 West End Ave., Summit, NJ 07901. *E-mail*—Artisanpub@home.com.

Career

American Maze Co., freelance graphic designer.

Writings

SELF-ILLUSTRATED

The Butterfly Seeds, Tamborine, 1995.

ILLUSTRATOR

Pete Watson, *The Market Lady and the Mango Tree,* Tamborine, 1994.
Cheyenne Cisco, *Hare's Big Tug-of-War,* Harcourt, 1996.
Lucy Floyce, *Grandma J,* Harcourt, 1996.
Anna Grossnickle Hines, *My Own Big Bed,* Greenwillow, 1998.

Work in Progress

Some Place Like Home, a book about interfaith shelters for the homeless.

Sidelights

From her career as a graphic artist, Mary Watson has gone on to design appealing illustrations for several children's books, including one by her husband, Pete Watson. In addition to her success as a picture book illustrator, Watson has also tried her hand at writing. In her 1995 effort, *The Butterfly Seeds,* Watson creates a story about renewal that *School Library Journal* reviewer Marilyn Taniguchi described as "heartfelt and appealing." Working with opaque paints, Watson's illustrations have been praised for their realism and their ability to capture and inspire the optimism of young people. Commenting on Watson's work in Ana Grossnickle Hines' *My Own Big Bed,* a *Publishers Weekly* contributor noted that "Watson's combination of neatly framed vignettes and full-bleed spreads makes skillful use of painterly realism."

Born in 1953 in Redbank, New Jersey, Watson attended the School of Visual Arts shortly after high school graduation, and received her bachelor of fine arts degree in 1976. "Like a lot of young artists in the '70s, I graduated from art school and went immediately into graphic arts," Watson explained to *SATA.* "For a while it was interesting, first doing paste up and later learning computer graphics. But ten years down the road I realized something was missing." Watson decided to go back to the School of Visual Arts to attend a night class in children's book writing and illustrating. "The class was taught by Bruce Degan, now famous for his *Magic School Bus* books," Watson noted. "Bruce began the class by saying, 'I was in advertising for years and then one day I realized that I had forgotten the reason I became an artist in the first place . . . because it was fun to sit down and draw.' It seemed like such a simple

remark. But then I realized that when I was drawing or painting it was not working, I was having fun."

A year later, Watson and her husband, Pete, completed their first collaborative children's book. "I made color copies of the illustrations, packaged it up with the story, and sent it off to my number-one choice, Tambourine Books," Watson related. "I figured a big company like [that] would take at least six months to respond. Two days later, I received what was probably the happiest phone call of my life: an offer to publish our book." The book, titled *Market Lady and the Mango Tree,* was released to bookstores in early 1994. Written by Pete and illustrated by Mary, the book relates the plan of a West African village woman to trap all the fruit of a local mango tree for herself. With all the fruit in her possession, she grows wealthy by selling it to the village children, until a bad dream teaches her that "you can't earn a living by selling what's free." Calling *The Market Lady and the Mango Tree* "a spirited, authentically flavored morality tale that hints at the contradictions . . . in human nature," *Booklist* contributor Stephanie Zvirin also praised Mary Watson's paintings with their "rich colors" and "expressive," humorous characters. Praising the book as "a different kind of story," *School Library Journal* reviewer Carol Jones Collins also applauded Watson's illustrations, calling them "lovely, dramatic, and bold in design. The village and the main character come vividly to life." In *Publishers Weekly,* the book was described by a reviewer as "deftly illustrated with realistic, warmly hued paintings."

In 1995 Watson completed her first solo effort, *The Butterfly Seeds.* Taking place near the turn of the twentieth century, the book introduces readers to Jake, a young immigrant traveling with his family to a new life in a multicultural ethnic community in New York City. Homesick, Jake is comforted by a box of seeds given to him by his grandfather, seeds he is told will attract hundreds of butterflies to his garden after they are planted. "Watson effectively relates the simple yet affecting tale of a child's separation from his old home and beloved relative," noted Taniguchi in her *School Library Journal* critique of *The Butterfly Seeds.* The book's illustrations also received critical praise; Taniguchi deemed them "vibrant and lovely, with "expressive" characters, and in *Booklist,* Hazel Rochman maintained that "Watson's realistic double-spread paintings are as upbeat as the story."

Watson remains modest about the praise that has been bestowed upon her books for children, but looks forward to continuing her success. "I realized that I was very fortunate and that many talented people have to try many times to get their start," she explained to *SATA.* "But I believe that you are already successful if you haven't lost sight of what it is that makes you happy."

Works Cited

Collins, Carol Jones, review of *The Market Lady and the Mango Tree, School Library Journal,* June, 1994, p. 115.

A young girl is both proud and fearful of sleeping in her new bed in Anna Grossnickle Hines's **My Own Big Bed,** *illustrated by Mary Watson.*

Review of *The Market Lady and the Mango Tree,*
    Publishers Weekly, February 21, 1994, p. 253.
Review of *My Own Big Bed, Publishers Weekly,* November
    9, 1998, p. 76.
Rochman, Hazel, review of *The Butterfly Seeds, Booklist,*
    September 1, 1995, p. 90.
Taniguchi, Marilyn, review of *The Butterfly Seeds, School
    Library Journal,* November, 1995, p. 83.
Watson, Pete, *The Market Lady and the Mango Tree,*
    Tamborine, 1994.
Zvirin, Stephanie, review of *The Market Lady and the
    Mango Tree, Booklist,* February 15, 1994, p. 1094.

For More Information See

PERIODICALS

Booklist, October 15, 1998, p. 427.

WHITE, Ruth (C.) 1942-
(Ruth White Miller)

Personal

Born March 15, 1942, in Whitewood, VA; daughter of John Edward (a coal miner) and Olive (a hospital food server; maiden name, Compton) White; divorced; children: Dee Olivia. *Education:* Montreat-Anderson College, A.A., 1962; Pfeiffer College, A.B., 1966; Queens College, Charlotte, NC, library media specialist, 1976. *Politics:* Democrat.

Addresses

Home—2409 Radium Springs Rd., Albany, GA 31705; *Office*—Dougherty Junior High School, 1800 Massey Dr., Albany, GA 31705.

Career

Mt. Pleasant Middle School, Mt. Pleasant, NC, English teacher, 1966-76; Boys Town, Pineville, NC, house mother, 1976-77; Harleyville-Ridgeville High School, Dorchester, SC, librarian, 1977-81; Dougherty Junior High School, Albany, GA, librarian, 1981—.

Awards, Honors

Citation for the best children's book by a North Carolinian, North Carolina chapter of the American Association of University Women, 1977, for *The City Rose; Belle Prater's Boy* was named a Newbery Honor Book, 1997; *The City Rose* was nominated for the Georgia Children's Book Award and voted favorite book by six thousand Indiana school children; Notable Book, American Library Association, for *Sweet Creek Holler; Weeping Willow* was named a Best Book for Young Adults by the American Library Association and One of the New York Public Library's 100 Titles for Reading and Sharing.

Writings

(Under name Ruth White Miller) *The City Rose,* McGraw, 1977.
Sweet Creek Holler, Farrar, Straus, 1988.
Weeping Willow, Farrar, Straus, 1992.
Belle Prater's Boy, Farrar, Straus, 1996.
Memories of Summer, Farrar, Straus, 2000.

Adaptations

Weeping Willow and *Belle Prater's Boy* were recorded as audiobooks.

Sidelights

School librarian Ruth White is the award-winning author of novels for middle grade and young adult readers, including *Sweet Creek Holler, Weeping Willow,* and *Belle Prater's Boy.* Her stories are set in the South, in

Twelve-year-old Gypsy and her cousin Woodrow become friends and overcome the tragedy of losing a parent in Ruth White's Newbery Honor Book. (Cover illustration by Ericka Meltzer.)

particular, the coal-mining region of western Virginia, where she grew up. Commentators have praised White for her characterizations, depiction of locale, and sensitive treatment of such difficult subject matter as the death of a parent and rape. In 1997 White's much-acclaimed novel *Belle Prater's Boy* was named a Newbery Honor Book.

Growing up poor in western Virginia during the 1950s gave White both incentive and fodder for her later writing career. "Born in the poverty-stricken coal mining region of Virginia, I was the fourth daughter of a coal miner who died when I was six," White told *SATA*. Because her family had no television, they read aloud and performed music. Ruth developed her imagination and "managed to get the most out of the public school system and go on to a better life" as a school teacher, school librarian, and writer.

White is particularly interested in the challenges teenage girls face, and the action in many of her novels takes place in the 1950s, when White was a girl. She told *SATA*, "I work with and write for adolescent girls

because that was the time in my life when I was most confused and unhappy. I can relate to these girls now because I remember the pain of trying to grow up, trying to find my identity, and trying to be an individual in a conformist's world. Adolescents today have basically the same problems, only more of them. It is a very hard time in which to grow up."

In *Sweet Creek Holler* six-year-old Ginny and her older sister June must deal with the rumors that swirl around them when they move to a new town. They are the object of these rumors because their father was shot to death, leaving them and their beautiful mother to fend for themselves. During the six years they live in the small mining town of Sweet Creek Holler, they witness the tragic effect gossip can have on sensitive souls. Reviewers found much to like in *Sweet Creek Holler.* Joanne Johnson, writing in *Voice of Youth Advocates,* praised White's "carefully drawn characters," portrayal of small-town life in Appalachia, and "well-thought out and presented" relationship between Ginny and her friend Lou Jean. *Horn Book* critic Nancy Vasilakis judged the novel to be "stronger in its delineation of character and in its evocation of time and place than in its narrative development," yet she praised White's obvious "affection for the indigent folk of its Appalachian locale."

Weeping Willow, set in 1956, tells the story of fourteen-year-old Tiny, who is the eldest child in her family. As she grows into adulthood, she must deal with her stepfather's unwanted sexual advances, as well as the typical challenges of life in high school. This young adult novel garnered mixed reviews. Writing in *Voice of Youth Advocates,* Myrna Feldman praised the novel for its characters, setting, and details, deeming it to be an "exceptionally fine book." Moreover, she asserted that the plot elements "are handled consistently, sensitively, and in relationship to Tiny's disturbing secret" and declared the book to be "honestly written and difficult to put down." Less enthusiastically, Linda Lee, a critic for the *New York Times Book Review,* commented, "While the sweep of the novel is admirable ... the main conflict between a young girl and her abuser seems somehow of no more import than the wearing of saddle oxfords when everyone else wears white bucks." Lee was also disturbed by what she interpreted as White's message that, in Lee's words, "incest is a bad thing, but it can be lived with." "Most annoying for a teenager in any era, Tiny has a secret, invisible friend named Willa, who counsels her long after the young woman should be making decisions on her own," complained Lee. Although she praised the novel's detailed setting and "strong" voice, Alice Casey Smith contended in her *School Library Journal* review, "Unfortunately, the main components of plot do not integrate; ... [*Weeping Willow*] has too, too many threads that don't weave together." Betsy Hearne voiced the opposite opinion. In her review for *Bulletin of the Center for Children's Books,* she called the novel "fine," praising its "vividly rendered" characters and "plot following variably but believably from their [the characters'] patterns of action."

In *Belle Prater's Boy,* White explores the nature of friendship, loss, and love. Despite its title, the novel revolves around twelve-year-old Gypsy, who is known in Coal Station, Virginia, for her long hair and her father who died tragically seven years earlier. When her cousin Woodrow moves in next door after the mysterious disappearance of his mother, Gypsy and he develop a rare friendship, one that, according to a *Publishers Weekly* reviewer, allows both of them to "face tragedy and transcend it—and the ability to pass along that gift to the reader." Reviewers praised *Belle Prater's Boy* highly. Writing in *Kliatt,* Jana Whitesel deemed it a "rare" book that "transcends age with its timeless story," though the story takes place during the 1950s. In the *New York Times Book Review,* Meg Wolitzer declared, "It takes a writer of real lyricism and energy to tell a good young-adult story, and Ruth White is one." Several critics applauded White for her characterizations and depiction of the locale. Remarking that "White has an eye for telling detail, and her descriptions of small-town life in a bygone era feel both nostalgic and authentic," Wolitzer added, "The author's vivid and accurate eye has helped her fashion an ideal backdrop for the story and its element of suspense." "White's characters are strong ... and her storytelling is rich in detail and emotion," asserted Maeve Visser Knoth in her *Horn Book* review. Likewise, *Booklist* reviewer Stephanie Zvirin praised White for her "humor and insight," "solid picture of small-town life," "unpretentious, moving story," and "strongly depicted characters." *Belle Prater's Boy* "balances disturbing emotional issues with the writer's light touch," summed up a critic in *Voice of Youth Advocates.*

Grateful for the opportunities public school education opened up for her, White has worked as a teacher and a librarian in public schools since the mid-1960s. "I am a great believer and a great supporter of the public education system in our country," she told *SATA.* "I will always work in the public school system and try to give back something of what was given to me. I love children. I love working with children and writing for children."

Works Cited

Review of *Bell Prater's Boy, Publishers Weekly,* March 11, 1996, pp. 65-66.

Review of *Belle Prater's Boy, Voice of Youth Advocates,* June, 1997, p. 87.

Feldman, Myrna, review of *Weeping Willow, Voice of Youth Advocates,* October, 1992, p. 234.

Hearne, Betsy, review of *Weeping Willow, Bulletin of the Center for Children's Books,* June, 1992, p. 284.

Johnson, Joanne, review of *Sweet Creek Holler, Voice of Youth Advocates,* December, 1988, p. 244.

Knoth, Maeve Visser, review of *Belle Prater's Boy, Horn Book,* September-October, 1996, p. 601.

Lee, Linda, review of *Weeping Willow, New York Times Book Review,* August 23, 1992, p. 26.

Smith, Alice Casey, review of *Weeping Willow, School Library Journal,* July, 1992, p. 91.

Fourteen-year-old Tiny survives high school and incest in White's emotional novel. (Cover illustration by Hilary Mosberg.)

Vasilakis, Nancy, review of *Sweet Creek Holler, Horn Book,* November-December, 1988, p. 785.

Whitesel, Jana, review of *Belle Prater's Boy, Kliatt,* May, 1998, p. 42.

Wolitzer, Meg, review of *Belle Prater's Boy, New York Times Book Review,* October 27, 1996, p. 44.

Zvirin, Stephanie, review of *Belle Prater's Boy, Booklist,* April 15, 1996, p. 1434.

For More Information See

PERIODICALS

Booklist, June 1, 1993, p. 1865.

English Journal, November, 1993, p. 79.

New York Times Book Review, November 13, 1988, p. 20.

Publishers Weekly, January 6, 1989, p. 52; November 4, 1996, p. 49; February 9, 1998, p. 26.

School Library Journal, October, 1988, p. 165.*

WIESNER, David 1956-

Personal

Surname is pronounced "*weez*-ner"; born February 5, 1956, in Bridgewater, NJ; son of George (a research manager at a chemical plant) and Julia (a homemaker; maiden name, Collins) Wiesner; married Kim Kahng (a surgeon), May 21, 1983; children: Kevin. *Education:* Rhode Island School of Design, B.F.A., 1978.

Addresses

Home—700 Westview, Philadelphia, PA 19119. *Agent*—Dilys Evans, P.O. Box 400, Norfolk, CT 06058.

Career

Author and illustrator of children's books. Has appeared as a guest on the *Today* show, NBC-TV, 1992. *Exhibitions:* Wiesner's paintings have been displayed in the Metropolitan Museum of Art, New York City, 1982, as well as in various galleries, including Master Eagle Gallery, New York City, 1980-89, Academy of Natural Sciences, Philadelphia, PA, 1986— (permanent exhibit), Museum of Art at Rhode Island School of Design, Providence, RI, 1989, Brooklyn Public Library, Brooklyn, NY, 1990, Muscarele Museum of Art, College of William and Mary, Williamsburg, VA, 1990, Society of Illustrators, New York City, 1991 and 1992, and Greenwich Public Library, Greenwich, CT.

Awards, Honors

Children's Picture Book Award, *Redbook,* 1987, for *The Loathsome Dragon;* Caldecott Honor Book, American Library Association (ALA), 1989, for *Free Fall;* notable children's book, ALA, 1991, Reviewer's Choice, *Sesame Street Parents' Guide,* 1991, "Ten Best Books of 1991," *Parenting Magazine,* and Caldecott Medal, ALA, 1992, all for *Tuesday;* Parent's Choice citation, 1992, for *June 29, 1999.*

Writings

SELF-ILLUSTRATED PICTURE BOOKS

(Reteller with wife, Kim Kahng) *The Loathsome Dragon,* Putnam, 1987.
Free Fall, Lothrop, 1988.
Hurricane, Clarion, 1990.
Tuesday, Clarion, 1991.
June 29, 1999, Clarion, 1992.
Sector 7, Clarion, 1999.

ILLUSTRATOR

Gloria Skurzynski, *Honest Andrew,* Harcourt, 1980.
Avi, *Man from the Sky,* Knopf, 1980.
Nancy Luenn, *The Ugly Princess,* Little, Brown, 1981.
David R. Collins, *The One Bad Thing about Birthdays,* Harcourt, 1981.
Jane Yolen, *The Boy Who Spoke Chimp,* Knopf, 1981.

Yolen, *Neptune Rising: Songs and Tales of the Undersea Folk,* Philomel, 1982.
Mike Thaler, *Owly,* Harper, 1982.
Vera Chapman, *Miranty and the Alchemist,* Avon, 1983.
Allan W. Eckert, *The Dark Green Tunnel,* Little, Brown, 1984.
William Kotzwinkle, *E. T.: The Storybook of the Green Planet* (based on a story by Steven Spielberg), Putnam, 1985.
Eckert, *The Wand: The Return to Mesmeria,* Little, Brown, 1985.
Dennis Haseley, *Kite Flier,* Four Winds, 1986.
Nancy Willard, *Firebrat,* Knopf, 1988.
The Sorcerer's Apprentice: A Greek Fable, retold by Marianna Mayer, Bantam, 1989.
Laurence Yep, *The Rainbow People,* HarperCollins, 1989.
Tongues of Jade (Chinese-American folk tales), retold by Laurence Yep, HarperCollins, 1991.
Eve Bunting, *Night of the Gargoyles,* Clarion, 1994.
Dilys Evans, *Looking for Merlyn,* Scholastic, 1997.

Adaptations

Free Fall has been adapted into a videocassette with teacher's guide, distributed by American School Publications, 1990; *Tuesday* has also been adapted into a videocassette, distributed by American School Publications, 1992.

Sidelights

"I create books I think I would have liked to have seen when I was a kid," David Wiesner remarked in an interview with *Something about the Author* (*SATA*). "I loved being able to get lost in paintings and to get involved in all the details." Winner of the 1992 Caldecott Medal for his picture book *Tuesday,* Wiesner combines his imaginative powers with his talent for illustration, producing award-winning works like *Free Fall, Hurricane,* and *The Loathsome Dragon.* He was born into a creatively inclined family—art and music number among his siblings' interests—and grew up in an environment that encouraged his own flair for drawing. "I never had the sense that I had to rebel at home so my parents would let me be an artist," he recalled in his interview. "They made my love of drawing seem like something natural—I thought it was the norm." Eventually, his love of drawing fused with his fascination for storytelling, and he found his niche in children's literature, particularly in picture books. He works primarily in watercolors, and expresses his passion for creativity in humorous and inventive tales. "What I really find interesting is that opportunity to take a normal, everyday situation and somehow turn it on its end, or slightly shift it. I love to introduce a 'what if?,' or juxtapose things that aren't normally together. Those just happen to be the kind of ideas I generate."

Born in 1956 to George and Julia Wiesner, David found the diverse landscape of his Bridgewater, New Jersey, hometown well-suited to his active imagination. Making use of the local cemetery, the river that bordered it (which neighborhood kids called a swamp), the nearby woods, and the town dump, Wiesner and his friends concocted all sorts of games, among which "army" was a particular favorite. "We had very specific rules when we played army," Wiesner remembered in his interview, "that said if you were chasing someone and came to a road in the cemetery (which was to us a river), you had to shuffle your feet and hold your hands over your head to keep your gun dry (which was usually a stick). As soon as you got to the other side you could run again because you'd be on dry land." Ordinary objects were also transformed by the young Wiesner's creativity: wire hangers and plastic bags formed homemade hot-air balloons for a pastime called UFO, and a simple tree and some sticks made wonderful tree forts. "There was that constant ability to transform the everyday world into the pretend. We continually reinvented the world around us when we played."

Even though neighborhood companions in Bridgewater were in abundance, Wiesner enjoyed spending long stretches of time by himself, so much so, he laughingly admitted to *SATA*, that "there were times my parents were probably worried that, somehow, I didn't have any friends." During these periods of solitude, Wiesner often found himself drawing. "Art has always been a part of my life. I can't pinpoint the exact time when I began drawing; it was something I was always doing, and it became part of how I was perceived. It also defined my personality to a certain extent: clearly when relatives were aware of my interest in art, I would get various art supplies on Christmas and birthdays, and a lot of hand-me-downs—boxes of pastels, watercolors—from Carol, my oldest sister, and George, my brother, who are both pretty artistically inclined. I loved to watch them draw things."

Wiesner's penchant for drawing was fueled further by a television show he watched when he was about six or seven years old. Hosted by artist Jon Gnagy and originally aired in the late 1940s, *You Are an Artist* marked one of TV's first forays into instructional programming. Wiesner, who caught the telecast in

stalking the mighty leopard.

A tree uprooted by a hurricane inspires two brothers' imaginations in Wiesner's self-illustrated **Hurricane.**

reruns, was fascinated with Gnagy's work, particularly with the artist's attention to perspective, light, and scale. The youngster bought Gnagy's instruction books and earnestly practiced drawing all the pictures first in charcoal in black and white, then in color. "The books and program probably provided my first formal exposure to techniques and ideas about drawing," Wiesner recalled in his *SATA* interview. "Gnagy could stand there and in fifteen or twenty minutes turn out these drawings. I thought it was just miraculous. I still keep a framed picture of him on my wall."

By junior high school Wiesner had discovered the Renaissance and Surrealism, two creative movements that helped shape his artistic style. The Renaissance artists of the late fifteenth and early sixteenth centuries appealed to the youngster because of their sensitivity to space and perspective. He found himself particularly enchanted by the works of Michelangelo, Leonardo da Vinci, Albrecht Durer, and Pieter Brueghel the Elder—"the real draftsmen," he declared in an interview for *Clarionews*. "[I] could sit and look at those paintings for hours. There was so much happening in them, from the foreground back to the very, very far distance. You could follow things back to deep space." Surrealism, a twentieth-century art movement committed to the distorted portrayal of reality, also captured Wiesner's attention. "When I finally came across the surrealists," he told *SATA*, "it was like all hell broke loose—not only because they were painting with a similar quality that I saw in the Renaissance painters, but because the subject matter was just unbelievable. I really responded to it. Conceptually, I was really taken with the imagery, the bizarreness, that other-worldliness, that weirdness—it was really very appealing."

That love of the fantastic found its way into Wiesner's creative outlets throughout his teenage years. Horror movies and sci-fi films provided favorite forms of entertainment, and one film in particular, Stanley Kubrick's *2001: A Space Odyssey,* even helped inspire his enthusiasm for wordless storytelling. "I remember going to see *2001* in 1968," Wiesner recalled in *Clarionews*. "I don't want to be too dramatic, but I remember coming out of the theater a changed person. It was unlike anything I'd ever seen. It's almost a silent film; there's very little dialogue. It's all pictures, which tell a remarkably complex story and set of ideas, up there for the viewer to decipher."

Drawing continued to engage Wiesner's interest throughout high school, and he especially enjoyed sketching "sort of odd subjects," he recalled to *SATA*. "I would conjure up images that usually got some very strange responses. It was really a direct response to the surrealist work that I saw—lots of weird, creepy, floating and flying things which have always been part of the work I do." His own anti-hero super-hero creation, Slop the Wonderpig, grew out of his love of comic books, and his own film, *The Saga of Butchula,* about a Milquetoast-turned-vampire who avenges an attack by young thugs, grew out of his desire to experiment with the storytelling process. "Showing *Butchula* at the senior

talent show at Bridgewater Raritan East was one of the high points of high school," Wiesner exclaimed to *SATA*, "because the audience reacted at all the right points. I experienced this incredible feeling. It was great!"

High school provided Wiesner with one other strong creative influence: his art teacher Robert Bernabe. "In Mr. Bernabe I finally found someone I could talk to about art," Wiesner revealed in his *SATA* interview. "He essentially encouraged me to follow whatever inclinations I had and was willing to do what he could to facilitate that. This was the first time something like that had happened. He became a sort of confidant for me—I think that to a large degree art is this very personal thing, and Mr. Bernabe was someone with whom I could share my work. He didn't so much influence the projects I was pursuing as he provided me with a sense of encouragement."

However strong an interest art was for Wiesner, he scarcely entertained the idea of turning his craft into a career, until a student from the Rhode Island School of Design (RISD; pronounced "*riz-dee*") visited his art class. "He gave this presentation to the class," Wiesner explained to *SATA*, "and brought along these eight millimeter films of some of the projects he had completed at RISD—interactive sorts of things that were set up in the middle of school. He brought some little contraptions he had made as well as a commercial he had developed for one of his classes. I was just amazed at all the wonderfully creative stuff. I thought, 'Here's a place where everybody is doing art all the time, as opposed to once a week,' and it finally dawned on me that I could actually keep doing this and go to school and study it and make this my living. I kept expecting someone to say, 'okay, now you have to figure out what you want to do before you go to college for four years.' It finally became clear that I could in fact be an artist."

With encouragement from his parents, Wiesner applied to five art schools in 1973, including New York's Pratt Institute, the Philadelphia College of Art, the Cleveland Institute of Art, and RISD. Accepted by all five, there was no question as to which one he would attend: "I was totally ready for RISD and ready to immerse myself in what the school had to offer," Wiesner told *SATA*. The aspiring artist was greeted with a "pretty intense first year"—one in which he had to unlearn many old habits and absorb new ideas and ways of thinking about art. "I remember going to my life-drawing class and noticing that while the teacher didn't really respond to my work, he would look at another student's work and say, 'this is really terrific,' or something like that. I would look at the same work and wonder, 'Why is he saying that? He doesn't understand.' Yet by the end of the year I was able to look at that same work and realize 'that's great stuff.' RISD helped me reorient myself and helped me get rid of some of my preconceived notions."

In short, though Wiesner's experience at RISD was an active one, it was hardly a painful one. In fact, when asked to describe just one highlight he recalls from the

Frogs float through the air and explore a neighborhood in Wiesner's self-illustrated, award-winning **Tuesday.**

school, he is at a loss for words; there were too many, he explained. However, one project does stand out in his memory with particular fondness. The assignment was simply the word "metamorphosis"—a vague suggestion that Wiesner finds challenging; a ten-foot-long, forty-inch-tall painting was the result. "I had this big piece of paper I'd been waiting to use," Wiesner explained to *SATA,* "and I started to play around with these images that began to change and metamorphosize. I suppose it also relates to Dutch artist M. C. Escher (whose work I admire), who tended to focus on flat, graphic objects that shift and change from one to the other. I began the painting with images of oranges, then drew the orange sections falling away and turning into sailing ships. The ground then turned into water, and the ships changed and mutated into giant fish swimming out in the ocean. When I finished I knew I was on to something—the response in class was really good and I just kept thinking about it. Clearly there was more I could do with this."

The thought of expanding the painting into a narrative—either with words or without—fascinated Wiesner, and his assignments at RISD began to reflect this interest. At first he directed his talent toward adult-fantasy, short, wordless sequences done in oils. As he gained experience, he began developing his own style, primarily using watercolors, and experimenting with characters, settings, and storylines of a lengthier nature. By his senior year he completed a forty-page wordless picture book for adults based on the short story "Gonna Roll the Bones" by Fritz Leiber. "The idea of wordless storytelling was really appealing to me," Wiesner told *SATA.* "I was learning how to compress information as well as how to convey that information visually."

As graduation loomed, Wiesner tossed around the idea of working as an illustrator in some kind of published format, possibly for adult fantasy magazines. Pursuing a career in children's literature hardly crossed his mind. "If you looked at the work I was doing, though," he admitted in his *SATA* interview, "it was obvious I should be going into children's books." Evidently Lester Abrams, one of his instructors at RISD, thought the same thing, for he encouraged his pupil to show his work to noted children's author and illustrator (and later Caldecott Medalist) Trina Schart Hyman, who happened to be speaking at RISD. Hyman, who in 1978 was art director for *Cricket,* a children's magazine recognized for its exceptional illustrations, took one look at Wiesner's work and promptly offered the young artist a magazine cover. Wiesner was both surprised and pleased to discover an audience for his work in children's literature. "I realized," he related to *SATA,* "that there really is this remarkable range in children's literature open to very different personal visions of books. Not all illustrations are fuzzy bunnies and little cute things."

In children's literature Wiesner found his artistic niche. After graduating with his bachelor of fine arts in illustration in the spring of that same year, he procured work illustrating textbooks, which allowed him to compile a professional portfolio and compelled him to work under a variety of constraints involving size, medium, and content. "It's funny," he pointed out to *SATA.* "One of the harder things to resolve coming out of school was moving from a situation in which I wasn't working with too many restrictions into an environment where someone would say, 'Okay, down here in these couple inches along the bottom and maybe partly up the side we want to see Robin Hood, his band of men, the archery contest, the bleachers in the back, the king, and the sheriff of Nottingham.' It's a very difficult thing to adapt to without losing some of your spontaneity. It took me a while to reconcile these different ways of working. Early on, it was somewhat intimidating."

Intimidating or not, Wiesner persevered, and in 1980 secured contracts (with the help of agent Dilys Evans) to illustrate two children's books: Gloria Skurzynski's *Honest Andrew* and Avi's *Man from the Sky.* By this time he had moved to New York City with Kim Kahng, who would later become his wife, and during the next few years, he kept busy illustrating a variety of children's books. He also used the time to experiment with and fine-tune his own technique and form. At first, as he candidly admitted to *SATA,* his work appeared a bit unpolished—due in part to his inexperience in the field and in part to having to work with preseparated art, in which color is added only at the printing stage. However, with experience came the development of his own distinctive style as well as the ever-increasing desire to pursue his own book ideas. (The idea for *Free Fall,* inspired by the ten-foot long painting he had completed at RISD, was already forming in his mind.) However, in 1983, his career was unexpectedly put on hold. The apartment building he and his wife, Kahng, lived in burned to the ground, destroying everything the newly married couple owned.

By the time the Wiesners rebuilt their lives, David faced pressing deadlines for illustrations that had been contracted for a year or two years down the road. Consequently, he was compelled to work on *Free Fall* only in pieces—he would complete a picture or two for

the book, then be forced to stop and work on other titles. The pattern continued throughout the 1980s, during which time he illustrated such works as William Kotzwinkle's *E. T.: The Storybook of the Green Planet,* Allan W. Eckert's *Wand: The Return to Mesmeria,* and Dennis Haseley's *Kite Flier.* In 1987 he tackled another self-illustrated project—*The Loathsome Dragon,* retold with Kahng and based on the English fairy tale *The Laidly Worm of Spindleston Huegh.* The narrative relates the story of the beautiful Princess Margaret, who becomes trapped inside the body of an enormous dragon through the sorcery of her evil, jealous stepmother. Only three kisses from Margaret's brother, Childe Wynd, who is traveling in a far-off land, will free the princess from the spell. Wiesner captured *The Loathsome Dragon*'s medieval setting with double-page watercolor paintings, which portray detailed landscapes and seascapes, sprawling castles, elaborate robes, jewelry, and armor, and the frightful, yet gentle dragon. Reviewers applauded Wiesner's carefully crafted and attractive scenes as well as his regard for historical accuracy. "Few artists depict the medieval world or labyrinthine castles ... as well," judged a *Publishers Weekly* reviewer. Wiesner's artwork is "delicate, misty, and enchanting, extending and harmonizing with the traditional motifs of this fairy

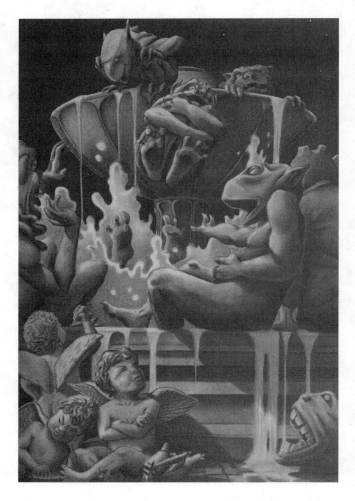

Wiesner's scary gargoyles are a good match for author Eve Bunting's spooky **Night of the Gargoyles.**

tale," noted *School Library Journal* contributor Constance A. Mellon. Perhaps the most flattering remarks came from 1991 Caldecott Medalist and RISD department head David Macaulay, who wrote in *Horn Book:* "Take a look at the watercolor landscapes [*The Loathsome Dragon*] contains and tell me you don't see a little da Vinci in there."

By the time *The Loathsome Dragon* was completed, Wiesner was nearly finished with *Free Fall.* "It had taken me longer than I had hoped to get to the point of completing *Free Fall,*" he revealed to *SATA,* "and the breaks in working on it were hard. But it was better than rushing it. Throughout that time I was focusing on the RISD assignment about metamorphosis—the continuous picture that tells a story. It was when I came up with the idea of the dream, using sleeping and then waking as a framework, that *Free Fall* really began to come together and make sense. The structure of the dream afforded me the opportunity to have the book be less a strict narrative and more a sort of free floating imagery—more impressionistic than a straight storyline."

Released in 1988, *Free Fall* is an imaginative, wordless picture book that follows a young boy through the fantastic journey he experiences during one of his dreams. Featuring images that continually transform into other images, the narrative opens as the youngster falls asleep while studying a book of maps. Reality fades as his bedspread metamorphosizes into a landscape, and he is transported along with exotic companions onto a chessboard with live pieces, to a medieval castle housing knights and a dragon, to rocky cliffs that merge into a city skyline, and to a larger-than-life breakfast table. Finally he floats among swans, fishes, and leaves back to his starting place. Especially characteristic of Wiesner's creative ingenuity are the many events and characters the young boy encounters during his dream; most of them correspond to objects in the youngster's bedroom—from the goldfish next to his bed, to the chess pieces stashed in his nightstand, to the pigeons hovering near his window, to the leaves sketched on his wallpaper.

"When I finished *Free Fall,*" Wiesner emphasized to *SATA,* "I realized that this was the type of work I really wanted to do. A lot of the sample pieces I had shown to publishers were geared toward typical fairy tale/folk tale kind of works, but there were also these other illustrations in the back of my portfolio that were just weird— editors would usually look at them and go 'oh, this is very interesting....' I would ask if they had any manuscripts to fit the drawings, and they'd invariably say 'no.' So I knew that ultimately I would have to invent my own ideas for books. *Free Fall* was the first true expression of the kind of work that I wanted to be doing."

Critical reaction to *Free Fall* was decidedly mixed. On one hand, reviewers admired the author's technical skill, his attention to architectural detail and form, and his visual creativity. The book is "an excellent replication of a dream," decided one *Bulletin of the Center for Children's Books* critic. On the other hand, some commentators found the book too complex to be readily understood by a young audience, and they criticized what they perceived as a murky narrative sequence. "The nameless protagonist's ... adventures are confusing, complicated, and illogical," assessed Julie Corsaro in *School Library Journal.* Instead of being upset by the critical response to his first book, Wiesner was amused: "I sort of enjoyed the fact that some reviewers got it," he confessed to *SATA.* "Some of the reviews were absolutely right on and connecting with everything, and others seemed not at all there. It was actually kind of interesting to get that very mixed reaction."

The mixed reaction did not extend to the committee selecting the Caldecott Honor Books in that year, for "the phone rang one Monday morning," Wiesner related to *SATA,* "and the chair of the committee said they had chosen *Free Fall* as an honor book. I experienced the classic reaction: I was left speechless—I just hung up the phone." After some time passed, Wiesner was able to verbalize his reaction: "Having *Free Fall* named a Caldecott Honor Book was a wonderful confirmation that 'yes, this does seem to be the way to go.' It felt really, really satisfying because all along I had the feeling I had been going in the right direction with the pieces I had done and conceived on my own. It was really encouraging that they [the committee] chose a work that isn't in the strict mold of the usual picture book—one that was even perceived by a lot of reviewers as difficult and something that kids wouldn't even relate to."

The same year *Free Fall* was named an honor book, Wiesner was asked by *Cricket* to design another cover (ironically, ten years from the time he illustrated his first *Cricket* cover). Given the artistic freedom to draw whatever he wished—the folks at *Cricket* told him only that the March issue would feature articles on St. Patrick's Day, frogs, and the like—Wiesner responded enthusiastically. "St. Patrick's Day didn't strike a chord—but frogs, they had potential," he said in his Caldecott acceptance speech, as reprinted in *Horn Book.* "I got out my sketchbook and some old *National Geographic*s for reference. Frogs were great fun to draw—soft, round, lumpy, and really goofy-looking. But what could I do with them?" The rhetorical question was no sooner asked by Wiesner, than it was answered. As he recounted to *SATA:* "I envisioned a frog on a lily pad, which reminded me of a flying saucer in a 1950s B movie. As soon as I saw that frog on the lily pad fly, the cover was pretty much right there—this whole bunch of frogs flying out of the swamp."

But a simple cover didn't satisfy the storyteller in Wiesner, who was already envisioning a narrative featuring the frogs. "I was sitting in an airplane, looking through my sketchbook," he continued in his Caldecott acceptance speech, "and I thought, Okay, if I were a frog, and I had discovered I could fly, where would I go? What would I do? Images quickly began to appear to me, and for fear of losing them I hastily scribbled barely legible shapes onto the page: a startled man at a kitchen

A young artist inspires clouds to form new shapes in Sector 7, written and illustrated by Wiesner.

table; a terrified dog under attack; a roomful of frogs bathed in the glow of a television. A chronology began to take shape, and within an hour I had worked out a complete layout, which remained essentially unchanged through to the finished book. Everything was there: the story, the use of the panels, the times of day, and the title." *Tuesday,* Wiesner's almost wordless 1991 picture book, was created.

Winner of the 1992 Caldecott Medal, *Tuesday* is a whimsical tale about a night when a crowd of frogs ascend to the sky on lily pads and soar over the surrounding neighborhood. Zooming past startled birds and an incredulous resident indulging in a late-night snack, the frogs speed through a clothesline (causing some minor entanglements), and spook Rusty, a sizable dog. They even sneak into a living room housing a sleepy elderly lady and watch some TV (one member of the assemblage operates the remote control with his spindly tongue). "I really felt good when I finished *Tuesday,*" Wiesner admitted in his *SATA* interview, "and the response was immediate from everyone who saw it." But winning the Caldecott was something Wiesner hardly imagined. His astonishment was yet apparent when he was asked by *SATA* to describe his reaction: "I couldn't quite really believe it had happened ... My reaction is hard to explain ... The Children's Book Council puts out little bookmarks that list all the

Caldecott winners back to 1938, and each year they just add the new winner. Looking at that list and seeing my name at the end of it as part of that tradition ... whatever else happens, that's there forever. It really felt good to be included in that."

Wiesner also received considerable recognition for 1990's *Hurricane* and 1992's *June 29, 1999*. The former is a well-received picture book drawn from an incident in Wiesner's youth. Depicting the warmth of a family gathered together to wait out a storm, the book also describes the fantastic explorations David and George (two youngsters appropriately named after the Wiesner brothers) imagine themselves undertaking after the hurricane downs a large elm on their neighbor's front lawn. The latter, *June 29, 1999,* is an amusing, innovative picture book that revolves around young Holly Evans, who sends an assortment of vegetable seedlings into the atmosphere as part of a science experiment for school. A little more than a month later, gigantic rutabagas, avocados, lima beans, artichokes, cucumbers, peas, and all sorts of other vegetables begin falling to the earth. Amazement, anxiety, and confusion overcome citizens. In addition, rumors spread ("4000 lb. Radish Has Face of ELVIS!" screams one tabloid headline); business opportunities in real estate flourish ("Gourd Estates" quickly sprouts in North Carolina); and at least one Iowa farmer is ecstatic ("At last, the blue ribbon at the state fair is mine!" he announces upon finding a gargantuan head of cabbage on his property).

Sector 7, published in 1999, is yet another self-illustrated airborne adventure told without words, this time featuring a human protagonist. An artistically-inclined boy on a field trip to New York's Empire State Building encounters a friendly cloud, who transports him to a vast Cloud Dispatch Center in the sky. As it turns out, the clouds are bored with the mundane shapes they are assigned to take on, and they encourage the boy to draw some new designs for them. He obliges and sketches shapes of various fish and octopuses, to the delight of the clouds. After the boy returns to earth, the sky becomes filled with gigantic aquatic patterns, to the amazement of humans, fish, and hungry cats alike. Reviewers praised *Sector 7* warmly. "Starting from a simple, almost obvious idea—once one has thought of it—Wiesner offers up an ingenious world of nearly unlimited possibilities," commented a critic in *Publishers Weekly.* The reviewer continued, "The work as a whole is an inspired embodiment of what seems to be this artist's approach to story and vision: the more you look, the more there is to see."

Wiesner told writer Cindi Di Marzo in a *Publishers Weekly* interview that he originally conceived of the clouds taking on the shapes of dinosaurs, but was later attracted to the visual possibilities of fish. There were certain storytelling problems Wiesner had to overcome to make his book work. "The idea was to have a child who draws and used art to transform a situation," he explained to Di Marzo. "But I had to get him up in the clouds. Since I've always been fascinated with New York and enchanted by steel, stone and the hustle and bustle, I thought, 'Well, the child could ride a cloud up to the top of the Empire State Building.' When the cloud took on a personality and a relationship grew between it and the boy, [the story] came together."

Wiesner continued to collaborate with writers during the 1990s as well, earning favorable notice for his illustrations for Eve Bunting's story *Night of the Gargoyles.* This oddly macabre tale of stone gargoyles at play while the city sleeps is interpreted by Wiesner with a surreal sense of whimsy. "Wiesner's duotone charcoal illustrations capture the huge heaviness of the stone figures and their gloomy malevolence as they bump and fly and tumble free in the dark," wrote reviewer Hazel Rochman in *Booklist.* Claiming "If anyone could bring gargoyles to life pictorially, it's Wiesner," *School Library Journal* contributor Julie Cummins applauded the artist's work, saying the illustrations combine to "creat[e] a deliciously eerie, spooky scenario."

If there is one common thread running through Wiesner's works, it is that his books are entertaining. "I'm hoping kids have fun when they read my books," he expressed in his *SATA* interview. Wiesner has fun creating them—the abundance of innovative, imaginative, and fantastic events and characters in his works attest to that—yet he also enjoys the challenge of expressing his ideas in a visual format. "I have found that wordless picture books are as enriching and as involving as a book with words in it. In a wordless book, each reader really completes the story; there is no author's voice narrating the story. In books like *Free Fall* or *Tuesday,* there is a lot going on there, and you really need to *read* the picture. A reader can't just flip through the book; all the details add up to more fully tell the story. It's exciting to me to develop that visual literacy."

Works Cited

Corsaro, Julie, review of *Free Fall, School Library Journal,* June-July, 1988, p. 95.

Cummins, Julie, review of *Night of the Gargoyles, School Library Journal,* October, 1994, p. 86.

Di Marzo, Cindi, interview with David Wiesner, *Publishers Weekly,* November 22, 1999, p. 22.

Review of *Free Fall, Bulletin of the Center for Children's Books,* May, 1988, p. 193.

"An Interview with David Wiesner," *Clarionews,* spring, 1992.

Review of *The Loathsome Dragon, Publishers Weekly,* October 30, 1987, p. 70.

Macaulay, David, "David Wiesner," *Horn Book,* July-August, 1992, pp. 423-28.

Mellon, Constance A., review of *The Loathsome Dragon, School Library Journal,* March, 1988, p. 178.

Rochman, Hazel, review of *Night of the Gargoyles, Booklist,* October 1, 1994, p. 331.

Review of *Sector 7, Publishers Weekly,* August 30, 1999, p. 83.

Wiesner, David, "Caldecott Acceptance Speech," *Horn Book,* July-August, 1992, pp. 416-22.

Wiesner, David, telephone interview with Denise E. Kasinec for *Something about the Author,* conducted August 27, 1992.

Wiesner, David, *June 29, 1999,* Clarion Books, 1992.

For More Information See

BOOKS

Pendergast, Sara, and Tom Pendergast, editors, *St. James Guide to Children's Writers,* St. James, 1999, pp. 1118-19.

Silvey, Ann, editor, *Children's Books and Their Creators,* Houghton Mifflin, 1995, pp. 679-80.

PERIODICALS

Booklist, September 15, 1999, p. 270.

Bulletin of the Center for Children's Books, November, 1990, p. 74; November, 1992, pp. 93-94.

Horn Book, January-February, 1991, pp. 61-62; January-February, 1992, p. 84; September, 1999, p. 603.

New York Times Book Review, September 25, 1988, p. 51; August, 1988, p. 99.

Publishers Weekly, July 25, 1986, pp. 187-88; May 12, 1989, p. 294; September 20, 1991, p. 134; August 8, 1994, p. 436; November 1, 1999, p. 57.

School Library Journal, January, 1986, p. 66; November, 1986, p. 78; August, 1988, p. 99; May, 1990, pp. 107-08; October, 1990, p. 104; December, 1990, p. 25; January, 1991, p. 56; May, 1991, p. 86; December, 1991, p. 132.*

*   *   *

WILD, Robyn 1947-

Personal

Born January 24, 1947, in Sydney, Australia; daughter of George (a motor mechanic) and Norma (a teacher; maiden name, McDonnel) Joseph; married Brian Wild (an agricultural scientist), March 28, 1969; children: Donna, Grant. *Education:* Riverside City College, A.A., 1976. *Hobbies and other interests:* Reading, walking, spiritual development.

Addresses

Home—Lot 3, Blaxland Court, Terrigal, New South Wales 2260, Australia.

Career

Worked as early childhood teacher and director of private and community-based child care centers in Gosford, Australia, 1980-95; teacher at local community college. Volunteer with Meals on Wheels, Red Cross, and World Vision (Australia).

Writings

Benjamin's Basket, illustrated by Elizabeth Lieselotte Cullen, Rocky River Publishers (Shepherdstown, WV), 1997.

Sidelights

Robyn Wild told *SATA:* "When teaching in child care centers, I told the children stories when they were settling down for their midday naps. Usually the stories were about my cat and dog. The children enjoyed hearing about all the adventures my pets were having (all make-believe) and would often jump into their beds asking for more stories. It was fun seeing how much the children enjoyed these make-up stories, and I realized just how much I enjoyed telling them. That's when I decided to write a children's book! I guess I inherited this trait from my dad, who used to tell me stories when I was a little girl.

"In 1976 my husband Brian decided to do his doctorate. We went to Riverside, California (from Australia) and were there for nearly four years at the University of California. We lived in student housing, I went to the local city college, Donna went to the local elementary school, and Grant went to the children's center. When Brian graduated we returned home to Australia after a wonderful experience."*

*   *   *

WINCH, John 1944-

Personal

May 25, 1944, in Sydney, Australia; son of Jack and Jean (Cook) Winch; married, wife's name, Madeleine (an illustrator), August 26, 1967; children: Martina, Jessie. *Education:* National Art School, diploma in design; Alexander Mackie C.A.E., graduate diploma; also attended Sydney Teachers College for three years. *Politics:* "None." *Religion:* "None."

Addresses

Home—36 Merton St., Rozelle, 2034, New South Wales, Australia. *Office*—P.O. Box 7, Stuart Town, 2820, New South Wales, Australia.

Career

Self-employed artist, illustrator, and writer since c. 1967.

Awards, Honors

I.B.B.Y. Honour Book, Australia, for *The Old Woman Who Loved to Read;* Winch has also received seventeen prizes for painting in Australia.

Writings

SELF-ILLUSTRATED

One Sunday, Angus & Robertson, 1988.
One Saturday, Walter McVitty Books, 1989.
The Old Man Who Loved to Sing, Scholastic, 1993.
The Old Woman Who Loved to Read, Holiday House, 1997.
Millennium Book of Myth and Story, Millenium, 1997.
Leonardo Pigeon of Siena, Margret Hamilton, 1998.

Keeping Up with Grandma, Holiday House, 2000.
Game of the Goose, Viking, 2000.

Also author of *The Folly,* 2000, and *The Boatman,* 2000.

Sidelights

John Winch told *SATA:* "I live in the 'bush' five hours west of Sydney in an old mining town of the gold rush era. Nothing has changed much, except the steam train is now a flash silver streak. With the help of the other four or five artists that have fled here from the city, we are trying to keep the town in the last century. Here most of my work is based on simple country life—the struggles with the seasons, drought, fire, floods, clinging onto old values.

"Apart from writing children's books, I am also an artist and my work encompasses printmaking, sculpture, painting, and ceramics. I have had exhibitions in Paris at the Bibliotheque National, and my work is in major museums throughout the world. I often feel I am spreading myself too thin over so many activities instead of concentrating on one media—but I'm having fun—which after all is more important that having a glowing reputation."

John Winch's picture books celebrate the joys of the Australian "bush" where he lives. Both *The Old Man Who Loved to Sing* and *The Old Woman Who Loved to Read* feature main characters who, like the author, moved to a rural area to enjoy the natural silence only to be found there. In *The Old Man Who Loved to Sing* the old man loves the sound of music—and of his own singing voice—so much that he moves to the country, where he can listen to both undisturbed by the noises of the city. At first his music disturbs the animals in his care, and they are later disturbed by its absence, when the old man becomes so elderly that he forgets to sing, whistle, or play his gramophone records while he performs his chores. The animals decide to remind the man of music by beating their tails, croaking, or trilling, thus making their own variety of noise. Their plan works, and the man bursts into song. "Winch's beautifully detailed paintings give this slight tale tremendous charm," averred Janice Del Negro in *Booklist.* Ellen Fader, writing in the *Horn Book,* similarly observed that while Winch's story "possesses a simple elegance," the illustrations "command the most attention." Executed in gouache and watercolor on paper made to look like it has been torn from an old book, the illustrations for *The Old Man Who Loved to Sing* are distinguished by unusual perspectives and animals with human expressions.

In *The Old Woman Who Loved to Read* the main character leaves the city behind and rents a farm in search of the peace and quiet she needs to be able to read all the books she owns. But living on a farm entails numerous chores, and every season brings its own emergency, from a newborn lamb that needs bottle feeding in the spring to bush fires in the summer to autumnal rains that bring a flood. The old woman never contributor Ellen Mandel remarked of *The Old Woman Who Loved to Read,* "It's a simple story line that finds rich and humorous embellishment in Winch's engagingly detailed watercolors." In his illustrations, which again feature animal portraits, Winch allows the realism of the basic story line to expand to include some elements of fantasy without abandoning what a reviewer in *Publishers Weekly* called the book's "core of recognizable feelings." "All of it—house and inhabitants—are cunningly, winsomely painted by Winch, who makes his story gently wry," concluded a reviewer in *Kirkus Reviews.*

Works Cited

Del Negro, Janice, review of *The Old Man Who Loved to Sing, Booklist,* April 15, 1996, p. 1447.

Fader, Ellen, review of *The Old Man Who Loved to Sing, Horn Book,* July-August, 1996, p. 458.

Mandel, Ellen, review of *The Old Woman Who Loved to Read, Booklist,* March 1, 1997, p. 1175.

Review of *The Old Woman Who Loved to Read, Kirkus Reviews,* February 15, 1997, p. 308.

Review of *The Old Woman Who Loved to Read, Publishers Weekly,* February 10, 1997, p. 84.

For More Information See

PERIODICALS

School Library Journal, April, 1996, pp. 121-22; May, 1997, p. 117.

John Winch (right) with children's literature educator and writer Maurice Saxby.

finds the time to read until the middle of winter finds her sitting before a fire with a book in her lap—falling asleep! Reviewers noted that Winch keeps his text to a minimum, as he did in *The Old Man Who Loved to Sing,* and lets the pictures extend the narrative thread. *Booklist*

Autobiography Feature

Dianne Wolfer

1961-

Doncaster, Melbourne

My life seems to have been a series of journeys. My first memories of home are in Doncaster, a suburb of Melbourne, Australia's second largest city. During the 1960s, Doncaster's orchards were making way for suburbia. Our family was part of that transition.

My older sister, Karen, and I grew up with a tribe of neighbourhood kids. We free-ranged together, played, had squabbles, and made cubbies. Building cubbies is one of my strongest childhood memories. Perhaps because cubby building involves fantasy and make-believe. Imagination was always an essential part of our games.

There were so many cubby variations. In summer we leapt into the long grass next door to create instant cubbies. In winter, blankets over chairs or tables created a cosier version. I can still remember how the world changed when we were tucked away in a cubby. We could be anyone and go anywhere. Such power was magical.

We had a spooky cubby, a "dungeon" under the house for scary, rainy day expeditions. My sister would frighten me by rising slowly out of her toy-box "coffin" as a vampire. There was also an *I Dream of Jeannie* cubby in my sister's small cupboard. I would climb in, imagine myself in a bottled harem, and await Larry Hagman's call.

Tree cubbies consisted of planks in the tall gum trees in our backyard. Their popularity depended on how prolific the population of furry emperor caterpillars was at the time. The best cubby of all, Heifer House (we were mad about cows), was a more permanent arrangement involving an old billboard which we leant against a fence to make a fabulous all-weather cubby, a hideaway that we could sleep in on hot summer nights.

The cubby was shared with Donna, the neighbour's daughter. She was a year older than me and a year younger than my sister—a source of constant jealousy regarding whose friend she really was. Her brother, who was my age, liked to chase me with caterpillars and put blue-tongue lizards down my back. He wasn't invited into our cubbies.

Early childhood was a happy time. Looking back, I'm sure that having the space and freedom to "imagine" contributed much to that happiness.

Every second Sunday my beloved grandma would sleep over. My sister and I put on shows for Doey, did her hair in curlers, and listened to her read from a well-worn copy of *Dot and the Kangaroo*. Other books I enjoyed as a young child were *The Muddle-headed Wombat* and *Winnie-the-Pooh*. On rainy days, I also loved sitting by the crackling record player listening to *The Elephant's Child* being spanked for his insatiable curiosity.

When I was two, my other grandmother made a fabric draft-stopper for the door. I called it Eeyore, and we became inseparable. My Eeyore was unlike his sad namesake. He listened to my hopes and fears, ate sugar, won races with me on his back, cuddled me in bed, and later travelled with us on a jumbo jet to Thailand. Together we enjoyed all sorts of adventures.

Clear school memories begin around Grade Two. My teacher at the time, Miss Leembrugen, wore a miniskirt and had the most amazing beehive hairdo. She wasn't a born teacher, but she let us put on shows for the other classes. This provided more scope for my active imagination.

I particularly remember the end of year Christmas play she organised. All the girls were angels with tinsel haloes and floaty dresses, but I kept tripping up when I was meant to curtsy. Miss Leembrugen decided I was better suited to the role of narrator. She told me it was a more important position, but I remember feeling humiliated.

After that I was often the narrator. In the playground I became director, too, when we reenacted scenes from Enid Blyton's *The Magic Faraway Tree*. I was a bossy little thing and insisted on playing Silky, the elf, to the boy next door's Moonface.

I had a great teacher in Grade Three. A man, very strict, who organised, amongst other things, for Fred Bear and the cast of TV's *Breakfast a Go-Go* to visit our class and watch our own copycat version of their show.

Around this time I began writing stories and still have a homemade book entitled *Plinky Pig*. It's a cliched story about two pigs who meet, fall in love, and escape a wicked fox. I loved reading animal stories and enjoyed *Black Beauty*, *The Call of the Wild*, and *Ring of Bright Water*.

To get to school we cut across a huge paddock with what we believed were wild horses. There were tall trees to hide behind and a dam full of slippery tadpoles. As we walked, we told secrets and had adventures. On winter mornings we jumped onto thinly frozen puddles and marvelled at the magic of frosty cobwebs. It makes me sad that few kids now have that unsupervised walking-to-school experience.

Other early memories include my sister and I having punch-ups. Being a younger sister was a test in endurance. Karen was better than me at everything, and she knew it. She liked to lock me in the *Jeannie* cupboard and cut my dolls' hair into punk styles that were years ahead of her time.

But we were also friends and spent many happy hours squashing rose petals for our latest perfume concoctions, dressing pee-wee dolls for camping trips in shoe-box caravans, and creating art shows for which we charged our parents two cents admission.

My parents were ambitious and wanted to get ahead. Dad, a working-class boy, had risen to the level of manager. Mum, a farm girl, was a home economics teacher helping city kids learn to cook. She went back to work once I was at school, which was unusual for women then.

My parents saved and one year bought an above-ground pool. The cubbies were abandoned, and we became very popular with the neighbourhood kids. Summer was spent swimming, sunbaking, and making whirlpool currents. I remember once complaining that our neighbour, Donna, got more Easter eggs and pocket money than we did. Mum told me we were saving for a special holiday.

Sure enough, when I was eight, we went on a cargo-passenger cruise to Fiji. It wasn't a luxury ship, but we had great fun with the handful of other kids. In Suva, we saw brown-skirted policemen directing traffic and big women in floral frocks. Our taxi driver took us home to meet his family, and we shared their spicy Indian meal. We watched boys climb tall palm trees for coconuts and drank the strange milk. I was later seasick. It was a great experience for a young girl from the suburbs, and so began my lifelong love of travel.

Besides that adventure, my primary school years were pretty normal. Each year we travelled four hours interstate to visit relatives in Albury, New South Wales. I remember lying on the back seat of Dad's Holden, watching gum trees whiz by upside down.

Two years after the Fijian trip, I was progressing in school, trying out for the rounders team and hoping to become sports captain, when my parents announced that Dad had a new job. We were moving to Bangkok. I still remember the devastation of that announcement. It was a bombshell. I curled up, tried to hide my tears, and imagined the worst.

Thailand

But the move wasn't bad, and the two years we spent in Thailand were crammed with new experiences. This is an extract from a piece I wrote a few years ago, describing my early impressions:

First night in Bangkok. Incense, spice and sewers—strange smells for a ten year old. Humidity welcomed us at the airport. It was like opening the oven door without mitts, then stepping inside to be baked. Even when the thermometer topped the century, Melbourne summers were never like this.

Dianne Wolfer (photo courtesy Border Morning Mail).

Overdressed in groovy, wine-coloured cord overalls with matching flower-power shirt, I followed my parents from the terminal. The hot air sucked the sweat from my body whilst I snuck covetous glances at my sister's white clogs. Mum said I was too young for them.

We drove from the airport at night and I watched the fairy lights of thousands of spirit houses flicker. Our driver smelt like curried rice and we gaped at the night vendors perching on their haunches, before he braked half-heartedly to avoid a dog. I clutched Eeyore and remembered my grandma's tears at the airport. It was 1972 and for her, Bangkok was almost a suburb of Vietnam.

Our new home was near a market, and we couldn't believe the smells. Thick, brown, oozing, fishy odours which hung in the air, lightened by the occasional whiff of ripe fruit. My sister and I, overwhelmed by homesickness, pretended we were tired and spent the first night plotting our escape—back to freshly mown, lawn-smelling, suburban safety. But we fell asleep between whispers, and in a few days the market smells disappeared. Mum said our noses had acclimatised.

Our international school followed the American calendar, and as it was summer in the U.S., we were on vacation. We spent the time exploring temples and trying to learn Thai.

One day Mum took us to the floating market, and I was knocked flat by the cute, but spoilt, baby elephant seen in the movie *Live and Let Die* (we appeared a few days after filming and I had sugar bananas behind my back). Two weeks later I was bitten by a monkey at a Thai theme park (he didn't want to share my peanuts with his mates).

The bite healed but Mum had to ring the keeper for daily reports. If one of the monkeys developed rabies, I'd be in for a two-week course of injections through the stomach. My sister thought this hilarious and pretended to froth at the mouth whilst making rabid-little-sister jokes. My grandma read my letters and worried.

There were so many things to discover. Mangy dogs and spirit houses. Monsoonal floods when we waded through our front yard catching fish with umbrellas. The candlelight of *Loy Krathong* festival, as thousands of banana leaf rafts floated down the local *klong,* their wicks fizzing as they sank. The *klong* has since been paved over to make way for yet another road.

One wonderful evening, Dad came home with a bike. We took turns to ride our new dragster up the soi to the market, plastic whirligigs from the cereal packet spinning on the spokes.

The market was an amazing place. There were slimy fish of all sizes, flicking in near-death experiences until a bucket of water revived them, chooks in baskets with their legs tied together, crabs and eels and mountains of fish paste. We always hurried past the food stalls towards the main entrance where old women sat threading scented, heart-shaped flowers and orchids onto leis to drape around the necks of golden Buddhas.

On the way home we'd pass immaculately clean schoolgirls stepping out of impossibly grimy hovels. Occasionally we went to banquets, some in our honour. After the first week, Mum told the maid not to make our beds for us.

The holidays ended and we began school at Ruam Rudi International School. I remember holding hands and giggling with my Spanish-speaking Filipina classmate—best friends until the day she offered me some of her special play-lunch. She peeled shell from the boiled egg and took a bite before passing it to me. Through her smile, I saw wings, feathers, and a half-formed beak as she chewed happily. I ran away and hid. In time I found another friend, an Australian girl a year older than me who ate peanut butter sandwiches for lunch. Soon, embryonic chooks faded into a bad memory.

In October 1973 we experienced what would be the first of several student uprisings. Bomb threats were made to the nearby police station, and for the first time I sensed fear in adults. Our contingency plan for fire was to swim the nearby, snake-infested swamp. For bombing we'd stand under our reinforced concrete porchway and cross our fingers. The station wasn't bombed, but although there was no fire, machine guns were heard at the end of our lane. Before Dad and our friend's father came home, a diplomat reported that all Australians were safe. Mum said later that if you weren't with the embassy, you didn't count.

Other memories of Bangkok involve strange food: rambutans, mangosteens, lychees, and our maid's back-to-front toasted cheese sandwiches for lunch. One morning she skewered five baby cobras with the rake. She said the mommy and daddy would probably be nearby.

On our way to swim at the British Club we passed beggars in the streets—young children, old men, mothers of deformed babies. My friend told me some parents injured their children so that they earned more. After a while we learnt not to see them, yet I still remember some of their faces. There was a lot to think about for an eleven-year-old.

We wore wattle-coloured Speedos to training. The strong smell of chlorine permeates those memories of breaststroke, butterfly, and individual medleys. One afternoon a champion swimmer visited our team. I was too young to be impressed, but my sister wasn't. Karen trained twice a day and became the first foreigner to represent Thailand in swimming.

Each morning we caught a tuk-tuk to school, where we learnt about hot dogs, cheerleaders, and American slang. There were whispers about "the drug problem" in the lanes behind the school and warnings to keep our distance. After school we'd watch seniors stroll that way.

On weekends, ice-cream vendors on bicycles rang their bells to attract our three Thai dogs—relatives of the dingo, who loved coconut milk treats. We went on trips up-country to the River Kwai, the Surin elephant roundup, and to see transvestites at Pattaya. Two years crammed with new experiences, growing breasts before I was ready, and learning rude words in Thai, experiences that even now I draw on in my writing.

People at home clicked their tongues. They said it was irresponsible to take children to South-east Asia. What about the political unrest, disease, and the Situation in Vietnam? But we found saffron-robed monks offering their bowls every morning for our virtuous neighbours to fill with food, a city skyline of roofs curving upwards to ward off evil spirits, while Buddhas wearing enigmatic smiles reclined in temples. And every evening, in every home, the smell of incense burning, portraits of the king and the glow of candles warming thousands of spirit houses.

After two years in Bangkok, however, my parents' marriage was on the rocks. Dad's alcohol problems had ruined his health. He was admitted to hospital, and Mum decided it was time to leave. Our house in Melbourne had tenants, and as she needed the support of family, we went to Albury.

Albury

The first months back in Australia were a messy time. Because we'd taken leave a few weeks before it was due, Dad's company said that he'd abandoned his post. They refused to send our belongings, so for several months we lived out of suitcases. It soon became clear that we wouldn't return to Bangkok, so when a rambling Tudor-style restaurant with on-site housing came onto the market, my parents sold our home in Melbourne, bought the restaurant, and tried to make a go of it.

Dianne (left) with sister, Karen, 1964.

Things went okay for a while. My sister and I attended the local high school. Mum opened a small business above the restaurant selling Thai artefacts. Silk flowers and embroidered caftans were a novelty in country Australia. They sold well, and Mum branched into importing silver jewellery, brass, and celadon ware.

Unfortunately Dad was still drinking heavily. This affected his management of the business, and the restaurant lost money. After about six months he was admitted to a rehabilitation hospital. Mum's health also suffered, and we had to sell the restaurant. Our family was broke.

For a while we moved in with my maternal grandmother. Mum took a job teaching at a Catholic boys' school while we continued our studies at the high school. In 1974 Albury High was a huge country school (there were seven English classes per year level) with students from both town and the surrounding farms. The mostly conservative staff taught traditional subjects, so it wasn't until I went to college that I realised city schools offered choices like literature, politics, and Indonesian.

Although my Year Eight English teacher encouraged us to write creatively, writing in senior high consisted mainly of producing essays on Shakespeare and the Bronte sisters' work. Besides these unimaginative school essays, the writing I did at this time was mainly outpourings of teenage love and angst into a journal.

Albury at that time was a town of approximately thirty thousand people. It was large enough to have a movie theatre, drive-in, and bowling alley, but small enough for adolescents to walk or cycle most places. The first friends I made lived on farms, so weekends were a bit lonely. After a while, though, I became friendly with the town kids and we had a lot of fun together. In summer we spent most of our spare time jumping off the highway bridge into the river and chatting as we floated downstream. Once we got our licenses we were able to drive to the Hume Weir where we also swam, sunbaked, and gossiped. Although the characters in my YA novels are fictitious, I draw on memories of how my friends and I felt during our high school years.

College in Melbourne

My first year at college was fantastic. I boarded at International House, residential student digs affiliated with Melbourne Uni. It catered to country kids and overseas students (mainly Chinese Malaysians).

There were twelve girls living in our wing. We were studying different courses but met each evening when we had to wear our black academic robes to the huge hall for dinner. There were parties, theme nights, and in the evenings, after studying for a few hours, we often walked to the local pub for a mug (or two) of cider.

At the end of the year I moved into a Victorian terrace house with four other students, two girls and two fellows. We lived together for a couple of years and became a strange family who shared the bills, shopping, and cleaning. We knew everything about each other and became good friends.

At college, I majored in literature, art, and philosophy. I loved learning about kids' books, so a highlight of the course was a field trip to Dromkeen, the children's

literature museum/library housed in a gracious old homestead on the outskirts of Melbourne.

In first year, each student was allocated a home school for their teaching practicals. My school, Footscray North, was home to multicultural kids from a disadvantaged area of the city. It was here that I discovered the importance of books as a bridge to literacy and began to build up a personal library of picture books and novels that "worked" in classrooms.

I was also taking Aboriginal Studies as an elective and was keen to teach indigenous kids in an outback school. The college administration told me that if I could get to the Northern Territory, they'd arrange a school. Mum offered to pay my train fare, so in my final year I travelled over two thousand kilometres to northern Australia and spent a month at Roper Valley Station.

In 1982, Roper Valley was a non-operational cattle station four hours' drive east of the small town of Mataranka (which is about three hundred kilometres south of Darwin). The station home was abandoned, and Anne, the teacher, lived in a demountable house with her husband, who did occasional butchering and kept the water bores open for the cattle.

The station was hundreds of kilometres in size. I was told that it was being used as a tax incentive for a middle-eastern, multinational group, but I never found out the details, or indeed if it was true. It made an interesting story at the time.

Every morning we'd drive a minibus into camp, collect our students, and ferry them back to the two adjoining schoolrooms. While I was there, Anne put me in charge of the junior grades.

One day a new kid came in from the bush, a boy aged about six. He had a severe louse infestation, and his head was covered in pus and bloody sores where he'd scratched the skin raw. Anne rang the flying doctor, and following his relayed instructions, I cut the lad's hair strand by strand before smearing on antiseptic cream and bandaging his head. Throughout it all he didn't whimper. We took him back to class, and it was incredible to watch his amazement as he explored the toys and books. I would love to capture that look of wonder in words.

Travelling

After finishing teacher's college, I worked for three months in my mother's shop to save money to go backpacking through Asia. Soon after my parents' divorce, Mum had moved her business closer to the main street and was employing part-time staff to help manage customers while she focused on the book work. Christmas was her busiest period, so when I finished college in November 1982, I was fortunate to be able to step into a job which I knew well. At the time I also worked in the evenings as a waitress in an Italian restaurant.

The idea of travelling in Asia had been a dream for several years. At the end of high school, I wanted to work in the refugee camps along the Thai/Kampuchean border. A perceptive career adviser told me that I'd be more useful if I had some training. I'd been interested in journalism or teaching as a career, so I followed his advice and trained as a teacher.

"A sleep-over with my best friends from high school: (from left) Fleur, Jill, Dianne, and Nill," 1977.

In January 1983, I had my certificate, two thousand dollars in the bank, and a handful of traveller's cheques. I was ready to go.

My journey began in Bali, an island crammed with tourists and backpackers. Mum had insisted that I pre-book the first few nights' accommodation. After settling into my *losman,* I ventured out for dinner and began talking to another Australian traveller. It turned out that she was also from Albury, had been travelling for two years, and this was her last night before flying home. I've always believed in omens, so I took this as a good sign.

After a few days in Kuta and Ubud, I travelled by bus to northern Bali where I caught the ferry to Java, then travelled overland to Yogyakarta. I quickly learnt the hazards of a woman travelling alone through a Moslem country. Even though I dressed like Indonesian women in a sarong and baggy shirt, I was constantly harassed by men and once even groped by a temple guardian. Putting a ring on my third finger and inventing stories of a fiance made absolutely no difference.

The situation worsened as I travelled through Sumatra, the more mountainous island. I spent several days on bumpy bus trips where I was so tired that all I could stomach were banana fritters and digestive biscuits.

As I travelled, I wrote chunks of a novel about a girl working at an outback pub. Although I have long since abandoned the story, the experience was my first attempt at plotting a novel. I'd often been compelled to write down my thoughts during school and college years, but all of a sudden I had the time to explore this interest. I kept a journal and began to collect ideas for stories and articles.

Halfway across Sumatra I bumped into a Dutch man that I'd met at a hostel in Yogyakarta. We travelled to Lake Toba and the Orangutan Rehabilitation Centre together. It was such a relief not to be on my guard the whole time. He was amazed at the different reaction I received as a woman.

Wim was a journalist who'd been on the trail for almost a year. He listened to my ideas and asked helpful questions when I said I was trying to write a book. This was perhaps my first encouragement to take my writing seriously.

Although I'd travelled with my family, being overseas on my own gave me so much to think and write about. For the first time ever, I had unlimited time to read. Swapping novels with backpackers from various countries led me to an eclectic blend of books I may not have otherwise found. *Midnight's Children, Cry the Beloved Country, The Brothers Lionheart,* and *Siddartha* were just a few of the titles I remember.

After Indonesia, I travelled the backpacker path from Penang along the Malay Peninsula to Bangkok. There I met up with my mother, who was leading a small tour on a hike around the lower mountains out of Pokhara, Nepal.

Nepal

Whilst working in my mother's shop, I'd met a missionary who'd lived in Nepal for twenty years. When I mentioned that I was planning on visiting Nepal, she gave me an address to contact in Kathmandu. If I wanted teaching work, there was plenty to do. So after farewelling my mother and the members of her group, I rang the United Mission to Nepal.

"You're here at last," they said. There was a position as tutor in Jumla, western Nepal, available, and they hoped that I'd agree to fill it. I was young and ready for an adventure, so the more I heard about the remote and difficult conditions, the more I wanted to go.

The tiny market town of Jumla lies in a 2,700-metre valley on the trade route between Tibet and India. The "hills" surrounding the valley are around 3,000 metres high, and the pass often clouds over as planes from Kathmandu approach, forcing them to return. Alternatively you can hike in from Surkhet on the Indian border, a two-week, leech-ridden trip.

After several weeks of delay, we flew via Nepalganj. I wrote about the trip for an Australian project entitled *Flightpaths,* which until recently could be viewed on the Internet.

The nine months I spent in Jumla were an amazing time. It was my first real teaching job. Six mornings a week I taught a thirteen-year-old boy and his bright ten-year-old sister. The boy's horse often joined us in the mudroom that served as schoolhouse. "Dusty" also starred in our production of *The Highway Man.*

The reason these hard-working Mennonite missionaries from Iowa needed me was that life in Jumla was so challenging. They had no time to supervise their kids' correspondence. All vegies, water, and milk had to be boiled; pebbles picked from the rice; and newspaper cut into squares for toilet paper. We suffered regular doses of amoebic dysentery, and I was often grateful that the schoolroom was across the path from the toilet.

Marijuana plants grew outside the classroom. They were taller than my students, who liked to play trucks amongst the stalks. Twice weekly I puffed up the steep mountain path to a pair of wild twins who loved to wait and ambush me. The twins were five and hadn't been to school. We made alphabet books and invented songs together.

Whilst living in Nepal I learnt how differently English speakers use the language. I became interested in the American habit of dropping articles, as in "ride horse" and "jump rope," and also the differences in spelling. I learnt interesting expressions and colloquialisms such as *Are your BMs okay?* That one threw me for a while; however with rats, fleas, and our regular bouts of dysentery, bowel movements (BMs) were indeed never far from our thoughts and conversations.

During my free time I contemplated life and wrote. I penned letters, kept a journal, and fiddled around with my first attempts at writing short stories. A life-changing moment occurred on a three-day hike to Rara Lake near the Tibetan border. I was with three fellows, two British and one Nepali. It began raining, and we took a wrong turn at the top of a pass. As we tried to find our way down, we had to cross a steep, snow-filled ravine. It was terrifying. The only thing that kept us going was the thought of black bears appearing after nightfall. In nine months I experienced

enough to keep me writing for the rest of my life, and yet I still haven't found time to mine this part of my life fully.

One short story, "The Red Bucket," set in Jumla, has been commended in competitions. Several others are still in first-draft format. When I returned to Albury, I discovered that not only had my mother read my letters to anyone who ventured into the shop, but she'd also filed them neatly into a folder. They're an interesting record of my time in Jumla, and I hope one day to find time to rework more of my experiences into stories.

One snippet that interested me as I re-read my Nepal journals was this entry written after an exhausting evening of writing:

> . . . enough, enough, but the words keep flowing, vain attempts to explain the images and sensations confronting me. In the absence of company, words flow into my pen. Must a writer's life then be by necessity a lonely one?

To answer this contemplative twenty-one-year-old's question, I do believe that a writer needs plenty of time alone. This doesn't mean they should be lonely, just able to create space for freethinking time. During quiet times, ideas form and take shape. For me it's an important part of the writing process. I find this happens best when my physical self is busy doing something else, something like swim-

College student Dianne, backpacking through Tasmania, Australia's southern island.

ming at the beach, doing laps in a pool, walking alone, or even long-distance driving. Lolling in the bath is good, too!

As winter and the prospect of being snowed in for three months approached, I had to decide whether to accompany my host family on vacation in India or to leave and continue my own travels. I'd already caught and named twenty-one rats in my mud hut and was wearing most of my clothes to bed because of the cold. When I saw my washing frozen on the line one morning, I decided it was time to leave. I had also just received an important letter.

During my last year at college I had enjoyed a whirlwind romance with the man who would later become such an important part of my life. When we met, Reinhard had sold his house and was about to drive across the Nullarbor Plain to Western Australia to take up a transfer with IBM. For three weeks we spent as much time as we could together. He had to go, and I couldn't leave college. I also knew that I needed to go travelling on my own before making a commitment to anyone.

Reinhard was seven years older and had lived in Berlin and Finland. Although he urged me to move west after completing my studies, Reinhard respected my decision to travel. Over the two years we'd been apart, our correspondence had become sporadic, so his warm letter to Jumla was very welcome. I answered immediately. He wrote

Dianne and Reinhard Wolfer on their wedding day, 1984.

back, and we decided to meet in Europe the following summer. In the meantime I wanted to see India and Kashmir.

However when I came down from the hills (with an American accent), I discovered that the backpacker trail had lost its sparkle. I was tired of being hassled by men and sick of being sick. I'd been away for almost a year, and my plan of eating a Toblerone on the steps of the Taj Mahal no longer seemed such a great way to spend Christmas.

On the spur of the moment I decided to start heading home. I'd always wanted to spend more time in the northern areas of Thailand, so I booked a flight from Kathmandu to Bangkok.

After spending Christmas with family friends I set out alone again. I was going to explore the ruined temples of Sukhothai. However as I bumped along on the bus, I couldn't stop thinking about home. After a day trudging around ruins in the rain, I sent Reinhard a telegram saying I was on my way back to Australia and that I would fly via Perth. Once I'd decided to return I couldn't get there quickly enough.

Reinhard met me at the airport, and it was as if we'd never been apart. Eleven months later we were married in my mum's garden. Before that lovely occasion, however, I experienced one of the most challenging times of my life.

Carnarvon

West Australia is about three times larger than Texas. There are 1.6 million people in the state and most of them (1.1 million) live in Perth. I'd been trained in the eastern state of Victoria. To get a teaching position in Perth I would first have to go bush. Although willing to try anything, I especially wanted to work in what was then called Special Education.

A supervisor in the education department promised that if I filled a challenging position for six months, she'd try to offer me a city job the year after. Reinhard and I had planned our wedding for December, the end of the school year. We'd survived two years apart, what difference would another six months make? I packed my bags and travelled one thousand kilometres north to Carnarvon.

My class was the senior special class—a jumble of nine, mostly indigenous children with a mixture of learning difficulties. I won't go into their problems, but several were so traumatised by the things they'd experienced during their short lives that being in a mainstream class wasn't possible.

As a young white woman, I wasn't the teacher they needed, but I was all that was available. It was a difficult time. I did my best, but the situation was exacerbated by the teacher I had to share lodgings with. She didn't want a housemate and had driven off several before me. She insisted we buy separate milk, bread, sugar, etc., and rarely spoke to me.

Things became impossible, and at last I moved into another government house with a wonderfully kind, born-again Christian girl who taught first graders and was always singing hymns or songs about the three bears.

Carnarvon was five hours' drive from the nearest big town and had more than its fair share of social problems. I once tried to write about this time but found it too depressing. Perhaps one day I'll be able to.

Dianne on Dusty with a local lad in Nepal. "Our schoolroom was on ground floor of building above Dusty's mane."

The upside of this experience was that I made some good friends. On weekends we'd pile into a four-wheel drive and explore the Pilbara countryside. One area we visited was the (now famous) dolphin beach at Monkey Mia.

In those days you could buy a bucket of fish for two dollars and feed the dolphins for as long as you liked. Now busloads of tourists arrive every day. Visitors form a long line, and only the lucky few are selected by a ranger to offer fish. This must be done to protect the dolphins, but I'm glad I visited Monkey Mia before it was widely discovered. I'm sure that at a subconscious level, my experience with these dolphins influenced the writing of my first novel, Dolphin Song.

After our wedding in December 1984, Reinhard and I spent a five-week honeymoon backpacking through Japan. Whilst I'd been grappling with basic Hindi in Nepal, he'd been learning Japanese at night school. Although I wanted to learn German, Reinhard convinced me to study Japanese for a year, so that when we left I'd be able to ask for food and basic directions.

We had a wonderful honeymoon backpacking from the Okinawa islands in the south across Kyushu and Honshu to beautiful Hokkaido in the north. It was a carefree, happy time. We loved the intricacies and multi-layers of Japanese culture. I'll never forget my first experience of Japanese politeness. After practising for a moment, I approached an elderly, kimono-clad woman and asked if "this *telephone*

was going to Shinjuku station" (the word for train is *densha* while telephone is *denwa*). The old lady smiled graciously, bowed, and said that "yes, indeed it was." Meanwhile, Reinhard, who was within listening distance, was almost wetting himself with laughter.

We stayed in youth hostels, Japanese inns, and the smaller *minshuku* (family inns) and hoped that soon we'd be back in Japan for a longer period.

Perth, Western Australia

I began married life working as a teacher at a centre for language-impaired children in Perth. On weekends we often escaped the city to go bushwalking or canoeing. Two evenings a week we continued our Japanese studies.

Around this time I summoned the courage to join the Society of Women Writers. I remember how nervous I was, and this memory helps me understand the reticence new writers feel attending the creative writing sessions that I now teach.

The WA SWW holds monthly meetings, which I couldn't attend because of work commitments, but they also have magazine groups, one of which I joined.

Eight women are assigned to each group. One woman acts as editor and compiles the work sent to her each month into a folder. This magazine circulates via the mail, and each member comments on the other seven submissions. For me as a new writer, this feedback was very helpful. All these years later, I still belong to a magazine called *Kaleidoscope,* a group specifically interested in writing for kids.

Through the SWW monthly newsletter I found out about competitions and opportunities for writers. I was able to set myself specific goals, and in 1985 my first article, "Eating out in Kathmandu," was published along with thirteen photographs in *Let's Travel* magazine. I was ecstatic.

It took a while for me to show my creative scribblings to Reinhard. It still amazes me that although I'd vowed to share my life, body, and soul with this man, I was nervous about sharing my writing. I was worried that he'd find my work silly.

As it turned out, Reinhard was a fabulous sounding board. He encouraged me to strive for excellence and to believe in myself. From him I learnt to combine my creativity with the discipline needed to set goals and work from home. When he died in 1995 I felt for a long time like a boat drifting without an anchor. But I'll write more about that later.

Like me, Reinhard loved to travel. As a young couple, both working, we were able to take an annual summer holiday. During one Christmas vacation we went to Germany so that I could meet my new in-laws. Having relatives from different cultural backgrounds is a wonderful experience. Reinhard's sister, Verena, married Sandy, a Chinese-Malaysian, and Auntie Ingrid has since married a Nigerian fellow. Family get-togethers are interesting and have inspired me to try and write from different cultural viewpoints.

After spending Christmas in Munich we hitchhiked to Berlin. "The Wall" was a sobering sight, as was the museum at Checkpoint Charlie. We caught a train through East Germany, then a boat to Scandinavia.

Winter in the Arctic Circle wasn't my idea of a holiday, but Reinhard had spent several years in Finland. He spoke Finnish fluently, loved cross-country skiing, and promised that I'd change my mind.

In Germany with cows decorated for the almabtrieb (last stage of the cows' journey from high alpine meadows to their winter barn).

We arrived in Helsinki early. There was a plane leaving for Lapland that afternoon. We could get a fantastic package, one week in a remote cabin and all transfers, but we had to hurry. The flight left at three. After a mad shopping frenzy we made the plane with twenty minutes to spare.

Our hut (with triple glass and open fire) was in a popular ski resort out of Rovaniemi, but as nobody came at *karmos,* we had the resort to ourself.

Karmos, the time of darkness. It was January and there were only a few hours' sunlight a day. But those hours were a swirl of dusky dawn colours, as the sky became an amazing palette of blue, pink, mauve, and even green. We spent hours skiing across powder-white countryside hoping to meet reindeer, but the lamp-lit trails led us to snowbound service stations, where strong coffee, dark Finnish bread, and thick soup warmed us. Once our eyelashes and gloves had defrosted we set off again.

Back at the cottage, we played Scrabble or Battleship, ate our supplies, and enjoyed the sauna. Reinhard showed me how to make snow angels by dragging my arms over my head. The print in the snow was like a Yuletide stencil, and the tingle of shocked flesh when I ran back inside was bizarre. A combination of pins and needles and tickling, but nicer.

Every evening we scanned the heavens for the Northern Lights. On the last night we were lucky. At 2 a.m. the sky went berserk. It was like a science experiment, full of flashing electrical lines and ghostly shawls of green light. I've never seen anything like it. We piled on all our clothes and ran out into minus forty degrees. For ten minutes, or maybe twenty, we stared and sighed and gasped (not too deeply because of the cold). Then we ran inside, stripped off our icy gear, and perched by the fire.

When we were warm, we put on our clothes and ran out again. We spent hours gazing at this miracle, until the night sky lightened. Then it was time to pack and go home. Home to Perth summer—forty degrees at Scarborough beach.

I wrote an article about this experience but was unable to get it published. Despite my love of travel, I've found breaking into the travel-writing genre difficult. It's an area I hope to pursue further.

Tokyo

After our honeymoon taste of Japanese culture, we decided to take a year off and return to Japan. In 1987 I was offered a job at the Japan International School, beginning in September. Reinhard had work commitments until November, so I went ahead to find somewhere for us to live. With limited Japanese this was difficult.

I eventually found a shoe-box, ten minutes' walk from the station in the exclusive suburb of Den-en-Chofu. The flat was tiny, damp, and would be prone to mould in Tokyo's humid summer, but the leafy walk from the station was lovely.

We'd assumed that with Reinhard's language skills he'd easily find work, but to image-conscious language schools, a German name wasn't an asset in an English teacher. He looked for other positions, one of which was a job as computer systems manager at the Australian embassy. Besides Australians, the shortlist included people

Dianne and Reinhard in Japan during cherry blossom season.

from several nationalities. Reinhard got the job, and after years of enjoying permanent resident status in Australia, he decided to stop procrastinating and take out citizenship.

On October 13, 1988, Reinhard became the first (and probably only!) German to become an Australian citizen in Japan. We crammed a bunch of friends into our apartment, drank Fosters, and sang Aussie songs before heading out to a local *yakitori* bar for a celebratory dinner.

One of the best things about our three years in Tokyo was the fantastic friends we made. Our closest mates were a Japanese/American couple, Martha and Hideki. We met often to escape for weekends at *onsen* (Japanese hot springs) or to eat at our favourite Indian restaurant in Shibuya. Martha also taught at Japan International School.

JIS turned out to be a strange school. There were daily intrigues, and it wasn't unusual for teachers to be fired on a whim of the principal. There were few resources and no playground. I was disappointed with the teaching conditions, so at the end of the year I gave my notice.

There was plenty of work for an English-speaking teacher in Tokyo, and I thought that it might be fun to get a job in the real world; teaching English to businessmen and women with one of Japan's large corporations. Before making such a radical move, I applied for positions at two other international schools. Let fate decide, I thought. It did and I landed a wonderful job at the American School in Japan.

ASIJ was established in 1903 and is perhaps the most prestigious international school in Asia. My position involved teaching four- and five-year-olds at the central Nursery-Kindergarten campus.

Working at ASIJ was everything education should be. The theories, activities, and ideas I learnt at college could at last be fully realised. The equipment was fabulous, the teachers were dedicated, and there were extra funds for each class to use on special projects. My teaching partner, Fumiko, was one of those special, selfless people that one rarely encounters in life. Her father was a diplomat, so coincidentally she'd been born in Australia, spent part of high school in New Zealand, and her older siblings had attended Ruam Rudi International School in Bangkok!

My other colleagues were American, British, and Japanese. The kids we taught came from all corners of the globe and were often the product of interesting marriage combinations. I learnt such a lot during this time: about education, different cultures, and professionalism. Although I didn't have much time to write (school commitments kept me busy), I received an honourable mention in the Japan Air Lines Haiku Contest. Besides a love of haiku poetry, our time in Japan gave me a rich tapestry of experiences to use in my writing.

However a day in August 1990 changed everything. Our school was visiting a park when the caretaker received a phone call for Dianne. There was an American mom called Diane, so I assumed the call was for her. After a moment she hurried back. It was for me.

Her expression made me run to the phone. Richard, our principal, told me not to panic, but that Reinhard had collapsed at work. He said a car would be waiting at the embassy to take me to the hospital.

I stumbled out of the office asking where the nearest train station was. Or should I catch a taxi? But what about the traffic? Maybe a train would be quicker? Fumiko thrust money into my hand, pointed out the direction of the station, and I began to run—in the wrong direction. One of the mums ran after me. She knew where the station was. There were taxis parked out the front. I jumped into one and directed the driver to the Australian embassy.

A car was waiting. They told me Reinhard had collapsed with a grand mal seizure. He was at the nearby hospital having tests. It was a short drive, and I was relieved to see Reinhard perched on a bed arguing that he was fine.

Reinhard usually jogged five or ten kilometres before work, then ate a fruit meal around ten o'clock. He'd been busy, forgotten to eat, and was sure that his collapse was due to low blood sugar. The doctor wasn't convinced. He ran an EEG, then ordered a CT scan.

Hours later, another doctor, a neurologist, came in to discuss the results. We stared at the ugly black shadow on the X-ray. Reinhard had an astrocytoma on his right parietal lobe. He was so fit and healthy, we couldn't believe it.

The doctor advised us to return to Australia. Although there were skilled neurosurgeons in Tokyo, Japanese radiotherapy patients had to remain in hospital during their five-week treatment. After a few minutes with Reinhard, he could see this would be a problem. He also said that we'd need family support.

We gripped each other's hand and stared out the window as the driver returned us to our apartment. At home we clung to each other and cried. My mother was away, but we were able to contact my stepsister. Robin was great. She rang the Royal Melbourne Hospital, explained the situation, and organised an appointment with a top neurosurgeon.

Reinhard rang his sister in Germany. Before he could explain, she excitedly told him that she'd found their father. Alfred had left when they were children. Reinhard had searched for him before leaving Berlin, without success. After an absence of twenty-five years, he was there with Verena! Reinhard greeted his father as best he could, then told Verena the news.

Our colleagues from ASIJ and the embassy were wonderful. After three hellish days of organising tickets and packing, we were on a plane. Mum met us in Melbourne and ferried us to the neurosurgeon. Until then we were hopeful that there was a mistake, some misinterpretation of the scan.

The neurosurgeon, however, was brutally honest. Astrocytomas are invasive, star-shaped tumours. Like tree roots, their tentacles infiltrate deep into the brain. Surgery involves a balance between removing as much cancerous growth as possible without causing permanent damage. After the operation Reinhard would undergo five weeks of radiotherapy treatment. The best we could hope for was no loss of function and five more years.

We left his office and staggered to the nearby park, a place where we'd strolled years before, during those three weeks we spent together in Melbourne. It seemed ironic somehow.

We had to wait another week for the operation to go ahead. It was a sad, scary time, most of which we spent walking through Melbourne's autumn-coloured parks.

The surgery was as successful as possible, and Reinhard was out of intensive care for his thirty-fifth birthday. Then the radiotherapy treatment began.

Serious illness changes both the patient and their carers—sometimes for the better. Reinhard's cancer taught us to cherish each day, to appreciate what we had and not waste time. Loving someone with a life-threatening illness is a bittersweet thing. Innocence and peace of mind were the casualties of accepting mortality. We tried to squeeze as much joy into the time we had, and yet there was always a shadow hanging over us.

I've written a few stories based loosely on these events, none of which have been published. They're too personal. Spending hours with Reinhard in hospitals I saw so many brave people. Trying to guess their stories helped pass the time, but it was depressing.

Around this time we became interested in alternative therapies. We learnt about the courageous work of Ian Gawler, the Simontons, and Bernie Siegel. Their books guided our lives and gave Reinhard inspiration for living with the tumour. Despite their theories, though, it was hard to understand why young children with bandaged heads sat beside us in the waiting room.

After the treatment, Reinhard wanted to go back to Tokyo. He felt that returning to normal life was the best

Daughter Sophie with a tiny orphaned joey whose mother was hit by a car.

approach. I wanted whatever was best for him. We had a couple of weeks before the school year started, so I organised a week at a quiet resort island on the Great Barrier Reef. From there we flew to Papua New Guinea to spend time with my sister, Karen.

Returning to Japan was strange. Reinhard was such a strong person. He worked hard at being healthy, but we'd both changed. He more than me. Sometimes it was hard to keep up. We had our share of misunderstandings, however on the whole, the experience brought us closer together.

We spent another year working in Japan, but an increase in Reinhard's seizures made us realise that we needed a quieter lifestyle. After directing the kindergarten's 1990 summer school program, I packed our things and we returned to Australia via Germany.

The three months we spent in Europe were a healing time. We hired a car, and after meeting Reinhard's father and visiting relations, we travelled through Bavaria and Austria's Tirol region. We stayed in small villages, watched harvest and almabtrieb (cows returning from the high meadows) festivals, and hiked in the alps. Reinhard participated in the Karwendel Marsch, a fifty-three-kilometre run through the mountains. This was a tremendous boost to his self-confidence.

Perth Again

In Perth, I was offered a part-time job teaching Japanese in five primary schools, and Reinhard returned to his job with IBM. Although he'd changed too much to accept the game playing and backstabbing of the corporate world, we hoped to start a family, so he was reluctant to give up financial security.

In November 1991 Sophie was born. She was a spirited baby who grew into an active, loving toddler. I taught adult education one night a week, rejoined the SWW, and wrote short stories whenever I had a spare moment. Life was busy and happy.

Before Sophie's birth I'd attended a writer's retreat organised by the SWW. Every evening participants came together to share their work. One night I read a story about a girl who finds a beached dolphin. West Australian author Deborah Lisson encouraged me to expand the piece into a novel for teenagers. Despite my teaching background, I'd never specifically written for children.

I roughed out a framework for how the story could be fleshed into a novel. Then I started writing. I kept on writing and finally sent a twenty-six-thousand-word manuscript to Deborah's publisher. They told me it was too short, but that it had potential. That was all the encouragement I needed to rewrite and eventually send it back.

Although they liked my story, the publishing house was streamlining commitments and said they couldn't publish it. I put the manuscript in a bottom drawer and concentrated on being a mother.

I also continued writing short fiction and in 1992 experienced my first taste of success when a story, "Gokiburi" (meaning cockroach in Japanese), was commended in the South-West Literary Awards. Later in the year it went on to win the SWW's Bronze Quill Award. At last I felt as if I was getting somewhere.

I kept writing. More stories were short-listed for prizes. I won the South-West Literary Awards for a one-act play and had articles and reviews published in magazines.

However, my writing had to take a back seat to the needs of my husband and young daughter. Of the twelve years I shared with Reinhard, half were spent living in the shadow of the tumour. We adjusted our lifestyle and worked out strategies to prevent the onset of grand mal seizures. On the surface Reinhard was able to continue with little change. He cycled, swam, canoed, and jogged.

I learnt a lot during this time. Reinhard taught me about courage, strength, dignity, and pain. We learnt to be positive and live each day to the full (a skill that came in handy during Sophie's toddler days), and finally I had to learn about letting go.

Reinhard changed jobs but was still unhappy at work. Meanwhile I dreamt of opening a boutique guesthouse in the country or the historic port city of Fremantle. Eventually Reinhard agreed that my plan was worth a try, and I began researching properties.

Around the same time, I rescued the dolphin manuscript from my bottom drawer, reworked the story, and sent it to local publishers, Fremantle Arts Centre Press. They suggested I liaise with their children's editor, Alwyn Evans, who gently guided me through further editing.

Dolphin Song was published in January 1995. The launch was a wonderful evening. I felt that I'd taken another step along the path to becoming a writer, and I was a happy wife and mother. All was well in my world. All was well until June.

In early June we found an ideal Fremantle property to renovate into a guest house. Our offer was accepted, and we sold our own house. Reinhard had agreed to take the plunge and leave the stressful computer world behind. Financially it was scary, but exciting.

Every six months Reinhard was supposed to have a checkup. In past years his CT scans had been fine. There was a fluid-filled area which triggered seizures, but the tumour had not regrown. The day he went for his checkup Reinhard was a picture of health. The architect's plans were in my bag. I'd gone into the city to meet a friend while Reinhard had his appointment. He surprised us by visiting the park on his way to the doctor. He was being silly, doing somersaults to make the kids laugh, before hurrying off to the clinic. That was the last time I saw Reinhard smile without sorrow.

I knew as soon as I saw his face. The tumour had regrown. He needed another operation. We both knew how bad this was. He'd already had the maximum radiotherapy. Chemotherapy was the only alternative, and it wasn't overly effective in fighting brain tumours.

Reinhard's brother, Frank, flew over from Germany. He stayed with us while Reinhard was in hospital and helped us get through this difficult time. After the operation we decided to spend time recovering in Queensland. Despite medication, however, the swelling quickly increased. Reinhard became disoriented and began having falls. We returned to Western Australia.

Our house was sold, our furniture was in storage, and we couldn't go ahead with the guest house. I'd always wanted to move to the country, so we drove south and looked at real estate. We found a spacious home in a quiet lane just out of the town of Denmark. Meanwhile Reinhard's health was deteriorating. After a quick settlement we moved in.

Denmark, Western Australia

People experience grief differently. For me it was like losing my anchor. If it weren't for Sophie I wonder how I could have gone on. Although we were blessed to experience such a deep love, when you've found your soul mate and life partner, the pain of losing them is hard to bear. People said time would soften the pain. They were right, but that was cold consolation during those first awful months.

We'd only been in Denmark a short time when Reinhard died. My mother flew over to help with Sophie and the nursing. The care we received from the Silver Chain nurses was wonderful, and Reinhard was able to remain at home until the last few days.

Brain tumours affect different skills as they grow. Reinhard was a challenging patient. He wanted so much to live and he had such willpower that letting go was very hard for him. His sister, Verena, flew over from Canada to be with us towards the end. Even with three of us taking shifts, caring for Reinhard became too difficult and he was admitted to the nearby country hospice. He died at Christmas 1995.

Dianne Wolfer with mother and daughter in Munich, 1999.

Mum stayed with us for a few weeks after Reinhard's death. She helped unpack boxes and made sure we ate, before returning to be with Geoff, her own terminally ill partner.

Being the mother of a young child leaves limited time to wallow, and the support of friends helped. I wrote a lot of grief out of my system via a journal and spent hours walking when Sophie was at pre-primary.

Working at writing also helped me keep sane. Soon after Reinhard died, I set myself the goal of completing the novel I'd been researching, before his birthday. It would be a final gift for him.

Western Australia's isolation has protected it from starlings, a bird that has colonised and caused millions of dollars' damage to farmers in eastern Australia. The Nullarbor is a vast plain separating South Australia and the West. Although cunning, starlings can only enter WA through a land bottleneck between the rugged Southern Ocean and the desert.

Before writing *Border Line,* I'd read an interesting article about a five-man team based at the border. Their full-time job is to track and shoot the starlings that try and get into WA. These men abseil over limestone cliffs to destroy nests and track birds for days on four-wheel motorbikes, before shooting them with rifles fitted with silencers. They take their job very seriously, and I felt this would make a fascinating theme and setting for a book.

I posted my manuscript the day before Reinhard's birthday. *Border Line* was published in January 1998 and has been short-listed for the West Australian Young Readers' Book Awards and the Wilderness Society's Environment Award.

Writers are renowned stickybeaks, and I am fascinated by people—their problems, habits, and courage. Writing about environmental themes is something I am passionate about, but I'm also interested in stories that involve mortality, cutting through polite conversation, and looking beneath the masks people wear.

In 1998 I won the Mary Grant Bruce Short Story Award for "Donkey Ears." Although suffering a degenerative illness, Kent, the central character, is sick of being mollycoddled. He wants to be treated like a normal kid, so he finds his own way to rebel. The idea for this story was sparked by a boy I saw sitting in a wheelchair at Kings Park and was perhaps a product of the hours spent in hospitals.

With each manuscript I feel I'm learning more about the craft of writing and becoming a stronger writer. I have hundreds of story ideas jotted in notebooks and filed on my computer. All I need is the time and space to write them—a big ask sometimes!

Being a single parent is a challenge. I miss not having a partner to bounce ideas off and to help make decisions. Although there is so much I want to do, at present my life revolves around Sophie and for the moment that feels right.

Something about the West Australian air seems to nurture writers. Perth is called "the most isolated city in the world." The nearest cities are Adelaide (South Australia) and Jakarta (Indonesia). And here in Denmark, we live a five-hour drive south of this "most isolated" city.

Isolation has both good and bad points. Most WA writers have space to think. The writing community is large enough to hold an interesting mix of opinions, yet small enough to be friendly. The catty element that exists elsewhere is uncommon here.

The small town where I live is a microcosm of most things you could find across Australia. We have traditional farmers living beside boutique wineries, and many locals rely on tourism for their livelihood. Alternative lifestylers live in the forests while closer to town there are retirees, young families, tradespeople, shopkeepers, butchers, bakers, and even candlestick makers (in rainbow *chakra* colours). Living in Denmark, I don't think I'll ever have a problem finding inspiration for characters to write about.

The southern coastline is a dramatic blend of wild beaches, rock pools, and national parks. This natural beauty refreshes my creative energy. We have kangaroos living on the public golf course and at the end of our lane. In spring, the bush hides hundreds of orchids as well as the more showy banksia and kangaroo paws. The local bird-life is fabulous (in part because there are few "bully birds" like starlings to steal their nests), and each time pelicans or a mob of black cockatoos wheel overhead screeching, I think how lucky we are to be here.

At present my travel urge is limited to holidays and short residencies. I don't want to uproot my daughter by moving. Denmark has become her home, and she had enough turmoil in her early years. Besides, I can't think of anywhere better to live. We've been here four and a half years now, the longest I've stayed in one place since high school.

Luckily we have relatives living in diversely beautiful parts of the world who keep asking us to visit, so that keeps the travel bug in check. My sister-in-law and her family are in Vancouver, and my other in-laws live in Munich and southern Germany. My stepsiblings, Robin, Wendy, and Alan, live in tropical Queensland with their families, while Mum is near the southern snowfields.

Karen has settled in far north Queensland with her partner, Owen, and their baby, Tolina. Their business, South Pacific Tours, organises eco-tours in the South Pacific and Kokoda Trail treks in Papua New Guinea. Sometimes they need people to try out new locations for them, and last year our family spent New Year on an uninhabited island in Marovo Lagoon (Solomon Islands), which was fabulous.

So, here I am at thirty-eight, parent of a beautiful eight-year-old girl, living in an interesting country town with a manic spotted dog and two guinea pigs. It's four years since Reinhard's death. The scars have almost healed, and I'm ready to enjoy life again. Reinhard wanted to live life to the full, and I try and do so for both our sakes.

I teach adult education at TAFE once a week and do regular workshops at schools. This gives me a chance to keep in touch with kids' interests. I'm a member of two bookgroups. We meet monthly to discuss our chosen book and catch up on each other's gossip.

Early next year, my third YA novel, *Choices,* will be published by Fremantle Arts Centre Press. I have two manuscripts for younger readers in semi-completed draft form and ideas for more YA novels. I'm also interested in writing a collection of short stories for adults with a linked Japanese theme. Three stories have been completed, but the others are still ideas and notes.

Like everyone, I've had ups and downs in my life. Sometimes I miss the excitement and opportunities the city could offer, but then I look out my window and realise that the grass is not always greener . . . .

Writings

FICTION FOR YOUNG ADULTS

Dolphin Song, Fremantle Arts Centre Press, 1995.
Border Line, Fremantle Arts Centre Press, 1998.

Choices, Fremantle Arts Centre Press, 2001.

Contributor of children's story "Seven-Five-Three" to *Lucky,* no. 6, 1997. Adult short stories "Gokiburi" anthologized in *Going Down South,* 1992, and *In Perspective,* SWW, 1993; and "Made in China" in *Going Down South Two,* 1993. Contributor of short stories, articles, and poems to magazines including *Infant Times, Let's Travel, Nature and Health, Well-Being, Western Review,* and *Western Word.* Contributor of "Theosophy in an Eight-Seater" to *Flightpaths* Internet site, 1997.

WOODS, Lawrence
See LOWNDES, Robert A(ugustine) W(ard)

Cumulative Indexes

Illustrations Index

(In the following index, the number of the *volume* in which an illustrator's work appears is given *before* the colon, and the *page number* on which it appears is given *after* the colon. For example, a drawing by Adams, Adrienne appears in Volume 2 on page 6, another drawing by her appears in Volume 3 on page 80, another drawing in Volume 8 on page 1, and so on and so on....)

YABC

Index references to *YABC* refer to listings appearing in the two-volume *Yesterday's Authors of Books for Children,* also published by The Gale Group. *YABC* covers prominent authors and illustrators who died prior to 1960.

Author Index

The following index gives the number of the volume in which an author's biographical sketch, Autobiography Feature, Brief Entry, or Obituary appears.

This index includes references to all entries in the following series, which are also published by The Gale Group.

YABC—*Yesterday's Authors of Books for Children: Facts and Pictures about Authors and Illustrators of Books for Young People from Early Times to 1960*
CLR—*Children's Literature Review: Excerpts from Reviews, Criticism, and Commentary on Books for Children*
SAAS—*Something about the Author Autobiography Series*

Author Index